# Teacher's Resources
## for use with

# Children
## The Early Years

by
**Dr. Celia Anita Decker**
Professor of Family and Consumer Sciences, retired
Northwestern State University of Louisiana
Natchitoches, Louisiana

Publisher
**The Goodheart-Willcox Company, Inc.**
Tinley Park, Illinois

# Contents

## Teacher's Resources

|  | Teacher's Resources | Text | Student Activity Guide |
|---|---|---|---|

# Introduction

*Children: The Early Years* is a comprehensive text designed to help students understand children's physical, intellectual, and social-emotional development from the prenatal period through the school-age years. In addition to the student text, the *Children: The Early Years* learning package includes the *Student Activity Guide, Teacher's Wraparound Edition, Teacher's Resource Guide, Teacher's Resource Portfolio,* and *Teacher's Resource CD with GW Test Creation Software.* Using these products can help you develop an effective child development program tailored to your students' unique needs.

## Using the Text

The text *Children: The Early Years* is designed to help your students learn how children grow and develop. Students will learn basic information about meeting children's needs in each stage of development.

The text is divided into 6 parts with a total of 25 chapters. The material is organized and presented in a logical sequence of topics for the study of child development. Although the text was written to be studied in its entirety, individual chapters and sections are complete enough to be studied independently.

*Children: The Early Years* contains components developed to support your curriculum and help you meet your students' needs. The text is thorough and up-to-date. Hundreds of photographs, charts, and illustrations attract student interest and emphasize key concepts. The copy references all illustrations, which helps students associate the written material with the visual image. This reinforces learning.

The text includes both brief and expanded tables of contents to give students an overview of the wide variety of topics they will study. The running glossary throughout the text and complete glossary at the back of the book help students learn terms related to child development. A complete index helps them find information they want quickly and easily.

Each chapter includes several features designed to help students study effectively and review what they have learned.

*Case Studies.* Each chapter opens with a case study related to chapter content. Reading the case study can increase student interest in the chapter concepts. Revisiting the case study after studying the chapter may help students see what they have learned. Discussion questions for each case study appear in the *Teacher's Wraparound Edition.*

*Objectives.* A set of behavioral objectives appears at the beginning of each chapter. These are performance goals you can expect students to achieve after studying the chapter. Review the objectives in each chapter with students to make them aware of the skills they will be building as they read the chapter material.

*Terms.* A list of vocabulary terms is found at the beginning of each chapter. Terms are listed in the order they are used within the text. These terms are set in red type throughout the text so students can recognize them while reading. A running glossary box in the lower-right corner of each spread also sets the vocabulary apart for student use. Discussing these terms with students helps them learn concepts to which they are being introduced. To familiarize students with these terms, you may want to ask them to

→ look up, define, and explain each term;
→ relate each term to the topic being studied;
→ match terms with definitions; and
→ find examples of how the terms are used in current newspapers and magazines, reference books, and other related materials.

*Ties with Family and Community boxes.* Each chapter includes one or more of these special boxes. Each box suggests a project or activity students could do to apply chapter learnings related to family and community life.

*Summary.* A chapter summary, called *Summing It Up,* is located at the end of each chapter. This section reviews the major concepts covered in the chapter.

*Reviewing Key Concepts.* The review questions at the end of each chapter cover the basic information presented. This section consists of a variety of true/false, completion, multiple choice, and short essay questions. It is designed to help students recall, organize, and use the information presented in the text. Answers to these questions appear in the margins of the *Teacher's Wraparound Edition* pages that contain the questions. These answers are given again in the *Teacher's Resources* products.

*Using Your Knowledge.* The activities in this end-of-chapter section offer students opportunities to increase knowledge through firsthand experiences. These activities encourage students to apply many of the concepts learned in the chapter to real-life situations. Suggestions for both individual and group work are provided in varying degrees of difficulty. Each activity is designated with the name or names of specific academic, career, or personal development areas it was written to enhance. Therefore, you may choose and assign activities according to students' interests and abilities.

**Making Observations.** The observations in this section are intended to expand student thinking and follow up on the content in each chapter. The observations are meant to be thought-provoking exercises that reinforce chapter content with real-life examples. They should motivate students to seek further information and to exchange their thoughts and opinions with other class members.

**Thinking Further.** These activities at the end of each chapter encourage critical thinking. Thought-provoking questions require students to apply chapter material to their own lives. The use of imagination and problem-solving techniques are promoted.

# Using the Student Activity Guide

The *Student Activity Guide* designed for use with *Children: The Early Years* helps students recall and review material presented in the text. It also helps them think critically about chapter content and form their own conclusions.

The activities in the guide are divided into chapters that correspond to the chapters in the text. The text provides the information students will need to complete many of the activities. Other activities will require creative thinking and research beyond the textbook.

You may want to use the exercises in the *Student Activity Guide* that are directly related to textual material as introductory, review, or evaluation tools. Ask students to do the exercises without looking in the book. Then they can use the text to check their answers and answer questions they could not complete. The pages of the *Student Activity Guide* are perforated so students can easily turn completed activities in for evaluation.

The *Student Activity Guide* includes various activities. Some have specific answers related to text material. Students can use these activities to review for tests and quizzes. Answers to these activities appear in the *Teacher's Resources* products.

Other activities ask for students' thoughts or opinions. Answers to these activities cannot be judged as right or wrong. These activities let students form their own ideas by considering alternatives and evaluating situations thoughtfully. These thought-provoking exercises can often be used as a basis for classroom discussion by asking students to justify their answers and conclusions.

The use of each activity in the *Student Activity Guide* is described in the *Teacher's Resources* products as a teaching strategy under the related instructional concept. Activities are identified by name and letter. In the margins of the *Teacher's Wraparound Edition,* teaching elements labeled Resource also describe the use of the activities in the *Student Activity Guide.*

# Using the Teacher's Wraparound Edition

The *Teacher's Wraparound Edition* for *Children: The Early Years* is a special edition of the student text. It is designed to help you more effectively coordinate materials in the *Student Activity Guide* with text concepts. It also provides you with additional suggestions to help you add variety to your classroom teaching.

Teaching elements are located in the margins of most text pages. These teaching elements appear in the order of coverage in the text. The chart on the following page details the types of teaching elements used in the wraparound edition.

In addition to teaching elements placed in the margins throughout the student text, the *Teacher's Wraparound Edition* includes a special front section. It begins with a detailed introduction explaining how to use the various components in the teaching package for *Children: The Early Years*. This section also contains several features designed to help you prepare meaningful lessons for your students.

The *Teacher's Wraparound Edition* also places the answers to chapter review questions alongside the review questions at the end of each chapter.

## Scope and Sequence

A *Scope and Sequence* chart, located near the end of the introduction, identifies the major concepts presented in each chapter of the text. This special resource will help you select for study those topics that meet your curriculum needs.

# Using the Teacher's Resource Guide

The *Teacher's Resource Guide* for *Children: The Early Years* suggests many methods of presenting the concepts in the text to students. It begins with some of the same helpful information found in the *Teacher's Wraparound Edition,* including teaching suggestions and the Scope and Sequence chart.

| Teaching Element | Description |
| --- | --- |
| Case Study Questions | Presents questions that spark discussion about the case study that opens each chapter. This discussion helps students link the case study with chapter concepts. |
| Vocabulary | Suggests vocabulary reinforcement activities such as defining terms, using terms in sentences, looking up terms in the glossary, or comparing important new terms. |
| Discuss | Discussion questions that reteach or reinforce learning. For single-answer questions, answers are given as part of the teaching element. These answers appear in italic type and are placed just after the question in parentheses. |
| Reflect | Questions to ask students to think about regarding the concepts presented, often by applying the content to their own lives. These questions are often more personal than the discussion questions are. |
| Activity | Activities related to the chapter that would reteach and reinforce concepts. |
| Note | Additional points the instructor might want to make regarding the chapter, or to spark student interest in the discussion. Points might include statistics, interesting facts, or historical notes. These may also be notes to the instructor regarding the subject matter. |
| Example | An example to use in illustrating an important point in the chapter material. |
| Enrich | Activities that relate to the concept, but are more involved and challenging for students. Examples include role-playing, research topics, interviews, debates, surveys, bulletin boards, field trips, or guest speakers. |
| Resource | An activity from the *Student Activity Guide* or a reproducible or transparency master from the *Teacher's Resources* that is appropriate for use with this section of the chapter. |

## Correlation of National Standards for Human Development with *Children: The Early Years*

In 1998, the National Standards for Family and Consumer Sciences Education were finalized. This comprehensive guide provides family and consumer sciences educators with a structure for identifying what learners should be able to do. This structure is based on knowledge and skills needed for work life and family life, as well as family and consumer sciences careers. The National Standards Components include 16 areas of study, each with a comprehensive standard that describes the overall content of the area. Each comprehensive standard is then broken down into content standards that describe what is expected of the learner. Competencies further define the knowledge, skills, and practices of the content standards and provide the basis for measurement criteria.

By studying the text *Children: The Early Years,* students will be prepared to master the competencies listed for the area of study called *Human Development*. To show you how this can be accomplished, a *Correlation of National Standards for Human Development* with *Children: The Early Years* has been included in the *Teacher's Resources* products. If you want to make sure you prepare students to meet the National Standards for Family and Consumer Sciences Education, this chart should interest you.

## Basic Skills Chart

Another feature of the *Teacher's Resource Guide* is a Basic Skills Chart. This chart has been included to identify those activities that encourage the development of the following basic skills: verbal, reading, writing, mathematical, scientific, and analytical. (Analytical skills involve the higher-order thinking skills of analysis, synthesis, and evaluation in problem-solving situations.) The chart includes activities from the "Using Your Knowledge" section of the text, activities from the *Student Activity Guide,* and strategies from the *Teacher's Resources* products. Incorporating a variety of these activities into your daily lesson plans will provide your students with vital practice in the development of basic skills. Also, if you find that students in your classes are weak in a specific basic skill, you can select activities to strengthen that particular skill area.

## Chapter-by-Chapter Resources

Like the *Student Activity Guide*, the *Teacher's Resource Guide* is divided into chapters that match the chapters in the text. Each chapter contains the following features:

*Objectives.* These are the objectives that students will be able to accomplish after reading the chapter and completing the suggested activities.

*Bulletin Board Ideas.* Bulletin board ideas are described for each chapter. Many of these ideas are illustrated for you. Creating bulletin board displays can be a stimulating student activity.

*Teaching Materials.* A list of materials available to supplement each chapter in the text is provided. The list includes the names of all the activities contained in the *Student Activity Guide* and all the masters contained in the *Teacher's Resources* products.

*Introductory Activities.* These motivational exercises are designed to stimulate your students' interest in the chapter they will be studying. The activities help create a sense of curiosity that students will want to satisfy by reading the chapter.

*Strategies to Reteach, Reinforce, Enrich, and Extend Text Concepts.* A variety of student learning strategies are described for teaching each of the major concepts discussed in the text. Each major concept appears in the guide as a heading followed by the teaching suggestions for that concept. Suggestions for using the activities from the *Student Activity Guide* are given to help you plan daily lessons. They are identified with the letters *SAG* following the title and letter of the activity. (example: *Bedtime Rituals,* Activity A, SAG.)

The number of each learning strategy is followed by a code in bold type. These codes identify the teaching goals each strategy is designed to accomplish. The following codes have been used:

**RT** identifies activities designed to help you reteach concepts. These strategies present the chapter concepts in a different way to allow students additional learning opportunities.

**RF** identifies activities designed to reinforce concepts to students. These strategies present techniques and activities to help clarify facts, terms, principles, and concepts. These activities make chapter concepts easier for students to understand.

**ER** identifies activities designed to enrich learning. These strategies help students learn more about the concepts presented by involving them more fully in the material. Enrichment strategies include interviews, demonstrations, field trips, guest speakers, panels, and surveys.

**EX** identifies activities designed to extend learning. These strategies promote thinking skills, such as critical thinking, creative thinking, problem solving, and decision making. Students must analyze, synthesize, and evaluate in order to complete these activities.

*Answer Key.* This section provides answers for review questions at the end of each chapter in the text, for activities in the *Student Activity Guide*, for the reproducible masters in the *Teacher's Resources* products, and for the chapter tests in the *Teacher's Resources.*

*Reproducible Masters.* Several reproducible masters are included for each chapter. These masters enhance the presentation of concepts in the text. Some provide related material beyond the scope of the text. Some masters are designated as transparency masters for use with an overhead projector. These are often charts or graphs that can serve as a basis for class discussion of important concepts. They can also be used as student handouts. Other masters are activities designed to be photocopied and given to students to encourage creative and critical thinking.

*Chapter Test Masters.* Individual tests with clear, specific questions that cover all the chapter topics are provided. True/false, multiple choice, and matching questions are used to measure student learning about facts and definitions. Essay questions are also provided in the chapter tests. Some of these require students to list information, while others encourage students to express their opinions and creativity. You may wish to modify the tests and tailor the questions to your classroom needs.

# Using the Teacher's Resource Portfolio

The *Teacher's Resource Portfolio* for *Children: The Early Years* combines the *Teacher's Resource Guide* with color transparencies. These transparencies enhance your classroom lecture as you discuss topics from the text with your students. Some transparencies are useful in illustrating and reinforcing concepts presented in the text. Others will give you an opportunity to extend learning beyond the scope of the text. Attractive colors are visually appealing and hold students' attention. Suggestions for how the transparencies can be used are included in the teaching strategies for each chapter of the *Teacher's Resources* products, and also in the teaching elements of the *Teacher's Wraparound Edition*.

All of the materials are included in a convenient three-ring portfolio binder with a carrying handle. Reproducible materials can be removed easily. Handy dividers included with the portfolio binder help you organize materials so you can quickly find the items you need.

# Using the Teacher's Resource CD with GW Test Creation Software

The *Teacher's Resource CD* includes all the contents of the *Teacher's Resource Portfolio* plus the *GW Test Creation Software*. This format lets you view and print *Teacher's Resource Portfolio* pages from your computer. Links in the table of contents connect directly to each specific page. To create overhead transparencies, print transparency master pages onto acetate film designed for your printer.

*GW Test Creation Software* database includes all the test master questions from the *Teacher's Resources* products plus an additional 25 percent new questions prepared just for this product. You can choose specific questions from the database or add your own questions to customize tests to meet your classroom needs. You may want to make different versions of the same test. Answer keys are generated automatically to simplify grading.

# Strategies for Successful Teaching

You can make the *Children: The Early Years* subject matter exciting and relevant for your students by using a variety of teaching strategies. Many suggestions for planning classroom activities are given in the teaching supplements that accompany this text. As you plan your lessons, you might also want to keep the following points in mind.

## Helping Your Students Develop Critical Thinking Skills

As today's students leave their classrooms behind, they will face a world of complexity and change. They are likely to work in several career areas and hold many jobs. Besides providing young people with a knowledge base of facts, principles, and procedures, you must help prepare them to solve complex problems, make difficult decisions, and assess ethical implications. In other words, you must help students learn how to use critical thinking skills. These skills are often referred to as the higher-order thinking skills. Benjamin Bloom listed these as

→ analysis—breaking down material into its component parts so its organizational structure may be understood;

→ synthesis—putting parts together to form a new whole; and

→ evaluation—judging the value of material for a given purpose.

In a broader perspective, students must be able to use reflective thinking in order to decide what to believe and do. According to Robert Ennis, students should be able to

→ define and clarify problems, issues, conclusions, reasons, and assumptions;

→ judge the credibility, relevance, and consistency of information; and

→ infer or solve problems and draw reasonable conclusions.

Students have the right to learn critical thinking skills. These skills cannot be an optional part of the curriculum. To think critically, students must have knowledge. However, critical thinking goes beyond memorizing or recalling information. Critical thinking cannot occur in a vacuum; it requires individuals to apply what they know about the subject matter. It requires students to use their common sense and experience. It may also involve controversy.

Critical thinking requires *creative thinking* to construct all the reasonable alternatives, consequences, influencing factors, and supporting arguments. To help students develop this type of thinking, you need to encourage learners to seek perspectives outside the obvious.

Teaching critical thinking does not require exotic and highly unusual classroom approaches. You can incorporate complex thought processes in the most ordinary and basic activities. With careful planning and skillful execution, you can even incorporate complex thought into reading, writing, and listening exercises.

Help your students develop their analytical skills and go beyond what they see on the surface. Rather than allowing students to blindly accept what they read or hear, encourage them to examine ideas in ways that show respect for others' opinions and different perspectives. Encourage learners to think about points raised by others. Ask students to evaluate how new ideas relate to their attitudes about various subjects.

Debate is an excellent way to explore opposite sides of an issue. You may want to divide the class into two groups, each taking an opposing side of the issue. You can also ask students to work in smaller groups and explore opposing sides of different issues. Each group can select students from the group to present the points for their side.

## Problem-Solving and Decision-Making Skills

An important aspect in the development of critical thinking skills is learning how to solve problems and make decisions. Some very important decisions lie ahead for your students, particularly those related to their future education and career choices. As you discuss with students how to make decisions about child development, you can encourage them to apply the decision-making process to all their important decisions.

Simulation games and role-plays are activities that allow students to practice solving problems and making decisions in nonthreatening circumstances. Role-playing allows students to examine others' feelings as well as their own. It can help students learn effective ways to react or cope when confronted with similar situations in real life.

## Using Cooperative Learning

The use of cooperative learning groups in your classroom will give students a chance to practice teamwork skills, which are critical in today's workplace. During cooperative learning, students learn interpersonal and small-group skills that will allow them to function as part of a team. These skills include leadership, decision making, trust building, communication, and conflict management.

Working in the early childhood lab provides an excellent opportunity for students to work cooperatively. When planning for cooperative learning, you will have a particular goal or task in mind. You will first specify the objectives for the lesson. You will match small groups of learners to complete the task or goal. Mix groups in terms of abilities and talents to create more opportunities for students to learn from one another.

You or the group will assign each group member a role. As groups work together over time, rotate the roles so everyone has an opportunity to practice and develop different skills.

Interdependence is a basic component of any cooperative learning group. Success is not measured only in terms of outcome. It is also measured in terms of the successful performance of each group member in his or her role. Students understand that one person cannot succeed unless everyone succeeds. The worth of each group member is affirmed as learners work toward their goal.

You will need to monitor the effectiveness of cooperative groups. Intervene as necessary to provide task assistance or to help with interpersonal and group skills. Finally, evaluate students' achievement and help them discuss how well they worked together.

## Helping Students Recognize and Value Diversity

Your students will be entering a rapidly changing workplace—not only in the area of technology, but also in the diverse nature of the workforce. Years ago, the workforce was dominated by white males, but 85 percent of the new entrants into the workforce at the start of this century were women, minorities, and immigrants. The workforce is also aging. Over half the workforce will be people between ages 35 and 54 years. Because of these changes, young workers will need to be able to interact effectively with people who differ from themselves.

Appreciating and understanding diversity is an ongoing process. The earlier and more frequently young people are exposed to diversity, the better able they will be to bridge cultural differences. If your students are exposed to various cultures within your classroom, they can begin the process of understanding cultural differences. This is the best preparation for success in a diverse society. In addition, teachers have found the following strategies to be helpful:

→ Actively promote a spirit of openness, consideration, respect, and tolerance in your classroom.

→ Use a variety of teaching styles and assessment strategies.

→ Use cooperative learning activities whenever possible. Make sure group roles are rotated so everyone has leadership opportunities.

→ When grouping students, make sure the composition of each group is as diverse as possible with regard to gender and ethnic group. If the groups present information to the class, make sure all members have a speaking part. (Sometimes females and minorities are underrepresented in speaking roles.)

→ Make sure one group's opinions are not overrepresented during class discussions. Seek opinions of underrepresented persons/groups if necessary.

→ If a student makes a sexist, racist, or other offensive comment, ask the student to rephrase the comment in a manner that will not offend other members of the class. Remind students that offensive statements and behavior are inappropriate in the workplace as well as the classroom.

→ If a difficult classroom situation arises based on a diversity issue, ask for a time out and have everyone write down thoughts and opinions about the incident. This allows everyone to cool down and allows you to plan a response.

→ Arrange for guest speakers who represent diversity in gender, age, and ethnicity even when the topic does not relate to diversity.

→ Have students change seats from time to time throughout the course, having them sit next to people they do not know, and introducing themselves.

→ Several times during the course, have students do anonymous evaluations of the class, asking them if there are any problems about which you are unaware.

# Using Other Resources

Much student learning in your class can be reinforced by allowing students to see, analyze, and work with examples. Your providing samples of pictures, demonstration samples, and articles related to a variety of family and consumer sciences topics can greatly enhance student learning. Students can use these items in many activities related to the text.

You may be able to acquire some items through local stores. Old items can be purchased inexpensively. Many stores may be willing to donate items. You may be able to obtain pamphlets and project ideas by contacting consumer product manufacturers.

Magazines, catalogs, and sales brochures are excellent sources of photos. Having a large quantity available for clipping and mounting photos will be helpful to students. Students may analyze and discuss the pictures in a variety of activities.

Current magazines and journals are also good sources of articles on various family and consumer sciences topics. Having copies in the classroom will encourage students to use them for research and ideas as they study family and consumer sciences. The following publications may be helpful to you or your students:*

*The American Montessori Society Bulletin*
American Montessori Society (AMS)
(212) 358-1250
www.amshq.org

*The Black Child Advocate*
(202) 833-2200
www.nbcdi.org

*Child Development and Child Development Abstracts and Bibliography*
Society for Research in Child Development
(734) 998-6578
www.srcd.org

*Childhood Education*
Association for Childhood Education International (ACEI)
(800) 423-3563
www.udel.edu

*Children Today*
Superintendent of Documents
www.access.gpo.gov/catalog

*Child Welfare*
Child Welfare League of America (CWLA)
(202) 638-2952
www.cwla.org

*Developmental Psychology*
American Psychological Association
(800) 374-2721
www.apa.org/journals

*Early Childhood News*
www.earlychildhood.com

*Early Childhood Research Quarterly*
National Association for the Education of
Young Children (NAEYC)
(800) 424-2460
www.naeyc.org

*Educational Researcher*
American Educational Research
Association (AERA)
(202) 223-9485
www.aera.net

*Education Leadership*
Association for Supervision and
Curriculum Development (ASCD)
(703) 578-9600; (800) 933-ASCD
www.ascd.org

*ERIC/EECE Newsletter*
University of Illinois Children's Research
Center
(800) 583-4135
Web site: ericeece.org/pubs/eece-nl.html

*Exceptional Children*
Council for Exceptional Children
(703) 620-3600; (888) CEC-SPED
www.cec.sped.org

*Gifted Child Quarterly*
National Association for Gifted Children
(202)785-7628
www.nagc.org

*Instructor*
Scholastic, Inc.
(212) 343-6100
www.scholastic.com/instructor

*Journal of Family and Consumer Sciences*
American Association of Family and
Consumer Sciences (AAFCS)
(703) 706-4600
www.aafcs.org

*Journal of Research in Childhood Education*
Association for Childhood Education
International
www.udel.edu

*Young Children*
NAEYC
www.naeyc.org

The following are resources for children:

*Babybug, Cricket, Ladybug,* and *Spider*
magazines
Carus Publishing Company
(800) 827-0227
www.cricketmag.com

*Ranger Rick* and *Your Big Back Yard* magazines
National Wildlife Federation
(800) 822-9919
www.nwf.org

*Sesame Street*
Sesame Workshop
(212) 595-3456
www.sesameworkshop.org

*Stone Soup*
Children's Art Foundation
(800) 447-4569
www.stonesoup.com

*Turtle*
Children's Better Health Institute
(317) 634-1100
www.cbhi.org

*U.S. Kids*
Children's Better Health Institute
(317) 636-8881
www.cbhi.org

Other information may be obtained through various professional organizations. The following may be able to provide you with some resources:

*American Association of Family and Consumer
Sciences (AAFCS)*
(703) 706-4600
www.aafcs.org

*American Educational Research Association
(AERA)*
(202) 223-9485
www.aera.net

*American Montessori Association (AMS)*
  (212) 358-1250
  www.amshq.org

*Association for Supervision and Curriculum
  Development (ASCD)*
  (703) 578-9600; (800) 933-ASCD
  www.ascd.org

*Children's Defense Fund*
  (202) 628-8787
  www.childrensdefense.org

*Child Welfare League of America (CWLA)*
  (202) 638-2952
  www.cwla.org

*Council for Exceptional Children*
  (703) 620-3660; (888) CEC-SPED
  www.cec.sped.org

*International Reading Association*
  (302) 731-1600
  www.reading.org

*National Association for the Education of
  Young Children (NAEYC)*
  (800) 424-2460
  www.naeyc.org

*National Association for Gifted Children*
  (202) 785-4268
  www.nagc.org

*National Black Child Development Institute
  (NBCDI)*
  (202) 833-2200
  www.nbcdi.org

*National Committee to Prevent Child Abuse*
  (312) 663-3520
  www.childabuse.org

*National Education Association (NEA)*
  (202) 833-4000
  www.nea.org

*Society for Research in Child Development*
  (734) 998-6578
  www.srcd.org

*Note: The contact information for these resources
may have changed since the publication of this
*Teacher's Resources* product.

## Teaching the Learner with Special Needs

Adapting daily lessons to meet the needs of all your students in the same classroom setting is a challenge. This challenge is magnified when the students in your classroom represent a wide range of ability levels. The chart on the following page provides descriptions of several of the special learning needs that may be present among your students. It includes some strategies and techniques to keep in mind as you work with students who have special needs.

## Using Evaluation Techniques

A variety of evaluation tools can be used to assess student achievement. Try using the reproducible forms *Evaluating Individual Participation, Evaluating Individual Reports,* and *Evaluating Group Participation,* included with the introductory material in the *Teacher's Resources* products. These rating scales let you observe a student's performance and rank it on a continuum. This enables students to see what levels they have surpassed and what levels they can still strive to reach.

In some situations, having students evaluate their own work is worth while. When evaluating an independent study project, for example, students may be the best judges of whether they met their objectives. Students can think about what they have learned and note how they have improved. They can analyze their strengths and weaknesses.

You may ask students to evaluate peers from time to time. This gives the student performing the evaluation an opportunity to practice giving constructive criticism. It offers the student being evaluated the opportunity to accept criticism from his or her peers.

Tests and quizzes are also effective evaluation tools. These may be given in either written or oral form. In either case, however, both objective and subjective questions should be used to help you adequately assess student knowledge and understanding of class material.

| | Learning Disabled* | Mentally Disabled* | Behaviorally Emotionally Disabled* |
|---|---|---|---|
| **Description** | Students with learning disabilities (LD) have neurological disorders that interfere with their ability to store, process, or produce information, creating a "gap" between ability and performance. These students are generally of average or above average intelligence. Examples of learning disabilities are distractibility, spatial problems, and reading comprehension problems. | Students with mental disabilities (MD) have subaverage general intellectual functioning that exists with deficits in adaptive behavior. These students are slower than others their age in using memory effectively, associating and classifying information, reasoning, and making judgments. | Students with behavioral or emotional disabilities exhibit undesirable behaviors or emotions, which may, over time, adversely affect educational performance. Their inability to learn cannot be explained by intellectual, social, or health factors. They may be inattentive, withdrawn, timid, restless, defiant, impatient, unhappy, fearful, unreflective, unmotivated, negative, and accusing. |
| **Teaching Strategies** | • Help students get organized.<br>• Give short oral directions.<br>• Use drill exercises.<br>• Give prompt cues during student performance.<br>• Let students with poor writing skills use a computer.<br>• Break assignments into small segments and assign only one segment at a time.<br>• Demonstrate skills and have students model them.<br>• Give prompt feedback.<br>• Use continuous assessment to mark students' daily progress.<br>• Prepare materials at varying levels of ability.<br>• Shorten the number of items on exercises, tests, and quizzes.<br>• Provide more hands-on activities. | • Use concrete examples to introduce concepts.<br>• Make learning activities consistent.<br>• Use repetition and drills spread over time.<br>• Provide work folders for daily assignments.<br>• Use behavior management techniques, such as behavior modification, in the area of adaptive behavior.<br>• Encourage students to function independently.<br>• Give students extra time to both ask and answer questions while giving hints to answers.<br>• Avoid doing much walking around while talking to MD students as this is distracting for them.<br>• Give simple directions and read them over with students.<br>• Use objective test items and hands-on activities because students generally have poor writing skills and difficulty with sentence structure and spelling. | • Call students' names or ask them questions when you see their attention wandering.<br>• Call on students randomly rather than in a predictable sequence.<br>• Move around the room frequently.<br>• Improve students' self-esteem by giving them tasks they can perform well, increasing the number of successful achievement experiences.<br>• Decrease the length of time for each activity.<br>• Use hands-on activities instead of using words and abstract symbols.<br>• Decrease the size of the group so each student can actively participate.<br>• Make verbal instructions clear, short, and to the point. |

* We appreciate the assistance of Dr. Debra O. Parker, North Carolina Central University, with this section.

| Academically Gifted | Limited English Proficiency | Physical Disabilities | |
|---|---|---|---|
| Students who are academically gifted are capable of high performance as a result of general intellectual ability, specific academic aptitude, and/or creative or productive thinking. Such students have vast resources of general knowledge and high levels of vocabulary, memory, and abstract reasoning. | Students with a limited proficiency in the English language generally speak English as their second language. Such students may be academically quite capable, but they lack the language skills needed to reason and comprehend abstract concepts. | Students who have physical disabilities include individuals who are orthopedically impaired, visually impaired, speech-impaired, deaf, hard-of-hearing, hearing-impaired, and health-impaired (cystic fibrosis, epilepsy). Strategies will depend on the specific disability. | Description |
| • Provide many opportunities for creative behavior.<br><br>• Make assignments that call for original work, independent learning, critical thinking, problem solving, and experimentation.<br><br>• Show appreciation for creative efforts.<br><br>• Respect unusual questions, ideas, and solutions these students provide.<br><br>• Encourage students to test their ideas.<br><br>• Provide opportunities and give credit for self-initiated learning.<br><br>• Avoid over-supervising these students.<br><br>• Avoid relying too heavily on prescribed curricula.<br><br>• Allow time for reflection.<br><br>• Resist immediate and constant evaluation. This causes students to be afraid to use their creativity.<br><br>• Avoid comparisons with other students, which applies subtle pressure to conform. | • Use a slow, but natural rate of speech; speak clearly; use shorter sentences; repeat concepts in several ways.<br><br>• Act out questions using gestures with hands, arms, and the whole body. Use demonstrations and pantomime. Ask questions that can be answered by a physical movement such as pointing, nodding, or manipulating materials.<br><br>• When possible, use picture, photos, and charts.<br><br>• Write key terms on the chalkboard. Point to the terms as you use them.<br><br>• Corrections should be limited and appropriate. Do not correct grammar or usage errors in front of the class, causing embarrassment.<br><br>• Give honest praise and positive feedback through your voice tones and visual articulation whenever possible.<br><br>• Encourage students to use language to communicate, allowing them to use their native language to ask/answer questions when they are unable to do so in English.<br><br>• Integrate students' cultural background into class discussions.<br><br>• Use cooperative learning where students have opportunities to practice expressing ideas without risking language errors in front of the entire class. | • Seat visually and hearing-impaired students near the front of the classroom. Speak clearly and say out loud what you are writing on the chalkboard.<br><br>• To reduce the risk of injury in lab settings, ask students about any conditions that could affect their ability to learn or perform.<br><br>• Rearrange lab equipment or the classroom and make modifications as needed to accommodate any special need.<br><br>• Investigate assistive technology devices that can improve students' functional capabilities.<br><br>• Discuss specific solutions or modifications with the physically disabled student. He or she has experience with overcoming his or her disability and may have suggestions you may not have considered.<br><br>• Let the student know when classroom modifications are being made and allow him or her to test them out before class.<br><br>• Ask advice from a special education teacher, school nurse, or physical therapist.<br><br>• Plan field trips that can include all students. | Teaching Strategies |

# Marketing Your Program

Your class is likely to be the child development class some of your students have taken. Many students and their parents may have preconceived ideas about what child development curriculum includes. You need to identify these preconceptions and, if necessary, gently alter them to give students and their parents a more accurate idea of what your class entails. You may need to make them aware of the value child development classes hold for students at a variety of levels.

Students and their parents are not likely to be the only ones who are not totally aware of the importance of child development classes. You can make people more aware through good public relations. It pays to make the student body, faculty, and community aware of your program. With good public relations, you can increase your enrollment, gain support from administrators and other teachers, and achieve recognition in the community. Following are some ways to market your program:

→ Create visibility. It is important to let people know what is going on in your program. Ways to do this include announcements of projects and activities at faculty meetings and in school bulletins or newspapers, displays in school showcases or on bulletin boards, and articles and press releases in school and community newspapers. Talk about your program with administrators, other teachers, and students. Invite them to visit your classes.

→ Interact with other subject matter areas. Child development information is related to many fields of learning. You can strengthen your program and contribute to other disciplines by cooperating with other teachers. For example, you can work with a science teacher to present information on the genetic principles involved in prenatal development. The more interaction you can generate, the more you promote your class.

→ Contribute to the educational objectives of the school. If your school follows stated educational objectives and strives to strengthen specific skills, include these overall goals in your teaching. For example, if students need special help in developing verbal or writing skills, select projects and assignments that will help them in these areas. Show administrators examples of work that indicate student improvement in needed skills.

→ Serve as a resource center. Child development information is of practical use and interest to almost everyone. You can sell your program by making your department a resource center of materials related to pregnancy; parenting; safety and health; healthful food choices for pregnant women and children of all ages; child development from conception to adolescence; and child-related careers. Invite faculty members, students, and parents to tap into the wealth of child development information available in your classroom.

→ Generate involvement and activity in the community. You are teaching concepts students can apply in their everyday lives. You can involve students in community life and bring the community into your classroom through field trips, interviews with businesspeople and community leaders, surveys, and presentations from guest speakers. You may be able to set up cooperative projects between the school and community organizations around a variety of topics.

→ Connect with parents. If you can get them involved, parents may be your best allies in teaching child development. Let parents know when their children have done good work. Moms and dads have had experiences related to many of the issues you discuss in class. They have experienced pregnancy, childbirth, and parenting. Call on them to share individually or as part of a panel addressing a specific topic. Parents can be a rich source of real-life experience. Keep them informed about classroom activities and invite them to participate as they are able.

→ Establish a student sales staff. Enthusiastic students will be your best salespeople. Encourage them to tell their parents and friends what they are learning in your classes. You might create bulletin boards or write letters to parents that focus on what students are learning in your classes. Ask students to put together a newsletter highlighting their experiences in your child development class. Students could write a column from your department for the school paper.

# Goodheart-Willcox Welcomes Your Comments

We are continually striving to publish better educational materials. Therefore, we welcome your comments and suggestions regarding *Children: The Early Years* and its ancillaries. Please send any comments you may have to

Editorial Department
Goodheart-Willcox Publisher
18604 West Creek Drive
Tinley Park, IL 60477-6243

or to send a memo to the editor, visit our Web site at www.goodheartwillcox.com

# Evaluating Individual Participation

**Name** _____ **Date** _____ **Period** _____

The rating scale below shows an evaluation of your class participation. It indicates what levels you have passed and what levels you can continue to try to reach.

## Attentiveness

| 1 | 2 | 3 | 4 | 5 | 6 | 7 | 8 | 9 | 10 |
|---|---|---|---|---|---|---|---|---|----|

Completely inattentive. | | Seldom attentive. | | Somewhat attentive. | | | Usually attentive. | | Extremely attentive.

## Contribution to Discussion

| 1 | 2 | 3 | 4 | 5 | 6 | 7 | 8 | 9 | 10 |
|---|---|---|---|---|---|---|---|---|----|

Never contributes to class discussion. | | Rarely contributes to class discussion. | | Occasionally contributes to class discussion. | | | Regularly contributes to class discussion. | | Frequently contributes to class discussion.

## Interaction with Peers

| 1 | 2 | 3 | 4 | 5 | 6 | 7 | 8 | 9 | 10 |
|---|---|---|---|---|---|---|---|---|----|

Often distracts others. | | Shows little interaction with others. | | Follows leadership of other students. | | | Sometimes assumes leadership role. | | Respected by peers for ability.

## Response to Teacher

| 1 | 2 | 3 | 4 | 5 | 6 | 7 | 8 | 9 | 10 |
|---|---|---|---|---|---|---|---|---|----|

Unable to respond when called on. | | Often unable to support or justify answers when called on. | | Supports answers based on class information, but seldom offers new ideas. | | | Able to offer new ideas with prompting. | | Often offers new ideas without prompting.

**Comments:**

_____
_____
_____

# Evaluating Individual Reports

**Name** _____**Date**_____**Period**_____

The rating scale below shows an evaluation of your oral or written report. It indicates what levels you have passed and what levels you can try to reach on future reports.

**Report topic** _____**Oral** _____ **Written** _____

## Criteria:

## Choice of Topic

| 1 | 2 | 3 | 4 | 5 | 6 | 7 | 8 | 9 | 10 |
|---|---|---|---|---|---|---|---|---|----|
| Slow to choose topic. | | Chooses topic with indifference. | | Chooses topic as assigned, seeks suggestions. | | | Chooses relevant topic without assistance. | | Chooses creative topic. |

## Use of Resources

| 1 | 2 | 3 | 4 | 5 | 6 | 7 | 8 | 9 | 10 |
|---|---|---|---|---|---|---|---|---|----|
| Unable to find resources. | | Needs direction to find resources. | | Uses fewer than assigned number of resources. | | | Uses assigned number of resources from typical sources. | | Uses additional resources from a variety of sources. |

## Oral Presentation

| 1 | 2 | 3 | 4 | 5 | 6 | 7 | 8 | 9 | 10 |
|---|---|---|---|---|---|---|---|---|----|
| No notes or read completely. Poor subject coverage. | | Has few good notes. Limited subject coverage. | | Uses notes somewhat effectively. Adequate subject coverage. | | | Uses notes effectively. Good subject coverage. | | Uses notes very effectively. Complete coverage. |

## Written Presentation

| 1 | 2 | 3 | 4 | 5 | 6 | 7 | 8 | 9 | 10 |
|---|---|---|---|---|---|---|---|---|----|
| Many grammar and spelling mistakes. No organization. | | Several grammar and spelling mistakes. Poor organization. | | Some grammar and spelling mistakes. Fair organization. | | | A few grammar and spelling mistakes. Good organization. | | No grammar or spelling mistakes. Excellent organization. |

# Evaluating Group Participation

**Group**
**Members:** _____     _____
             _____     _____
             _____     _____

The rating scale below shows an evaluation of the efforts of your group. It indicates what levels you have passed and what levels you can try to reach on future group projects.

## Teamwork

| 1 | 2 | 3 | 4 | 5 | 6 | 7 | 8 | 9 | 10 |
|---|---|---|---|---|---|---|---|---|---|

| | | | | |
|---|---|---|---|---|
| Passive membership. Failed to identify what tasks needed to be completed. | Argumentative membership. Unable to designate who should complete each task. | Independent membership. All tasks completed individually. | Helpful membership. Completed individual tasks and then assisted others. | Cooperative membership. Worked together to complete all tasks. |

## Leadership

| 1 | 2 | 3 | 4 | 5 | 6 | 7 | 8 | 9 | 10 |
|---|---|---|---|---|---|---|---|---|---|

| | | | | |
|---|---|---|---|---|
| No effective leadership. | Group fragmented by several members seeking leadership roles. | Sought leadership from outside group. | One member assumed primary leadership role for the group. | Leadership responsibilities shared by several group members. |

## Goal Achievement

| 1 | 2 | 3 | 4 | 5 | 6 | 7 | 8 | 9 | 10 |
|---|---|---|---|---|---|---|---|---|---|

| | | | | |
|---|---|---|---|---|
| Did not attempt to achieve goal. | Were unable to achieve goal. | Achieved goal with outside assistance. | Achieved assigned goal. | Achieved goal using added materials to enhance total effort. |

Members cited for excellent contributions to group's effort are:

_____     _____

_____     _____

Members cited for failing to contribute to group's effort are:

_____     _____

_____     _____

# Correlation of National Standards for Human Development with
# Children: The Early Years

In planning your program, you may want to use the correlation chart below. This chart correlates the Family and Consumer Sciences Education National Standards with the content of *Children: The Early Years*. It lists the competencies for each of the content standards for Human Development. It also identifies the major text concepts that relate to each competency. Bold numbers indicate chapters in which concepts are found.

After studying the content of this text, students will be able to achieve the following comprehensive standard:

*12.0 Analyze factors that impact human growth and development.*

**Content Standard 12.1   Analyze principles of human growth and development across the life span.**

| Competencies | Text Concepts |
|---|---|
| **12.1.1** Examine physical, emotional, social, and intellectual development. | **1:** To be a responsible parent; what is child development?; individual life cycle; factors that influence growth and development; brain development; differences in the rate of growth and development; principles of growth and development; Havighurst's theory of developmental tasks; Maslow's theory of human needs; observing children<br>**4:** Conception; genetic factors and the unborn baby; stages in prenatal development<br>**5:** Factors that affect the baby's health; health habits during pregnancy; health hazards to avoid; bonding<br>**6:** Care for premature babies; physical traits of a newborn; reflexes; meeting the newborn's physical needs; meeting the newborn's intellectual needs; meeting the newborn's social-emotional needs<br>**7:** Skeletal growth of infants; motor development of infants; differences in physical development of infants<br>**8:** Brain development supports learning; perception; cognition; perceptual concepts; beginnings of language: brain development research<br>**9:** Temperamental differences in infants; the infant's growing social world; interacting with others; learning to trust; showing attachment; infants express emotions<br>**10:** Physical needs of infants; intellectual needs of infants; social-emotional needs of infants; recognizing developmental delays in infants<br>**11:** Body growth and development of toddlers; motor development of toddlers<br>**12:** How and what toddlers learn; beginning of thought; language abilities<br>**13:** Self-awareness of toddlers; extending social relations; emotions of toddlers<br>**14:** Physical needs of toddlers; intellectual needs of toddlers; social-emotional needs of toddlers; recognizing developmental delays of toddlers<br>**15:** Body growth and development of preschoolers; motor development of preschoolers<br>**16:** How and what preschoolers learn; language abilities increase<br>**17:** Developing social awareness during the preschool years; learning gender roles of preschoolers; feeling and controlling emotions<br>**18:** Physical needs of preschoolers; intellectual needs of preschoolers; social-emotional needs of preschoolers; recognizing developmental delays in preschoolers<br>**19:** Physical development of school-age children; intellectual development of school-age children; helping school-age children meet their intellectual needs; social-emotional development of school-age children; helping school-age children with their social-emotional needs; recognizing developmental delays in school-age children<br>**20:** Children and their world of play; stages of play; types of play; providing enrichment activities for children; books and literature<br>**21:** Protecting children from disease and illness; accident prevention; caring for an ill or injured child; caring for a terminally ill child<br>**23:** Children with developmental differences; children who are exceptional; exceptional children need special help<br>**24:** Sibling relationships |

| 12.1.2 Examine interrelationships among physical, emotional, social, and intellectual aspects of human growth and development. | **1:** Growth and development have interrelated parts<br>**6:** Meeting the newborn's physical needs; meeting the newborn's intellectual needs; meeting the newborn's social-emotional needs<br>**10:** Physical needs of infants; intellectual needs of infants; social-emotional needs of infants; recognizing developmental delays in infants<br>**14:** Physical needs of toddlers; intellectual needs of toddlers; learning through play; social-emotional needs of toddlers; recognizing developmental delays in toddlers<br>**18:** Physical needs of preschoolers; intellectual needs of preschoolers; social-emotional needs of preschoolers; recognizing developmental delays in preschoolers<br>**19:** Physical development of school-age children; intellectual development of school-age children; helping school-age children meet their intellectual needs; social-emotional development of school-age children; helping school-age children with their social-emotional needs; recognizing developmental delays in school-age children<br>**20:** Importance of play |
|---|---|

## Content Standard 12.2　Analyze conditions that influence human growth and development.

| Competencies | Text Concepts |
|---|---|
| **12.2.1** Investigate the impact of heredity and environment on human growth and development. | **1:** Factors that influence growth and development; heredity; environment; heredity and environment combined; heredity and environment interact<br>**2:** Roles of parents; parenting styles; characteristics of healthy families<br>**4:** Genetic factors and the unborn baby; multiple pregnancy<br>**5:** The unborn baby's environment; factors that affect the baby's health; health habits during pregnancy; health hazards to avoid; congenital problems; monitoring the baby's development; bonding<br>**6:** What brain research says about newborns; how can parents help their babies learn? meeting the newborn's social-emotional needs<br>**7:** Body growth and development of infants; differences in physical development<br>**8:** Brain development supports learning<br>**9:** Temperamental differences in infants; learning to trust<br>**10:** Intellectual needs; activities to stimulate the senses; problem-solving activities<br>**11:** Height and weight<br>**12:** Learning meanings: a major brain development activity; different rates in learning to talk<br>**19:** Height and weight<br>**20:** The adult's role in children's play |
| **12.2.2** Determine the impact of social, economic, and technological forces on individual growth and development. | **2:** Characteristics of healthy families; cultural influences on families<br>**3:** Deciding about parenthood; factors to consider; sharing parenting responsibilities; managing finances; managing careers; family planning; infertility and sterility<br>**5:** Medical care; ultrasound; chorionic villus sampling; amniocentesis<br>**6:** Medical care and testing; care for premature babies<br>**17:** Developing social awareness<br>**18:** Learning through observing; television<br>**19:** Peer groups<br>**24:** Sibling relationships; parental employment; balancing family and work; family moves<br>**25:** A market overview; seeking education and training; an inside view; careers in child-related fields; job training; communication skills; managing multiple roles |
| **12.2.3** Examine the effects of gender, ethnicity, and culture on individual development. | **1:** To be a responsible parent<br>**2:** Changes affecting families today; socialization; cultural influences on families; multicultural families<br>**17:** Learning gender roles; cultural factors<br>**18:** Aiding gender role learning<br>**19:** Extending gender role<br>**22:** Parent communication and participation; cultural diversity in group programs |

| 12.2.4 Examine the effects of life events on individuals' physical and emotional development. | **2:** Changes affecting families today; changes in family roles; family types; adoption; the family life cycle<br>**23:** Children with developmental differences; children who are exceptional; exceptional children need special help<br>**24:** Sibling relationships; parental employment; balancing family and work; children in self-care; coping with family moves; coping with death; coping with divorce; single parenting; remarriage and stepparenting; teens as parents; child abuse and neglect |
|---|---|

## Content Standard 12.3    Analyze strategies that promote growth and development across the life span.

| Competencies | Text Concepts |
|---|---|
| 12.3.1 Examine the role of nurturance on human growth and development. | **1:** To be a responsible parent; to protect children's rights<br>**2:** Roles of parents; nurturance; guidance and discipline; parenting styles<br>**3:** Learning parenting skills<br>**6:** Meeting the newborn's social-emotional needs<br>**9:** Separation anxiety; the infant's growing social world; learning to trust; showing attachment; infants express emotions<br>**10:** Social-emotional needs of infants<br>**13:** Self-awareness of toddlers; extending social relations; emotions<br>**14:** Social-emotional needs of toddlers; recognizing developmental delays<br>**17:** Developing social awareness during the preschool years; feeling and controlling emotions<br>**18:** Social-emotional needs of preschoolers; recognizing developmental delays<br>**19:** Social-emotional development of school-age children; helping school-age children with their social-emotional needs; recognizing developmental delays<br>**20:** Children and their world of play; stages of play; types of play; providing enrichment activities for children<br>**24:** Sibling relationships |
| 12.3.2 Examine the role of communication on human growth and development. | **8:** Beginnings of language: brain development research; how babies communicate; passive versus active vocabulary<br>**11:** Language abilities of toddlers; learning spoken language; different rates of learning to talk<br>**14:** Language activities for toddlers<br>**16:** Language abilities of preschoolers increase; articulation of preschool children; vocabulary of preschool children; grammar of preschool children<br>**18:** Preschoolers use symbols in language; learning through language<br>**19:** Language is mastered by school-age children<br>**20:** Language-logic play; literature<br>**22:** Parent communication and participation<br>**23:** Children with speech disorders; help for children with special needs<br>**24:** Helping children cope with death; coping with the effects of divorce; preparing for family changes<br>**25:** Communication skills |
| 12.3.3 Examine the role of support systems in meeting human growth and development needs. | **2:** Single-parent families; extended families; families with adopted children; foster families<br>**3:** Learning parenting skills<br>**5:** Postpartum mood disorders<br>**6:** Meeting the parents' needs<br>**17:** Extending social relations<br>**19:** Peers become important; guiding and modeling behavior<br>**21:** Preparing a child for routine and hospital care; caring for an ill or injured child; caring for a terminally ill child<br>**22:** Types of child care programs; choosing a group program; effects of group care on children; helping children adjust to group care<br>**23:** Helping children with special needs<br>**24:** Helping children cope with grief; family members need support throughout a divorce; helping children cope with living in a single-parent family; teens as parents; financial concerns; lifestyle changes; child abuse and neglect; treatment for victims; what are the causes of neglect and abuse? how can neglect and abuse be prevented? resources for children in crisis |

# Scope and Sequence

In planning your program, you may want to use the Scope and Sequence chart below. This chart identifies the major concepts presented in each chapter of the test. Refer to the chart to find the material that meets your curriculum needs. Bold numbers indicate chapters in which concepts are found.

## Part 1: Children in Today's World

### ■ Parenthood

**1:** Why study children? To understand yourself; To be a responsible parent; To protect children's rights

**2:** Changes affecting families today; Changes in family roles; Family types; The family life cycle; Roles of parents; Socialization; Nurturance; Guidance and discipline; Parenting styles; Characteristics of healthy families; Cultural influences on families

**3:** Why is it hard to be a good parent? Learning parenting skills; Deciding about parenthood; Reasons for choosing parenthood; Reasons for not choosing parenthood; How children affect relationships; Sharing responsibilities; Managing finances; Managing careers; Family planning

### ■ Principles of Growth and Development

**1:** Why study children? To be a responsible parent; What is child development? Individual life cycle; Factors that influence growth and development; Heredity and environment; Differences in the rate of growth and development; Principles of growth and development; Theories of growth and development; Havighurst's theory of developmental tasks; Maslow's theory of human needs; Developmental tasks; Observing children; Why observe children? What do researchers want to know? Ways to observe; Direct observations; Indirect observations; Guidelines for observations

**2:** The family life cycle; Types of discipline; Parenting styles

### ■ Physical Development

**1:** To be a responsible parent; Heredity and environment; Brain development

**2:** Nurturance

### ■ Intellectual Development

**1:** To be a responsible parent; To work with children; Brain development; Basic wiring occurs; Heredity and environment interact; Windows of opportunity; Brain plasticity

**2:** Nurturance; Guidance and discipline

### ■ Social-Emotional Development

**1:** Why study children? To understand yourself; To be a responsible parent; Developmental tasks

**2:** Socialization; Nurturance; Guidance and discipline; Parenting styles

## ◼ Caring for and Guiding Children

**1:** To be a responsible parent; To protect children's rights; To work with children

**2:** Changes affecting families today; Changes in family roles; Family types; The family life cycle; Roles of parents; Socialization; Nurturance; Guidance and discipline; Parenting styles; Cultural influences on families

**3:** Why is it hard to be a good parent? Learning parenting skills; Deciding about parenthood; Reasons for choosing parenthood; How children affect relationships; Sharing responsibilities

## ◼ Family Relationships

**1:** To be a responsible parent; Heredity and environment combined

**2:** Changes affecting families today; Changes in family roles; Family types; Two-parent families; Single-parent families; Extended families; Stepfamilies; Families with adopted children; Foster families; The family life cycle; Characteristics of healthy families; Cultural influences on families

**3:** Why is it hard to be a good parent? Learning parenting skills; How children affect relationships; Sharing responsibilities; Managing finances; Managing careers; Family planning

## ◼ Safety and Health

**1:** To be a responsible parent; To protect children's rights

**2:** Adoption options and rights; Adoption issues

**3:** Why is it hard to be a good parent? Learning parenting skills; Problems with family and work; Infertility and sterility

## ◼ Children with Special Needs

**1:** Why study children?

## ◼ Leadership and Careers

**1:** Why study children? To work with children; Observing children; Why observe children? What do researchers want to know? Ways to observe; Direct observations; Indirect observations; Guidelines for observations

**3:** Sharing responsibilities; Managing finances; Managing careers

# Part 2: Prenatal Development and the Newborn

## ◼ Parenthood

**5:** The role of the family; Family involvement; Bonding

**6:** Meeting the newborn's physical needs; Feeding; Clothing and dressing; Diapering; Bathing; Sleeping; Exercising; Scheduling; How can parents help their babies learn? Meeting the parents' needs; The need for rest; Organize tasks; Time to be with adults

## Prenatal and Postnatal Care and Development

**4:** Genetic factors and the unborn baby; Multiple pregnancy; Conception; Stages of prenatal development; Germinal stage; Embryonic stage; Fetal stage

**5:** Signs of pregnancy; Medical care; The unborn baby's environment; Factors that affect the baby's health; Mother's age; Mother's physical health; Rh factor; Mother's emotional health; Health habits during pregnancy; Nutrition; Weight gain; Hygiene practices; Rest and sleep; Physical activity and exercise; Health hazards to avoid; Diseases or illnesses in the mother; Radiation exposure; Complications of pregnancy; Monitoring the baby's development; Ultrasound; Chorionic villus sampling; Amniocentesis; The role of the family; Family involvement; Family decisions concerning childbirth; Stages of labor; Bonding; Postpartum care

**6:** Medical care and testing; Care for premature babies; The Apgar test; Neonatal assessment scales; Other hospital care; Reflexes

## Principles of Growth and Development

**5:** Bonding

**6:** What can newborns do?

## Physical Development

**5:** Factors that affect the baby's health; Mother's age; Mother's physical health; Mother's emotional health; Health habits during pregnancy; Weight gain; Health hazards to avoid; Monitoring the baby's development; Time to be born; Bonding

**6:** Medical care and testing; Care for premature babies; Physical traits of a newborn; Reflexes; Meeting the newborn's physical needs; Feeding; Clothing and dressing; Diapering; Bathing; Sleeping; Exercising; Scheduling

## Intellectual Development

**5:** The role of the family; Family involvement; Bonding

**6:** Meeting the newborn's intellectual needs; What brain research says about newborns; What can newborns do? How can parents help their babies learn?

## Social-Emotional Development

**5:** Factors that affect the baby's health; Mother's emotional health; The role of the family; Family involvement; Bonding

**6:** Meeting the newborn's social-emotional needs; Alertness of newborns; Soothing a fussy baby

## Caring for and Guiding Children

**5:** The role of the family; Family involvement; Bonding

**6:** Meeting the newborn's physical needs; Meeting the newborn's social-emotional needs

## Family Relationships

**5:** The role of the family; Family involvement; Bonding

**6:** Meeting the parents' needs

## ◼ Safety and Health

**4:** Conception; Genetic factors and the unborn baby; Chromosomes and genes; Dominant and recessive traits; Sex chromosomes; Multiple pregnancy; Fraternal births; Identical births; Mixed types

**5:** Signs of pregnancy; Medical care; The first appointment; The unborn baby's environment; Factors that affect the baby's health; Mother's age; Mother's physical health; Rh factor; Mother's emotional health; Health habits during pregnancy; Nutrition; Weight gain; Hygiene practices; Rest and sleep; Physical activity and exercise; Health hazards to avoid; Diseases or illnesses in the mother; Pregnancy-induced hypertension (PIH); Sexually transmitted diseases (STDs); Drugs; Radiation exposure; Environmental pollution; Complications of pregnancy; Miscarriage; Congenital problems; Monitoring the baby's development; Ultrasound; Chorionic villus sampling; Amniocentesis; Family decisions concerning childbirth; Time to be born; Complications of delivery; Hospital care; Bonding; Postpartum care

**6:** Medical care and testing; Care for premature babies; The Apgar test; The neonatal assessment scales; Other hospital care; Well-baby checkup; Meeting the newborn's physical needs; Feeding; Bathing; Exercising; Scheduling; Clothing and dressing; Diapering; Sleeping

## ◼ Children with Special Needs

**5:** Factors that affect the baby's health; Health hazards to avoid; Complications of pregnancy; Congenital problems; Ultrasound; Chorionic villus sampling; Amniocentesis; Complications of delivery; Cesarean births

**6:** Care for premature babies; The Apgar test; The neonatal assessment scales; Other hospital care

## Part 3 Infants

## ◼ Parenthood

**10:** Physical needs; Establishing routines; Intellectual needs; Social-emotional needs; Baby-adult interaction; Handling special problems; Recognizing developmental delays

## ◼ Principles of Growth and Development

**7:** Head-to-foot development; Center-to-extremities development

**8:** Cognition; Perceptual concepts

**9:** Temperamental differences in infants; Learning to trust; Showing attachment

**10:** Recognizing developmental delays

## ◼ Physical Development

**7:** Skeletal growth; Length and weight; Body proportions; Bones and teeth; Motor development; Head-to-foot development; Center-to-extremities development; Differences in physical development

**10:** Physical needs; Feeding; Weaning; Clothing; Diapering a baby; Tub bathing; Establishing routines; Rest and sleep; Places for sleep and play

## Intellectual Development

**8:** How infants learn; Brain development supports learning; Thinking and memory centers; Perception; Cognition; Sensorimotor stage; Piaget's stages of cognitive development; What infants learn; Perceptual concepts; Object constancy or sameness; Object concept; Depth perception; Beginnings of language: Brain development research; How babies communicate; Passive versus active vocabulary

**10:** Intellectual needs; Activities to stimulate the senses; Problem-solving activities; Sensory stimulation activities; Language activities; Recognizing developmental delays

## Social-Emotional Development

**9:** Temperamental differences in infants; The infant's growing social world; Interacting with others; Learning to trust; Erikson's stages of personality development; Showing attachment; Bonding and attachment; Development of attachment behaviors; Infants express emotions; Love; Fear; Anxiety; Anger

**10:** Social-emotional needs; Baby-adult interaction; Helping babies develop self-awareness; Handling special problems; Recognizing developmental delays

## Caring for and Guiding Children

**10:** Physical needs; Feeding; Weaning; Clothing; Diapering a baby; Tub bathing; Establishing routines; Places for sleep and play; Intellectual needs; Activities to stimulate the senses; Problem-solving activities; Motor activities; Language activities

## Safety and Health

**10:** Physical needs; Sudden Infant Death Syndrome; Rest and sleep; Recognizing developmental delays

## Children with Special Needs

**7:** Differences in physical development

## Part 4 Toddlers

## Parenthood

**14:** Physical needs; Intellectual needs; Social-emotional needs; Recognizing developmental delays

## Principles of Growth and Development

**13:** Self-awareness; Achieving autonomy
**14:** Recognizing developmental delays

## Physical Development

**11:** Body growth and development; Height and weight; Other body changes; Growth from birth to age two years; Average height and weight from one to three years; Motor development; Large-muscle development; Small-muscle development

**14:** Recognizing developmental delays

## ■ Intellectual Development

**12:** How and what toddlers learn; Discovering new ways to solve problems; Beginning of thought; Language abilities; Learning spoken language; The tool of communication; Different rates of learning to talk

**14:** Intellectual needs; Learning through activities; Learning through play; Sensory stimulation activities; Problem-solving activities; Motor activities; Language activities; Recognizing developmental delays

## ■ Social-Emotional Development

**13:** Self-awareness; Achieving autonomy; Erikson's stages of personality development; Promoting a toddler's autonomy; Extending social relations; Self-esteem; Emotions; Affection; Fear; Anxiety; Anger

**14:** Social-emotional needs; Discipline; Balancing self-assertion and obedience; Guidance: Helping toddlers control their emotions; Planning self-awareness activities; Recognizing developmental delays

## ■ Caring for and Guiding Children

**14:** Physical needs; Feeding; Clothing; Rest and sleep; Hygiene; Toilet learning; Intellectual needs; Learning through activities; Learning through play; Sensory stimulation activities; Problem-solving activities; Motor activities; Language activities; Discipline; Guidance: Helping toddlers control their emotions; Planning self-awareness activities

## ■ Safety and Health

**14:** Feeding; Hygiene; Toilet learning; Recognizing developmental delays

## ■ Children with Special Needs

**14:** Recognizing developmental delays

# Part 5 Preschoolers and School-Age Children

## ■ Parenthood

**18:** Physical needs; Meeting nutritional needs; Selecting the right clothes; Handling sleep and toileting problems; Providing needed space and furnishings; Learning responsibility; Intellectual needs; Discipline: Helping with initiative and mistakes; Sharing responsibility; Aiding gender role learning; Providing time for friendships; Helping children with emotional control; Recognizing developmental delays

**19:** Helping school-age children meet their intellectual needs; Guiding intellectual development; Preparing the child to enter school; Guiding the child to school; Guiding television viewing; Assisting computer use; Helping school-age children with their social-emotional needs; Guiding and modeling behavior; Enjoying family ties; Providing time for friendships; Listening; Helping children control their emotions; Helping children improve their self-esteem; Recognizing developmental delays

## ■ Principles of Growth and Development

**16:** How preschool children learn; Obstacles to logical thinking

**17:** Taking the initiative

**19:** How school-age children think; Seeing from the viewpoint of others; Focusing on more than one part; Using reversibility logic; Using deductive and inductive reasoning; What school-age children learn

## ◼ Physical Development

**15:** Body growth and development; Height and weight; Other body changes; Motor development; Gross-motor development; Fine-motor development

**18:** Physical needs; Meeting nutritional needs; Recognizing developmental needs

**19:** Physical development of school-age children; Body growth and development; Motor development; Providing for school-age children's physical needs; Recognizing developmental delays

## ◼ Intellectual Development

**16:** How preschool children learn; Obstacles to logical thinking; Piaget's stages of cognitive development; What preschool children learn; Concepts children learn; Language abilities increase; Articulation of preschool children; Vocabulary of preschool children; Grammar of preschool children

**18:** Intellectual needs; Learning through observing; Learning through problem solving; Learning through symbolizing; Using symbols in art; Using symbols in language; Learning through motor skills; Learning through language; Computers and learning; Recognizing developmental delays

**19:** Intellectual development of school-age children; Piaget's stages of cognitive development; How school-age children think; Using reversibility logic; Noting transformations; Using deductive and inductive reasoning; What school-age children learn; Language is mastered; Helping school-age children meet their intellectual needs; Guiding intellectual development

## ◼ Social-Emotional Development

**17:** Developing social awareness; Taking the initiative; Erikson's stages of personality development; Show responsibility; Learning gender roles; How does gender role develop? Cultural factors; Extending social relations; Feeling and controlling emotions; Dependency; Fear and anxiety; Anger and aggression; Jealousy

**18:** Social-emotional needs; Discipline: Helping with initiative and mistakes; Sharing responsibility; Aiding gender role learning; Providing time for friendships; Helping children with emotional control; Fear and anxiety; Anger and aggression; Recognizing developmental delays

**19:** Social-emotional development of school-age children; Developing the self-concept; Showing social awareness; Erikson's stages of personality development; Controlling emotions

## ◼ Caring for and Guiding Children

**17:** Learning gender roles; How does gender role develop? Cultural factors; Extending social relations

**18:** Physical needs; Meeting nutritional needs; Selecting the right clothes; Handling sleep and toileting problems; Providing needed space and furnishings; Learning responsibility

**19:** Helping school-age children meet their intellectual needs; Guiding intellectual development; Preparing the child to enter school; Getting the child to school; Reinforcing school tasks; Guiding television viewing; Assisting computer use; Helping school-age children with their social-emotional needs; Guiding and modeling behavior; Balance dependent with independence; Extend gender role; Encourage work and industry; Extend children's horizons; Keep family communication open; Listening; Enjoying family ties; Providing time for friendships; Helping children control their emotions; Helping children improve their self-esteem; Recognizing developmental delays

## ■ Family Relationships

**17:** Learning gender roles; How does gender role develop? Cultural factors; Extending social relations

**19:** Keep family communication open; Listening; Enjoying family ties

## ■ Safety and Health

**18:** Preventing eating problems

**19:** Encouraging health and safety practices; Physical activity and other good health practices; Safety practices

## ■ Children with Special Needs

**18:** Recognizing developmental delays

**19:** Recognizing developmental delays

# Part 6 Guiding and Caring for Children

## ■ Parenthood

**20:** The adult's role in children's play; Allow freedom to play; Allow time to explore; Display the right attitude toward play; Select toys with care

**21:** Protecting children from disease and illness; Accident prevention; Childproofing the environment; Safety devices and safety measures; Preparing a child for routine or hospital care; Caring for an ill or injured child; Caring for a terminally ill child

**22:** Choosing a group program; Parent communication and participation; Helping children adjust to group care

**24:** Family togetherness; Balancing family and work

## ■ Principles of Growth and Development

**20:** Children and their world of play; Importance of play; Play and physical development; Play and mental development; Play and social-emotional development; Stages of play; Types of play; Active-physical play; Manipulative-constructive play; Language-logic play; Providing enrichment activities for children; Stages of development in visual arts; Manipulative stage; Representation stage

**24:** Sibling relationships; Sibling interactions; Birth order and development; Traits affected by birth order; Children of multiple births

## ■ Physical Development

**20:** Play and physical development; Active-physical play; Manipulative-constructive play

## ■ Intellectual Development

**20:** Play and mental development; Imitative-imaginative play; Language-logic play; Providing enrichment activities for children

## ■ Social-Emotional Development

**20:** Children and their world of play; Importance of play; Play and social-emotional development; Stages of play

**22:** Effects of group care on children; Effects on social development

**24:** Social life changes

## ■ Family Relationships

**20:** Adult's role in stimulating art experiences; Reacting to children's art; The adult's role in guiding music experiences; The adult's role in encouraging science activities

**24:** Family togetherness

## ■ Caring for and Guiding Children

**20:** The adult's role in children's play; Allow time to explore; Display the right attitude toward play; Providing enrichment activities for children; The adult's role in stimulating art experiences; Reacting to children's art; The adult's role in guiding music experiences; The adult's role in encouraging science activities; Selecting books for children

**21:** Protecting children from disease and illness; Childhood diseases; Allergies; Accident prevention; Anticipating possible hazards; Helping children meet goals in a safe way; Childproofing the environment; Safety lessons; Preparing a child for routine or hospital care; Caring for an ill or injured child; Giving medication and proper care; Caring for a terminally ill child; Helping the ill child cope

**22:** Types of child care programs; Choosing a group program; Quality of group programs; Helping children adjust to group care

**24:** Financial concerns

## ■ Safety and Health

**21:** Nutrition, rest, cleanliness, and physical activity; Medical and dental care; Immunization; Medical attention during illness; Childhood diseases; Allergies; Accident prevention; Creating a safe environment; Supervising children; Anticipating possible hazards; Helping children meet goals in a safe way; Childproofing the environment; Safety devices and safety measures; Safety lessons; Preparing a child for routine or hospital care; Caring for an ill or injured child; Giving medication and proper care; Caring for a terminally ill child

**22:** Choosing a group program; Regulations; Housing and equipment; Staff; Program activities; Cultural diversity in group programs; Providing child care for children with special needs; Quality of group programs; Effects of group care on children; Effects on health; Effects on mental development

**23:** Help for children with special needs; How many children have special needs? What kinds of help are needed?

**24:** Children in self-care; Coping with family moves; Coping with death; Health risks for the teen mother and her baby; Consequences of teen parenting; Family violence; Child neglect and abuse; What happens to the victims? Physical scars; Myths and realities of sexual abuse; Mental scars; Emotional scars; New brain development research findings; Treatment for victims; What are the causes of neglect and abuse? How can neglect and abuse be prevented? Risk factors for neglect and abuse; Recognizing and reporting neglect and abuse; Signs of child neglect and abuse; Resources for children in crises

**25:** Concern for children

## ◼ Leadership and Careers

**22:** Types of group programs; Child care programs; Kindergartens; Nursery schools; Montessori schools; Head Start; Staff

**25:** Heading toward a career; Identifying your interests, aptitudes, and abilities; Learning about careers; A market overview; Seeking education and training; Career information; Develop a career plan; Short-term goals; Long-term goals; Job search skills; Writing a resume; Securing an interview; Completing a job application; Interviewing for a job; Careers in child-related fields; Types of careers; Personal qualifications for a child-related career; Concern for children; Leadership; Professional qualifications for a child-related career; Job training; Skills for job success; Human relations skills; Work ethic; Communication skills; Being a team player; Leadership skills; Managing multiple roles; Leaving a job in the right way

## ◼ Children with Special Needs

**22:** Providing child care for children with special needs

**23:** Children are more alike than different; Children with special needs; Children with gifts and talents; Children with physical disabilities; Children with speech disorders; Children with mental disabilities; Learning disabilities; Children with behavioral disorders

# Basic Skills Chart

The chart below has been designed to identify those activities in *Children: The Early Years* text, *Student Activity Guide*, and *Teacher's Resources* products that specifically encourage the development of basic skills. The following abbreviations are used in the chart:

**Text:** End-of-chapter activities in the text called *Using Your Knowledge*.

**SAG:** Activities in the *Student Activity Guide* (designated by chapter and letter).

**TR:** Strategies described in the *Teacher's Resources* products (referred to by number).

Activities listed as *Verbal* include the following types: class or group discussions, role-playing, conducting interviews, oral reports, and debates.

Activities listed as *Reading* may involve actual reading in and out of the classroom. However, many of these activities are designed to improve reading comprehension of the concepts presented in each chapter. Some are designed to improve understanding of vocabulary terms.

Activities that involve writing are listed under *Writing*. These include activities that allow students to practice composition skills, such as letter writing, informative writing, and creative writing.

The *Math/Science/Technology* list includes activities that require students to use computation skills in solving typical problems they may encounter in everyday living. Activities related to the sciences and computers are also listed.

The final category, *Analytical*, lists activities that involve higher-order thinking skills of analysis, synthesis, and evaluation. Activities that involve decision making, problem solving, and critical thinking are also included in this section. In addition, all the questions under the *Thinking Further* section at the end of each chapter in the text are in this category.

| | Verbal | Reading | Writing | Math/Science/Technology | Analytical |
|---|---|---|---|---|---|
| **Chapter 1** | Text: 1<br>SAG: A, D<br>TR: 1, 3, 8, 9, 11, 14, 15, 16, 17, 24, 25, 28, 30, 31, 34, 35, 36, 40, 41, 43, 45, 47, 52, 53, 54, 56, 58, 60, 61, 63, 64, 65, 66 | Text: 1, 2, 3, 4<br>SAG: B, G<br>TR: 6, 12, 14, 21, 24, 25, 28, 33, 35, 37, 42, 45, 69, 70 | Text: 4<br>SAG: A, B, C, D, E, F, G, H<br>TR: 1, 2, 5, 6, 7, 12, 18, 33, 48, 62, 73 | Text: 2, 3<br><br>TR: 36, 38, 39, 45 | SAG: D, E, F, H<br>TR: 1, 7, 15, 23, 25, 26, 28, 30, 31, 34, 36, 39, 40, 46, 47, 48, 55, 58, 60, 61, 65, 66, 67 |
| **Chapter 2** | Text: 2<br>SAG: C, D<br>TR: 1, 2, 3, 4, 8, 10, 11, 12, 15, 18, 19, 20, 21, 22, 24, 25, 27, 29, 30, 35, 37, 40, 41, 42, 43, 44, 46, 48 | Text: 4<br><br>TR: 1, 9, 13, 17, 32, 45 | Text: 1, 4<br>SAG: A, B, C, D<br>TR: 5, 6, 8, 14, 28, 31, 39, 45, 57 | Text: 4 | SAG: A, C, D<br>TR: 1, 4, 17, 21, 22, 23, 25, 30, 34, 35, 37, 39, 47 |
| **Chapter 3** | SAG: B, C, E<br>TR: 4, 5, 7, 12, 13, 14, 15, 17, 18, 19, 20, 22, 23, 24, 30, 31, 32, 33, 37, 43, 44, 48, 49, 50, 57 | Text: 5<br>SAG: B<br>TR: 1, 9, 19, 27, 48, 49, 57, 59 | Text: 1, 3, 5<br>SAG: D<br>TR: 8, 10, 24, 27, 29, 38, 41, 44, 47, 48, 51, 53, 60 | Text: 1, 3, 4, 5<br>SAG: E<br>TR: 23, 35, 36, 37, 38, 39 | SAG: A, D, E<br>TR: 1, 2, 5, 7, 12, 13, 19, 21, 22, 23, 28, 29, 30, 33, 41, 42, 43, 44, 46, 49, 53, 60 |
| **Chapter 4** | SAG: B, C<br>TR: 2, 6, 8, 9, 10, 12, 13, 17, 18, 20 | Text: 1<br>SAG: A, C, D<br>TR: 1, 9, 12, 13 | Text: 1, 5<br>SAG: A, C<br>TR: 12, 17 | Text: 1, 2, 4<br>SAG: A, B, C, D<br>TR: 6, 8, 9, 14, 19 | Text: 4<br>SAG: B, D<br>TR: 10, 20, 21 |

| | Verbal | Reading | Writing | Math/Science/Technology | Analytical |
|---|---|---|---|---|---|
| Chapter 5 | Text: 2<br>SAG: C<br>TR: 1, 3, 4, 6, 8, 11, 12, 13, 16, 18, 19, 21, 23, 28, 32, 33, 35, 36, 37, 39, 40, 42, 44, 45, 48, 53, 55, 56, 58, 61, 63 | Text: 5<br>SAG: C<br>TR: 14, 16, 28, 30, 34, 37, 46, 48, 57, 60, 64 | Text: 1, 5, 6<br>SAG: A, C, D, E, F<br>TR: 2, 5, 7, 14, 22, 23, 37, 38, 39, 46, 49, 52, 54, 56, 59, 64 | Text: 1, 5<br>SAG: A, B, C<br>TR: 11, 14, 20, 21, 23, 26, 31, 32, 35, 37, 39, 62, 64 | Text: 4<br>SAG: A, E<br>TR: 10, 12, 32, 38, 56, 57, 62 |
| Chapter 6 | Text: 1, 4, 5<br>SAG: C<br>TR: 1, 2, 5, 9, 13, 14, 17, 18, 22, 30, 34, 35, 38, 40, 41, 42, 45, 46 | SAG: C<br>TR: 6, 9, 20, 37 | Text: 4<br>SAG: A, D, E, F<br>TR: 1, 4, 7, 20, 23, 25, 31, 46 | Text: 1, 2, 5<br>SAG: A, B, C, D, E, F<br>TR: 6, 8, 28 | Text: 2, 3<br>SAG: D, E<br>TR: 1, 10, 15, 16, 39, 45 |
| Chapter 7 | Text: 1, 4<br>TR: 3, 6, 8, 9, 13, 14, 15, 20, 22, 28 | Text: 5<br>TR: 4, 5, 11, 17, 18, 21 | Text: 3, 5<br>SAG: A, B, C<br>TR: 2, 3, 10, 11, 27 | Text: 1, 5<br>SAG: A, C<br>TR: 7, 23, 26, 27 | Text: 4<br>SAG: C<br>TR: 23, 26, 27 |
| Chapter 8 | Text: 2, 5<br>TR: 1, 2, 3, 4, 5, 9, 19, 22, 24, 25, 28, 30, 31, 32, 36, 37, 38, 39 | SAG: C<br>TR: 10, 16, 23 | Text: 1<br>SAG: A, B, D<br>TR: 1, 6, 8, 23, 25, 27, 33 | Text: 1, 2<br>TR: 11, 12, 14 | SAG: A, C<br>TR: 3, 7, 14, 17, 18, 20, 22, 23, 30, 31 |
| Chapter 9 | Text: 2, 3, 4<br>SAG: C<br>TR: 1, 2, 6, 7, 8, 9, 10, 11, 13, 14, 20, 21, 22, 24, 25, 30, 31, 32, 33, 34, 35, 39 | TR: 3, 15, 37 | Text: 1<br>SAG: A, B, C, D<br>TR: 7, 9, 18, 27, 28, 29 | Text: 3 | TR: 3, 4, 6, 15, 27, 32, 34, 38 |
| Chapter 10 | Text: 5<br>TR: 1, 2, 7, 8, 11, 12, 14, 15, 17, 19, 20, 25, 34, 35, 36, 38, 40, 41, 43, 45, 46, 47, 48, 50 | TR: 21, 23, 39 | Text: 2, 4<br>SAG: A, B, E<br>TR: 3, 4, 5, 7, 22, 23, 25, 27, 28, 38, 44, 49, 50 | Text: 3<br>TR: 13 | Text: 1<br>SAG: B, C, D<br>TR: 4, 13, 15, 18, 32, 45 |
| Chapter 11 | Text: 4, 5<br>TR: 3, 7, 9, 15, 18, 22, 25, 26, 27 | TR: 1, 4, 14, 23, 24 | Text: 1, 5<br>SAG: B, C<br>TR: 1, 10, 12, 19, 20, 21, 24 | Text: 1, 3, 4<br>SAG: A<br>TR: 7, 8 | Text: 3<br>SAG: C<br>TR: 13 |

| | Verbal | Reading | Writing | Math/Science/ Technology | Analytical |
|---|---|---|---|---|---|
| Chapter 12 | Text: 2, 3, 4<br>SAG: D<br>TR: 1, 2, 9, 10, 14, 16, 17, 23, 24 | TR: 18, 21, 22 | Text: 2<br>SAG: A, B<br>TR: 3, 6, 11, 12, 15 | SAG: A<br>TR: 19, 20 | SAG: C |
| Chapter 13 | Text: 1, 3,5<br>SAG: C<br>TR: 1, 2, 3, 4, 7, 10, 12, 14, 15, 16, 21, 22, 23, 24, 25, 27, 28, 29, 30 | Text: 3, 4<br>TR: 6, 29 | Text: 2, 4<br>SAG: A, B, C<br>TR: 8, 9, 12, 17, 18, 20 | SAG: B, D, E<br>TR: 4 | |
| Chapter 14 | Text: 3, 4, 5<br>SAG: D, H, J<br><br>TR: 2, 3, 6, 7, 8, 15, 16, 17, 18, 21, 24, 29, 32, 33, 37, 41, 45, 50, 53, 56, 57, 59, 62 | TR: 20, 50, 51, 55 | SAG: A, B, C, D, E, F, G, H, J<br>TR: 1, 19, 28, 29, 35, 36, 38, 41, 49, 54, 58, 61 | Text: 1<br><br><br>TR: 14 | Text: 1, 3, 5<br>SAG: E, I<br><br>TR: 3, 9, 10, 12, 13, 21, 27, 47, 51, 54 |
| Chapter 15 | Text: 2, 3<br><br>TR: 1, 2, 6, 7, 13, 14, 16, 17, 19, 23, 25, 26 | TR: 9, 22 | Text: 1, 5<br>SAG: B<br>TR: 1, 4, 10, 11, 18, 24 | Text: 2, 5<br>SAG: A<br>TR: 1 | Text: 4<br>SAG: C<br>TR: 3, 4, 15, 21 |
| Chapter 16 | Text: 1, 2, 3<br><br>TR: 1, 3, 4, 7, 8, 14, 15, 16, 17, 19, 20, 24, 25, 26, 27, 28, 30, 33 | Text: 4<br>SAG: A<br>TR: 6, 18, 25, 33 | Text: 5<br>SAG: B, C<br>TR: 9, 12, 15, 22, 23, 31, 33 | Text: 2, 3, 4<br><br>TR: 5, 11, 12 | Text: 1, 3, 5<br>SAG: C<br>TR: 2, 9, 18, 32 |
| Chapter 17 | Text: 1, 3<br><br>TR: 4, 7, 8, 12, 13, 15, 16, 17, 18, 20, 22, 24, 26, 27, 29, 30, 31, 32, 33, 34, 35, 36, 38 | Text: 5 | Text: 3, 5<br>SAG: A, B, C, D<br>TR: 1, 2, 3, 5, 11, 14, 28, 32, 36, 37, 38 | Text: 5 | Text: 1<br>SAG: B<br>TR: 10 |
| Chapter 18 | Text: 2, 5<br>SAG: G<br>TR: 4, 5, 7, 10, 15, 16, 17, 18, 22, 23, 24, 27, 28, 33, 35, 36, 38, 40, 42, 44, 45, 46, 47, 48, 49, 52, 55, 56, 57, 59, 62, 65 | TR: 39, 47, 53, 54 | Text: 4<br>SAG: A, B, C, D, E, F<br>TR: 3, 8, 14, 17, 19, 20, 30, 32, 57, 58, 60, 61, 63 | Text: 4<br><br>TR: 7, 41, 42, 43 | Text: 2<br>SAG: B<br>TR: 1, 2, 8, 12, 19, 22, 25, 27, 34, 54 |

| | Verbal | Reading | Writing | Math/Science/Technology | Analytical |
|---|---|---|---|---|---|
| Chapter 19 | Text: 5<br>SAG: E, F, I<br>TR: 3, 4, 5, 6, 10, 11, 16, 17, 20, 24, 25, 26, 29, 31, 33, 34, 37, 38, 40, 41, 42, 44, 46, 48, 50, 51, 54, 56, 57, 58, 59, 60, 62, 67 | Text: 3<br><br>TR: 21, 52 | SAG: A, B, C, D, E, F, G, H<br>TR: 7, 15, 23, 27, 35, 50, 52, 53, 55, 65, 66 | Text: 2, 3<br><br>TR: 4, 8, 14, 23 | Text: 1, 2, 3<br>SAG: B<br>TR: 2, 23, 25, 27, 28, 36, 39, 41, 42, 47, 63, 64 |
| Chapter 20 | Text: 1, 5<br><br>TR: 1, 2, 3, 6, 7, 9, 10, 11, 13, 18, 20, 22, 24, 26, 27, 28, 29, 31, 32, 35, 39, 41, 42, 44 | Text: 5<br><br>TR: 15, 25, 31, 36, 43 | Text: 4<br>SAG: A, B, C<br>TR: 4, 10, 12, 16, 19, 34, 38, 40 | Text:2, 4<br>SAG: C<br>TR: 35, 39 | Text: 2<br>SAG: A, C<br>TR: 6, 17, 23, 32 |
| Chapter 21 | Text: 1, 2<br>SAG: B, E<br>TR: 3, 5, 7, 8, 10, 12, 14, 15, 16, 17, 18, 19, 20, 25, 27, 29, 31, 33, 34, 35, 39, 40, 42, 43, 44, 47, 49, 54, 55 | Text: 2<br><br>TR: 10, 11, 13, 17, 22, 28, 50, 55 | SAG: A, C, D, E, F<br>TR: 21, 22, 30, 50, 51 | Text: 2, 3, 5<br><br>TR: 4, 7, 9, 18, 35, 36 | Text: 3<br>SAG: C, D<br>TR: 1, 12, 15, 23, 30, 36, 44, 45, 46, 48 |
| Chapter 22 | Text: 1, 2, 4<br>SAG: C<br>TR: 5, 6, 7, 9, 11, 13, 14, 17, 18, 19, 21, 25, 26, 27, 28, 32, 33, 34, 35, 36, 37, 38, 40, 41, 42 | Text: 3<br>SAG: A, B<br>TR: 5, 15, 20, 24, 32 | Text: 3, 5<br>SAG: A, C, D, E<br>TR: 1, 15, 23, 27, 39 | Text: 3 | Text: 2, 3, 4<br><br>TR: 9, 11, 12, 14, 19, 21, 22, 36 |
| Chapter 23 | Text: 1, 2<br>SAG: A, B<br>TR: 2, 4, 5, 9, 13, 15, 16, 17, 19, 20, 21, 22, 23, 24, 26, 27, 28, 31, 32, 33 | Text: 1, 2, 4<br>SAG: A, C<br>TR: 3, 6, 7, 16, 18, 21, 23, 29, 30, 33 | Text: 4<br>SAG: A, B, C<br>TR: 3, 11, 12, 14, 18, 21, 25, 32 | Text: 3, 4<br><br>TR: 20 | Text: 3<br><br>TR: 1, 4, 26 |
| Chapter 24 | Text: 5<br>SAG: A, B<br>TR: 5, 6, 8, 10, 11, 14, 15, 16, 17, 18, 19, 22, 23, 24, 26, 27, 28, 29, 30, 34, 37, 38, 39, 40, 41, 42, 43, 45, 46, 49, 51, 52, 53, 54, 57, 59, 61 | Text: 2<br>SAG: B, E<br>TR: 2, 11, 41 | Text: 1, 3, 4<br>SAG: A, B, C, D, E, F<br>TR: 3, 4, 11, 13, 31, 32, 41, 50, 58 | Text: 4<br><br>TR: 45, 47, 48, 59, 60 | SAG: C, D, F<br>TR: 1, 14, 16, 28, 33, 34, 36 |
| Chapter 25 | Text: 2, 3<br>SAG: B, E, F<br>TR: 3, 4, 5, 6, 8, 9, 14, 15, 17, 19, 20, 21, 24, 25, 26, 28, 29, 32, 36, 38, 40, 42, 43, 44, 45, 46, 47, 48, 49, 50, 51, 52, 53, 55, 59, 60, 64, 65, 68, 69, 71, 72, 73, 74, 75, 76, 77, 80, 81 | SAG: F<br>TR: 1, 2, 11, 12, 14, 54, 65, 66 | Text: 5<br>SAG: A, B, C, D, E, F<br>TR: 2, 11, 21, 27, 28, 30, 35, 37, 50, 54, 55, 56, 57, 58, 61, 66, 70, 79 | Text: 5 | Text: 1, 4<br>SAG: D, E<br>TR: 2, 14, 17, 59, 60, 61, 63, 66, 67, 72, 78, 81 |

**Children in Today's World**

# Learning About Children

# 1

## Objectives

After studying this chapter, students will be able to

→ list reasons for learning about children.

→ define the term *child development*.

→ describe the individual life cycle.

→ describe three factors that promote growth and development.

→ explain how brain development occurs.

→ identify differences in the rate of growth and development.

→ explain and give examples of some major principles and theories of growth and development.

→ develop observation skills.

## Bulletin Boards

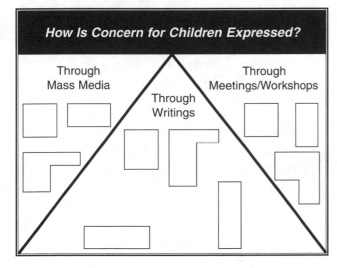

### Title: *How Is Concern for Children Expressed?*

Divide the bulletin board into sections as shown. Place the title and the following three subheadings on the board: (1) Through Mass Media, (2) Through Writings, (3) Through Meetings/Workshops. Under the subheadings students display examples, such as radio or TV listings, newspaper and magazine articles, book jackets, and announcements of meetings and workshops. Students can change the examples throughout the instructional period.

### Title: *Children Are...*

Instruct students to find pictures of children (of themselves as babies or from magazines) to place under the following headings: (1) Curious and Inquisitive, (2) Loving, (3) Fun, (4) Challenging, (5) Creative, (6) Active, (7) All Different, (8) Sometimes Difficult to Understand. Students may add other titles as they discuss the development of children.

### Title: *Reasons for Studying Children*

Divide the bulletin board into five sections, one for each of the following headings: (1) To Understand Yourself, (2) To Be a Responsible Parent, (3) To Protect Children's Rights, (4) To Work with Children. Illustrate each section with pictures.

## Teaching Materials

**Text,** pages 18-49
*Reviewing Key Concepts*
*Using Your Knowledge*
*Making Observations*
*Thinking Further*

**Student Activity Guide**
A. *Parents Aid Children's Growth and Development*
B. *Individual Life Cycle*
C. *Heredity or Environment?*
D. *Is the Brain More Than a Computer?*
E. *A Look at Tomorrow*
F. *The Wholeness of Growth and Development*
G. *Children Fulfill Their Needs*
H. *Observation: Children at Play*

**Teacher's Resources**
*The Subject Matter of Child Development*, reproducible master 1-1
*Why Is It Important to Study Children?* reproducible master 1-2
*Wiring of Brain Cells*, color transparency CT-1A
*Analyzing Brain Research*, reproducible master, 1-3

*Changes in Growth and Development Patterns,* transparency master 1-4
*Developmental Tasks,* transparency master 1-5
*Maslow's Hierarchy of Human Needs,* color transparency CT-1B
*Observation Guidelines,* transparency master 1-6
Chapter 1 Test

# Introductory Activities

1. Have students write brief descriptions of their views of children and share their impressions in class. Collect and save the descriptions. Contrast these descriptions with the students' impressions of children at the end of the course.
2. *The Subject Matter of Child Development,* reproducible master 1-1. Students should complete the master before reading the chapter. Encourage them to match the statements about children with the areas of knowledge and then discuss reasons for their responses.

# Strategies to Reteach, Reinforce, Enrich, and Extend Text Concepts

## Why Study Children?

3. **RT** Encourage students to explain the difference between wanting to meet children's needs and knowing how to do so.
4. **RT** Have students list reasons it is difficult to know how to meet children's needs.
5. **ER** Have students write a newspaper article entitled "The Century of the Child" or "How the Needs and Rights of Children Have Been Abused."
6. **ER** Invite students to suggest reading materials for parents and others interested in child development.
7. **RF** *Why Is It Important to Study Children?* reproducible master 1-2. For each reason given, students are asked to add a message, drawing, or magazine clipping to its box to illustrate it.

## To Understand Yourself

8. **ER** Instruct students to spend at least 30 minutes with a baby or child. Invite students to share in class what they learned or enjoyed.
9. **RT** A person's upbringing affects how he or she acts as a parent and on the job. Ask students to imagine some hypothetical examples of this statement.

## To Be a Responsible Parent

10. **RF** *Parents Aid Children's Growth and Development,* Activity A, SAG. Students are asked to give examples of ways that parents meet children's needs.
11. **RT** Conduct a student discussion of the question "Of children's many needs (physical, intellectual, social, trust, and love/discipline), which needs are parents most likely to have limited knowledge for meeting?"
12. **ER** Have students explore the contents of books and/or parenting programs and then write a paper on the topics often included.
13. **RT** Ask students to give examples of how parenting practices should change as children's needs change.

## To Protect Children's Rights

14. **ER** Give students a reading assignment that shows how children often were mistreated before child labor laws were established. Have students discuss their findings.
15. **EX** Invite students to list questions that concern the protection of children. (An example is whether violence should be shown on the TV programs children watch.)
16. **ER** Encourage students to interview a social worker about his or her role in protecting children. The interview should focus on why children need protection and how various government services protect children.
17. **ER** Instruct students to interview a juvenile court judge. They should ask the judge to give a simple interpretation of your state's laws concerning (a) the rights of children when neglected or abused by parents; (b) the rights of juveniles accused of offenses; (c) the responsibilities and rights of parents, teachers, and other adults who work with children; (d) the reasons parental rights may be altered in child custody cases; and (e) the "gray areas" between parents' rights and children's rights. (An example is when parents refuse medical care for a child in a life-threatening situation.)

## To Work with Children

18. **RT** Ask students to list child-related careers that are available in your area.
19. **ER** Panel discussion: Encourage students to invite several people who work in child-related careers to discuss how they use their knowledge of children in their work.

## What Is Child Development?

20. **RT**  Invite students to describe the differences between fact and opinion and discuss the following questions: (a) Are opinions always wrong? (b) Are facts presented in research always correct? (c) Why are sciences, including child development, subject to change?

21. **RF**  Bring a research report to class for students to examine. Ask them to identify parts of the report, such as what was studied, how children were chosen, how information was collected, how information was analyzed, and how researchers reached conclusions. (Students do not need to understand the sampling techniques or analyses. This activity is designed to show them that researchers follow strict rules.)

## Individual Life Cycle

22. **RF**  *Individual Life Cycle*, Activity B, SAG. Students are asked to complete a chart about the individual life cycle.

23. **RF**  Use poster board to create a wheel similar to that of a bicycle. On each section of the wheel, write the name of a stage of the individual life cycle that applies to children. Use a metal brad to attach the wheel to a second poster board, on which one arrow has been drawn to touch the wheel. Have each student spin the wheel to select a stage. For the stage selected, the student should offer one descriptive word or fact about children in this stage.

## Factors That Influence Growth and Development

24. **RT**  Instruct students to check the meaning of the terms *heredity* and *inheritance* in a dictionary. Encourage them to discuss the relationship between the words.

25. **RT**  Have students check the meaning of the term *environment* in a dictionary. Students also should look at the term *environ*. Have students discuss how the terms are related.

26. **RT**  Discuss with students words that convey the meaning of the term *heredity* (such as *internal* or *inside*) and the meaning of the term *environment* (such as *external* or *outside*).

27. **RF**  Using one circle, diagram the relationship between heredity and environment for students.

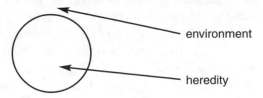

## Heredity

28. **RT**  Invite students to give examples of traits they believe they inherited.

29. **ER**  Have students read the story of Gregor Mendel who, in the mid-1800s, discovered that inheritance followed natural laws.

## Environment

30. **RF**  Ask students to share in class examples or pictures of objects and people that are usually part of a child's life. Each student should explain how the object or person might promote change in a child as he or she grows.

31. **RF**  Ask each student to share one environmental influence in his or her own life. For example, this might include the effects of family geographical location, rural or urban residence, family size or structure, family occupation(s), or family hobbies and recreation.

## Heredity and Environment Combined

32. **RF**  *Heredity or Environment?* Activity C, SAG. Students are asked to list their traits or skills and classify them as the products of heredity or environment.

33. **ER**  Instruct students to research a case study or biographical information on a celebrity or political leader. Students should then write a paper on the person that includes the following information: (a) ways in which heredity affected the person's development, (b) ways in which environment affected the person's development, (c) ways the person's childhood compares to the principles of growth and development.

## Brain Development

34. **RT** Ask each student to offer one reason that studying brain development is important in understanding children and their development.
35. **ER** Divide the class into four groups. Each group should research on the Internet one of the following brain imaging techniques: Computed Tomography Scan (CT-Scan), Position Emission Tomography (PET), Magnetic Resonance Imaging (MRI), and Functional Magnetic Resonance Imaging (FMRI). Each group should describe how its chosen technique is done and what it measures.

## Basic Wiring Occurs

36. **ER** Using photos from biology books or the Internet, ask students to describe the appearance of the human brain. (You may want to add that if the brain folds were spread out, it would cover the surface of a pillowcase.)
37. **RT** Have students look up in a dictionary the original meanings of *axon* (from *axle* meaning straight line or thread), *dendrite* (branching tree-like form), and *synapse* (to fasten).
38. **RT** *Wiring of Brain Cells,* color transparency CT-1A. Use this transparency to point out how brain cells "connect" with one another through stimulation.
39. **ER** Ask students to name other electrical impulses or charges that jump a gap. (Charge from an engine's spark plugs and lightning are two examples.)

## Heredity and Environment Interact

40. **ER** Preselect four or five toys for infants and/or young children. Divide the class into four or five groups and give each group one toy. Ask the students to play with the toy and list what type of wiring (learnings) might occur as a child plays with this toy. Each group should share ideas with the class. Ask whether this procedure would be a good way for parents to choose toys for their children.
41. **RT** Ask a student whose primary language is not English to explain which English sounds are difficult for him or her to make. Have students practice some sounds unique to other languages. The reason the sounds are difficult or impossible to make is the pruning of auditory connections for sounds not heard or made in one's primary language. (A foreign language teacher can also conduct this activity.)
42. **RF** Rewrite the nursery rhyme, "Mary, Mary, Quite Contrary," to incorporate the concepts of making brain connections grow or pruning them. The rhyme could begin as: "Mary, Mary, Quite Contrary, How do your connections grow?" or "Mary, Mary, Quite Contrary, How are your connections pruned?"

## Windows of Opportunity

43. **ER** Invite a child development specialist who is trained in early brain development to class. Ask the speaker to share with the class the windows of opportunity for various skills. What effects do the timing of these windows have on a child's development?
44. **RF** Discuss with students why trying to introduce a skill before the window of opportunity opens is a problem. (Before the window opens, the brain is not prepared to learn this new skill and has a slim chance of success in learning it.) Also explain why trying to introduce a skill after the window closes is a problem. (After the window closes, the brain has lost its best opportunity for learning this skill. Pruning may also have occurred that makes the brain incapable of learning the skill after the window closes.)

## Brain Plasticity

45. **RT** Before reading this section of the text, have students look up the meaning of the term *plasticity*. After reading this section, ask them to explain why this is an appropriate term to describe the brain.
46. **ER** Write the following elements on the board and ask the students to elaborate on each as positive for the brain's development: *nutrition, positive environment, appropriate activities,* and *early identification and treatment of problems.*
47. **EX** Have a class discussion on why the early years are the most important ones in terms of brain development.
48. **ER** Write *Unfavorable Environment* and *Favorable Environment* on the chalkboard. Under these headings, ask students to write an example of either a favorable or unfavorable environment for brain development.

49. **EX** Following the completion of Activity D, SAG, have students do a large Venn diagram of the comparisons for a bulletin board. Descriptions could be word processed, cut as strips of paper, and tacked to the correct part of the overlapping circles as shown below.

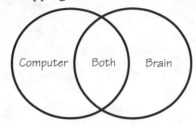

(The two circles should overlap by about half. One of the circles should be labeled *Computer* and the other labeled *Brain*. The portion where one circle overlaps the other should be labeled *Both*. Then the strips of paper labeled with the functions of either or both should be tacked in place.)

50. **RF** *Is the Brain More Than a Computer?* Activity D, SAG. In this activity, students are asked to write phrases comparing and contrasting the human brain with a computer.

51. **EX** *Analyzing Brain Research,* reproducible master 1-3. Use this handout to help students examine how thinking about brain development has changed and what implications the changes in thinking have for helping children.

## Differences in the Rate of Growth and Development

52. **RT** Ask students to give examples of differences in the rates of growth and development in children they know.

53. **RT** Have students work in groups to role-play parents of children at a park who are similar in age but show differences in their rates of growth and development.

## Principles of Growth and Development

54. **ER** Ask a pediatrician to discuss principles of growth and development with students. Have students prepare a list of questions in advance.

55. **RF** On index cards, write the names of various motor skills. Have students take turns drawing two cards and telling which skill, according to the principles of head-to-toe and center-to-extremities development, develops first.

## Growth and Development Are Constant

56. **RT** Invite students to give an example of some aspect of their growth and development that has been rather constant.

58. **RT** Ask students to share examples of words people use to describe personality. Foster a discussion of the question, "Why would the term *personality* be meaningless if constancy did not occur in growth and development?"

59. **RF** *A Look at Tomorrow*, Activity E, SAG. Students are asked to complete descriptions of children in ways that show constancy.

## Growth and Development Are Gradual and Continuous

60. **RT** Invite students to give examples of how children can "catch up" in their development and areas where they cannot.

61. **RF** *Changes in Growth and Development Patterns*, transparency master 1-4. There are times in the life of most children when smooth patterns of growth and development change. It takes children time to regain balance and calm as they adjust to these changes. Use this transparency to point out times when children's growth and development are very fast, very slow, or seem to have stopped. Ask students to give examples of breaks in growth and development patterns.

## Growth and Development Happen in Sequenced Steps

62. **RT** Have students list the sequence of steps that lead to walking. (You may want to keep students' responses and have them check their answers after studying chapter 7 in the text.)

63. **RT** Invite students to describe a skill they learned recently that had to be grasped in steps.

64. **RT** Encourage students to give examples of children who are under social pressure to achieve a task they are not ready to perform. Discuss with students what can happen to these children.

## Growth and Development Happen at Different Rates

65. **RF** Have students observe on their own children of nearly the same age in a group setting. Students should look for differences in rates of development. Ask students to share their observations in small groups.

66. **RT** Have students explain why knowing the average rate of growth and development can be useful.

## Growth and Development Have Interrelated Parts

67. **RT** Have students discuss how the physical, mental, and social aspects of growth and development are involved in language learning.
68. **RF** *The Wholeness of Growth and Development,* Activity F, SAG. Students should describe how different aspects of growth and development affect each other.

## Theories of Growth and Development

69. **RF** Have students find the definition of *theory* in the dictionary. Discuss what a theory is, how it is developed, and how it reaches wide acceptance in its field.
70. **ER** Have students research current theories of growth and development and present their findings to the class.

## Havighurst's Theory of Developmental Tasks

71. **RF** *Developmental Tasks,* transparency master 1-5. Use this transparency to outline for students Havighurst's developmental tasks for children from birth to age 12 years.
72. **RF** Have students discuss the developmental tasks as indicated by Havighurst.
73. **RF** Ask students to write a definition of the term *developmental tasks* using their own words.

## Maslow's Theory of Human Needs

74. **RT** *Maslow's Hierarchy of Human Needs,* color transparency CT-1B. Use this transparency to explain each level of needs and with students how parents can help children meet these needs.
75. **RF** Using a list of Maslow's hierarchy of needs, have students describe how their various needs were met on a given day.
76. **RF** Have students discuss and give specific examples of how Maslow's needs could be fulfilled differently in various cultures. (For example, nutritional requirements can be met with many types of foods.)
77. **RF** *Children Fulfill Their Needs,* Activity G, SAG. Students are asked to identify the needs being met in each activity based on Figure 1-19 in the text.

## Observing Children

78. **RT** Ask students to give examples of how the senses are used in observation.
79. **RT** Invite students to explain how observation skills might be learned through imitation.
80. **RT** Have students discuss how some people "see" more than others see in certain situations.

## Why Observe Children?

81. **RT** Discuss with students reasons researchers study children.
82. **RF** Foster a student discussion. Ask students what they can learn by observing children and how these learnings will help them.

## Ways to Observe

83. **RT** Have students list places where children can be directly observed.
84. **RT** Ask students for examples of indirect observations.

## Guidelines for Observing

85. **RT** Encourage students to discuss the importance of following each of the guidelines for observing.
86. **RF** *Observation Guidelines,* transparency master 1-6. Use this transparency to outline for students the proper methods of observation. Use it as a basis for discussion on the methods expected when students observe.
87. **RF** *Observation: Children at Play,* Activity H, SAG. Help students choose a child's behavior or characteristic to observe. Students are asked to follow the guidelines in the text as they observe and record their findings on the observations sheet.

# Answer Key

## Text

*Reviewing Key Concepts,* page 48

1. false
2. (List four:) to understand yourself, to be a responsible parent, to protect children's rights, to work with children
3. the scientific study of children from conception to adolescence
4. prenatal stage, neonatal stage, infancy stage, toddler stage, preschool stage, school-age stage
5. heredity, environment, heredity and environment combined
6. false

7. does
8. true
9. Developmental acceleration is when a child performs like an older child. Developmental delay is when a child performs like a younger child.
10. (Student response.)
11. C.   The steps in which most children grow and develop occur in about the same order. The order of the steps in growth and development is about the same for most children.
12. physical growth—B; social pressures—A; inner pressures—C
13. (Student response. See pages 40–42 in the text.)
14. (List five:) know your objectives, obtain permission to observe, know what to do at the site, observations should not distract children from their regular activities, observe carefully and objectively, record accurately, protect the rights of all observed

## Student Activity Guide

### Is the Brain More Than a Computer?
### Activity D

(Exact wording will be student response.)
1. Organ made of living tissue, bathed in fluids to reduce shock, and housed in bone (the skull).
2. Each person's brain is unique.
3. The brain is "turned on" long before it is completed. The brain changes throughout one's life but dramatically in the first 10 years of life.
4. Also uses electrical signals.
5. Uses chemicals to transmit signals.
6. Has energy that comes from nutritional foods. (The brain needs sugars and oxygen.) Exercise helps the brain get needed oxygen, too.
7. Transmits all the time, even during sleep.
8. Some diseases and a negative environment can make the brain sick.
9. Brain plasticity allows the brain to be repaired from some illnesses provided that it gets early and good treatment.
10. Learns by experiences including mistakes. Learnings become stronger with repetition.
11. Has the ability to learn something previously unknown.
12. Does several things at once such as one can breathe, walk, think, and talk at the same time.
13. Is a faster processor.
14. Always able to learn new things as needed.

### Children Fulfill Their Needs, Activity G

1. physiological
2. belonging and love
3. belonging and love
4. esteem
5. safety
6. physiological
7. aesthetic
8. esteem
9. esteem
10. safety
11. safety or belonging
12. esteem
13. physiological
14. safety
15. aesthetic
16. belonging and love
17. safety
18. esteem
19. esteem
20. physiological or safety

## Teacher's Resources

### The Subject Matter of Child Development, reproducible master 1-1

| | |
|---|---|
| 1. A | 6. D |
| 2. B | 7. B |
| 3. C | 8. D |
| 4. D | 9. B |
| 5. A | 10. C |

### Chapter 1 Test

| | | | |
|---|---|---|---|
| 1. F | 10. T | 19. A | 28. L |
| 2. T | 11. F | 20. D | 29. H |
| 3. F | 12. T | 21. B | 30. K |
| 4. F | 13. F | 22. C | 31. A |
| 5. T | 14. D | 23. B | 32. G |
| 6. T | 15. A | 24. B | 33. I |
| 7. T | 16. A | 25. E | 34. J |
| 8. F | 17. C | 26. D | 35. C |
| 9. F | 18. D | 27. F | |

36. prenatal stage, neonatal stage, infancy stage, toddler stage, preschool stage, and school-age stage
37. (List four. Student response.)
38. physical growth, social pressures, inner pressures (Student response for explanations.)
39. (Student response.)
40. (Student response.)

# The Subject Matter of Child Development

**Name** _____ **Date** _____ **Period** _____

The content of child development includes almost everything people know about children. Match the following areas of knowledge and statements about children. (As you study the text, you will read similar statements again.)

*Statements About Children*

_____ 1.   Newborns average about 17 hours of sleep per day.

_____ 2.   During the first year, infants babble syllables, such as *da da*.

_____ 3.   Babies become anxious when beloved adults leave them even for a short time.

_____ 4.   Children are proud when they can do tasks for themselves.

_____ 5.   After the first year, babies continue to grow rapidly but less rapidly than during the first year.

_____ 6.   Toddlers are attached to adults who care for them.

_____ 7.   School-age children can learn symbol systems used in reading and math.

_____ 8.   Brothers and sisters are built-in playmates for each other.

_____ 9.   Children are curious and eager learners.

_____ 10.   Children with speech impairments may lack self-esteem.

*Areas of Knowledge*

A.   way children's bodies grow and develop

B.   way children think and learn

C.   way children feel about themselves

D.   way children interact with others

Reproducible Master 1-2

# Why Is It Important to Study Children?

**Name** _____ **Date** _____ **Period** _____

Each box is labeled with a reason studying children is important. In the space inside each box, write, draw, or find pictures to illustrate reasons this is important.

### To Protect Children

### To Be a Better Parent

### To Work with Children

### To Understand Yourself Better

### Other

### Other

# Analyzing Brain Research

| Past Concepts | Present Concepts |
|---|---|
| Basic question—Is heredity or environment more important? | Basic question—How do heredity and environment interact? |
| Brain development mainly depends on heredity and good nutrition. | Brain development is the result of heredity, nutrition, and environmental experiences with people and objects. |
| The brain develops steadily throughout life. | The brain develops far faster in the first three years than at other times although it keeps developing for a lifetime. |
| Adult brains are most active. | Adult brains are half as active as three-year-old brains. |
| The brain develops as a whole like arms and legs do. | Different skills and learnings develop in different regions of the brain; these regions are "wired" at different times. |
| Brain development mainly influences mental development. | Brain development influences intellectual and social-emotional development. Without a positive environment, a child's brain will be 20 to 30 percent smaller than normal for his or her age. Stress prunes the brain's "wiring" in the region that controls emotions. |
| Environment affects the general way the brain develops; that is, good nutrition and experiences aid overall development. | Environment affects how the brain develops and how it is "wired." When used, connections develop and strengthen patterns for doing certain tasks, such as relating to others. Strong patterns will be useful for a lifetime. If needed patterns are missing or incorrect, problems will likely always exist. |
| Children three years and older who have negative experiences or lack needed stimulation suffer the most severe brain development problems. | Infants and toddlers who have negative experiences or lack appropriate stimulation have the most serious and long-term developmental problems. |
| Problems in brain development can be corrected any time during life with good results. | To be most effective, intervention must occur early in life—preferably within the first 3 years and no later than the first 10 years. After this time, correcting a brain pattern is much more difficult and can be impossible. (Plasticity lessens with age.) |

## Implications for Helping Children

| Current Practices Based on Past Concepts | Desired Practices Based on Present Concepts |
|---|---|
| Prenatal care and good nutrition are needed for gene protection. (Heredity is the main influence on brain development.) | Prenatal care and good nutrition are vital, but brain development only starts there. Adults need training as the brain's first teachers. (Environment has a large influence on brain development.) |
| Quality experiences must begin in preschool or school years. | Quality experiences must begin in infancy and be continued throughout life. |
| Researchers were unsure when a given learning or skill was the easiest for children to master. | Research now suggests some answers about the best times (windows of opportunity) for learning certain concepts. Much more research needs to be done. |
| Help for children who have developmental problems or negative environments is often delayed four or five years. | Delaying diagnosis and treatment is not in any child's best interest. Intervention in the first three years of life is most effective. |

# Changes in Growth and Development Patterns

| Most likely to occur when there are: | Examples |
|---|---|
| → changes in environment | → moving to a new location |
| → changes in physical development | → rapid growth spurts, such as during the late childhood or early teen years |
| → changes in status | → change in family structure, such as a new baby, divorce, marriage, or death |
| → changes in roles | → going to child care, preschool, or school for the first time |
| → changes in the kind and amount of emphasis placed on certain skills | → weakened math skills after concentrating hard on reading skills |

# Developmental Tasks

Children go through predictable patterns of growth and development. The skills learned during these stages are called developmental tasks.

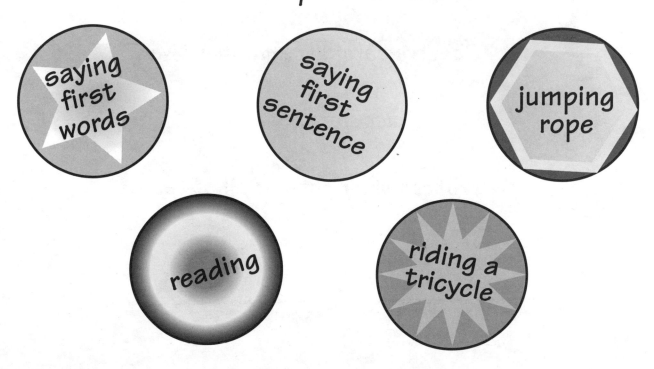

# Observation Guidelines

- Know your objectives.

- Obtain permission to observe.

- Know what to do at the site.

- Be sure observations do not distract children from regular activities.

- Observe carefully and objectively.

- Record accurately.

- Protect the rights of all observed.

# Learning About Children

**Name** _____

**Date** _____ **Period** _____ **Score** _____

## Chapter 1 Test

True/False: Circle *T* if the statement is true or *F* if the statement is false.

T    F     1. Heredity alone determines growth and development.

T    F     2. Learning about children helps adults enjoy being with them.

T    F     3. Development ends when the human becomes an adult.

T    F     4. The sole focus of child development is on physical growth.

T    F     5. The term *development* implies change in a person.

T    F     6. Heredity affects some aspects of growth and development more than others.

T    F     7. The environment is a powerful force in growth and development.

T    F     8. A developmental delay is when a child performs like an older child.

T    F     9. Principles of growth and development fit all people in the same way.

T    F    10. Some developmental tasks are the same for all cultures.

T    F    11. Genetics is the study of environmental factors that affect development.

T    F    12. Brain cells called neurons send and receive messages between various parts of the brain.

T    F    13. The baby's large head size at birth indicates that brain development is complete.

Multiple Choice: Choose the best response. Write the letter in the space provided.

_____ 14. Protection of children has been the concern of _____.
         A. the United Nations
         B. parents
         C. U. S. federal and state courts
         D. All of the above.

_____ 15. Which of the following statements about brain plasticity is false?
         A. Brain development is mostly the result of heredity.
         B. Brain connections can be strengthened or pruned.
         C. The brain has prime times for developing various skills.
         D. Experiences can affect brain development and brain health in both
            positive and negative ways.

_____ 16. Development is best described as a _____.
         A. process
         B. product
         C. period in a person's life
         D. None of the above.

_____ 17. Child development is defined by the text as _____.
         A. an understanding of parent-child relations
         B. knowledge about children
         C. the scientific study of children
         D. social changes that occur as children become older

*(Continued)*

**Name** _____

_____ 18. Which of the following promote healthy brain development?
A. Prenatal care.
B. Loving relations between young children and adults.
C. Quality experiences.
D. All of the above.

_____ 19. Genes can affect _____.
A. both the existence and range of certain traits
B. neither the range nor the existence of traits
C. only the existence of certain traits
D. only the range of certain traits

_____ 20. Environment includes _____.
A. physical conditions
B. what people learn by listening and reading
C. what people learn as they interact with people and the world around them
D. All of the above.

_____ 21. Which of the following is a poor child observation practice?
A. Introduce yourself to the person in charge and state why you are there.
B. Don't take a pencil and paper with you because that will interfere with your observations.
C. Leave promptly when finished.
D. Try not to distract children or adults from their activities.

_____ 22. Before Sarah can learn to read, she must learn many skills, such as how to move her eyes from top to bottom and from left to right on the page. Learning this and other skills before reading is an example of _____.
A. continuous growth and development
B. constancy of growth and development
C. sequenced steps in growth and development
D. the effect of heredity on growth and development

_____ 23. Which of the following statements is *not* true about the rate of growth and development?
A. The rate of growth and development is determined by a person's desire to achieve.
B. The rate of development is determined by environment but not by heredity.
C. The rate of growth and development are different for all children.
D. The rate of growth and development changes throughout a child's life.

*(Continued)*

**Name** _____

Matching: Match the following terms and identifying phrases.

_____ 24. A process through which babies gradually change into adults.

_____ 25. Traits of blood kin passed through parents.

_____ 26. Everything that affects people except traits of blood kin.

_____ 27. Brain cell that consists of cell body, axon, and dendrites.

_____ 28. Network of brain fibers.

_____ 29. Brain's ability to weed out unused connections.

_____ 30. Prime times in a child's life for specific types of brain stimulation.

_____ 31. Brain's ability to adapt to the environment.

_____ 32. Results of studies that describe how humans are alike.

_____ 33. Learnings or skills in growth and development that follow one another in rather exacting ways.

_____ 34. The time in a person's life when the body is ready, society requires, and he or she desires to master a task.

_____ 35. Skills a person should master at a certain stage in life.

A. brain plasticity

B. development

C. developmental task

D. environment

E. heredity

F. neuron

G. principles of growth and development

H. pruning

I. sequenced steps

J. teachable moment

K. windows of opportunity

L. wiring

Essay Questions: Provide complete responses to the following questions or statements.

36. Name the six stages of the individual life cycle for children.

37. List four tips for adults who wish to promote brain development in young children.

38. Explain the three sources that combine to give rise to developmental tasks.

39. Explain how Maslow's hierarchy of human needs theory relates to the care of children.

40. Choose one of the guidelines for observing given in the chapter and explain why it is important.

# Families Today

2

## Objectives

After studying this chapter, students will be able to
→ describe changes affecting families today.
→ explain the role of families in today's society.
→ list the main advantages and disadvantages of living in different types of families.
→ explain changes that take place during the family life cycle.
→ describe the major roles of parents.
→ define three parenting styles.
→ list characteristics of healthy families.
→ describe ways that culture influences the family

## Bulletin Boards

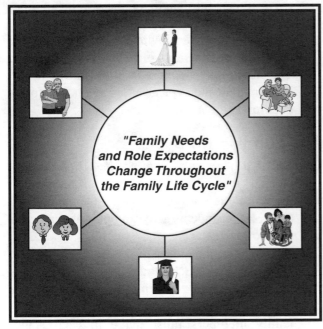

### Title: Family Needs and Role Expectations Change Throughout the Family Life Cycle

Place this title in the center of the board with lines leading to six squares around the center. Within each of the squares, have students place pictures of families that appear to be in each of the six stages of the family life cycle.

### Title: Families Come in Many Shapes and Sizes

Have students gather or draw pictures that depict each family type discussed in the text. Students should arrange the pictures on the board and label each family type.

## Teaching Materials

**Text**, pages 50-81
*Reviewing Key Concepts*
*Using Your Knowledge*
*Making Observations*
*Thinking Further*

**Student Activity Guide**
A. *Family Types*
B. *The Family Life Cycle*
C. *Types of Discipline*
D. *Parenting Styles*

**Teacher's Resources**
*Tasks of a Two-Parent Family,* reproducible master 2-1
*Types of Families,* reproducible master 2-2
*Studying the Family Life Cycle,* transparency master 2-3
*My Family's Cultural Priorities,* reproducible master 2-4
*Connecting in a Diverse World,* color transparency CT-2
Chapter 2 Test

## Introductory Activities

1. *Tasks of a Two-Parent Family,* reproducible master 2-1. Use this two-page master as a discussion-starter. Have students complete the charts indicating how family members would assign home-care tasks in each of two situations. Ask students to compare responses in small groups and conclude with class discussion.
2. Ask students to explain the relationship between the level of technology in a society and the years of childhood. Students should explain the reason

for the relationship. (The higher the level of technology in a society, the longer the years of childhood. More formal education is required for employment in a technical society.)

3. Encourage students to discuss why the family continues to be the basic unit of society.

# Strategies to Reteach, Reinforce, Enrich, and Extend Text Concepts

## Changes Affecting Families Today

4. **RF**  Conduct a brainstorming session, asking students to list changes that affect families today. Ask them if each change affects families positively or negatively.

5. **ER**  Have students write articles describing changes they think are affecting families today.

## Changes in Family Roles

6. **RF**  Instruct students to make a poster that depicts how the roles of parents have changed over the years.

7. **RT**  Have students give reasons families (rather than other social groups) can best meet the needs of children in their early years.

8. **ER**  Invite a grandparent or older person to class to talk about his or her early years of married life. Have the person describe the family roles he or she carried out and relationships with extended family. Students may write a summary of similarities and differences they see from that generation to the present.

## Family Types

9. **RF**  Instruct students to look up the terms *consanguine* and *consanguineous* in a dictionary. Ask them to explain the original meanings of these terms.

10. **RT**  Discuss with students stereotypical examples of the "typical" (two-parent) family as depicted in older books, movies, and television shows.

11. **EX**  Discuss with students what type of personality would fit best in an extended family.

12. **RT**  Ask students how other types of families can enjoy some of the same advantages as people living in the extended family structure. (An example might be visiting relatives for holidays.)

13. **RF**  Instruct students to look up the term *conjugal* in a dictionary. Have students explain the original meaning of this term.

14. **EX**  Because many single-parent families form unexpectedly, people often focus on the problems these families face. Ask students to list possible advantages for parents and children of living in a single-parent family.

15. **RF**  Many people focus on the problems of stepfamilies. Discuss advantages for both parents and children who live in stepfamilies.

16. **RF**  *Family Types*, Activity A, SAG. Invite students to describe each type of family listed and list strengths and weaknesses for each type.

17. **RF**  *Types of Families*, reproducible master 2-2. Have students read each scenario and identify the type of family it describes.

18. **ER**  Guest speaker: Ask an adoption agency caseworker to visit your class. The caseworker may explain the services available to birthparents and prospective adoptive parent(s). Ask the caseworker to describe the agency and legal procedures involved in an adoption. Other points might include the qualifications of adoptive parents, the length of the waiting period, and the cost for an adoption.

19. **ER**  Guest speaker: Invite a foster parent to talk about the satisfactions of being a foster parent. The parent may also discuss problems he or she encountered and typical adjustments for foster children and parents.

## The Family Life Cycle

20. **RF**  *Studying the Family Life Cycle*, transparency master 2-3. Use this transparency to introduce the various stages of the family life cycle. Have students give examples of characteristics of each stage.

21. **RT**  Discuss the family life cycle stages in class. Ask students which stages mark the family's expansion and which stages mark the family's decrease in size. Discuss adjustments family members must make in each stage. Which stages are likely to last the longest? Which stages are likely to last the shortest?

22. **RT**  On a chalkboard or blank transparency film, draw a line depicting the family life cycle. Draw a line from the center to the top of the circle. Ask a volunteer to draw another line depicting the first stage in the cycle and predict how many years an average couple might spend in this stage. Have another volunteer draw the line for the next stage and explain his or her rationale. Continue until all stages are depicted. Ask the class if the lines need to be adjusted. Discuss what determines the placement of the lines and how stages vary from family to family.

23. **RF**  Ask students to draw their families' life cycles, predicting the number of years their families will spend in each stage.
24. **EX**  Have students role-play each stage of the family life cycle. Several students role-play a family in a particular stage. Role-plays can portray joys, satisfactions, problems, and concerns that are common in this stage.
25. **RF**  Have students describe some customs they hope to develop or continue when they have children of their own. Ask students to describe customs and traditions in their current families, including dating, marriage, and parenting customs and holiday activities. Do these traditions tend to build family unity and strengthen family bonds?
26. **RF**  *The Family Life Cycle*, Activity B, SAG. Students are asked to define each stage of the family life cycle and write a short story describing a family's passage through the stages of the cycle.

## Roles of Parents

27. **RF**  Have the students discuss the different roles people play in life. Emphasize that each role has certain expectations, responsibilities, joys, and rewards.
28. **RF**  Ask students to draw a cartoon or write a paragraph explaining how a fictitious character manages multiple roles or feels about his or her role as parent.

## Socialization

29. **EX**  Looking at Figure 2-8 in the text, ask each student to comment on one aspect of his or her own culture.
30. **RT**  Ask students whether they think socialization is for the most part taught directly or learned indirectly by example. Ask them to explain their answers.
31. **RF**  *My Family's Cultural Priorities,* reproducible master 2-4. Students should write examples of their family's views. They should use Figure 2-9 in the text as a reference.

## Nurturance

32. **RF**  Have students look up the terms *nurturance* and *control* in a dictionary Students should compare the dictionary's definitions with the text's discussions of the topics.
33. **EX**  Guide students to speculate why women traditionally nurtured and men traditionally controlled children.

34. **RT**  Instruct students to contrast the attitudes of parents who blur the roles of nurturer and controller of children and those who prefer to make the roles distinct.

## Guidance and Discipline

35. **RT**  Discuss the concepts of *guidance* and *discipline*. Ask each student to compose a definition for each term. Have volunteers share their definitions, then discuss them. Do some definitions for discipline include punishment? Discuss the differences between discipline and punishment.
36. **EX**  *Types of Discipline*, Activity C, SAG. Students are asked to describe types of discipline and give an example of how each might be used. They are also asked to give and support their opinion of each type of discipline. You can use students' comments as the basis for class discussion.

## Parenting Styles

37. **RF**  Review the three parenting styles with students. Divide the class into small groups. Ask each group to list the pros and cons of each parenting style. Discuss in class.
38. **RF**  *Parenting Styles*, Activity D, SAG. Instruct students to unscramble the words pertaining to parenting roles and styles. Students then should arrange the circled letters to discover which parenting style is a more positive way to help children learn self-discipline.
39. **RF**  Instruct each student to complete the following sentence: "I believe the most effective parenting style is _____ because _____." Write a paper supporting the choice.

## Characteristics of Healthy Families

40. **ER**  Ask students to interview a family therapist about characteristics of healthy families. Have students prepare a list of questions in advance.
41. **RF**  Ask students to suggest ways parents can provide a healthy home environment for their families.

## Cultural Influences on Families

42. **RT**  Ask students to share examples of culture handed down by parents, teachers, religious leaders, youth leaders, and celebrities in all fields.
43. **ER**  Have students discuss the culture that may have been handed down to children in an earlier

historical period. Encourage students to speculate on the culture that might be handed down to
children in the year 2050.

44. **ER**  Invite students to share with the class
selections from books that show the handing
down of culture. For example, a student might
select examples from the writings of Amy Tan.

45. **EX**  Have students select and read a story or
book written about someone from a culture other
than their own. Each student should write a report
concerning two or three values or practices of the
culture.

46. **EX** *Connecting in a Diverse World,* color
transparency CT-2. Use this transparency to
stimulate discussion of how people can learn to
appreciate people from other cultures.

## Multicultural Families

47. **RT**  Ask students to list some of the possible joys
and challenges of living a multicultural family.

48. **EX**  As a class, discuss this question: Before
considering marriage to someone of another
culture, what are some specific things potential
spouses might need to discuss? Make a class
record of the key points in the discussion.

# Answer Key

## Text

### Reviewing Key Concepts, page 80

1. (Student response.)
2. F, A, A, B, D, E, C
3. C, A, D, E, F, B
4. socialization; nurturance; guidance, discipline
5. power assertion, love withdrawal, induction
   (Student response for effects.)
6. democratic
7. permissive
8. authoritarian
9. (List three:) shared values used to decide on
   family goals; consider family members as individuals; have commitment to family life; help
   each other; communicate
10. having more than one cultural group represented
11. (List five. See Figure 2-15.)

## Student Activity Guide

### Family Types, Activity A

(Student response for strengths and weaknesses.
Answers should be based on information from the
"Family Types" section in the text.)

**Two-parent family:** A family consisting of a
father, a mother, and their biological children.

**Single-parent family:** A family that is headed
by one adult.

**Stepfamily:** A family formed when a single
parent marries another person.

**Extended family:** A family in which two or
more generations of a family live together.

**Family with adopted children:** A family that
has at least one child who was the child of other
parents but who legally became the child of the new
parent(s).

**Foster-family:** A family in which the adults
provide a temporary home for children who cannot
live with their birthparents.

### The Family Life Cycle, Activity B

**Beginning stage:** A couple marries and gets to
know each other. This stage lasts until a child is born.

**Childbearing stage:** The couple has children.
This stage lasts until the birth of the last child.

**Parenting stage:** The couple focuses on
guiding their children through the school-age and
teen years. This stage lasts until children start to
leave home.

**Launching stage:** The couple's children begin
leaving home to live on their own. This stage ends
when all children have left home.

**Mid-years stage:** The couple focuses on their
marriage, planning for their future, and becoming
grandparents. This stage lasts until the couple retires.

**Aging stage:** The couple retires and adjusts
to this change in lifestyle. This stage lasts
throughout life.

### Types of Discipline, Activity C

**Power Assertion:** Occurs when parents use or
threaten to use some form of physical punishment.

**Love Withdrawal:** A discipline technique in
which parents threaten children or suggest some
form of parent/child separation.

**Induction:** Happens when parents discipline
by reasoning and explaining.

(Examples and opinions are student response.)

### Parenting Styles, Activity D

**Authoritarian:** A style in which the main
objective is to make children completely obedient.

**Permissive:** Parents give children almost no
guidelines or rules.

**Democratic:** A parenting style in which parents
set some rules but allow children some freedom.

# Teacher's Resources

## Types of Families, reproducible master 2-2

1. extended family
2. adoptive family
3. foster family
4. single-parent family
5. stepfamily
6. two-parent family

## Chapter 2 Test

| | | | |
|---|---|---|---|
| 1. T | 14. F | 27. A | 40. A |
| 2. T | 15. F | 28. D | 41. G |
| 3. T | 16. F | 29. D | 42. F |
| 4. T | 17. T | 30. D | 43. D |
| 5. F | 18. F | 31. B | 44. M |
| 6. T | 19. F | 32. C | 45. E |
| 7. T | 20. T | 33. C | 46. C |
| 8. F | 21. F | 34. A | 47. L |
| 9. F | 22. F | 35. D | 48. J |
| 10. F | 23. T | 36. D | 49. H |
| 11. T | 24. T | 37. A | 50. B |
| 12. F | 25. F | 38. K | |
| 13. T | 26. T | 39. I | |

51. (Student response.)
52. beginning stage: when the couple marries and gets to know each other and lasts until a child is born; childbearing stage: couple starts having children and lasts until the birth of the last child; parenting stage: couple focus on guiding their children and lasts until children start to leave home; launching stage: couple's children begin living on their own and lasts until all have left home; mid-years stage: couple focuses on their marriage, planning for their future, and becoming grandparents and lasts until the couple retires; aging stage: couple retires and lasts throughout life.
53. Democratic parenting style is best because it helps children learn self-discipline in a positive, encouraging setting.
54. (Student response.)

# Tasks of a Two-Parent Family

**Name** _____ **Date** _____ **Period** _____

Check the appropriate column to indicate which family member is best able to complete each task listed on the following charts. Check more than one column to indicate that two or more family members should share a task.

Complete the first chart based on a family of four. The father of this family works at home. The mother leaves the house for her job at 7:30 a.m. and returns at 5:30 p.m. The two children, ages 10 and 7 years, leave for school at 7:30 a.m. and return home at 4:00 p.m.

| Task | Dad | Mom | Child 1 (age 10) | Child 2 (age 7) |
|---|---|---|---|---|
| Wash dishes | | | | |
| Wash clothes | | | | |
| Buy groceries | | | | |
| Make beds | | | | |
| Sweep kitchen floor | | | | |
| Vacuum floors | | | | |
| Feed dog | | | | |
| Walk dog | | | | |
| Dust furniture | | | | |
| Prepare dinner | | | | |
| Prepare lunches | | | | |
| Care for car | | | | |
| Mow lawn | | | | |

*(Continued)*

**Name** _____ **Date** _____ **Period** _____

Complete the second chart based on the same family of four. When assigning tasks, consider a change in the
father's schedule. He now works outside the home and is away from 8:30 a.m. to 6:00 p.m. Check the last
column of this chart if you feel family members perform a certain task less often or pay others to do it
because of time constraints.

| Task | Dad | Mom | Child 1 (age 10) | Child 2 (age 7) | Task done less often or others paid to do task |
|------|-----|-----|------------------|-----------------|------------------------------------------------|
| Wash dishes | | | | | |
| Wash clothes | | | | | |
| Buy groceries | | | | | |
| Make beds | | | | | |
| Sweep kitchen floor | | | | | |
| Vacuum floors | | | | | |
| Feed dog | | | | | |
| Walk dog | | | | | |
| Dust furniture | | | | | |
| Prepare dinner | | | | | |
| Prepare lunches | | | | | |
| Care for car | | | | | |
| Mow lawn | | | | | |

# Types of Families

**Name** _____ **Date** _____ **Period** _____

Read these teen comments and write the family type in the blank beside each comment.

1. I moved into our old recreation room so
   Grandmother could have my bedroom on the
   ground floor. We don't want her to take a fall.       _____

2. Look at all these curls. My birthparents must
   have had really curly hair.                          _____

3. I can't go to your house after school today
   because the caseworker is coming to talk
   with my brother and me.                              _____

4. Do you know where any after-school jobs are
   available? I want to make some extra money.
   My mom works hard to support my sisters and
   me, but there's never enough money.                  _____

5. I guess it's hard on my new brother to have to
   share his room with me.                              _____

6. My parents and I like to do many of the same
   hobbies. The three of us often go swimming
   together on hot summer days.                         _____

# Studying the Family Life Cycle

 **Beginning Stage**

 **Childbearing Stage**

 **Parenting Stage**

 **Launching Stage**

 **Mid-Years Stage**

 **Aging Stage**

# My Family's Cultural Priorities

**Name** _____**Date** _____**Period** _____

Open your text to Figure 2-9. After reading the statements under each heading, write a brief paragraph about your family's cultural priorities in the following categories:

**Family and family roles:** _____

_____

_____

_____

**Parenting methods:** _____

_____

_____

_____

**Health practices:** _____

_____

_____

_____

**Moral learnings:** _____

_____

_____

_____

**Achievement:** _____

_____

_____

_____

**Attitudes:** _____

_____

_____

_____

# Families Today

Name _____

Date _____ Period _____ Score _____

## Chapter 2 Test

True/False: Circle *T* if the statement is true or *F* if the statement is false.

T    F    1. Throughout history the family has played a major role in meeting children's needs.

T    F    2. Today childhood is considered a special time for children to learn and be as free from stress as possible.

T    F    3. In two-parent families, parents often share responsibilities.

T    F    4. Single-parent families are most often headed by women.

T    F    5. Children of divorced parents seem to adjust better when their parents have joint custody.

T    F    6. As a whole, members of most stepfamilies have good relationships.

T    F    7. An extended family is made up of several generations of one family living together.

T    F    8. Learning to get along with many people may be a disadvantage of living in an extended family.

T    F    9. In extended families task roles are most often blurred, with family members doing different jobs from time to time.

T    F    10. Decisions in extended families are based on the special needs of each family member rather than the needs of the entire family.

T    F    11. Adoption ends the rights and responsibilities between a child and his or her birthparents.

T    F    12. An illegal market adoption is a legitimate way to adopt a child.

T    F    13. A quick transition to parenthood is a common problem for parents with adopted children.

T    F    14. Foster families provide temporary homes for children but can never adopt these children.

T    F    15. The first stage in the family life cycle is the launching stage.

T    F    16. Every family goes through each stage in the family life cycle.

T    F    17. A nurturing parent sees that his or her child's physical, emotional, and social needs are met.

T    F    18. The goal of discipline is to punish children for doing wrong.

T    F    19. Most parents believe children will learn right from wrong eventually on their own and disciplining children will lead to more problems than it will solve.

T    F    20. Power-assertive techniques can lead to child abuse.

T    F    21. In the induction technique of guidance and discipline, the child is spanked in order to learn self-control.

T    F    22. Authoritarian parents feel that children should be punished for bad behavior and always rewarded for good behavior.

T    F    23. Many parents believe that some rules must be set, but they allow some flexibility.

T    F    24. Shared priorities of parents are important for the health of the family.

T    F    25. Culture affects everyone in about the same ways.

T    F    26. Cultural priorities determine family practices.

*(Continued)*

Multiple Choice: Choose the best response. Write the letter in the space provided.

_____ 27. The needs of children first met by the family were _____.
A. physical
B. intellectual
C. social-emotional
D. None of the above.

_____ 28. The family that has been considered the typical family in the United States is the _____.
A. stepfamily
B. extended family
C. single-parent family
D. two-parent family

_____ 29. The single-parent family often _____.
A. has less money
B. needs help with household and child care tasks
C. needs emotional support from other adults
D. All of the above.

_____ 30. Adoption in which the birthparents and the adoptive parents share information and sometimes have contact with each other is called a (an) _____.
A. agency adoption
B. closed adoption
C. independent adoption
D. open adoption

_____ 31. Which of the following is *not* true of foster families?
A. Foster children are being protected through court action.
B. The overall goal is to take children away from their birthparents.
C. Foster families can offer a stable, secure home for children.
D. Counseling is often provided to birthparents while children live in foster families.

_____ 32. When parents set rules and regulations but allow some freedom, they are using what parenting style?
A. authoritarian
B. permissive
C. democratic
D. nurturance

_____ 33. A positive type of self-discipline is learned through what parenting style?
A. authoritarian
B. permissive
C. democratic
D. None of the above.

_____ 34. Which of the following is *not* true about cultural influences on the family?
A. Most cultures have the same concepts of the family.
B. Some cultural concepts are taught directly, but more are learned indirectly.
C. Parents model and reward what their culture values.
D. The importance of the family varies with the culture.

_____ 35. Language for a given culture includes _____.
A. spoken language
B. body language
C. choice of words
D. All of the above.

*(Continued)*

_____  36. Multicultural families may have problems because of _____.
  A. communication problems across cultures
  B. differing cultural expectations
  C. differing views regarding family life
  D. All of the above.

_____  37. Most children from multicultural homes are *not* _____.
  A. confused about their identity
  B. happy
  C. high achievers
  D. respectful toward others

Matching: Match the following terms and identifying phrases.

_____ 38. Families with members from two or more
  cultural groups.

_____ 39. A situation in which divorced parents share
  decision-making and child care responsibilities
  regarding their children.

_____ 40. A state-funded private agency licensed by the
  state to handle adoptions.

_____ 41. Type of adoption arranged by the birthparents,
  adoptive family, and usually one other person.

_____ 42. An adoption in which payments are made
  beyond the actual cost of the adoption process.

_____ 43. Stages that depict family changes.

_____ 44. Training children receive to help them live
  in a group.

_____ 45. Words and actions that parents use to influence
  children's behavior.

_____ 46. Part of guidance concerned with techniques used
  to help children learn self-control.

_____ 47. Form of discipline in which parents use or threaten
  to use some form of physical punishment.

_____ 48. Form of discipline in which parents threaten children
  or suggest some form of parent/child separation.

_____ 49. Form of discipline in which parents reason and explain.

_____ 50. Having more than one culture represented among a
  group of people, such as a nation.

A. adoption agency

B. cultural diversity

C. discipline

D. family life cycle

E. guidance

F. illegal market adoption

G. independent adoption

H. induction

I. joint custody

J. love withdrawal

K. multicultural families

L. power assertive

M. socialization

Essay: Provide complete responses to the following questions or statements.

51. Describe two changes you believe are affecting families today.

52. List and briefly describe the six stages in the family life cycle.

53. Name the most positive style of parenting and state why it is a good method.

54. Name three characteristics of healthy families.

# Preparing for Parenting

## Objectives

After studying this chapter, students will be able to
→ explain why parenting is more difficult than other jobs.
→ analyze some of the motivations for and against parenthood.
→ identify factors to consider before becoming a parent.
→ describe effects of family planning.
→ explain physical and psychological problems of infertility.
→ describe fertility methods.

## Bulletin Boards

**Why Don't Babies Come with Instructions?**

### Title: Why Don't Babies Come with Instructions?

Have students select one or more cartoons that show funny situations caused by lack of knowledge on how to care for children. If a single cartoon is chosen, have students enlarge it to fill the board. Otherwise, students may arrange several cartoons on the board.

### Title: Am I Cut out to Be a Parent?

Use stick figures to border the top and bottom of the bulletin board. Make a silhouette of a pair of scissors near the title. Have students find pictures of parents interacting with children, such as feeding, changing, playing, cuddling, and bathing and attach these to the board.

## Teaching Materials

**Text**, pages 82-106
*Reviewing Key Concepts*
*Using Your Knowledge*
*Making Observations*
*Thinking Further*

**Student Activity Guide**
A. *Comparing Parenting to Other Careers*
B. *Child Development Resources*
C. *Is This a Good Reason for Choosing Parenthood?*
D. *Couple Relationships Affect Parenthood*
E. *The Cost of Parenthood*

**Teacher's Resources**
*Reasons for Parenthood Choices,*
    reproducible master 3-1
*Children Learn What They Live,*
    transparency master 3-2
*Are You Ready for Parenthood?*
    color transparency CT-3A
*Parenting: A Time-Consuming Job,*
    reproducible master 3-3
*Children Grow More Expensive,*
    color transparency CT-3B
*Calculating Foregone Income,*
    reproducible master 3-4
*Birth Control Options,*
    reproducible master 3-5
Chapter 3 Test

## Introductory Activities

1. *Reasons for Parenthood Choices,* reproducible master 3-1. Before reading the text, have students list reasons couples might give for choosing or not choosing parenthood. After students have read the chapter, they should add reasons that were not on their list.
2. Students should contrast the amount of training people receive to prepare for skilled jobs with the amount of training most receive to prepare for parenting. Note the importance of each job. Discuss which job may last longer as well as which may influence government, politics, social mores, societal beliefs, community responsibility, and the country's economy.

3. Point out that at age 12 years, a person might be ready biologically to have a child but not socially, emotionally, or mentally. On the chalkboard, make columns with the headings *Physical, Social, Emotional,* and *Mental.* In each column, write negatives of teen parenting.

# Strategies to Reteach, Reinforce, Enrich, and Extend Text Concepts

## Why Is It Hard to Be a Good Parent?

4. **RT** Discuss with students the qualities of good relationships. Why might differences between two people sometimes make a good relationship difficult?
5. **RT** Ask students to explain why parenting is a one-sided relationship for many years.
6. **ER** *Comparing Parenting to Other Careers*, Activity A, SAG. Students should use this activity to compare parenting to other careers.
7. **RT** Invite students to discuss whether parenting today is easier or more difficult now than in the past.
8. **ER** Ask students to write a paragraph entitled "A Good Parent Is…."
9. **ER** *Children Learn What They Live*, transparency master 3-2, a poem by Dorothy Law Nolte. Use this poem to help students understand the importance of good parenting and the impact parenting skills have on the life of a child.

## Learning Parenting Skills

10. **RF** Ask students to list ways parents can learn child care skills.
11. **ER** *Child Development Resources*, Activity B, SAG. Students should identify professionals, classes, and other resources available in the community to help parents and parents-to-be learn more about parenting.

## Deciding About Parenthood

12. **RF** Discuss each of the following statements: (1) Feelings about parenting should be discussed before marriage. (2) For the sake of a couple's relationship, the decision to parent should be mutual. (3) For the sake of the child, the decision to parent should be mutual.

13. **RF** Ask students to explain why a person who wants parenthood for selfish reasons is apt to be disappointed. Students should explain how unfair it is for a child to be born or adopted into a family where he or she doesn't measure up to a parent's selfish expectations.
14. **EX** *Are You Ready for Parenthood?* color transparency CT-3A. Use this transparency to lead a discussion contrasting qualities of couples who are ready for parenthood to those who are not ready.

## Reasons for Choosing Parenthood

15. **ER** Have students interview two or more parents about the joys and responsibilities of parenting. The interview may focus on the following themes: (1) How does the responsibility of parenting compare with other responsibilities in their life? (2) What, in general, do they feel parents should teach children? (3) What have they learned from their children? (4) What have they most enjoyed about the parent-child relationship?
16. **RF** *Is This a Good Reason for Choosing Parenthood?* Activity C, SAG. Instruct students to work in small groups to plan and present a skit depicting poor reasons for becoming parents.
17. **RF** Ask students to prepare and present skits about good reasons for choosing parenthood.
18. **EX** Ask students to suggest possible reasons for parenthood in other cultures, such as royal families to have heirs to the throne or farming communities to have help with work on family farms.
19. **EX** Ask students whether some of the reasons given in the text could lead parents to abuse or neglect their children. (For example: How might a parent react to a premature baby or a baby with special needs if a "cute" baby was their main reason for having a child?)

## Reasons for Not Choosing Parenthood

20. **RF** Divide the class into six groups. Ask each group to suggest ways that couples who really want children can overcome one of the reasons given for not choosing parenting. Share each group's ideas in class discussion.
21. **EX** Ask each student to rank the six reasons in the list in order of priority and give the rationale for their choices.

22. **EX**  Use the following questions to stimulate a class discussion:
    → Is choosing parenthood ever risk-free?
    → What other problems might occur if one waits too long to have children and later decides to have children?

## Factors to Consider

23. **ER**  Have students work in small groups to prepare an oral report on one of the following: (1) The Costs of Parenting; (2) Challenges of Single Parenting; (3) Challenges of Parenting a Child with Disabilities; (4) Challenges and Costs of Finding Quality Child Care. After groups have given their reports, ask students whether they think these are valid reasons for choosing not to have children.
24. **RF**  Students should identify and list ways that having children changes a person's life. Allow volunteers to share answers with the class.

## How Children Affect Relationships

25. **RF**  *Couple Relationships Affect Parenthood*, Activity D, SAG. Ask students to list words or phrases that describe strong and weak couple relationships.
26. **RT**  Discuss with students how a couple's feelings for others have a direct bearing on how effective they will be as parents.
27. **ER**  Instruct students to research the Foster Grandparent Program funded by the federal government. Students should write a paper on how this program helps both children and the elderly.
28. **EX**  Ask students to reflect on the following questions: Can you recall a strong relationship you had with an adult outside your immediate family? In what ways did this help you learn to accept others and get along with them?

## Sharing Responsibilities

29. **RF**  Students should list all the responsibilities adults must take during the first two months of parenthood.
30. **ER**  *Parenting: A Time-Consuming Job*, reproducible master 3-3. Students should ask three parents who have children of different ages to complete the chart. Help students analyze the results and present their findings in class.
31. **ER**  Invite a couple with a full-time home-maker and a dual-career couple to class. Ask each couple to discuss how the spouses share home and child care tasks. Encourage students to ask questions.

32. **EX**  Invite students to role-play scenes depicting a couple's conflicts in sharing home care responsibilities.
33. **RT**  Ask students to brainstorm ways couples can share home care responsibilities before and after they become parents.
34. **RT**  Discuss with students the importance of knowing how a potential spouse feels about sharing home care responsibilities before marriage.

## Managing Finances

35. **RT**  *Children Grow More Expensive*, color transparency CT-3B. Use this transparency to illustrate the types of expenses parents incur as children grow.
36. **RF**  Divide the class into groups. Have members of each group sample the costs of items in categories of child-related expenses, such as food, clothing, furniture, toys, and services for children. Students should make posters showing the expenses.
37. **RT**  Discuss Figure 3-9 in the text. Ask students if they are surprised at the total cost. What years are most costly for parents?
38. **RF**  Have students list some ways families can adjust their budgets to meet the costs of children.
39. **EX**  *Calculating Foregone Income*, reproducible master 3-4. Use the form to review the steps in calculating foregone income with students. You may want to instruct students to research specific amounts of costs for step 1.
40. **ER**  *The Cost of Parenthood*, Activity E, SAG. Have students interview a parent about the costs involved in parenting and record information in the space provided.

## Managing Careers

41. **RT**  Instruct students to list advantages and disadvantages of both parents working outside the home.
42. **RT**  Discuss with students what they would say to a new mother about working outside the home and its effects on her child's development.
43. **ER**  Invite students to plan and present two skits. One skit should show a parent giving complete focus to a child's needs. The other should show a parent giving only partial focus to a child's needs. After the skits, discuss with students how adults feel when others give them only partial attention during a conversation. How might partial attention actually be dangerous?

## Maternity and Paternity Leave

44. **RF** Ask students to list advantages and disadvantages of maternity and paternity leaves.

45. **ER** Interview a mother who took maternity leave. Ask her what she noted as advantages and disadvantages of the leave. Ask how she would rewrite her employer's maternity leave policy if she could.

46. **RT** Ask the class to brainstorm reasons that fathers take paternity leave far less often than women take maternity leave.

47. **EX** Have students list things a father could do for his wife and baby while on paternity leave.

48. **ER** Have students use the Internet to research the provisions of the Family Medical and Leave Act and prepare a written or oral report on their findings.

## Problems with Family and Work

49. **RT** Divide the class into six groups. Assign each group one of the questions given in the bulleted list on page 96 of the text. Have groups brainstorm ways a couple might plan to resolve each issue. Ask groups to share their ideas to help form a master list of key suggestions.

50. **ER** Interview a local child care advocate about the availability of quality child care for infants and young children in your community.

## Family Planning

51. **RT** Students should list concerns of family planning.

52. **RF** Discuss with students how relationships differ when siblings are close in age versus when siblings have wider age differences.

53. **RF** Have students list pros and cons of being an only child.

54. **RF** Discuss with students the advantages and disadvantages of having fewer children versus many children.

55. **EX** *Birth Control Options,* reproducible master 3-5. If appropriate for your class, use this master to describe the various methods of birth control available. If appropriate, you can also photocopy this list and distribute to students for their reference. **Note:** Abstinence is described in more depth in the section *Why Wait?* on pages 669 and 670 of the text.

## Infertility

56. **RT** Share with students why infertility is an increasing problem. (Increased age of those wanting to conceive, increased rate of STDs, and increase in other health problems are leading to more cases of infertility.)

57. **ER** Have students find magazine articles about fertility problems. Students should give short reports summarizing the articles in class.

58. **RT** Discuss with students how infertility and sterility can affect a marriage.

## Overcoming Infertility

59. **RT** Using a dictionary, ask students to find in a dictionary each word of the three assisted reproductive technologies (ART) described in the chapter. Point out that understanding the meanings of these words helps in learning what each process does.

60. **EX** Ask students possible reasons more couples today choose to try ART methods. (Student answers might include availability of these technologies, increase in fertility problems, and increased acceptance of ART.)

61. **EX** Ask students to list reasons people may choose *not* to use ART methods. (Student responses might include relatively low success rate, high costs, travel, missed work days, moral or ethical beliefs, health risks, and emotional trauma of failed attempts.)

# Answer Key

## Text

*Reviewing Key Concepts,* page 104

1. false

2. (List three:) We want to share our love with a child. Wouldn't it be nice to have a cute little baby? Our parents want grandchildren. Our older child needs a brother or sister. A child can make us proud. Others will see me as a stable, reliable person. A child will comfort us in our old age.

3. D

4. having enough time and energy for both roles, finding good child care services

5. potential income lost by not being in the workforce

6. gives her time to recover from the pregnancy, labor, and delivery; allows her to adjust to her new role of meeting the baby's constant and many needs; allows time to bond with the baby

7. law that protects the rights of many employed women and men to take unpaid maternity or paternity leave

8. Family planning affects how many children a couple will have and when they will have children.

9. false
10. Infertility is emotionally painful. Couples often feel sad and helpless about their life plans. The spouse with the problem may feel damaged or guilty. Seeking treatment is time-consuming, expensive, and often ineffective.
11. by using assisted reproductive technologies or by parenting adopted or foster children

# Teacher's Resources

## *Reasons for Parenthood Choices,* reproducible master 3-1

(Exact student responses may vary.)

**Reasons for choosing parenthood:**
1. to share love with a child
2. to have a "cute little" baby
3. to satisfy parents' desires to be grandparents
4. to satisfy a child's desire for a sibling
5. to seem stable and reliable to others
6. to have someone for comfort in old age
7. to renew love in a couple's relationship

**Reasons for not choosing parenthood:**
1. a couple's lack of maturity
2. high cost
3. loss of free time
4. interference with careers
5. likelihood of having a disabled child
6. fear of becoming a single parent

## Chapter 3 Test

| | | | |
|---|---|---|---|
| 1. T | 10. F | 19. B | 28. I |
| 2. T | 11. T | 20. D | 29. J |
| 3. F | 12. T | 21. A | 30. D |
| 4. T | 13. F | 22. D | 31. C |
| 5. T | 14. T | 23. C | 32. B |
| 6. F | 15. T | 24. D | 33. H |
| 7. F | 16. B | 25. C | 34. E |
| 8. T | 17. B | 26. G | 35. A |
| 9. F | 18. A | 27. F | 36. K |

37. Training for parenting is much less specific than training for other careers. Unlike many careers, the new parent is given total responsibility almost immediately. In other careers, a new employee assumes tasks more gradually. Parents do not get paid for meeting their parenting responsibilities. People can change jobs if they desire, but parenting is permanent.
38. Couples must examine the strengths and weaknesses of their relationships with each other, relatives, and friends. Couples must also decide how they would meet parenting responsibilities such as sharing household and child care tasks, managing financial resources, planning who will care for the child, finding child care services, and planning for the future.
39. Artificial insemination is a medical procedure in which sperm are introduced into the vagina or uterus. In vitro fertilization is a procedure in which the mother's eggs are surgically removed and fertilized with sperm in a laboratory dish before being placed into the uterus for implantation. Gamete intrafallopian transfer is the placing of a mixture of sperm and eggs directly into the mother's fallopian tubes for fertilization.

# Reasons for Parenthood Choices

**Name** _____ **Date** _____ **Period** _____

One of the most important decisions couples make as they consider marriage is whether they will become parents. This decision will affect many aspects of their marriage. Before reading your text, list all the reasons couples might give for wanting or not wanting to become parents. You do not need to agree with a reason to list it.

| For Being a Parent | For Not Being a Parent |
|---|---|
| | |

After reading your text, list other reasons for being or not being a parent that were not included in your first list.

| For Being a Parent | For Not Being a Parent |
|---|---|
| | |

# Children Learn What They Live

*If a child lives with criticism, he learns to condemn.*

*If a child lives with hostility, he learns to fight.*

*If a child lives with ridicule, he learns to be shy.*

*If a child lives with shame, he learns to feel guilty.*

*If a child lives with tolerance, he learns to be patient.*

*If a child lives with encouragement, he learns confidence.*

*If a child lives with praise, he learns to appreciate.*

*If a child lives with fairness, he learns justice.*

*If a child lives with security, he learns to have faith.*

*If a child lives with approval, he learns to like himself.*

*If a child lives with acceptance and friendship, he learns to find love in the world.*

**Dorothy Law Nolte**

# Parenting: A Time-Consuming Job

**Name** _____ **Date** _____ **Period** _____

Parents are busy people. Effective parenting takes much time. Ask three adults—the parent of a baby, the parent of a preschooler, and the parent of a school-aged child—to complete the items needed for the following chart. In the space that follows, record the time they spent parenting for one week. (Make copies of the charts for each parent.)

## For Infants

| Scheduled Items | Day 1 | Day 2 | Day 3 | Day 4 | Day 5 | Day 6 | Day 7 | Total |
|---|---|---|---|---|---|---|---|---|
| food preparation | | | | | | | | |
| laundry/mending | | | | | | | | |
| hygienic care of child, such as bathing | | | | | | | | |
| housekeeping chores related to child | | | | | | | | |
| shopping for child's needs | | | | | | | | |
| chauffeuring child | | | | | | | | |
| conversations with persons in child care services, such as physicians or child care workers | | | | | | | | |
| interacting with child (beyond the above items) | | | | | | | | |
| other | | | | | | | | |

Total ☐

*(Continued)*

**Name** _____

# For Preschoolers

| Scheduled Items | Day 1 | Day 2 | Day 3 | Day 4 | Day 5 | Day 6 | Day 7 | Total |
|---|---|---|---|---|---|---|---|---|
| food preparation | | | | | | | | |
| laundry/mending | | | | | | | | |
| hygienic care of child, such as bathing | | | | | | | | |
| housekeeping chores related to child | | | | | | | | |
| shopping for child's needs | | | | | | | | |
| chauffeuring child | | | | | | | | |
| conversations with persons in child care services, such as physicians or child care workers | | | | | | | | |
| interacting with child (beyond the above items) | | | | | | | | |
| other | | | | | | | | |

Total ☐

*(Continued)*

**Name** _____

# For School-Age Children

| Scheduled Items | Day 1 | Day 2 | Day 3 | Day 4 | Day 5 | Day 6 | Day 7 | Total |
|---|---|---|---|---|---|---|---|---|
| food preparation | | | | | | | | |
| laundry/mending | | | | | | | | |
| hygienic care of child, such as bathing | | | | | | | | |
| housekeeping chores related to child | | | | | | | | |
| shopping for child's needs | | | | | | | | |
| chauffeuring child | | | | | | | | |
| conversations with persons in child care services, such as physicians or child care workers | | | | | | | | |
| interacting with child (beyond the above items) | | | | | | | | |
| other | | | | | | | | |

Total [ ]

*(Continued)*

**Name** _____

Did the parents used in your study express surprise at the total amount of time they spent parenting?

_____

_____

_____

_____

Based on the three homes you studied, how did the time spent for scheduled items change with the age of child?

_____

_____

_____

_____

_____

_____

# Calculating Foregone Income

**Name** _____ **Date** _____ **Period** _____

## Step 1

Add costs of earning an income.                                                    $ _____

    taxes on earned income                                     $ _____

    FICA                                                       $ _____

    transportation to and from work                           $ _____

    food away from home                                        $ _____

    costs to update skills (required seminars, courses,

       and conferences paid for by employee)                  $ _____

    clothing appropriate for job—including

       uniforms or safety equipment                           $ _____

    professional or union dues                                 $ _____

    child care costs while working or updating skills          $ _____

    incidental costs (gifts, office parties, or other)         $ _____

Total                                                                              $ _____

## Step 2

Subtract costs of earning an income from gross income.

    gross income                                               $ _____

    costs of earning income                                    $ _____

    foregone income                                            $ _____

Foregone income is an estimate because exact costs are impossible to calculate and fringe benefits may increase gross income.

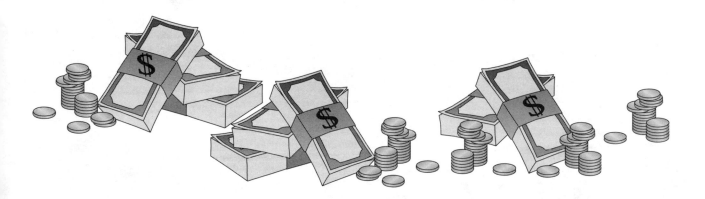

# Birth Control Options

| Option | Effectiveness | Advantages | Possible Problems |
|---|---|---|---|
| Abstinence | 100% | No medical or hormonal side effects<br><br>Endorsed by many religious groups<br><br>Prevents STDs<br><br>Costs nothing | Lack of willpower<br>Lack of commitment by one or both partners |
| **Hormonal methods (estrogen, progestin, or combinations)**<br>*Certain drugs and illnesses can interfere with hormones' effectiveness | | | |
| Birth control pill (oral contraceptive) | 95 to 99%*<br>No protection against STDs | Less acne<br>Fewer premenstrual symptoms<br>Less iron deficiency<br>Some protection against ovarian and uterine cancers | Must be taken daily<br>Temporary irregular bleeding<br>Breast tenderness<br>Weight gain or loss<br>Blood clots |
| 1-month injection | 99%*<br>No protection against STDs | (Same as the Pill) | (Same as the Pill) |
| 3-month injection | 99.7%*<br>No protection against STDs | Doesn't have to be taken daily<br><br>Reduces menstrual cramps and anemia<br><br>Some protection against ovarian and uterine cancer | Irregular bleeding<br><br>Change in frequency of periods with a 5-year use<br><br>May have trouble conceiving for a year after use is stopped<br><br>Side effects can continue for 8 months |
| Hormone implants<br><br>Match-size, soft plastic tubes placed under the skin in the upper arm. These are inserted and removed through a small incision. | 99.9%*<br>No protection against STDs | Effective for up to 5 years; can be removed at any time | Irregular periods and spotting<br><br>Decreased effectiveness in overweight women<br><br>Some increased risks of heart attacks and strokes |

*(Continued)*

| Option | Effectiveness | Advantages | Possible Problems |
|---|---|---|---|
| **Mechanical Devices** | | | |
| **Diaphragm or cervical cap**<br><br>Diaphragm is a latex dome that is inserted in the vagina and covers the cervix<br><br>Cervical cap is a thimble-shaped latex cap that fits over the cervix<br><br>Often combined spermicide for greater protection | 90 to 94% (80% effective with women who have had children) | Used only when needed<br><br>Can last several years<br><br>Reduces risk of cervical cancer<br><br>Some protection against STDs<br><br>May be used during breast-feeding | Must be inserted before each use and left in place a set number of hours after use<br><br>Messy<br><br>Cannot be used during vaginal bleeding or infection<br><br>Allergies to latex and spermicide can develop<br><br>Cannot be used by women with poor vaginal muscle tone<br><br>Diaphragm increases risk of bladder infection<br><br>Must be refitted after pregnancy, weight change, or abdominal or pelvic surgery<br><br>May be difficult to fit and difficult to use |
| **Male condom**<br><br>Condom is a sheath made of latex polyurethane, or animal membrane worn over the erect penis during intercourse | 88% | Easy to purchase<br><br>Latex condoms are effective against STDs<br><br>Can help relieve premature ejaculation<br><br>Can increase effectiveness if used with spermicide | Allergies to latex or to spermicide<br><br>Condom can break, tear, or slip off into the vagina |
| **Female condom**<br><br>Polyurethane pouch that lines the vagina to keep semen out | 79%<br><br>No protection against STDs | | Allergies to polyurethane |
| **Intrauterine Device (IUD)**<br><br>Small plastic device inserted into the uterus for up to 10 years | 98% (with hormones)<br><br>99.2% (with copper)<br><br>Increases the risk of STDs | Effective for up to 10 years<br><br>IUDs with hormones may reduce menstrual cramps | Temporary increase in cramps<br><br>Spotting between periods<br><br>Heavier and longer periods<br><br>Increased chance of fallopian tube infection<br><br>Usually not recommended for women who have not had children due to the size of the uterus |

*(Continued)*

| Option | Effectiveness | Advantages | Possible Problems |
|---|---|---|---|
| **Sterilization** | | | |
| **Tubal ligation**<br><br>Surgery of the female that closes, ties, or cuts the fallopian tubes (tubes that carry eggs from the ovaries to the uterus) | 99.6%<br><br>No protection against STDs | Permanent | Difficult or impossible to reverse<br><br>Possible medical side effects |
| **Vasectomy**<br><br>Surgery of the male that cuts and closes the vas deferens (tubes that carry sperm out of the male body) | 99.85% after first several weeks<br><br>No protection against STDs | Permanent | Difficult or impossible to reverse<br><br>Possible medical side effects |
| **Natural Planning** | | | |
| **Natural Family Planning**<br>(also called periodic abstinence, rhythm method, and fertility awareness)<br><br>Avoiding sex near the time of ovulation by: (1) noting and recording changes in cervical mucus; (2) noting and recording changes in body temperature; (3) sympto-thermal, which combines both (1) and (2); or (4) counting days in which ovulation should occur | 80% | Only costs are thermometer and calendar<br><br>No medical or hormonal side effects<br><br>Accepted by most religions | Uncooperative partner could interfere with method's effectiveness<br><br>Involves commitment to daily observing and recording<br><br>Ovulation is difficult to predict accurately; illness and stress make this even more difficult to predict<br><br>Method is ineffective with irregular menstrual cycles<br><br>Other biological factors can affect temperature or cervical mucus |

# Preparing for Parenting

**Name** _____

**Date** _____ **Period** _____ **Score** _____

## Chapter 3 Test

True/False: Circle *T* if the statement is true or *F* if the statement is false.

T   F   1. It is *not* easy to be a good parent.

T   F   2. Once a person is a parent, he or she will always be a parent.

T   F   3. The most important reason for having a child is the pride a child brings a parent.

T   F   4. Having children interferes with careers because parents do not think they can be effective parents and do worthwhile work outside the home at the same time.

T   F   5. Parenthood happens quickly, giving new parents full responsibility.

T   F   6. How a couple feels about other adults will have little effect on how they will feel about children.

T   F   7. All couples should equally divide all child care tasks because parenting is a 50-50 responsibility.

T   F   8. As a general rule, expenses will grow as children do.

T   F   9. Due to the Family Medical Leave Act, almost as many fathers as mothers are currently taking leave after the birth or adoption of a baby.

T   F   10. Finding quality child care is easy for most parents.

T   F   11. Providing adequate spacing between children is good for all members of a family.

T   F   12. Family planning is a personal decision a couple should make with the advice of their doctor.

T   F   13. All couples need fertility counseling.

T   F   14. In vitro fertilization is sometimes used to help couples have biological children.

T   F   15. The use of donor cells (eggs and/or sperm) in assisted reproductive technologies can cause ethical and legal issues.

Multiple Choice: Choose the best response. Write the letter in the space provided.

_____ 16. New parents are more skilled at parenting if they _____.
A. have a college degree
B. take classes to learn effective parenting skills
C. follow one child care book for every child care situation
D. do everything exactly like their own parents did

_____ 17. A decision *not* to parent _____.
A. is made by selfish people
B. need not always be a permanent choice
C. should only be made if a couple has fertility problems
D. needs to be made before a person chooses a career

*(Continued)*

**Name** _____

_____ 18. Which of the following is the most important reason for having a child?
    A. A person wants to welcome a child into his or her life and share his or her love and time with the child.
    B. A person feels an only child needs a brother or sister.
    C. A person feels a child will help the parents love each other more.
    D. A person feels having a child will make him or her appear to be a more stable member of the community.

_____ 19. All of the following are characteristics of effective parents *except* _____.
    A. They are sensitive to the needs of others.
    B. They are inflexible and have a hard time accepting changes.
    C. They recognize and respect the rights of others.
    D. They understand children's needs and are prepared to meet these needs.

_____ 20. Relatives and friends are important to children because they may _____.
    A. provide children with their first link to the outside world
    B. serve as a living bond to the past
    C. give children a deep sense they are cared for and loved
    D. All of the above.

_____ 21. All of the following are indirect costs of having children *except* _____.
    A. costs of diapers, clothes, and baby supplies
    B. the value of earnings foregone when a parent leaves the workforce to stay home with children
    C. the impact on the parent's career opportunities due to time out of the workforce
    D. not having time to pursue a personal hobby

_____ 22. Paternity leave seems to be positive because fathers who have taken this leave report they _____.
    A. have good relationships with their children
    B. better understand what it takes to be a stay-at-home parent
    C. realize they work for a better total life for their families rather than just economic support
    D. All of the above.

_____ 23. Children tend to do better when _____.
    A. mothers stay at home
    B. mothers work outside the home
    C. mothers have a positive attitude toward their work in or out of the home
    D. fathers stay at home and mothers work outside the home.

_____ 24. Family planning _____.
    A. is unimportant for married couples because it does not matter when they have children
    B. is needed only after the first child is born
    C. should be only the mother's decision because she is more likely to do child care tasks than the father
    D. None of the above.

_____ 25. Infertile couples _____.
    A. soon get over the emotional pain of not being able to have children
    B. can always have biological children through the use of assisted reproductive technologies
    C. face ethical, legal, and moral issues when considering the use of ART with a surrogate mother
    D. always learn the cause of their fertility problems through fertility counseling

*(Continued)*

**Name** _____

Matching: Match the following terms and identifying phrases.

_____ 26. Resources used to meet child-related expenses that could have been used to meet other goals.

_____ 27. Potential earnings given up by a parent who leaves the workforce to stay home and raise a child.

_____ 28. Time a woman takes off from work for the birth or adoption of a child.

_____ 29. Time a man takes off from work for the birth or adoption of a child.

_____ 30. Law that protects the rights of many men and women to take unpaid leave when a baby is born or adopted.

_____ 31. Decisions a couple makes about the desired number and spacing of future children.

_____ 32. Methods couples use to prevent conception.

_____ 33. Couple who are not able to conceive after a year of trying.

_____ 34. Medical evaluation that seeks to determine reasons for fertility problems and explore treatment options.

_____ 35. Methods infertile couples can use to help them conceive.

_____ 36. Woman who bears (or conceives and bears) a child for a couple.

A. assisted reproductive technologies (ART)

B. birth control

C. family planning

D. Family and Medical Leave Act

E. fertility counseling

F. foregone income

G. indirect costs

H. infertile

I. maternity leave

J. paternity leave

K. surrogate mother

Essay Questions: Provide complete responses to the following questions or statements.

37. Describe two differences between parenting and careers.

38. What types of decisions must those who are considering parenting make?

39. Name and describe three methods used to help couples overcome problems of not conceiving.

90

# Pregnancy

4

## Objectives

After studying this chapter, students will be able to
- describe what happens during conception
- explain how genetic factors affect prenatal development
- describe how a person inherits traits through genes.
- list the three different types of multiple pregnancies.
- describe the three main stages of prenatal development.

## Bulletin Boards

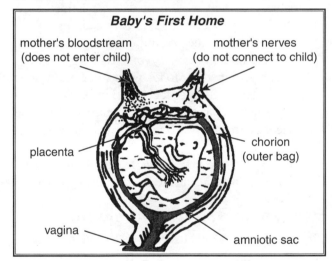

**Baby's First Home**

mother's bloodstream (does not enter child)

mother's nerves (do not connect to child)

placenta

chorion (outer bag)

vagina

amniotic sac

### Title: Baby's First Home

Have students draw or enlarge a drawing similar to illustration 4-12 in the text. Write labels on cards, and punch a hole near the bottom of each card. Attach a small ribbon or piece of yarn long enough to reach the drawing, and pin labels around the drawing. As you progress through the chapter, have students attach the free end of the ribbon or yarn to the proper place on the drawing.

### Title: Nine Months to Get Ready

Using a large calendar, separate pages for each month. Choose a date, circle it, and mark it *Conception*. Count ahead 270 days and mark that day *Due Date*.

Highlight one week around the due date and mark this as the *Due Week*. Mark also the beginning and ends of the germinal, embryonic, and fetal stages of pregnancy.

## Teaching Materials

**Text**, pages 108–127
  *Reviewing Key Concepts*
  *Using Your Knowledge*
  *Making Observations*
  *Thinking Further*

**Student Activity Guide**
  A. *Biology of Heredity Review*
  B. *Inheriting Unique Traits*
  C. *Multiple Births*
  D. *Development in the Unborn*

**Teacher's Resources**
  *Pregnancy Vocabulary*, reproducible master 4-1
  *Multiple Pregnancy*, transparency master 4-2
  *Stages of Prenatal Development*, color transparency CT-4
  Chapter 4 Test

## Introductory Activities

1. *Pregnancy Vocabulary*, reproducible master 4-1. Use this puzzle as a pretest of chapter terms. Have students try the puzzle again after studying the chapter to assess vocabulary comprehension.
2. Ask students to list any "wives' tales" they may have heard about pregnancy. Examples include the following: (1) Birthmarks are caused by being frightened during pregnancy. (2) If pregnant women have heartburn, the baby has lots of hair. (3) If pregnant women raise their arms over their heads, it will strangle the baby. Discuss why these myths are inaccurate.

# Strategies to Reteach, Reinforce, Enrich, and Extend Text Concepts

## Conception

3. **RT** Discuss with students the events that occur at conception.
4. **RT** Make magnetic or flannel board illustrations of: (a) the cross section of the female internal reproductive organs; (b) an egg; and (c) several sperm. Have a student trace (by moving the egg and sperm) the journey they take to the upper third of the fallopian tube where conception takes place.
5. **EX** Explain that *zygote* means to join. Ask the students what is joined at conception.

## Genetic Factors and the Unborn Baby

6. **RT** Ask students to describe how knowing the genetic backgrounds of both a mother and father would indicate some of the traits of their children.
7. **RF** *Biology of Heredity Review*, Activity A, SAG. Have students fill in the blanks in the provided story to review the terms and concepts of heredity.
8. **RT** Invite students to explain the roles of chromosomes, genes, and DNA in the heredity process.
9. **ER** Instruct students to research heredity using another book as a source. Students should find out what happens when the two factors for each trait (one from the mother and one from the father) carry different instructions. Traits could include: blue eyes and brown eyes, light-colored hair and dark-colored hair, curly and straight hair, and tall and short height. Students should report their findings in class.
10. **RT** Ask students to explain how a child may have one or more traits that no one else in the family possesses.
11. **ER** *Inheriting Unique Traits*, Activity B, SAG. Invite a biology teacher to class to discuss genetic mutations. Have students use the information from the speaker to answer the questions provided.
12. **ER** Students should research the work of Gregor Mendel or another noted genetic scientist. Instruct them to write a one-page paper and present their information to the class.
13. **ER** Have students research facts concerning ultrasound, amniocentesis, or chorionic villus sampling. They should learn the purpose of the chosen medical procedure and report findings to the class.

## Multiple Pregnancy

14. **RT** Describe how it can be determined whether children of multiple births are fraternal or identical.
15. **RF** *Multiple Births*, Activity C, SAG. Students should write answers to questions about multiple births.
16. **RF** *Multiple Pregnancy*, transparency master 4-2. Use this transparency to diagram for students (or have students diagram) various types of multiple pregnancies.
17. **ER** Invite students to interview twins about the joys and problems of being a twin. Students should then write a news or feature article based on the interview.
18. **ER** Invite the parents of multiple-birth children to speak to the class about the uniqueness of their family. Ask them to tell the class how they managed their time when the children were babies, as well as how they have helped their children develop individual personalities.
19. **EX** Point out the scientific name for identical multiple births is *monozygotic*. Ask why this is a meaningful word. (*Mono-* means one and *zygote* means fertilized egg. Identical births come from one zygote that splits one or more times.) The scientific name for fraternal multiple births is *dizygotic*. Ask why this is a meaningful name. (*Di-* means two and *zygote* means fertilized egg. Fraternal births result from separate zygotes.)

## Stages in Prenatal Development

20. **RT** Ask students to look at the point of a pencil or pen. Explain that a zygote is about the same size. Then have students discuss adjectives that could describe the happenings during the nine months of pregnancy.
21. **RT** *Stages of Prenatal Development*, color transparency CT-4. Use this transparency as an introduction to the three stages of prenatal development. Note the approximate length and major developments of each stage.
22. **RF** *Development in the Unborn*, Activity D, SAG. Students should match each phrase that describes happenings in prenatal development with its corresponding stage.

# Answer Key

## Text

### Reviewing Key Concepts, page 126

1. The ovum is released from the ovaries and swept into a fallopian tube. It floats about one-third of the distance down the tube and pauses. Sperm enter the body during intercourse. They "swim" through the woman's reproductive organs to the egg. Those sperm that survive the long journey surround the egg and try to enter. Only one sperm may eventually enter. Within several hours, the sperm has reached the center of the egg and a zygote is formed.
2. 23; 23
3. The male's sperm may have an X chromosome for producing a girl or a Y chromosome for producing a boy.
4. B
5. identical, fraternal, mixed type
6. fraternal
7. false
8. embryonic
9. false
10. bones
11. C

## Student Activity Guide

### Biology of Heredity Review, Activity A

1. ovum
2. sperm
3. conception
4. cell
5. nucleus
6. DNA
7. 46
8. genes
9. blue
10. germ
11. 46
12. divided
13. parents
14. baby
15. traits

### Development in the Unborn, Activity D

1. fetal stage
2. germinal stage
3. embryonic stage
4. fetal stage
5. fetal stage
6. germinal stage
7. fetal stage
8. embryonic stage
9. embryonic stage
10. germinal stage
11. fetal stage
12. fetal stage
13. fetal stage
14. embryonic stage
15. germinal stage
16. embryonic stage
17. fetal stage
18. fetal stage
19. fetal stage
20. fetal stage

## Teacher's Resources

### Pregnancy Vocabulary, reproducible master 4-1

1. sperm
2. ovum
3. conception
4. zygote
5. fallopian
6. uterus
7. amnion
8. placenta
9. embryo
10. fetus

### Multiple Pregnancy, transparency master 4-2

(For correct diagrams, see Figures 4-5, 4-8, and 4-11 in the text.)

### Chapter 4 Test

1. T
2. T
3. F
4. T
5. T
6. F
7. F
8. T
9. F
10. T
11. D
12. C
13. A
14. C
15. D
16. B
17. A
18. A
19. C
20. B
21. K
22. G
23. M
24. E
25. D
26. C
27. F
28. I
29. A
30. H
31. L
32. J

33. (Student response.)
34. The first stage of prenatal development is the germinal stage. In this stage the egg is fertilized by the sperm and then moves to the uterus. The fertilized egg, or zygote, begins to grow through cell divisions. Toward the end of the stage, the zygote begins to embed in the wall of the uterus. The second stage is the embryonic stage. At this point, the embryo can receive nourishment from the mother through the umbilical cord. Almost all the body systems develop during this stage. The stage lasts about six weeks. The third stage is the fetal stage. During the fetal stage, all the parts of the body mature and overall size increases. The fetus begins to move and develop to the point where it can survive outside the mother.
35. All traits are either dominant or recessive. The gene for a given trait will be either dominant or recessive. Because both parents provide a corresponding gene for most traits at conception, the child may receive two dominant genes, two recessive genes, or a dominant and a recessive gene. (For a few traits on the twenty-third chromosome, boys receive only

one dominant or recessive gene from the mother and no corresponding gene from the father.) For a trait to show, a child has to have only one dominant gene. Two recessive genes, one from the mother and one from the father, are most often required for these recessive traits to show; however, boys may show a few recessive traits that were inherited from the mother only (hemophilia and color blindness).

# Pregnancy Vocabulary

**Name** _____ **Date** _____ **Period** _____

Below are definitions commonly used in pregnancy. Read the definitions and write the term in the appropriate place.

1. The male germ cell is called the _____.
2. The female germ cell is called the _____.
3. _____ is the union of an ovum and a sperm at the beginning of pregnancy.
4. Ovum and sperm unite to form a (an) _____.
5. The two hollow _____ tubes extend from the right and left sides of the uterus.
6. The organ in which the baby develops and is protected until birth is called the _____.
7. The _____ is a fluid-filled sac that protects the baby until birth.
8. The _____ is an organ filled with blood vessels that are used to nourish the unborn baby.
9. In the second stage of prenatal development, the unborn baby is called a (an)_____.
10. In the final stage of prenatal development, the unborn baby is called a (an)_____.

1. ☐☐☐☐☐
2. ☐☐☐☐☐
3. ☐☐☐☐☐☐☐☐☐☐
4. ☐☐☐☐☐☐
5. ☐☐☐☐☐☐☐☐☐
6. ☐☐☐☐☐☐
7. ☐☐☐☐☐☐
8. ☐☐☐☐☐☐☐
9. ☐☐☐☐☐☐
10. ☐☐☐☐☐

# Multiple Pregnancy

## Fraternal Twins

## Identical Twins

## Identical Triplets

## Mixed Types Triplets

# Pregnancy

**Name** _____

**Date** _____ **Period** _____ **Score** _____

## Chapter 4 Test

True/False: Circle *T* if the statement is true or *F* if the statement is false.

T    F    1. The joining of an egg and a sperm is called *conception*.

T    F    2. The uterus is the organ inside which a baby develops and is protected until birth.

T    F    3. The egg and sperm typically unite as the egg enters the uterus.

T    F    4. Chromosomes are threadlike structures that carry genes in living cells.

T    F    5. Every germ cell contains 23 chromosomes.

T    F    6. A child who looks more like his or her father inherited more chromosomes from the father than from the mother.

T    F    7. Inheritance is an environmental factor that affects the unborn.

T    F    8. Despite advances in medical treatments, doctors remain especially concerned about the health of the babies in a multiple pregnancy.

T    F    9. Identical twins share the same fingerprints.

T    F    10. The genes of fraternal twins are less alike than those of identical twins.

Multiple Choice: Choose the best response. Write the letter in the space provided.

_____ 11. Which of the following statements is true about traits?
A. Dominant traits show in a person if only one gene in a gene pair is for that trait.
B. Recessive traits do not show in a person if only one gene is present except for a few traits seen in boys.
C. People can pass along (carry) traits to their children that do not show in them.
D. All of the above.

_____ 12. If a husband and wife both have brown eyes (a dominant trait), but also carry a trait for blue eyes (a recessive trait), what is known about their children's eye color?
A. The children's eyes will definitely be brown.
B. The children's eyes will definitely be blue.
C. The children's eyes might be blue or brown.
D. Eye color is random, so the children's eyes could be any color.

_____ 13. The gender of a child is determined by ___.
A. the father
B. the mother
C. neither the father nor the mother
D. conditions in the uterus

_____ 14. In order for twins to be identical, they must ___.
A. look alike in every way
B. share the same placenta before birth
C. show genetic matches through blood tests and skin grafts
D. have mirror images

*(Continued)*

**Name** _____

_____ 15. Mixed type pregnancies involve ___.
A. one boy and one girl
B. three identical children
C. three fraternal children
D. at least two identical children and one fraternal child

_____ 16. Drugs and diseases of the mother are most dangerous to the unborn in the ___ of prenatal development.
A. germinal stage
B. embryonic stage
C. fetal stage
D. all stages equally

_____ 17. During which stage does the placenta begin to develop?
A. germinal stage
B. embryonic stage
C. fetal stage
D. None of the above.

_____ 18. The age of viability is the ___.
A. earliest age at which most babies survive if born
B. earliest age at which all babies survive if born
C. age at which babies can take care of themselves
D. age at which babies reach full-term

_____ 19. In the ninth month of pregnancy, the ___.
A. the heartbeat of the fetus is first heard through a stethoscope
B. fetus grows slowly
C. fetus receives immunities from the mother
D. mother begins to feel the movements of the fetus

Matching: Match the following terms and identifying phrases.

_____ 20. The smallest unit of life that is able to reproduce itself.

_____ 21. Male sex cell.

_____ 22. Female sex cell; also called the *egg*.

_____ 23. Single cell formed at conception; also called a *fertilized egg*.

_____ 24. Traits passed through the genes from parent to child.

_____ 25. Term describing children of a multiple pregnancy that develop from two fertilized eggs and differ in genetic makeup.

_____ 26. Outer membrane that surrounds baby in the uterus.

_____ 27. Term describing children of a multiple pregnancy that develop from one fertilized egg and share genetic makeup.

_____ 28. Type of development that takes place between conception and birth.

_____ 29. A fluid-filled sac that protects the baby until birth.

_____ 30. An organ filled with blood vessels that nourishes the baby in the uterus.

_____ 31. Connects the baby to placenta.

_____ 32. Movements of the fetus that can be felt by the mother.

A. amnion

B. cell

C. chorion

D. fraternal

E. genetic factors

F. identical

G. ovum

H. placenta

I. prenatal development

J. quickening

K. sperm

L. umbilical cord

M. zygote

*(Continued)*

**Name** _____

Essay questions: Provide complete responses to the following questions or statements.

33. Explain why children are *not* exactly like their parents or their brothers and sisters.

34. List and describe the three stages of prenatal development.

35. Explain how dominant and recessive traits differ.

# Prenatal Care and Childbirth 5

## Objectives

After studying this chapter, students will be able to
- describe the early signs of pregnancy.
- explain the role of the environment on prenatal development.
- explain the relationship between the health of the mother and the health of the baby.
- describe how diseases, drugs, radiation, environmental pollutants, and congenital problems can harm the fetus.
- list ways family members can be involved during pregnancy.
- describe the birth process and some of the possible complications of delivery.
- describe physical and emotional changes in the mother during the postpartum period.

## Bulletin Boards

Be Good to Your Baby Before Birth

✓ Medical Care   ✓ Physical Activity

✓ Nutrition   ✓ Hygiene

### Title: *Be Good to Your Baby Before Birth*

Place a silhouette of a pregnant woman in the center of the board. Place the headings *Medical Care, Physical Activity, Nutrition,* and *Hygiene* on the board with space for a checklist under each. Have students develop checklists for expectant mothers to fit each category. Post each list under its appropriate heading.

### Title: *General Diet Versus Pregnancy Diet*

Display two food charts, one showing a general day's diet plan and the other specifying daily nutritional requirements for pregnant women.

## Teaching Materials

**Text**, pages 128-171
  *Reviewing Key Concepts*
  *Using Your Knowledge*
  *Making Observations*
  *Thinking Further*

**Student Activity Guide**
  A. *Mothers-to-Be Affect the Health of Their Unborns*
  B. *Menu for a Mother-to-Be*
  C. *Drugs and Diseases in Mothers-to-Be*
  D. *The Role of the Father-to-Be in Pregnancy*
  E. *Choices for Delivery*
  F. *Stages of Labor*

**Teacher's Resources**
  *Pregnancy and Health,* reproducible master 5-1
  *Prenatal Eating Habits,* color transparency CT-5
  *Hazards and the Unborn Baby,* reproducible master 5-2
  *Pain Medications for Labor and Delivery,* transparency master 5-3
  Chapter 5 Test

## Introductory Activities

1. Have students discuss the March of Dimes slogan "Be good to your baby before it is born." Students should debate the importance of following this slogan.
2. *Pregnancy and Health*, reproducible master 5-1. Have students write brief interpretations of the statements given. Use these written interpretations as a basis for a class discussion. You may have students rewrite their interpretations after they have studied the chapter so they can see what they have learned.

## Strategies to Reteach, Reinforce, Enrich, and Extend Text Concepts

### Signs of Pregnancy

3. **RT** Have students discuss how a woman and her doctor interpret signs of pregnancy.

4. **RT**  Discuss with students why it is better to think of pregnancy as a normal process rather than an illness. Why is it inaccurate to think that signs of pregnancy, such as morning sickness, are "all in a woman's head?"

## Medical Care

5. **ER**  Instruct students to develop a brochure that identifies sources of prenatal care (such as physicians, county health departments, WIC nurses, and certified nurse-midwives). The brochure should also include tips to evaluate care sources.

6. **ER**  Invite students to interview one or more physicians about what a prenatal care plan includes, such as the number of visits and childbirth classes. Students should report findings in class.

7. **RF**  Instruct students to make a list of questions parents-to-be should ask during the first prenatal checkup.

## The Unborn Baby's Environment

8. **EX**  Explain to students the word *environment* comes from the word *environ* meaning "to encircle" or "around." Ask them to name things in our surroundings. (Students may name things from both the physical and cultural environment.) Ask the students how the unborn baby's environment is always the same (always in the uterus) and yet can change with the activity level of mother, noise level of the mother's environment, foods eaten, harmful substances ingested, and stress.

9. **EX**  Play a recording from the womb so students can hear the sound of breathing, heartbeat, and blood flow in the uterus.

10. **RT**  Before reading the next section, have students suggest ways to make the unborn baby's environment healthy, safe, and secure. (Review this list after completing the next section in the chapter.)

## Factors That Affect the Baby's Health

11. **RT**  Ask students to explain the importance of learning about a pregnancy early for the sake of the unborn child's health.

12. **RT**  Have students list parental health practices they could take now to help a future child be born healthy. Discuss whether students think men, women, or both men and women should take these health measures. Students should justify their responses.

13. **ER**  Invite a dietitian to discuss with the class the importance of healthy eating practices and attaining a healthy weight before becoming pregnant.

14. **ER**  Instruct students to research how the Rh factor was first discovered and tested in the Rhesus monkey. (Students should note how the factor received its name.) Students then should write a short paper on their findings.

15. **RF**  Ask students to define *stress* and describe causes of stress. Explain that these causes of stress are called *stressors*. Make a class list of appropriate and inappropriate ways of coping with stressors. Note that people who cope with stressors appropriately are called *resilient*.

16. **RF**  Ask students to name some extra stressors that occur during pregnancy. (Students may want to skim Chapter 3 to review some of the concepts.)

## Health Habits During Pregnancy

17. **RT**  *Mothers-to-Be Affect the Health of Their Unborns*, Activity A, SAG. Ask students to identify positive and negative maternal characteristics and health habits associated with the health of the unborn.

18. **RF**  Ask students to explain why the amount of weight gain recommended in each trimester (three-month period) differs. This is because the recommendations follow the natural pattern of the baby's growth throughout the pregnancy. The baby grows slowly at first and then more rapidly later in the pregnancy.

19. **RF**  *Prenatal Eating Habits*, color transparency CT-5. Use this transparency to help students explore the importance of healthful eating habits and good nutrition during pregnancy.

20. **RF**  *Menu for a Mother-to-Be*, Activity B, SAG. Students should plan a three-day menu for a mother-to-be.

21. **RF**  Show the March of Dimes video "Inside My Mom." Discuss the implications of good maternal care.

22. **RF**  Instruct students to write a letter from the standpoint of a fetus writing to his or her mother about the importance of good health habits.

23. **ER**  Guest speaker: Invite a dietitian or nutritionist to speak about nutrition and nutritional supplements during pregnancy.

24. **RT**  Have students list good grooming habits important for the mother-to-be.

25. **RT**  Discuss with students the appropriateness of various physical activities during pregnancy.

## Health Hazards to Avoid

26. **RF** *Hazards and the Unborn Baby,* reproducible master 5-2. Distribute this master regarding health hazards and the unborn baby to students for their reference. Point out to students the effects of some of these substances on the fetus.
27. **ER** *Drugs and Diseases in Mothers-to-Be,* Activity C, SAG. Students should conduct a more in-depth study of a drug or disease that may cause a congenital problem. Have students give a class report on one congenital problem.
28. **ER** Have students use the Internet to find information (possibly including pictures) about babies born to drug-addicted mothers. How were children affected? Were there any long-term physical or mental problems? Students should report in class.
29. **RT** Discuss with students the major consequences to babies born with a low birthweight.
30. **RF** Find pictures (from books, magazines, slides, or videos) of babies born with fetal alcohol syndrome (FAS). Students should describe the characteristics and seriousness of this condition. Emphasize that no known quantity of alcohol is safe during pregnancy, so women are strongly advised to refrain from drinking any alcohol while pregnant.
31. **ER** Divide the class into these five groups on maternal health habits: nutrition; hygiene practices; rest and sleep; physical activities; and protection from drugs, diseases, and other substances. (Groups for nutrition and protection from drugs, diseases, and other agents should have more members because more information is available on these subjects.) Instruct each group to plan a class presentation on their subject. Students should create visual aids to use during their presentation.
32. **EX** Have students analyze actions families could take to reduce the risk of environmental pollutants that could endanger an unborn or newly born baby.
33. **ER** Invite a nurse to discuss the causes and effects of gestational diabetes, PIH, and STDs during pregnancy.

## Complications of Pregnancy

34. **ER** Using the Internet or other resources, find current statistics on babies born with congenital problems and infant mortality rates.
35. **ER** Ask a representative from the March of Dimes to discuss congenital problems with

students. Have them prepare a list of questions for the speaker in advance.
36. **EX** Have students identify local and national organizations that work to research and prevent congenital problems. Encourage students to serve as volunteers for one or more of these agencies.
37. **ER** Have students choose a congenital problem and research current developments in eliminating or dealing with this problem. Students should prepare a report and share their findings with the class.
38. **RT** Ask students to list some possible causes of miscarriage and some of the emotional effects of losing a baby through miscarriage or stillbirth.

## Monitoring the Baby's Development

39. **ER** Students should interview an obstetrician about what amniocentesis, chorionic villus sampling, or ultrasound can reveal about babies. Students should write a newspaper or magazine-style article about their findings.
40. **ER** Invite new parents to discuss their experience with ultrasound and possibly chorionic villus sampling or amniocentesis. Did the parents find out the gender of the baby before birth? Ask students whether they would want to learn the gender of their children before birth if possible.

## The Role of the Family

41. **RT** *The Role of the Father-to-Be in Pregnancy,* Activity D, SAG. Have students find or draw cartoons showing the "traditional" (and rather absurd) role of fathers during pregnancy and childbirth. Then have students write a description contrasting the cartoon and today's actual practices.
42. **RT** Discuss with students the statement "Mutual support between a husband and a wife is needed during a pregnancy." Students should give examples of how parents-to-be can give mutual support.
43. **RT** *Pain Medications for Labor and Delivery,* transparency master, 5-3. Use this transparency master as you cover Figure 5-13 in the text.
44. **ER** Invite a mother who has gone through Lamaze to visit the class. You may also invite a Lamaze instructor to speak to the class about this method of childbirth. Find out advantages and disadvantages of this method.
45. **ER** Guest speaker: Invite an obstetrical nurse to explain the type of prenatal childbirth preparation

parents-to-be receive. Your class may be able to attend the beginning session of a class.

46. **ER** Instruct students to read about the Leboyer method of childbirth. Students should write a report on their findings.

47. **RF** *Choices for Delivery*, Activity E, SAG. Students should list advantages and disadvantages of various delivery methods.

48. **ER** Have students research your community's options for birthing places and methods. Students should report findings to the class.

## Time to Be Born

49. **RF** Students should create a poster depicting a "to do" list before childbirth.

50. **RT** Discuss the term *labor* with students. Why does it appropriately describe the childbirth process? How does the term *false labor* contrast with actual labor?

51. **RT** *Stages of Labor*, Activity F, SAG. Using the drawings provided, students should describe the stages of labor in their own words.

## Complications of Delivery

52. **RF** Have students write a report on premature births. The report should cover causes, problems associated with delivery, and ways to prevent premature delivery.

53. **EX** Have students interview the parents of a child who was born prematurely. What problems and fears did this cause for the parents? In what ways was the child's health affected soon after birth? How is the child's health now, and what special needs (if any) does the child have?

54. **RF** Have students write a report on any of the delivery-aid techniques described in the text.

## Hospital Care

55. **ER** Field trip: Tour local facilities for giving birth and caring for newborns. Have students observe neonatal care in the nursery. Find out hospital policies about rooming-in and birthing rooms. What care is given to premature babies? How does the hospital care for babies who are born on the way to the hospital?

56. **EX** Have students interview two mothers—one whose child is younger than three years, and one whose child is older than twelve years. How did their hospital experiences differ regarding labor, delivery, and postpartum stay? What hospital policies were in place when each

mother delivered? Ask students to compare the two experiences they heard and summarize ways in which hospital care has changed over time.

## Bonding

57. **RT** Have students find the definition of the term *bond* in a dictionary. Ask students whether *bonding* seems to be an appropriate term to explain a parent's attachment for a newborn. Students should explain why or why not.

58. **ER** Invite students to find out whether local hospitals encourage the following aids to bonding: (a) fathers handling their newborns in the delivery (or recovery) room and postpartum room, (b) parents visiting and holding their newborns who are in ICNs, and (c) rooming in.

59. **ER** Instruct students to write a paragraph on the importance of bonding for both infant and parent.

## Postpartum Care

60. **RF** Instruct students to look up the term *postpartum* and explain the origin of this word.

61. **RT** Ask students to explain the postpartum period as a reversal process to a mother's prepregnant state. Emphasize how long this can take, especially if the mother is breast-feeding.

62. **RT** Students should give several reasons crash dieting to lose the extra weight of pregnancy is dangerous for a mother and possibly her baby (if she is nursing).

63. **ER** Interview new mothers to find out whether they experienced baby blues or other postpartum mood disorders. If so, how did they cope?

64. **RF** Have students write a report on PPD or PPP.

# Answer Key

## Text

*Reviewing Key Concepts,* page 170
1. B
2. 21 and 28 years
3. false
4. false
5. true
6. D
7. (Student response.)
8. the show—B; dilation of the cervix—C; birth of the baby—A; cutting of the umbilical cord—E; delivery of the placenta—D
9. false

10. A
11. true
12. Postpartum

## Student Activity Guide
### Mothers-to-Be Affect the Health of Their Unborns, Activity A

| | | |
|---|---|---|
| 1. + | 6. – | 11. – |
| 2. – | 7. + | 12. + |
| 3. – | 8. – | 13. + |
| 4. + | 9. + | 14. – |
| 5. + | 10. – | 15. – |

Answer to questions: Student response.

### Stages of Labor, Activity F

Stage 1: Dilation of the cervix. Contractions are 15 to 20 minutes apart; the uterus narrows; the baby pushes against the cervix; the cervix flattens and opens. Stage 2: Delivery of baby. Baby's head enters the birth canal; the mother's muscles push to move the baby down; head emerges, followed by shoulders, abdomen, and legs; the baby is free from the mother's body; the umbilical cord is cut. Stage 3: Delivery of the placenta. Mother has a few irregular contractions; placenta detaches from the uterus and descends.

## Teacher's Resources
### Chapter 5 Test

| | | |
|---|---|---|
| 1. T | 15. B | 29. A |
| 2. T | 16. D | 30. J |
| 3. T | 17. A | 31. I |
| 4. F | 18. C | 32. C |
| 5. F | 19. B | 33. F |
| 6. T | 20. D | 34. G |
| 7. F | 21. D | 35. H |
| 8. T | 22. D | 36. S |
| 9. F | 23. Q | 37. D |
| 10. F | 24. K | 38. M |
| 11. C | 25. P | 39. B |
| 12. B | 26. E | 40. N |
| 13. C | 27. L | 41. O |
| 14. B | 28. R | |

42. (Describe four:) cessation of menstruation, nausea, sleepiness, frequent urination, swelling and tenderness of breasts and abdomen, internal changes noted by doctor, include: fetal heartbeat, fetal movement, fetal image through ultrasound, fetal shape felt by physician, contractions noted by physician but not felt by mother, and presence of certain hormone levels
43. (List six. See pages 140 to 145 in the text.)
44. Fathers-to-be can serve as support persons for wives, as coaches in childbirth, and as partners in meeting the economic and adjustment needs of the changing family.
45. Bonding helps form a closer tie between parent and baby.

# Pregnancy and Health

**Name** _____ **Date** _____ **Period** _____

Write your own interpretations of the following statements.

1. "Good health habits started early in life lay the framework for having a healthy baby."

_____

_____

_____

_____

_____

_____

_____

_____

_____

_____

2. " 'Catch-up nutrition' and other such health practices do not work in pregnancy."

_____

_____

_____

_____

3. "It may be too late if a woman waits until after her pregnancy is confirmed to give up dangerous practices like using drugs, smoking, eating too much junk food, and getting too little rest and sleep."

_____

_____

_____

_____

_____

_____

_____

_____

_____

# Hazards and the Unborn Baby

| Hazard | Possible Effects on Baby |
|---|---|
| **Drugs** | |
| Hormones used for birth control or treatment of reproductive disorders | Limb malformations |
| Aspirin | Prolonged labor<br>Bleeding in mother and baby |
| Tranquilizers | Decreased activity in the baby<br>Cleft palate |
| Narcotics | Premature birth/delivery complications<br>Reduced growth rate/low birthweight<br>Breathing problems<br>Withdrawal symptoms |
| Steroids (such as Cortisone) | Cleft palate |
| Nicotine (tobacco products) | Fetal distress (heart rate abnormalities)<br>Miscarriage, stillbirth, or neonatal death<br>Low birthweight/premature birth<br>Breathing problems<br>Higher risk of SIDS<br>Smaller physical size, poor reading skills, and poor school adjustment |
| Alcohol | Increased activity level<br>Miscarriage or stillbirth<br>Low birthweight<br>Fetal alcohol syndrome or fetal alcohol effect<br>Mild to moderate developmental disabilities<br>Heart, joint, and eye problems<br>Smaller physical size and poor development |
| Tetracycline (antibiotic) | Teeth and bone problems |
| Sulfa drugs | Liver function problems |
| Vitamin supplements (excessive amounts)<br>K<br>D<br>B$^6$ | Severe anemia with possible brain damage or death<br>Circulatory damage<br>Convulsions |

*(Continued)*

| Hazard | Possible Effects on Baby |
|---|---|
| **Diseases** | |
| Rubella | |
| Diabetes | Increased change of pregnancy-induced hypertension in mother and related problems for fetus |
| | Increased size of baby at birth and related delivery problems |
| | Miscarriage or stillbirth |
| Fifth disease | Anemia |
| Lyme disease | Stillbirth |
| | Premature birth |
| | Heart problems |
| Toxoplasmosis | Developmental disabilities |
| | Deafness |
| | Blindness |
| **Other Substances** | |
| Radiation (X rays) | Slow growth |
| | Developmental disabilities |
| | Sterility |
| | Possible cancers in later life |
| Inadequate maternal diet | Developmental disabilities |
| | Brain development problems |
| | Physical disabilities |
| | Lowered resistance to infection |
| Changes in maternal hormones due to repeated or prolonged stress | Irritability in the baby |
| | Smaller or less well-wired brain |
| | Miscarriage |
| | Delivery complications |

# Pain Medications for Labor and Delivery

| Category | Uses |
|---|---|
| Sedation | Given by injection or IV. Used in labor to relax the mother and reduce pain. |
| Local anesthesia | Given by injection. Used in childbirth to numb vaginal area for delivery, incision, or sutures. |
| Regional anesthesia | Most commonly used type for childbirth is the epidural. Given through a catheter inserted in the small of the back to numb lower half of the body. |
| General anesthesia | Given by IV or inhaled as a gas. Used in childbirth only to put the mother completely to sleep for an emergency C-section. |

# Prenatal Care and Childbirth

Name _____

Date _____ Period _____ Score _____

## Chapter 5 Test

True/False: Circle *T* if the statement is true or *F* if the statement is false.

T    F    1. A couple's closeness in the prenatal stage may set the stage for better marriage relationships and for better parenting.

T    F    2. Parents-to-be should ask their physicians about any pregnancy-related issues that concern them.

T    F    3. Children born to women over age 36 usually have a greater chance of congenital problems than children born to younger women.

T    F    4. The Rh factor is a blood incompatibility problem that affects almost all pregnancies.

T    F    5. Caloric intake should be greatly increased in the last weeks of pregnancy.

T    F    6. Gestational diabetes is a type of diabetes that can develop during pregnancy.

T    F    7. Babies born to mothers who have AIDS automatically develop the syndrome.

T    F    8. The Lamaze method emphasizes breathing exercises for pain relief during labor and delivery.

T    F    9. Labor contractions are voluntary.

T    F   10. The third stage of labor includes the delivery of the baby.

Multiple Choice: Choose the best response. Write the letter in the space provided.

_____ 11. Which statement is true of prenatal development?
A. The mother's body affects the baby.
B. The baby's body affects the mother.
C. The bodies of mother and baby affect one another.
D. None of the above.

_____ 12. For a healthy baby, medical care and supervision should begin _____.
A. only for the mother's first baby
B. as soon as a woman thinks she might be pregnant
C. a few months before delivery
D. only if the mother does not feel healthy

_____ 13. Doctors who specialize in pregnancy and birth are called _____.
A. internists
B. gynecologists
C. obstetricians
D. pediatricians

_____ 14. Which of the following are environmental factors that can affect the unborn baby?
A. Sexually transmitted diseases (STDs).
B. Inherited traits.
C. Nutrition of the mother.
D. Fetal alcohol sydrome (FAS) or fetal alcohol effect (FAE).

*(Continued)*

**Name** _____

_____ 15. What effects does stress of the mother have on the unborn?
- A. Even a tiny amount of stress harms an unborn baby.
- B. Stress harms the unborn only if it is prolonged or severe.
- C. Stress has no effect on the unborn.
- D. It is not known whether stress has any effect on the unborn.

_____ 16. The pregnant woman's diet affects _____.
- A. her own weight gain during pregnancy
- B. her baby's brain development
- C. her baby's physical development
- D. All of the above.

_____ 17. Pregnant women should avoid _____.
- A. contact sports
- B. any unnecessary physical activity
- C. walking for exercise
- D. All of the above.

_____ 18. Commonly used tests to monitor an unborn baby's development include all of the following *except* ____.
- A. amniocentesis
- B. chorionic villus sampling (CVS)
- C. radiation
- D. ultrasound

_____ 19. Anxiety during childbirth _____.
- A. causes the baby to have birthmarks
- B. can be reduced through education and breathing techniques
- C. should always be reduced by drugs
- D. None of the above.

_____ 20. The Leboyer method of childbirth focuses mainly on the comfort of the _____.
- A. physician
- B. mother
- C. father
- D. baby

_____ 21. A cesarean section might be performed for any of the following reasons *except* _____.
- A. baby or mother is at medical risk
- B. baby is in breech birth position
- C. mother's pelvis shape will make vaginal birth too difficult
- D. mother wants the convenience of scheduled birth

_____ 22. Which of the following is true about postpartum mood disorders?
- A. They are less common among women in their forties.
- B. They are more common among women with strong support from family and friends.
- C. They are unrelated to stress.
- D. They vary in severity from one woman to another.

*(Continued)*

**Name** _____

Matching: Match the following terms and identifying phrases.

_____23.  Term describing a baby who is born too soon.

_____24.  Term describing a baby who weighs less than 5½ pounds at birth.

_____25.  High blood pressure caused by pregnancy.

_____26.  Physical or biochemical problem in a baby that is present at birth.

_____27.  Expulsion of a baby from the mother's body before week 20 of pregnancy.

_____28.  Loss of a baby after week 20 of pregnancy.

_____29.  Test in which a needle is inserted through the woman's abdomen into the amniotic sac and a sample of fluid is removed for cell study.

_____30.  Change in the baby's position that indicates birth is nearing.

_____31.  Process that moves the baby out of the mother's body.

_____32.  Persons who are specially trained to deliver babies but not handle problem deliveries.

_____33.  The opening of the cervix during labor.

_____34.  An incision made in the vagina to prevent tearing as the baby is born.

_____35.  A curved instrument that is used to help the doctor ease a baby down the birth canal.

_____36.  Technique that uses suction to help the doctor move the baby down the birth canal.

_____37.  Delivery method in which the mother's abdomen and uterus are surgically opened to remove the baby.

_____38.  The medical help a mother receives during the six to eight weeks following childbirth.

_____39.  Mild postpartum mood disorder that goes away on its own.

_____40.  Serious form of mood disorder after giving birth.

_____41.  An extreme form of mental illness that may result after giving birth.

A. amniocentesis

B. baby blues

C. certified nurse-midwives (CNM)

D. caesarean section

E. congenital problem

F. dilation

G. episiotomy

H. forceps

I. labor

J. lightening

K. low birthweight

L. miscarriage

M. postpartum care

N. postpartum depression (PPD)

O. postpartum psychosis (PPP)

P. pregnancy-induced hypertension (PIH)

Q. premature

R. stillbirth

S. vacuum extraction

Essay Questions: Provide complete responses to the following questions or statements.

42.  Describe four presumptive and positive signs of pregnancy.

43.  List six health hazards a pregnant woman should avoid to protect the health of her baby.

44.  What roles can involved fathers-to-be play in pregnancy and childbirth?

45.  Why is bonding important?

# The Newborn

## Objectives

After studying this chapter, students will be able to
- describe the characteristics of a newborn.
- identify a newborn's physical, intellectual, and social-emotional needs.
- explain how parents of newborns can meet their own needs.

## Bulletin Boards

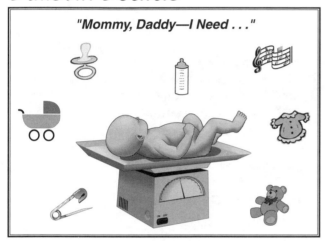

"Mommy, Daddy—I Need . . ."

### Title: Mommy, Daddy—I Need...

Place a picture of a newborn, perhaps on a weighing scale, in the center of a bulletin board. Around the baby, place pictures of a baby's various needs, such as clothing, toys, and equipment. Add new items as students further define the needs of a newborn.

### Title: And Baby Makes Three

Place three titles on the board: *New Mother, New Father,* and *New Baby.* Below the titles, add the subtitle: *All three view an ideal world.* After students have had a chance to read about each perspective in the text, have them discuss possible conflicts that might arise in the new family.

## Teaching Materials

**Text**, pages 172-201
*Reviewing Key Concepts*
*Using Your Knowledge*
*Making Observations*
*Thinking Further*

**Student Activity Guide**
    A. *Newborns and Parents Adapt*
    B. *Reflexes of the Newborn*
    C. *Shopping for the Newborn*
    D. *Learning Through the Senses*
    E. *Toys for Newborns*
    F. *Meeting New Parents' Needs*

**Teacher's Resources**
*What It Really Means to Be a Parent,*
    reproducible master 6-1
*Suggestions for Successful Nursing,*
    reproducible master 6-2
*New Baby Crossword Puzzle,*
    reproducible master 6-3
*Happy BIRTHday!* color transparency CT-6
*What's a Parent to Do?* reproducible
    master 6-4
Chapter 6 Test

## Introductory Activities

1. Ask students to write about their impressions of newborns. They should describe what they think newborns look like, how newborns act, and what newborns can do. Have the students discuss their impressions in class. Collect the written work and return it to students after they study the chapter. Students can use it to compare to their more informed impressions of newborns.
2. *What It Really Means to Be a Parent*, reproducible master 6-1. Have students interview the parents of newborns and discuss their findings in class.
3. *Newborns and Parents Adapt*, Activity A, SAG. Students should list the adaptations a newborn must make from the prenatal to neonatal stage and make suggestions to ease the transition to parenthood.

4. Write a short paragraph discussing how you would or would not be ready for parenthood based on the suggestions for enjoyable parenting.

# Strategies to Reteach, Reinforce, Enrich, and Extend Text Concepts

## Medical Care and Testing

5. **ER**  Ask students to interview a pediatrician or pediatric nurse about the impact of prenatal care on a newborn's health.
6. **ER**  Instruct students to check the statistics of the infant mortality rate and the rate of congenital problems in newborns. (Information is available through the Vital Statistics Bureau and the March of Dimes.)
7. **RT**  Students should list some of the tests newborns receive while they are in the hospital.
8. **RT**  Discuss with students why the second Apgar score (5 minutes after birth) rather than the first score (1 minute after birth) best predicts the newborn's chances for survival.
9. **ER**  Have students research in more detail some of the behavioral responses checked in the Neonatal Behavioral Assessment Scale, then report findings to the class.

## Other Hospital Care

10. **RT**  Have students explain the purpose of making footprints of the newborn and attaching name bands to the newborn's arm or leg.
11. **RF**  Draw a classification diagram to show students the relationship among the general physician, pediatrician, and neonatologist.

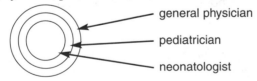

general physician
pediatrician
neonatologist

12. **ER**  Field trip: If possible, arrange for students to tour the facilities of an intensive care nursery (ICN).
13. **ER**  Guest speaker: Invite a pediatrician to demonstrate in class a well-baby checkup with a real baby or with a doll.
14. **ER**  Students should interview parents to find out what procedures they have seen pediatricians perform during a newborn's first well-baby checkup.

## Physical Traits of a Newborn

15. **RF**  Ask students to bring in pictures of babies used in advertisements or on baby products. Students should compare these photos to those of newborns in the text. Ask students what differences they note. Also ask them how old they think the baby is in each advertisement.
16. **ER**  If possible, arrange for students to view babies through the viewing window of a local hospital nursery. If some of the babies were born early, have students compare their appearance to that of the full-term infants.

## Reflexes

17. **RF**  Demonstrate the meaning of the term *reflex* by having students look at the changes in the pupils of their eyes while turning a nearby lamp off and on. (This reflex is called *pupillary reflex*.)
18. **RT**  Have students discuss why reflexes, even in adults, are important to a person's well-being.
19. **RF**  *Reflexes of the Newborn*, Activity B, SAG. Ask students to name the stimulus and the expected reaction associated with certain reflexes seen in newborns.

## Meeting the Newborn's Physical Needs

20. **RF**  After students have read the section on breast-feeding, have them design a poster on the theme, "Breast-Feeding...Your Best Choice." Students could focus on these five main points: breast milk is nutritional, protects from disease, provides ideal growth, promotes bonding, and benefits the mother.
21. **EX**  *Suggestions for Successful Nursing,* reproducible master 6-2. If appropriate for your class, hand out these suggestions for successful nursing. Point out to students that although it is a natural process, breast-feeding takes effort from mother and baby to be successful.
22. **EX**  Invite a lactation consultant from a local hospital to share information on topics, such as how a baby suckles, how mothers know whether their babies are getting enough milk, and how working mothers can continue to provide breast milk for their babies.
23. **EX**  Have students write a report on how breast milk is produced. The students should note that milk production is stimulated by the baby suckling.

24. **RT**  Discuss with students why smiling at, singing to, talking to, and cuddling a baby are important. Does a warm relationship with the baby help the baby's body to better digest food? What type of eating atmosphere is best for babies? for adults?

25. **RF**  Have students begin an index card file on child care techniques. On the top left corner of each card, have students write *Newborn*. Have students list the topic on the top right corner. Using the text and other resources, students should outline the technique on the card. Some suggested topics from this chapter are: (a) steps in preparing formula for bottle-fed babies, (b) burping, (c) clothing needs, (d) dressing/diapering, (e) bathing, (f) bedding needs, (g) exercising, (h) learning activities, and (i) soothing a baby.

26. **RF**  *Shopping for the Newborn*, Activity C, SAG. Instruct students to price the clothing of newborns and record their findings.

27. **RF**  Demonstrate (or have students demonstrate) for the class one or more of the following with a doll): bottle-feeding, dressing, diapering, bathing, and exercising.

## Meeting the Newborn's Intellectual Needs

28. **RF**  Begin a chart called "Our Brains Are Wired." List *Newborn* as the stage of development and describe what parts of the brain are wired at birth. If needed, have students conduct Internet to help them complete the chart. (This chart can be continued in upcoming chapters.)

29. **RF**  *Learning Through the Senses*, Activity D, SAG. Have students list some important sensory learnings of newborns.

30. **RT**  Ask students to give some examples of skills they have learned totally or partially by imitation.

31. **ER**  Pretending they are the directors of an infant program, students should prepare an article for a parent newsletter explaining why newborns need variety in their physical environment.

32. **RF**  Instruct students to make and display toys suitable for newborns. See chart 6-19 of the text for ideas.

33. **RF**  *Toys for Newborns*, Activity E, SAG. Have students identify objects that are appealing to newborns.

34. **RT**  Ask students to explain how talking to newborns helps their brain development even though the babies do not understand the words adults use.

## Meeting the Newborn's Social-Emotional Needs

35. **ER**  Have students observe very young babies and note how babies seem to have individuality at birth. Students should also note whether some babies are more alert or active than others. Students should report their findings to the class.

36. **RT**  Discuss with students ways to soothe a fussy baby. Demonstrate using a doll and have students practice various techniques. For a more realistic demonstration, play a tape of a baby crying in the background.

37. **RF**  *New Baby Crossword Puzzle*, reproducible master 6-3. Have students complete the crossword puzzle using terms defined in the chapter.

## Meeting the Parents' Needs

38. **RT**  *Happy BIRTHday!* color transparency CT-6. Use this transparency to introduce students to the changes a family experiences after a baby is born. Students should discuss the changing family scene and how members can adjust and adapt. Discuss what families can do to make life easier after the baby and mother come home from the hospital.

39. **RT**  Ask students to give examples of the physical, intellectual, and social-emotional needs of young adults. Students should explain how others help young adults meet their needs. (Note that unlike the newborn, young adults do not depend totally on others.)

40. **ER**  Guest speaker: Determine whether any employers in your community offer paid paternity leave. If so, ask the employer to share with the class some of the details of the leave plan and whether fathers who have used the plan feel it is valuable.

41. **ER**  Invite students to interview a father who has taken paternity leave. How did this affect him and his family?

42. **EX**  Instruct students to prepare and present skits showing couples planning ways to meet their own needs while still meeting the needs of their newborns.

43. **RT**  Discuss with students why parents are more apt to meet newborns' needs when their own needs are satisfied.

44. **EX**  *Meeting New Parents' Needs*, Activity F, SAG. Have students write suggestions to help new parents get organized and meet their own needs as well as their baby's needs.

45. **EX** *What's a Parent to Do?* reproducible master 6-4. Have students read the situation, analyze the family's problem, and complete the questions that follow.
46. **EX** Divide the class into three groups or two sets of three groups. Instruct each group to write on the topic "An Ideal First Four Weeks" from one of three perspectives—a newborn's perspective, a new mother's perspective, and a new father's perspective. Students may add the final drafts to the bulletin board for this chapter.

# Answer Key

## Text

### Reviewing Key Concepts, page 200

1. baby's pulse, breathing, muscle tone; responsiveness; and skin color
2. A reflex is an involuntary reaction that occurs in response to a certain stimulus, such as touch, light, or sound. Voluntary movements are movements that a person makes at will. (Students may describe any two of the reflexes described in the text.)
3. (Students may describe any of the features described in the text.)
4. (Students may describe any of the advantages of breast-feeding given in the text.)
5. Equation: 2 to 2.5 oz. × weight of child in pounds ÷ number of feedings per day

   Weight of Chris: 10 pounds

   | 2 oz. | 2.5 oz. |
   |---|---|
   | × 10 | × 10 |
   | 20 oz. | 25 oz. |

   2 oz. × 10 = 20 oz.
   2.5 oz. × 10 = 25 oz.
   Amount of formula per day: 20 to 25 oz.
   Number of feedings: 6 feedings
   20 oz. ÷ 6 = 3.3 oz.
   25 oz. ÷ 6 = 4.1 oz.
   Amount of formula Chris needs at each feeding: 3.3 to 4.1 oz.
6. false
7. (Student response. See pages 196 and 197 in the text.)

## Student Activity Guide

### Reflexes of the Newborn, Activity B

*Rooting Reflex*—Stimulus: Cheeks or skin around mouth is touched. Reaction: Head turns in direction of touch and mouth searches for food.

*Palmar Reflex*—Stimulus: Palm of hands stroked. Reaction: Babies grasp finger or object stroking palm.

*Plantar Reflex*—Stimulus: Ball of foot is stroked horizontally. Reaction: Toes curl around or down toward object.

*Babinski Reflex*—Stimulus: Outside sole of the foot stroked from heel to toe. Reaction: Babies spread their toes out and the big toe fans backward.

*Moro Reflex*—Stimulus: Loud noises, bright light, change in body position, or a cough or sneeze. Reaction: Babies arch back, throw head back, fling out the arms and legs, and rapidly flex limbs toward center of body.

*Walking Reflex*—Stimulus: While held upright, feet make contact with hard surface. Reaction: Legs are lifted alternately as in walking, but arms do not move.

*Withdrawal Reflex*—Stimulus: Feet are pricked. Reaction: The legs jerk or withdraw.

*Sucking Reflex*—Stimulus: Mouth comes into contact with object. Reaction: Drawing or pulling movement occurs in cheeks and tongue called sucking.

*(Name of reflex)*—(student response)
1. (Student response.)
2. (Student response.)
3. (Student response.)

### Toys for Newborns, Activity E

1. Object B
2. Object A
3. Object B
4. Object A
5. Object A
6. Object A

(Guidelines should be based on information from the text.)

# Teacher's Resources

## New Baby Crossword Puzzle,
reproducible master 6-3

```
                                              R    W
                                              E    E
                                              F    L
               B        A                     L    L
            P  R        PKU                    E    B
            E  A        G                      X    A
            D  Z        A                      E    B
      A                                             Y
     INTENSIVECARENURSERY                           C
      E     A     L     T  E                         H
      M     T     T     E  O                         E
   COLIC    R     O     S  NICU                      C
      A     I     N     T  A                         K
            C     S     T  T                         U
            I     C        E                         P
            A     A
            N     L
           NEONATOLOGY
```

## Chapter 6 Test

| | | |
|---|---|---|
| 1. F | 13. T | 25. D |
| 2. T | 14. T | 26. F |
| 3. F | 15. F | 27. D |
| 4. F | 16. B | 28. E |
| 5. T | 17. D | 29. G |
| 6. T | 18. C | 30. A |
| 7. T | 19. A | 31. H |
| 8. F | 20. C | 32. C |
| 9. T | 21. C | 33. I |
| 10. T | 22. C | 34. J |
| 11. T | 23. D | 35. B |
| 12. F | 24. C | |

36. For the best chance of healthy development, the medical care that was started in the prenatal stage needs to continue in the neonatal stage. The Apgar test is used to determine the baby's chances for survival in the first minutes after birth. Blood tests, careful examination of the baby's body, and tests of some of the reflexes help determine whether the baby is healthy during the neonatal well-baby checkups.

37. (Name three for baby and three for mother. See Figure 6-9 in the text or accept other valid responses.)

38. (List two:) locating the source of stimuli, such as turning their heads in the direction of a sound; becoming quiet and attending to many sensory stimuli; responding to human speech, human cries, and a parent's voice more intently than to nonhuman sounds and strangers' voices; responding to visual stimuli, such as following objects with their eyes and imitating gestures; paying more attention to a new sight or sound than to those they have seen or heard before

39. (Give four. See pages 196 in the text or accept other valid responses.)

40. Parenthood is abrupt because one day you are not a parent and the next day you are. With parenthood comes the never-ending task of meeting the child's needs. Many needs must be met immediately regardless of parents' fatigue. Along with these immediate responsibilities comes the realization that parenthood lasts a long time. Faced with this seemingly overwhelming task, many parents wonder how they can meet their own needs.

# What It Really Means to Be a Parent

**Name** _____ **Date** _____ **Period** _____

Interview the parent or parents of a newborn. Report their answers to the following questions in class.

1. How were your expectations about parenthood altered after you brought your baby home?

   _____

   _____

   _____

2. What child care technique was the most difficult at first? Why?

   _____

   _____

   _____

3. How did you cope with fatigue?

   _____

   _____

   _____

4. Were you surprised at the added expenses the newborn caused? What expenses were the most surprising?

   _____

   _____

   _____

5. What were your family's major adjustments?

   _____

   _____

   _____

6. Do you feel that all family members were well prepared for the realities of parenthood? What aspects did you need to know more about?

   _____

   _____

   _____

7. If you could begin again with your newborn, what would you do differently? What would you do the same?

   _____

   _____

   _____

   _____

# Suggestions for Successful Nursing

## Learn about nursing and get a good start.

- Begin nursing within an hour of delivery. (Baby is awake and sucking instinct is strong.)

- Find out how to breast-feed from a knowledgeable person. (Hospitals often have nurses or other staff members who help new mothers with nursing.)

- Nurse on demand. (Nursing on demand helps baby get the needed amount of milk and mother's breasts to produce plenty of milk.) Newborns often nurse 8 to 12 times in 24 hours. Doctors usually advise waking a newborn for feedings every three hours.

- Nurse before baby cries. Watch for alertness and rooting as signs of hunger.

- Delay the use of artificial nipples (pacifiers or bottles) for a week or two. (Babies are confused by the different sucking action required.)

## Make sure baby is properly nourished.

- Breast-feeding should be observed by a knowledgeable person during the first 24 to 48 hours after delivery.

- Baby and mother should be checked for the following 48 to 72 hours after hospital discharge: baby's weight, and jaundice and hydration check; daily record of breast-feedings and baby's urination and stools is checked; mother's breasts are checked; and nursing is observed.

## Take care of breasts.

- Air-dry nipples to prevent cracking.

- Feed frequently to prevent breast engorgement (becoming overfull of milk).

- Watch for fever, lumps, or redness in breasts, which are symptoms of breast infection. If noted, seek immediate help.

- Seek medical attention promptly anytime something seems wrong or questions arise. (Early hospital discharge and lack of follow-up help causes many women to quit breast-feeding.)

# New Baby Crossword Puzzle

Name _____ Date _____ Period _____

**Across:**
6. Abbreviation for a disease that can cause mental retardation if left untreated by diet.
8. Babies born with physical problems are often placed immediately in an _____ _____ _____.
10. A condition in which the baby has intense abdominal pain.
11. Abbreviation for heated, completely enclosed units used for newborns needing intensive care.
12. A branch of medicine concerned with the care, development, and diseases of newborns.

**Down:**
1. Automatic, unlearned behaviors.
2. A routine medical visit in which the doctor examines a baby for signs of good health and proper growth.
3. The _____ _____ tests for problems of newborns in four areas.
4. The newborn's physical condition is usually checked using the _____ _____, which predicts his or her chance of survival.
5. A doctor who cares for infants and children.
7. A low level of oxygen-carrying substances in the blood.
9. From birth to one month of age, the baby in medically known as a _____.

# What's a Parent to Do?

**Name** _____ **Date** _____ **Period** _____

Family relationships can become strained during times of change. New parents need to work on maintaining family harmony. Read the following story about a young couple and their baby. Answer the questions that follow the story.

Sarah and Rodney brought their newborn home from the hospital two weeks ago. They are excited and happy about their new little boy. Sarah was working, but is now taking maternity leave. Rodney's job still does not offer paid paternity leave, so he went back to work after the first few days. Sarah and Rodney live too far away from either set of parents to have any help with the baby. They are not close to their neighbors. The baby's care is totally up to them. They are sometimes overwhelmed by how much attention the baby requires. They are particularly distressed at night when the baby cries and cries. Sarah gets up to feed the baby several times each night, but she is near exhaustion. As a new mother, she still needs lots of rest. She has talked to Rodney about it, but his busy job has put him under a great deal of stress. Consequently, he needs sleep, too. He says Sarah can rest during the day while the baby sleeps.

1. Describe Sarah's feelings. _____

_____

_____

_____

_____

2. Describe Rodney's feelings. _____

_____

_____

_____

_____

3. What is the conflict? _____

_____

_____

_____

_____

4. How can it be resolved? _____

_____

_____

_____

_____

# The Newborn

**Name** _____

**Date** _____ **Period** _____ **Score** _____

## Chapter 6 Test

True/False: Circle *T* if the statement is true or *F* if the statement is false.

| | | | |
|---|---|---|---|
| T | F | 1. | Neonatal intensive care units are for all newborns. |
| T | F | 2. | The Apgar test measures the newborn's chance of survival. |
| T | F | 3. | The Brazelton scale measures the newborn's intelligence. |
| T | F | 4. | Coughing and sneezing among newborns always indicates a cold. |
| T | F | 5. | Some reflexes may help babies learn later voluntary behaviors, such as walking. |
| T | F | 6. | Breast-feeding is the best choice for most mothers and newborns. |
| T | F | 7. | Dressing newborns is similar to dressing rag dolls because newborns cannot push their arms and legs through garments. |
| T | F | 8. | The main reason to give newborns a sponge bath is because babies like to play with sponges. |
| T | F | 9. | Newborns need exercise. |
| T | F | 10. | Parents should follow the newborn's schedule for feeding and sleeping. |
| T | F | 11. | Parents can provide an environment that is stimulating for the newborn's brain development. |
| T | F | 12. | After birth, the newborn's brain must wire itself for heartbeat, breathing, and reflexes. |
| T | F | 13. | Parenting skills do *not* come automatically but are learned. |
| T | F | 14. | Fatigue is common among parents caring for newborns. |
| T | F | 15. | Except for emergencies, couples need to spend all their nonworking hours with their newborn. |

Multiple Choice: Choose the best response. Write the letter in the space provided.

_____ 16. The official time of birth is when the _____.
  A. baby's head first appears at the opening of the birth canal
  B. baby has cleared the mother's body
  C. baby starts breathing
  D. baby cries

_____ 17. Which of the following tips can help parents adjust to parenthood?
  A. Plan carefully.
  B. Live one day at a time.
  C. Accept responsibilities.
  D. All of the above.

_____ 18. A well-baby checkup includes all of the following *except* _____.
  A. measuring and weighing
  B. examining the baby from head to toe
  C. determining the cause of illness
  D. answering parent questions and making recommendations

_____ 19. Physical characteristics of newborns include _____.
  A. fast heart and breathing rates as compared to those of adults
  B. a head that is one-half the total length of the body
  C. chest that is rounded and stomach that is flat
  D. All of the above.

*(Continued)*

**Name** _____

_____ 20. The newborn's reflexes _____.
    A. show thinking on the baby's part
    B. serve no purpose
    C. lead to voluntary behaviors
    D. change each time

_____ 21. Nursing mothers should understand that _____.
    A. they need fewer calories than mothers who formula-feed their babies
    B. they may lose a tooth unless their diet is adequate
    C. certain foods they eat may cause reactions in the baby
    D. breast-feeding is impossible if they return to work

_____ 22. The newborn's sleep can be described as _____.
    A. short naps because of the need to be alert and ready for action often
    B. so "light" that parents and others need to be rather quiet
    C. short naps in which they may suck, wheeze, and gurgle
    D. filled with lots of movement, such as rolling over and throwing the covers off

_____ 23. Newborns learn mainly by _____.
    A. looking at mobiles hung above the bed
    B. playing with their toys
    C. being exposed to many new people right away
    D. being near parents and other caregivers

_____ 24. Newborns differ in all of the following *except* _____.
    A. the amount of time they are alert
    B. how much time they spend fussing and crying
    C. their use of crying as the main way to communicate
    D. the ease with which they are soothed

_____ 25. Newborns have _____.
    A. physical needs
    B. intellectual needs
    C. social-emotional needs
    D. All of the above.

Matching: Match the following terms and identifying phrases.

_____ 26. A baby who is one month or younger in age.

_____ 27. Heated, completely enclosed beds for newborns who require intensive care.

_____ 28. Branch of pediatrics concerned with the care, development, and diseases of newborns.

_____ 29. Doctor who specializes in the treatment of infants and children.

_____ 30. A low level of the oxygen-carrying material of the blood.

_____ 31. A disease that can cause mental retardation if untreated by diet.

_____ 32. A liver condition that makes the skin, tissues, and body fluids look yellow.

_____ 33. Automatic, unlearned behaviors.

_____ 34. Condition in which an infant who seems healthy dies without warning in his or her sleep.

_____ 35. Condition in which a baby has intense abdominal pain and cries inconsolably.

A. anemia

B. colic

C. jaundice

D. neonatal intensive care units (NICU)

E. neonatology

F. neonate

G. pediatrician

H. phenylketonuria (PKU)

I. reflexes

J. sudden infant death syndrome (SIDS)

*(Continued)*

**Name** _____

Essay Questions: Provide complete responses to the following questions and statements.

36. Explain the purpose of medical care and testing just after birth.

37. Name three benefits of breast-feeding for the mother and three benefits of breast-feeding for the baby.

38. What are two of the major learnings of newborns?

39. Give four tips for soothing a fussy baby.

40. Why is the newborn stage difficult for parents?

## Part 3 — Infants

# Physical Development of the Infant 7

## Objectives

After studying this chapter, students will be able to

- describe how an infant develops physically during the first year.
- describe the order in which an infant's motor skills develop.

## Bulletin Boards

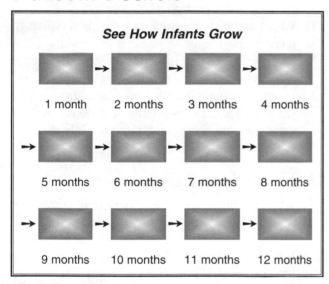

**See How Infants Grow**

| 1 month | 2 months | 3 months | 4 months |
| 5 months | 6 months | 7 months | 8 months |
| 9 months | 10 months | 11 months | 12 months |

### Title: *See How Infants Grow*

Display and label monthly pictures of one baby through the first year of life. Have students discuss the changes they note in the pictures.

### Title: *My Baby Picture*

Post each student's baby picture on a bulletin board. Ask students to match classmates with their pictures. Have each student identify his or her own picture and tell his or her age when photographed.

## Teaching Materials

**Text**, pages 204-217
  *Reviewing Key Concepts*
  *Using Your Knowledge*
  *Making Observations*
  *Thinking Further*

**Student Activity Guide**
  A. *Changes in Physical Growth*
  B. *Motor Skills Develop Rapidly*
  C. *Observation: Babies Use Motor Skills in Play*

**Teacher's Resources**
  *Heredity, Environment, and Development*, reproducible master 7-1
  *Appearance of Deciduous Teeth*, transparency master 7-2
  *Development of Gross-Motor Skills*, color transparency CT-7
  *Progression of Ability to Grasp Objects*, reproducible master 7-3
  Chapter 7 Test

## Introductory Activities

1. Display pictures of different full-grown animals and label each picture with the animal's age. Compare to humans at ages 20 or 21 years.
2. *Heredity, Environment, and Development*, reproducible master 7-1. Instruct students to write descriptions of a child's physical development during the first year. How do heredity, nutrition, illness, and activity affect development? After studying the chapter, students should revisit their responses and adjust as needed.
3. Invite students to make a large poster entitled "Infant Development We Can See." The chart should have the headings *Age, Skeletal Growth,* and *Motor Skills*. Students should also list ages *3, 6, 9,* and *12 months*. As students study the chapter they should list the average length, average weight, and expected deciduous teeth for each growth period. To address motor skills, students should write phrases describing the expected head-to-foot and center-to-extremities developmental milestones. Display the chart on a table under the suggested bulletin board. Discuss the chart while viewing the monthly pictures.

# Strategies to Reteach, Reinforce, Enrich, and Extend Text Concepts

## Skeletal Growth

4. **RF** Students should find the word *skeleton* in a dictionary. Ask students to explain the word's origin.
5. **ER** Instruct students to research and explain the purpose of the skeleton as a body system.

## Length and Weight

6. **RF** Discuss with students why doctors are more concerned with the rate of growth than total length and weight changes. Have students respond to the following questions: (1) How do physicians keep track of the growth rate? (2) If parents change the baby's physician, should health records be transferred? Why or why not?
7. **RT** Give students a hypothetical length and weight. Ask them to calculate the baby's length and weight for the first year using information from the text.

## Body Proportions

8. **RT** Have students explain why a small, receding jaw is helpful to a baby. (This shape makes it easier to suck during feedings.)
9. **ER** Guest speaker: Invite a parent to bring a four- to six-month-old baby to class. As the parent holds the baby, have students describe the "baby look."

## Bones and Teeth

10. **RF** Students should watch a baby play with his or her feet. Have students describe the baby's flexibility.
11. **ER** Instruct students to research and list sources of calcium and phosphorus, which are needed for healthy development.
12. **RF** Discuss with students why a baby's hands reach adult size before feet do (principle of head-to-toe development).
13. **ER** Have students prepare and present an oral report about the changes that occur as teeth develop in the jaw.
14. **RT** *Appearance of Deciduous Teeth*, transparency master 7-2. Display the transparency and have students explain when each type of tooth appears. Students should explain why certain teeth might appear first and certain teeth might appear last.

15. **ER** Invite a physician or nurse to discuss signs of teething and treatments parents can use to relieve a baby's pain.
16. **RF** *Changes in Physical Growth*, Activity A, SAG. Have students summarize the physical growth of infants by writing phrases that describe babies' length, weight, body proportions, and bones and teeth at various ages.

## Motor Development

17. **RF** Students should find the word *motor* in a dictionary and explain why the word is used to describe movement skills.
18. **RT** Have students refer again to chapter 6 to review the age norms for the disappearance of various reflexes.
19. **RT** Discuss why babies are apt to fall when someone talks to them as they are standing or walking without support.
20. **RF** Discuss with students what it was like to learn a new motor skill, such as needlework, a sport, or a musical instrument. Students should discuss the following questions: (1) How fast are your movements during the learning stage? (2) How are the movements of athletes, such as figure skaters and divers, slowed while they are in the "thinking" stage of learning a motor skill?

## Head-to-Foot Development

21. **RF** Instruct students to examine the drawings in chart 7-3 in the text. Explain how an infant's development follows head-to-foot development.
22. **RT** *Development of Gross-Motor Skills*, color transparency CT-7. Use this transparency to illustrate the progression of gross-motor skills in infants. Discuss with students the time frame of each major skill development. Note there is some difference in the exact time of each development, but the normal sequence is the same for all children.

## Center-to-Extremities Development

23. **RT** Students should sequence the development of infants from center-to-extremities. Have students identify the period in which each development first appears.
24. **RF** *Motor Skills Develop Rapidly*, Activity B, SAG. Have students sequence the skills in head-to-foot development and center-to-extremities development by identifying the quarter of the first year in which each skill listed should emerge.

25. **RF** *Observation: Babies Use Motor Skills in Play*, Activity C, SAG. Instruct students to observe a baby between ages six months and one year and record the motor skills observed.

26. **RT** *Progression of Ability to Grasp Objects*, reproducible master 7-3. Students should determine the proper order of the steps in development of grasping ability. (For a hands-on variation, you may wish to cut apart the master and have a student arrange the steps in the proper order.)

## Differences in Physical Development

27. **RT** Read this sentence from the text to the class: "The rate is affected by heredity, nutrition, illnesses, and activity." Ask students which of these factors are environmental (all but heredity). Have students list ways adults can provide a healthy environment. Keep the list and revisit it again after studying chapter 10.

28. **ER** Have each student interview a parent with two or more children ages two years or older. Ask the parent to recall the differences in the ages in which these children learned to creep, sit, pull to a stand, and walk. Ask the parent to speculate on the cause(s) of these differences. Share your responses.

# Answer Key

## Text

*Reviewing Key Points,* page 216

1. triple
2. true
3. false
4. increase in length of bones, ossification begins, changes in number of bones
5. false
6. true
7. D
8. sits without support with back straight—3; raises head while on abdomen—1; creeps—4; walks—6 or 7; rolls over from front to back—2; stands without help—5; picks up object with thumb used in opposition to finger—6 or 7
9. unlearned; learned

## Student Activity Guide

*Motor Skills Develop Rapidly,* Activity B

1. fourth quarter
2. third quarter
3. first quarter
4. first quarter
5. third quarter
6. fourth quarter
7. second quarter
8. second quarter
9. third quarter
10. third quarter
11. fourth quarter
12. second quarter
13. second quarter
14. third quarter
15. first quarter
16. second quarter
17. third quarter
18. second or third quarter (occurs in the sixth or seventh month)
19. second quarter
20. fourth quarter

## Teacher's Resources

*Appearance of Deciduous Teeth,* transparency master 7-2

(See Figure 7-2 on page 208 of the text.)

*Progression of Ability to Grasp Objects,* reproducible master 7-3

Stages should be placed in the following order:
1. no contact
2. contact only
3. hand grasp
4. superior palm grasp
5. forefinger grasp
6. superior forefinger grasp

## Chapter 7 Test

| | | |
|---|---|---|
| 1. F | 14. T | 27. L |
| 2. T | 15. T | 28. G |
| 3. T | 16. A | 29. B |
| 4. F | 17. C | 30. K |
| 5. F | 18. A | 31. F |
| 6. T | 19. B | 32. J |
| 7. F | 20. A | 33. I |
| 8. T | 21. D | 34. H |
| 9. F | 22. D | 35. A |
| 10. F | 23. A | 36. C |
| 11. T | 24. C | 37. D |
| 12. F | 25. A | 38. E |
| 13. T | 26. D | 39. M |

40. Failure to grow is often noted when growth charts kept by the baby's doctor indicate a decline in growth.

41. Bones bend without breaking. Bones are soft and easily misshapen. Because babies should always sleep on their backs, they need some "tummy time" when they can hold up their heads.

42. (Describe five:) soft and flexible bones; large head; protruding abdomen; short legs; long trunk; wide forehead; receding jaw; about equal sized head and chest

43. Infants are mainly alike in terms of the order or sequence of development. They are mainly different in terms of the rate in which they move through the sequence.

# Heredity, Environment, and Development

**Name** _____ **Date** _____ **Period** _____

Write a description of a baby. Show how heredity, nutrition, illness, and activity affected the baby's physical development. For each description, you can choose whether development was affected in a positive or negative way.

**Heredity:** _____

_____

_____

_____

_____

**Nutrition:** _____

_____

_____

_____

_____

_____

**Illness:** _____

_____

_____

_____

_____

_____

**Activity:** _____

_____

_____

_____

_____

_____

# Appearance of Deciduous Teeth

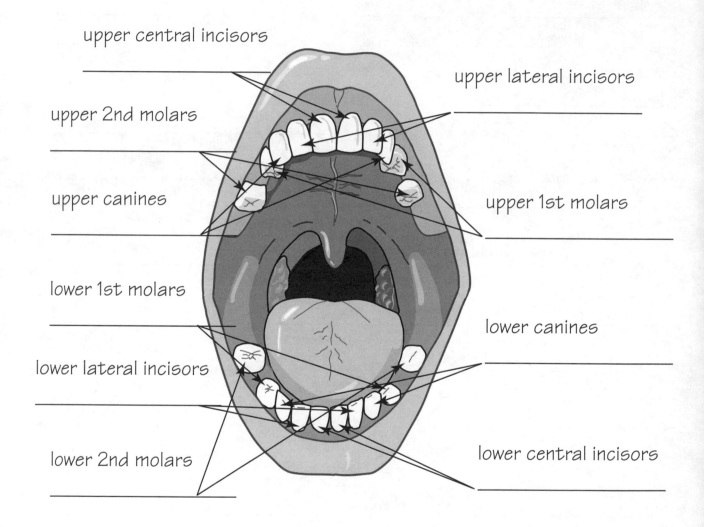

upper central incisors

upper lateral incisors

upper 2nd molars

upper canines

upper 1st molars

lower 1st molars

lower canines

lower lateral incisors

lower 2nd molars

lower central incisors

# Progression of Ability to Grasp Objects

**Name** _____ **Date** _____ **Period** _____

A baby's ability to grasp goes through stages. Examine the stages illustrated below. Determine the proper order of the steps and number each box accordingly.

| # _____ | # _____ |
|---|---|
| Superior Forefinger Grasp | Contact Only |
| # _____ | # _____ |
| No Contact | Forefinger Grasp |
| # _____ | # _____ |

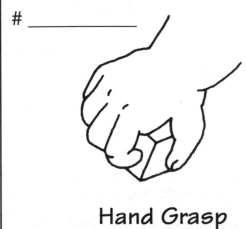

Hand Grasp

Superior Palm Grasp

# Physical Development of the Infant

Name _____

Date _____ Period _____ Score _____

## Chapter 7 Test

True/False: Circle *T* if the statement is true or *F* if the statement is false.

T   F   1. Human development is completed sooner than development in other living creatures.

T   F   2. Teeth are part of a human's skeletal system.

T   F   3. The head-to-toe measurement for babies is referred to as length because a baby does not stand at birth.

T   F   4. The chubby newborn begins to lose fat deposits under the skin soon after birth.

T   F   5. Body proportions of infants are so similar to those of adults that infants look much like miniature adults.

T   F   6. Newborns are flexible because large spaces between the bones help the joints bend easily without breaking.

T   F   7. Motor development includes gross-motor skills but not fine-motor skills.

T   F   8. Infants are more similar with regard to the order of their development than to the rate of this development.

T   F   9. Leaving a two-month-old asleep in the middle of an adult's bed is a safe child care practice.

T   F   10. Babies usually roll from back to front before they roll from front to back.

T   F   11. Sitting without support requires so much concentration that a baby is apt to topple over if distracted.

T   F   12. *Creeping* and *crawling* are different names for the same skill.

T   F   13. Some children begin walking when they are one year old.

T   F   14. The Palmar reflex is replaced with voluntary grasping in the first year.

T   F   15. Differences in physical development are due to both genetic and environmental factors.

Multiple Choice: Choose the best response. Write the letter in the space provided.

_____ 16. By the end of the first year, the length of the infant has _____.
    A. increased 1½ times
    B. doubled
    C. tripled
    D. None of the above.

_____ 17. By the end of the first year, the weight of the infant has _____.
    A. increased 1½ times
    B. doubled
    C. tripled
    D. None of the above.

_____ 18. Which of the following statements is *not* true of infant body proportions?
    A. The legs are long and slender.
    B. The head is about one-fourth of the infant's total length.
    C. The jaw is small and slopes backward.
    D. The infant has a "pot-bellied" look.

*(Continued)*

**Name** _____

_____ 19. Changes in bones include all of the following *except* _____.
   A. increasing length
   B. softening of bones
   C. changes in numbers
   D. ossification

_____ 20. Which of the following statements about deciduous teeth is true?
   A. It is normal for the first tooth to be present at birth, appear during the first year, or appear after the first birthday.
   B. Deciduous teeth are permanent teeth.
   C. The molars are the first teeth to come in.
   D. Deciduous teeth start to form in the jaw only days before they break through the surface of the gums.

_____ 21. Motor development includes the infant's ability to _____.
   A. turn
   B. walk
   C. grasp
   D. All of the above.

_____ 22. Which of the following is *not* a pattern of motor development?
   A. The baby develops from head to toe.
   B. The baby develops from general to specific.
   C. The baby develops from center to outward to the extremities.
   D. The baby develops from the fingers inward to the center of the body.

_____ 23. Trunk control is required for _____.
   A. sitting and rolling over
   B. writing and manipulating objects
   C. lifting the head and smiling
   D. crawling and grasping

_____ 24. Which of the following shows the correct order of appearance of the motor skills listed?
   A. sitting, walking, creeping
   B. walking, crawling, sitting
   C. crawling, creeping, cruising
   D. standing, rolling over, sitting

_____ 25. Which sentence is true about grasping?
   A. Grasping starts as a reflex but becomes a voluntary movement.
   B. Grasping starts as voluntary but becomes quick and reflexive.
   C. Voluntary grasping is a quick and easy task for babies to master.
   D. Grasping is an example of head-to-toe development.

_____ 26. Slower than average physical development may be due to _____.
   A. heredity problems
   B. poor nutrition or illness
   C. lack of opportunity to practice a movement
   D. All of the above.

*(Continued)*

**Name** _____

Matching: Match the following terms and identifying phrases.

_____ 27. The body system that includes bones and teeth.

_____ 28. A condition in which the child fails to grow at a healthy rate.

_____ 29. The relative size of body parts.

_____ 30. Hardening of bones caused by the depositing of the minerals calcium and phosphorus.

_____ 31. The first set of teeth.

_____ 32. The use and control of muscles that direct body movements.

_____ 33. Abilities to control and use large muscles.

_____ 34. Abilities to control and use small muscles.

_____ 35. A range of ages at which most children reach developmental milestones.

_____ 36. Moving by pulling with the arms but not lifting the abdomen.

_____ 37. Moving by pulling with the arms, using the hands and knees or hands and feet, and lifting the abdomen.

_____ 38. Walking by holding onto an object or person.

_____ 39. Movements, such as grasping, that are learned and controlled at will.

A. age norm

B. body proportions

C. crawling

D. creeping

E. cruising

F. deciduous teeth

G. failure to thrive

H. fine-motor skills

I. gross-motor skills

J. motor development

K. ossification

L. skeletal system

M. voluntary

Essay Questions: Provide complete responses to the following questions or statements.

40. Explain how failure to thrive can be diagnosed.

41. Give two facts about the bones of babies and describe how these affect the care needed.

42. Describe five physical characteristics of infants.

43. How are infants most alike in their physical development? How are they most different in their physical development?

# Intellectual Development of the Infant

## Objectives

After studying this chapter, students will be able to
- describe how and what infants learn.
- explain how infants express what they know through language.
- identify the order in which infants learn.

## Bulletin Boards

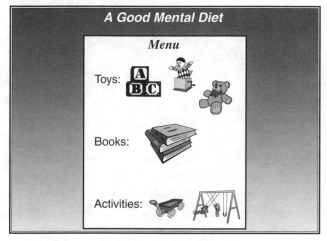

A Good Mental Diet

### Title: A Good Mental Diet

Have the bulletin board resemble a menu from which students can choose items that would stimulate the intellectual development of an infant.

### Title: Toys to Stimulate a Baby's Perception

After students complete SAG Activity 8A, instruct them to find pictures of the toys identified as appropriate for each age group. Have students place the pictures on the bulletin board. Under each group of toys, students should list the age group for which they would be most appropriate.

## Teaching Materials

**Text**, pages 218-237
*Reviewing Key Concepts*
*Using Your Knowledge*
*Making Observations*
*Thinking Further*

**Student Activity Guide**
A. *Toys to Stimulate a Baby's Perception*
B. *Mental Advances in the First Year*
C. *Object Identity*
D. *Learning to Talk—A Complex Skill*

## Teacher's Resources

*Errors in Perception*, reproducible master 8-1
*Object Permanence Is Developmental*, transparency master 8-2
*Depth Perception in Babies*, color transparency CT-8
*Observation: Children Learn to Communicate*, reproducible master 8-3
Chapter 8 Test

## Introductory Activities

1. Have students create a story, poem, or cartoon from the viewpoint of an infant. Students should use the work to reflect their views about an infant's intellectual development. Have students save and revisit these pieces at the end of the chapter. Were their initial perceptions (and portrayals) accurate? Discuss.
2. On the chalkboard or a transparency write "Why Adults May Underestimate Infants' Intellectual Development." Have students brainstorm reasons for the underestimation and create a master list. (For example, adults may think sensory organs like eyes are immature; adults may believe babies just want to sleep and eat; babies may lack language to "tell" adults what they know; and adults are too busy with routine physical care to notice how much babies know.) After studying the chapter, revisit this list and discuss the potential risks involved with underestimating infants' mental development.

## Strategies to Reteach, Reinforce, Enrich, and Extend Text Concepts

### How Infants Learn

3. **RT** Discuss with students the role that "wanting to learn" plays in the learning process. Ask students to suggest ways that babies show what they want to learn.
4. **EX** Ask the students to give other words for wanting to learn that might describe an infant.

## Brain Development Supports Learning

5. **RT** Ask students for examples of how brain development and the environment can affect the rate of intellectual development.

6. **RT** Instruct students to list learnings a baby may acquire from throwing toys or other objects from a high chair.

7. **RT** Have students visualize an infant's typical home environment and ask them to brainstorm available opportunities for babies to develop motor skills.

8. **RT** Have students make a vertical list of some gross-motor and fine-motor skills developed in infancy. (They can refer to chapter 7 if needed.) Next to each skill, have students write one or more new learnings made possible by the skill. (For example, a creeping infant can explore every inch of the floor, see undersides of furniture, chase toys that roll away, and follow parents, siblings, and pets from room to room.)

9. **RT** Ask students to explain what the phrase "a good mental diet" means.

10. **RT** Have students design a poster called "Food for Thought." As they read this chapter, they can add pictures or captions to the poster that represent objects or activities that stimulate babies' thoughts.

11. **RF** Have students add to the chart "Our Brains Are Wired" that was begun in chapter 6. (See teaching strategies in chapter 6 of this *Teacher's Resources* product for description.) Students should list *Infant* as the stage and list descriptions of what is wired in this first year of life. If needed, have students conduct Internet research to help them complete the chart. (This chart can be continued in upcoming chapters.) Point out to students that each area of brain wiring (motor, visual, and thinking) requires experience in that specific area.

## Perception

12. **EX** Discuss the following with students: Babies younger than seven or eight months usually go readily to any adult. After this time, a baby often cries when held by or left with an unfamiliar adult. What is the baby's likely perception of the parent (or other familiar adult) prior to seven months? (the adult is part of himself or herself) After seven months? (the adult is a separate person from the baby and can leave him or her.)

13. **RF** Students should make a chart listing the senses used in developing perceptions of form, space, weight, and number, and in developing social perceptions (such as ability to judge others' feelings from their behavior).

14. **RF** *Errors in Perception*, reproducible master 8-1. Students should complete the activities on errors in perception.

15. **RF** *Toys to Stimulate a Baby's Perception*, Activity A, SAG. Instruct students to identify toys that fit babies' changing needs.

## Cognition

16. **RT** Have students define the term *cognition*.

17. **RT** Ask students to describe the relationship between cognition and perception.

18. **RT** Ask students to describe Piaget's theory of intellectual development.

19. **RT** Have students give examples of ways very young children explore their world through their senses and motor skills.

20. **RT** Students should sequence the learning methods, as outlined by Piaget, of children who are in the sensorimotor stage.

21. **RF** *Mental Advances in the First Year*, Activity B, SAG. Instruct students to match the baby's learnings to the first four of Piaget's substages of the sensorimotor stage.

## What Infants Learn

22. **EX** Have students debate whether they agree or disagree with the following statement: "Even as an adult, a person's concepts continue to change." Ask students to give examples to support their position.

23. **RF** Students should write the definitions of the terms *perception* and *concept* as given in the text. Students should explain how sensory stimuli lead to perceptions and how perceptions lead to concepts.

## Perceptual Concepts

24. **RF** Have students explain what "rule" they would use to explain the apparent changes in objects in each of these cases: (a) You see a large jet take off and become smaller and smaller; (b) A car looks different as it approaches behind you, as it passes your car, and as you see ahead of you moving away; (c) Your yellow sweater looks greenish under fluorescent lights.

25. **RF** Instruct students to read about object constancy in the text and study Figure 8-10.

Each student should then select one common object in the home or yard. (Each student should choose a different object.) As a homework assignment, students should view the object from both an infant's crawling and standing height positions. Students should write a description of the object from an infant's visual perspective and present their descriptions in class.

26. **EX** *Object Identity*, Activity C, SAG. Students should use this activity to analyze a baby's concept of object identity.

27. **RF** *Object Permanence Is Developmental*, transparency master 8-2. For each stage given on this transparency, have students describe the development of object permanence in that stage. Write in their responses on the master. Sample answers are given in the answer key. Note that some older infants may advance to Stage 5.

28. **RF** Discuss with students why a baby would develop a concept of object permanence about a parent before developing the concept about a toy. Students should explain why the concept of object permanence for grandparents who live far away is developed long after the first year. Also have students explain what situation helps children develop object permanence.

29. **RT** *Depth Perception in Babies*, color transparency CT-8. Use this color transparency to present the concept of depth perception in babies. Have students discuss the importance of depth perception. Explain that even though depth perception is well developed by seven to nine months of age, babies still are not safe from falls.

30. **RT** Ask students to give examples of situations in which a child's depth perception was not fully developed. Have them explain the outcomes of these situations.

## Beginnings of Language Development: Brain Development Research

31. **RF** Using only words and no actions, have students explain how to do a task or describe a person or place. Students should discuss the difficulty of communicating only with words.

32. **RF** Ask students the following questions: Have you noticed that after you learn a new word you begin to hear it or see it in print "for the first time?" Why do you think this situation occurs?

33. **RT** Have students explain how rich experiences can lead to a more extensive vocabulary that, in turn, leads to greater mental growth. Students should diagram these relationships as a mental growth cycle.

## How Babies Communicate

34. **RF** Ask students to tape record examples of babies crying, cooing, babbling, and saying early words. Other students should try to interpret these sounds.

35. **RF** *Learning to Talk—A Complex Skill*, Activity D, SAG. Instruct students to list ways adults can aid the speech development of babies.

36. **RT** Discuss with students how parents' language habits affect the language skills of their babies.

37. **ER** Guest speakers: Invite students or adults with a first language other than English to share which English sounds are difficult for them. Ask the guests to share some sounds made in their language that are not made in English.

## Passive Versus Active Vocabulary

38. **RT** Ask students to explain the difference between passive and active vocabulary.

39. **ER** *Observation: Children Learn to Communicate*, reproducible master 8-3. Students should observe the vocabulary of children under two years of age. What words are included in their active vocabulary? Other than words, how else do they communicate? Have students give examples of children's use of passive vocabulary.

# Answer Key

## Text

*Reviewing Key Concepts,* pages 236-237

1. false
2. the baby's physical development (mainly brain growth) and the environment
3. B
4. A. 3-D objects
   B. solid-colored cards
   C. patterned cards
   D. human face
   E. curved lines
   F. new objects
5. true
6. false

7. true
8. A
9. A—2; B—3; C—1; D—5; E—4
10. A—Joe; B—Tyrone; C—Maria
11. 1—crying; 2—cooing; 3—babbling;
    4—reduplication babbling; 5—first words

## Student Activity Guide

### Mental Advances in the First Year,
Activity B

| | | |
|---|---|---|
| 1. B | 8. D | 15. B |
| 2. C | 9. C | 16. A |
| 3. C | 10. B | 17. D |
| 4. D | 11. D | 18. D |
| 5. A | 12. C | 19. A |
| 6. C | 13. A | 20. C |
| 7. B | 14. B | |

## Teacher's Resources

### Object Permanence Is Developmental,
transparency master 8-2

Stage 1: Newborns—Baby tries to follow an object being moved in front of his or her eyes. If the object goes out of sight, the baby does not search for it.

Stage 2: 1 to 4 Months—Baby follows an object being moved. As the object leaves the field of vision, the baby stares at the place from which the object disappeared. (Baby does not turn to locate the object.)

Stage 3: 4 to 8 Months—Baby will search for a partially hidden object, but will not search for a completely hidden object.

Stage 4: 8 to 12 Months—Baby will search for completely hidden objects. If the object is hidden under one box and is moved in full view of the attentive baby to a position under a second box, the baby will look for it under the first box and stop searching.

Stage 5: 12 to 18 Months—Toddler will search under the last box where the toy was seen even if toy is hidden under a box and then moved to be hidden under another box. If three boxes are moved with the toy remaining hidden underneath, toddlers look under the box that ends up in the position where the toy was last seen. If nothing is there, toddlers give up the search.

## Chapter 8 Test

| | | |
|---|---|---|
| 1. T | 14. F | 27. C |
| 2. F | 15. D | 28. O |
| 3. T | 16. C | 29. G |
| 4. T | 17. B | 30. D |
| 5. T | 18. A | 31. J |
| 6. F | 19. C | 32. I |
| 7. T | 20. C | 33. K |
| 8. F | 21. D | 34. L |
| 9. T | 22. C | 35. F |
| 10. T | 23. D | 36. E |
| 11. F | 24. B | 37. H |
| 12. T | 25. P | 38. M |
| 13. T | 26. N | 39. A |

40. motor center, vision center, thinking center, memory centers, auditory center for language sounds

41. Language is closely related to intellectual development. The brain is wired for language and speech. Vocabulary is often considered a measure of intellectual development but cannot be used as such until children are older. Language is also related to social-emotional development. Language is used to express feelings and emotions, make friends, and get along with others. Infants do not have the needed language skills to use language to meet their social-emotional needs.

42. Passive vocabulary has more words because infants understand many more concepts and words than they can express in spoken words.

# Errors in Perception

**Name** _____ **Date** _____ **Period** _____

Perceptual development depends on information that comes to you through your senses. Of course if your sense organs are not perfect (for example if you have poor eyesight), the information sent to your brain is less than perfect. People are likely to make other errors in perception just because they are human. Answer the following questions in the spaces below. (Be honest with yourself!)

1. **Visual Perceptual Errors**
   Look at each of these figures and respond to the questions:

   Figure 2

   Figure 1

   Figure 3

   a. In Figure 1, do the slanting lines look as though they would meet when extended inward? _____
      Use a straight edge. Do they meet? _____
   b. In Figure 2, do line segment A and line segment B appear to be the same length? _____
      Measure them. Are they the same length? _____
   c. In Figure 3, do the two lines seem to run exactly parallel to each other? _____
      Measure them. Are they exactly parallel? _____

2. **Auditory Perceptual Errors**
   a. When you hear the sound of a moving jet, where is the jet?

   b. What was the error of the child who heard someone sing, "Gladly, the cross I bear," and who later
      drew a picture of "Gladly, the cross-eyed bear"? _____

      _____

3. **Tactual Perceptual Errors**
   Try this experiment. Fill three basins of water—one hot, one lukewarm, and one cold.
   a. Plunge one hand into the hot water and then into the lukewarm water. How does the lukewarm
      water feel? _____

      _____

   b. Plunge the other hand into the cold water and then into the lukewarm water. How does the
      lukewarm water feel?_____

      _____

*(Continued)*

4. **Using Perceptual Errors**

a. How does an interior decorator use perceptual errors to make a small room seem larger or smaller?

_____

_____

_____

_____

b. How does a fashion designer use perceptual errors to downplay figure flaws? _____

_____

_____

_____

_____

c. What entertainment area(s) is(are) based solely on perceptual errors?_____

_____

5. Look up the term *illusion* in your dictionary. What does it mean?_____

_____

6. What are some possible synonyms for the term *illusion*?_____

_____

_____

7. Respond to the old saying "Seeing is believing." _____

_____

_____

_____

_____

# Object Permanence Is Developmental

Stage 1: Newborns

Stage 2: 1 to 4 Months

Stage 3: 4 to 8 Months

Stage 4: 8 to 12 Months

Stage 5: 12 to 18 Months

# Observation: Children Learn to Communicate

**Name** _____ **Date** _____ **Period** _____

Children communicate in many ways. Observe the communication methods of several children ages two years and younger. Write your response to the information requested.

1. Names and ages of children observed _____
   _____

2. Location of observations _____
   _____

3. In what ways did the children communicate? _____
   _____
   _____

4. What words did they use? _____
   _____
   _____
   _____
   _____
   _____

5. Give examples of any reduplication babbling you may have heard. _____
   _____
   _____
   _____
   _____

6. Can you and others easily understand what the children are "saying" or do only those who know them well seem to understand them? _____
   _____
   _____
   _____
   _____

7. Give examples of any passive vocabulary observed. _____
   _____
   _____
   _____
   _____

8. Time observation began _____ Time observation completed _____

# Intellectual Development of the Infant

**Name** _____

**Date** _____ **Period** _____ **Score** _____

## Chapter 8 Test

True/False: Circle *T* if the statement is true or *F* if the statement is false.

T    F     1. Babies come into the world using all their sense organs and react to stimuli with certain reflexes.

T    F     2. Babies do *not* want to learn, but the environment pressures them to learn.

T    F     3. Both new and repeated experiences are necessary for learning.

T    F     4. Brain wiring for vision occurs in early infancy.

T    F     5. Perception is dependent on the maturing sense organs.

T    F     6. Infants are unable to tell the differences in high- and low-pitched sounds at birth.

T    F     7. Cognition is a more advanced mental behavior than is perception.

T    F     8. The first stage of Piaget's cognitive development is called the accommodation stage.

T    F     9. Reflexes are the basis of all learnings in the first stage of intellectual development.

T    F    10. Before babies are a year old, they can see a connection between what they do and what happens.

T    F    11. If two people share an identical environment, their concepts of that environment would also be identical.

T    F    12. Depth perception is developed to a great extent in the first year of life.

T    F    13. Infants may "talk" through cooing and crying.

T    F    14. Saying fewer than 10 words by the first birthday is abnormal.

Multiple Choice: Choose the best response. Write the letter in the space provided.

_____ 15. Intellectual development consists of _____.
    A. how people learn
    B. what people learn
    C. how people express what they know through language
    D. All of the above.

_____ 16. Which of the following statements about learning is untrue?
    A. A person learns by trying to cause actions to happen.
    B. A person learns by trying to figure out what is happening.
    C. A person learns without exerting effort.
    D. A person learns by using his or her sensory organs.

_____ 17. Perceptual learning during infancy does *not* involve _____.
    A. organizing information that comes through the senses
    B. giving names to objects
    C. the speed in which people organize information
    D. the way in which people select among sensory experiences

*(Continued)*

**Name** _____

_____ 18. Babies do *not* prefer _____.
    A. highly complex over moderately complex objects
    B. slow-moving over stable objects
    C. patterned over solid-colored objects
    D. 3-D over 2-D objects

_____ 19. The major theorist who described children's intellectual development is _____.
    A. Erikson
    B. Havighurst
    C. Piaget
    D. Maslow

_____ 20. In the first stage of mental development, infants learn primarily through their _____.
    A. senses
    B. motor skills
    C. senses and motor skills
    D. own reasoning

_____ 21. Concepts change from _____.
    A. simple to complex
    B. concrete to abstract
    C. inaccurate to accurate
    D. All of the above.

_____ 22. An example of babbling is _____.
    A. a monotone speaking voice
    B. repeating the same vowel sound
    C. a series of combined consonant and vowel sounds
    D. a "word" understood only by a baby's parent(s)

_____ 23. First words are formed rather directly as a result of _____.
    A. cooing
    B. gesturing
    C. simple babbling
    D. reduplication babbling

*(Continued)*

**Name** _____

Matching: Match the following terms and identifying phrases.

_____ 24. The ability to fuse an image in the brain so it appears as one image using both eyes.

_____ 25. Sound, light, and other sensations that influence the activity of the sense organs.

_____ 26. Organizing information obtained through the senses.

_____ 27. Act or process of knowing or understanding.

_____ 28. Stage of intellectual development in which babies learn through senses and movements.

_____ 29. To copy or mirror the actions of others.

_____ 30. Idea formed by combining what is known about a person, object, place, quality, or event.

_____ 31. Knowing that objects remain the same even if they appear different.

_____ 32. Understanding that objects, people, and events are separate from one's interactions with them.

_____ 33. Understanding that an object stays the same from one time to the next.

_____ 34. Concept that people, objects, and places still exist even when they are no longer seen, felt, or heard.

_____ 35. Ability to tell how far away something is.

_____ 36. A light, happy sound made by babies around two months of age.

_____ 37. Changes in pitch used to express happiness, demands, and questions; opposite of *monotone*.

_____ 38. Words a person understands but does not say.

_____ 39. Words a person uses in talking or writing.

A. active vocabulary

B. binocular vision

C. cognition

D. concept

E. coo

F. depth perception

G. imitating

H. inflections

I. object concept

J. object constancy

K. object identity

L. object permanence

M. passive vocabulary

N. perception

O. sensorimotor stage

P. stimuli

Essay Questions: Provide complete responses to the following questions or statements.

40. What five areas of the brain are wired during infancy?

41. What is the relationship of language to intellectual and social-emotional development?

42. Which contains more words among infants—passive vocabulary or active vocabulary? Explain.

# Social-Emotional Development of the Infant

9

## Objectives

After studying this chapter, students will be able to
- identify temperamental differences in babies.
- describe the infant's major first-year social tasks.
- explain the roots of four emotions—love, fear, anxiety, and anger.

## Bulletin Boards

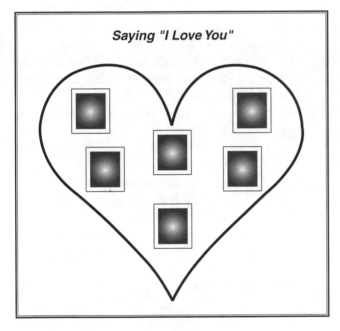

**Saying "I Love You"**

Title: *Saying I Love You*

Illustrate the bulletin board with pictures showing ways people may show an infant affection, such as smiling, holding, and hugging. Writing captions may help clarify the meanings of pictures.

Title: *Babies Express a Wide Range of Emotions*

On the bulletin board place the following words in bold letters: love, fear, anxiety, and anger. Leave space for students to add pictures, sayings, or illustrations that depict babies experiencing each emotion.

## Teaching Materials

**Text**, pages 238-253
*Reviewing Key Concepts*
*Using Your Knowledge*
*Making Observations*
*Thinking Further*

**Student Activity Guide**
A. *Difficult Babies Make Parenting Stressful*
B. *Building a Trusting Relationship*
C. *Observation: Attachment Behaviors*
D. *Helping to Ease Separation Anxiety*

**Teacher's Resources**
*Infant Needs*, reproducible master 9-1
*Cycles of Trust and Mistrust*, transparency master 9-2
*Pleasant vs. Unpleasant Emotions*, color transparency CT-9
Chapter 9 Test

## Introductory Activities

1. Have a class debate on the statement "The personality you are born with is the personality you have throughout life." Students should cite examples that support or do not support the statement. After reading the text description of temperamental differences, discuss the issue again.
2. Ask students whether they know children who fit into the temperament categories of easy, slow to warm up, or difficult. Students should give characteristics of children that fit each description.

## Strategies to Reteach, Reinforce, Enrich, and Extend Text Concepts

### Temperamental Differences in Infants

3. **RT** Instruct students to research the origin of the word *temperament* in a dictionary. The origin of this word is further explained by the meaning of the term *humor*. (Students should find this

term as well.) Ask students whether *temperament* is more often used positively or negatively, as in the description "temperamental artist."

4. **EX**  Students should brainstorm words that describe a person's disposition.

5. **RF**  *Difficult Babies Make Parenting Stressful*, Activity A, SAG. Discuss with students positive responses to the descriptions of difficult babies. Point out that it is the temperament style that is difficult rather than the child.

6. **RT**  Ask students how parents can distinguish between a difficult temperament and ineffective parenting. Discuss answers in class.

## The Infant's Growing Social World

7. **ER**  Have students list categories of social relationships with which children must eventually cope, such as relationships with family members and neighborhood friends. You may have students diagram the expanding social world with concentric circles.

8. **RF**  Using specific examples, discuss with students how parents can affect a baby's social development in the first year.

## Interacting with Others

9. **ER**  Each student should ask a parent to share stories of interactions between an older child and an infant. Students should then write newspaper- or magazine-style articles on how infants interact with older children.

10. **EX**  Ask students whether they remember any interactions with grandparents when they were little. What part do they feel grandparents should play in the life of grandchildren?

11. **RT**  Discuss with students what can happen to children when they have too few children and adults with whom to interact.

12. **EX**  Use the following case study to start a class discussion. Both Darrell and Samantha are six months old. Darrell's caregiver spends a lot of time with him, cuddling, talking, smiling, and socializing him with adults who interact similarly. Samantha's caregiver is reserved and self-conscious, experiencing discomfort cuddling, talking to, and smiling at her. Samantha is rarely around other people. How do you think the caregivers have affected and will affect the social-emotional development of these babies?

## Learning to Trust

13. **RT**  Ask students to explain why Erikson believes trust is the basis of social interaction.

14. **RT**  Students should discuss how they feel when their basic needs are met and there is a sameness in their environment versus when they are hungry, tired, and cold and are in a different environment. Compare this to the way children develop trust and mistrust.

15. **RF**  *Infant Needs*, reproducible master 9-1. In this activity, students will compare Erikson's basic trust versus basic mistrust stage to Maslow's hierarchy of human needs. Students will need to use the text and other resources to research the theories.

16. **RT**  *Cycles of Trust and Mistrust*, transparency master 9-2. Use this transparency as you explain how the interaction between parents and babies leads the baby to trust or mistrust others.

17. **RT**  Discuss with students why it is important to keep babies' environments fairly consistent. Give examples of what this entails.

18. **RF**  *Building a Trusting Relationship*, Activity B, SAG. Ask students to give specific examples of how adults can provide the consistency children need to develop trust.

19. **RF**  Ask students to complete the following sentence: "Babies learn to trust others and believe in their world when …"

20. **EX**  Explain to students that Erikson believed mistrust in infancy and childhood would lead to a generalized mistrust in the teen and adult years. Ask students how they can recognize general mistrust in teens and adults and why mistrusting people are so unhappy. Often people who mistrust are suspicious of others' motives by saying that others are carrying out their "hidden agendas." Ask students how suspicious people affect teamwork in school and in the world of work and how mistrust might affect family relations.

21. **RF**  Instruct students to use a doll to demonstrate a physical care task that is done with slow, cuddling movements and a quiet voice rather than with impatience and a hurried attitude.

## Showing Attachment

22. **ER**  Panel discussion: Invite several parents to discuss expressions of love between parents and infants. Parents should discuss ways they show love to their children as well as ways the infants show love to them.

23. **ER** *Observation: Attachment Behaviors, Activity C, SAG.* Students should observe the way or ways a child expresses strong feelings for others.
24. **RT**   Ask students to explain how feelings of attachment can help babies' intellectual development.

## Infants Express Emotions

25. **RT**   For each emotion described in the text (love, fear, anxiety, and anger), ask students for two examples of a thought that can trigger the emotion and a change in the body.
26. **ER** *Pleasant vs. Unpleasant Emotions,* color transparency CT-9. Use this color transparency to present the concept of emotions and babies.
27. **ER**   Have students defend or refute the following statement: People need to express a range of emotions—from happy to unhappy—for healthy emotional development. Students should also address whether a person can express unhappy emotions in age-appropriate ways. If students believe this is true, they should give examples.
28. **RF**   Students should chart emotional development during the first year of life. They could use the following age categories: 0 to 3 months, 3 to 6 months, 6 to 9 months, and 9 to 12 months. Instruct students to chart the appearance of the emotions love, fear, anxiety, and anger. They should list actions that reveal the emotion on the chart. (For example, evidence of fear at 0 to 3 months might be seen in the jerk or startle reflexes.)

## Love

29. **ER**   Instruct students to write a short paper on how their concept of love differs from that of an infant's concept of love.
30. **RT**   Ask students to describe some objects that adults become attached to that are somewhat similar to the baby's attachment objects, such as pacifiers, blankets, stuffed toys.

## Fear

31. **RT**   Ask students why they think babies are not afraid of young children.
32. **EX**   Have students analyze and discuss how an adult can instill enough fear to increase a child's safety and still avoid making a child overly afraid.
33. **RT**   Discuss with students how fear can affect physical and intellectual growth.

## Anxiety

34. **RT**   Ask students whether they think adults have more anxieties or more fears. Explain.
35. **EX**   Students should explore ways to deal with children who are experiencing strong separation anxieties. Ask students to explain what a caregiver can do when a child cries and cries as a parent leaves. How can the caregiver ease the child's fear and anxiety?
36. **RF** *Helping to Ease Separation Anxiety,* Activity D, SAG. Instruct students to write suggestions for adults to help relieve an infant's feelings of separation anxiety.

## Anger

37. **RT**   Students should examine the three major conditions under which babies show anger. Ask students what the underlying reason is for anger in all these situations.
38. **EX**   Instruct students to compare adult anger to infant rage. Students should answer the following questions: Are there similarities between adults and infants in the underlying reasons for anger? Do adults, like infants, show a variation in the frequency and intensity of their anger?
39. **RT**   Discuss with students the problems that can occur when adults model anger in response to a baby's anger.

# Answer Key

## Text

### Reviewing Key Concepts, page 252

1. true
2. (Name two:) heredity, prenatal conditions, ease of birth, environment after birth
3. cries, coos, smiles
4. true
5. false
6. E
7. (List two:) trying to stay close to the adult, following the adult, clinging to the adult, smiling at the adult, crying for the adult, calling to the adult
8. false
9. D
10. false
11. A; B; D; A; B; B; C; D

# Teacher's Resources

## Infant Needs, *reproducible master 9-1*

| Maslow's Needs | Erikson's Basic Trust |
|---|---|
| Self-Actualization | |
| Esteem | |
| Love and Acceptance | Cuddling and Play |
| Safety and Security | Communicating and Consistent Environment |
| Physical Needs | Food, Cleansing, Warmth, and Sleep |

## Chapter 9 Test

| | | | | | |
|---|---|---|---|---|---|
| 1. | F | 12. | F | 23. | J |
| 2. | T | 13. | F | 24. | D |
| 3. | T | 14. | A | 25. | K |
| 4. | F | 15. | C | 26. | I |
| 5. | T | 16. | B | 27. | G |
| 6. | T | 17. | D | 28. | B |
| 7. | F | 18. | D | 29. | E |
| 8. | T | 19. | C | 30. | A |
| 9. | F | 20. | D | 31. | H |
| 10. | T | 21. | A | 32. | C |
| 11. | T | 22. | A | 33. | F |

34. Babies have the physical abilities to send signals of distress and pleasure to others, such as through crying and smiling. Babies also have the mental abilities to locate the direction of the human voice, to move in rhythm to human speech, and to learn meanings of the social messages others send.

35. Erikson called his first stage basic trust versus basic mistrust. He believed consistency in having needs met and sameness in the environment lead to feeling the world is reliable. The baby develops a sense of basic trust. If the world is not seen as reliable, basic mistrust develops.

36. Emotions require thoughts. For example, babies must know adults help them before love can develop. They must know they can be hurt before fear develops. Babies must understand that others are separate from them and can leave them before anxiety develops. Babies must understand their own goals cannot be met before frustration and anger develop. Emotions lead to physical changes in the body, such as increased heart rate. Severe distress can interfere with healthy physical development.

# Infant Needs

**Name** _____ **Date** _____ **Period** _____

Research Erikson's stage of basic trust versus basic mistrust and Maslow's hierarchy of human needs. On the chart below, show the relationship between the components of the two theories. Write a short explanation underneath. List the resources you used below your explanation.

| Maslow's Needs | Erikson's Basic Trust |
|---|---|
| | |

_____

_____

_____

_____

## Resources Used

_____

_____

_____

_____

# Cycles of Trust and Mistrust

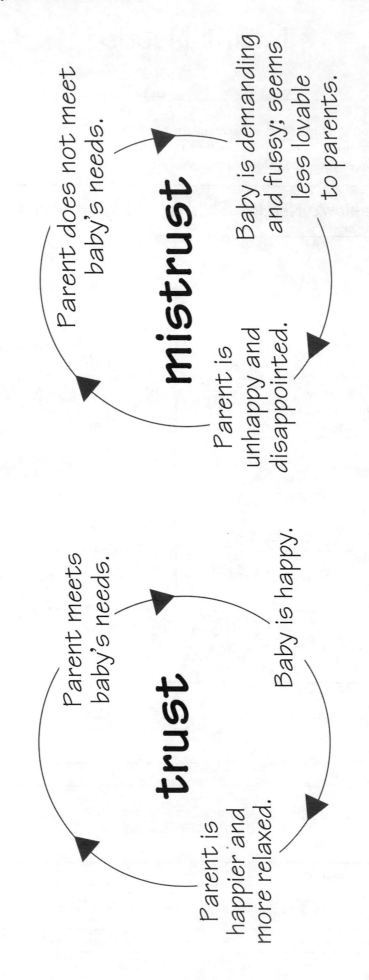

**trust**

Parent meets baby's needs.

Baby is happy.

Parent is happier and more relaxed.

**mistrust**

Parent does not meet baby's needs.

Baby is demanding and fussy; seems less lovable to parents.

Parent is unhappy and disappointed.

# Social-Emotional Development of the Infant

**Name** _____

**Date** _____ **Period** _____ **Score** _____

## Chapter 9 Test

True/False: Circle *T* if the statement is true or *F* if the statement is false.

T    F    1. Social-emotional development is slow in the first year.

T    F    2. A person's disposition is part of his or her social-emotional development.

T    F    3. Babies with slow to warm up temperaments take longer to adapt than babies with easy temperaments.

T    F    4. Babies with difficult temperaments are mainly spoiled.

T    F    5. Babies know how others feel about them by the way they are looked at and held.

T    F    6. The rate of social development increases with advanced motor skills.

T    F    7. According to Erikson, feelings of trust and mistrust in infants do *not* affect feelings toward others in later life.

T    F    8. Bonding is an attachment feeling.

T    F    9. Babies who show strong attachment behaviors are always more attached to their parents than babies who show less intense attachment behaviors.

T    F    10. Because thinking changes, the situations that cause emotions change over the years.

T    F    11. Emotional responses should change as a person matures.

T    F    12. Babies have an attachment to their parents immediately after birth.

T    F    13. Caring very much for a blanket, pacifier, or toy is seldom seen in babies and can be considered abnormal.

Multiple Choice: Choose the best response. Write the letter in the space provided.

_____ 14. Which of the following statements is most accurate?
A. Temperament joined with a person's environment shapes personality most.
B. Culture shapes personality most.
C. Genes shape personality most.
D. Parents and other adults shape personality most.

_____ 15. Social development is shaped by _____.
A. how adults affect babies
B. how babies affect adults
C. how adults and babies affect each other
D. None of the above.

_____ 16. Quickly soothing a crying baby _____.
A. increases cooing and babbling responses
B. reduces crying
C. increases crying as a way to get attention
D. spoils the baby

*(Continued)*

**Name** _____

_____ 17. Babies interact with young children by _____.
   A. watching them
   B. following them
   C. playing with toys laid down by them
   D. All of the above.

_____ 18. A baby's trust is built by _____.
   A. meeting a baby's needs without too much delay
   B. meeting a baby's needs each time
   C. providing sameness in the baby's environment
   D. All of the above.

_____ 19. Babies' early responses to their world are _____.
   A. general distress
   B. general excitement
   C. general distress and excitement
   D. love, fear, anxiety, and anger

_____ 20. Fear _____.
   A. has its roots in a reflex
   B. is directed toward the unknown
   C. is learned from direct experiences and the warnings of others
   D. All of the above.

_____ 21. Anxiety is _____.
   A. concern about the future
   B. a neurotic fear
   C. a sign of delayed development
   D. All of the above.

_____ 22. With time, anger becomes _____.
   A. more directed toward a certain person or object
   B. less directed toward a certain person or object
   C. more intense
   D. more physical

Matching: Match the following terms and identifying phrases.

_____ 23. Consists of a person's basic disposition as well as interacting with others and showing feelings.

_____ 24. A person's general mood.

_____ 25. Tendency of a person to react in a certain way to events.

_____ 26. Brothers and sisters.

_____ 27. The most serious form of not trusting.

_____ 28. Closeness between people that remains over time.

_____ 29. Thoughts that lead to feelings and cause changes in the body.

_____ 30. Proper, healthy ways to express emotions based on a person's age.

_____ 31. Emotion common among babies caused by the fear that loved ones who leave them will not return.

_____ 32. Reliance of one person on another to fill his or her needs.

_____ 33. Wanting to do things for oneself.

A. age-appropriate behaviors

B. attachment

C. dependence

D. disposition

E. emotions

F. independent

G. mistrust

H. separation anxiety

I. siblings

J. social-emotional development

K. temperament

(Continued)

**Name** _____

Essay Questions: Provide complete responses to the following questions or statements.

34. What beginning tools for social development do babies possess?

35. Name and describe Erikson's first stage of social-emotional development.

36. Explain how emotions are closely tied to intellectual and physical development.

# Providing for the Infant's Developmental Needs

10

## Objectives

After studying this chapter, students will be able to
- plan ways to meet the developmental needs of babies in their first year.
- demonstrate skills that meet babies' physical needs.
- stimulate babies' mental development.
- enhance babies' growing awareness of themselves.

## Bulletin Boards

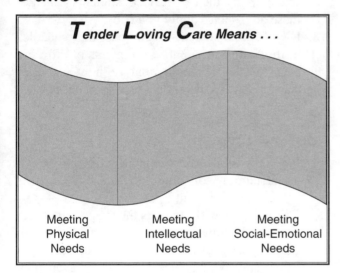

**Tender Loving Care Means . . .**

| Meeting Physical Needs | Meeting Intellectual Needs | Meeting Social-Emotional Needs |

### Title: *Tender Loving Care Means...*

Place a large piece of pastel paper across the center of the board to resemble a section of ribbon. Divide the ribbon into thirds. Place one of the following labels under each third: "Meeting Physical Needs," "Meeting Intellectual Needs," and "Meeting Social-Emotional Needs." Have students draw or collect pictures that show adults meeting these needs with infants. Place the pictures in the appropriate sections of ribbon.

### Title: *Establish Routines But Keep Them Flexible*

Place a picture of a large clock in the center of a bulletin board. Around the edge place the words *Sleeping, Bathing, Feeding, Napping,* and *Playing.*

## Teaching Materials

**Text**, pages 254-287
 *Reviewing Key Concepts*
 *Using Your Knowledge*
 *Making Observations*
 *Thinking Further*

**Student Activity Guide**
 A. *Foods Babies Should Not Eat*
 B. *Choices in Baby Foods*
 C. *Wise Clothing Choices*
 D. *Play Throughout the House*
 E. *How's the Baby-Adult Interaction?*

**Teacher's Resources**
 *Successful Caregiving Survey*, reproducible master 10-1
 *Sensory Stimulation Activities*, reproducible master 10-2
 *Spatial Concepts*, color transparency CT-10
 *Problem-Solving Activities*, reproducible master 10-3
 *Babies Solve Problems*, reproducible master 10-4
 *Gross-Motor and Fine-Motor Games*, reproducible master 10-5
 *Action Rhymes*, transparency master 10-6
 *Meeting Infant's Developmental Needs*, reproducible master 10-7
 Chapter 8 Test

## Introductory Activities

1. Ask students to discuss experiences they have had caring for babies 1½ years old or younger. What were some enjoyable experiences? Were some experiences difficult? How do they like being around children this age?
2. *Successful Caregiving Survey*, reproducible master 10-1. Invite students to interview caregivers and record hints to ease difficulty or solve problems in caring for infants. Have students share their findings with the class in the following order of topics: feeding, weaning, clothing, diapering, bathing, providing rest and sleep time, establishing routines, providing sleep and play spaces, meeting intellectual needs, and meeting social-emotional needs.

# Strategies to Reteach, Reinforce, Enrich, and Extend Text Concepts

## Physical Needs

3. **RT** Ask students to give some examples of how babies, children, and adults suffer mentally and socially-emotionally when physical needs are not met.

4. **RF** Students should list the physical needs of babies in the first year. Students should compare babies' needs with those of adults.

5. **ER** After students study the entire section on "Physical Needs" of infants, ask them to add to the list made in strategy 27, chapter 7 of this *Teacher's Resource* product concerning the ways adults can aid infant's physical development.

## Feeding and Weaning

6. **EX** *Choices in Baby Foods*, Activity B, SAG. Prepare homemade baby food with students. Students should compare the homemade food with similar commercially prepared foods.

7. **ER** Invite students to interview several parents about when and how they weaned their babies. Students should ask about difficulties parents experienced in the weaning process. Instruct students to write a paper based on their findings.

8. **ER** Instruct students to observe a baby self-feeding. Students should note how the baby holds the food, how fast the baby can self-feed, what problems the baby encounters, and the mess at the end of the feeding. Have students share their findings in class.

9. **RF** *Foods Babies Should Not Eat*, Activity A, SAG. Students should give reasons that babies should not eat the foods listed.

## Clothing

10. **RF** *Wise Clothing Choices*, Activity C, SAG. Instruct students to select several garments for a baby and rate various features of each garment.

11. **RT** Discuss with students why infants do not need shoes until they are walking outside and why some shoes worn during infancy can even interfere with healthy foot growth and development.

12. **ER** Guest speaker: Invite a pediatrician to speak about recommended fabrics for baby clothing and products.

## Diapering a Baby

13. **EX** Instruct students to compare the costs of cloth and disposable diapers and prepare a pros and cons chart for each.

14. **RF** Students should suggest ideas for interacting with babies during diapering.

## Tub Bathing

15. **ER** Ask students to set up a display of types of bathing equipment. Students should discuss the advantages and disadvantages of each item.

16. **RF** Using a doll, demonstrate the procedure for a tub bath, including positive interactions with the baby. Have students practice the procedure.

## Establishing Routines

17. **RT** Discuss with students the advantages of a schedule in their life. Ask students whether these advantages apply to a baby.

18. **EX** Instruct students to compare the schedules of three or four parents with infants of differing ages. Students should analyze how activities change with time. How does time spent on activities change?

## Rest and Sleep

19. **RT** Ask students to explain why the mental understanding of object permanence causes babies to cry at night.

20. **RT** Discuss with students the suggested procedure for handling a crying baby at night. Ask students what problems they can foresee when adults stay with babies all night or even play with them during the family's sleeping hours.

## Sudden Infant Death Syndrome

21. **ER** Students should research different theories of causes of Sudden Infant Death Syndrome.

22. **RT** Have students make a poster or create a public service announcement on ways to help prevent SIDS.

23. **EX** Ask students to read an article or story of the trauma faced by a family who lost a child to SIDS. After reading the selection, students should write a few paragraphs on the nature of the trauma.

## Places for Sleep and Play

24. **RF** *Play Throughout the House*, Activity D, SAG. Students should collect or make toys that

are suitable for play by infants aged seven months to one year. Each student should arrange for a parent to use the toys with the baby and offer feedback to the student.

25. **ER**  Field trip: Arrange for students to visit a child care center with a room designed for infants. Have a center representative discuss what types of toys, objects, and activities are used with the infants and which seem to be the most popular.

## Intellectual Needs

26. **EX**  Have students explain the rationale for each of the following points: (a) Activities are not special in themselves–the warmth and feelings parents and others have for babies seem to make games worth while. (b) Activities for babies are best woven into the routines of the day. (c) Babies' own activities should not be stopped in order to play games adults have planned.

27. **RF**  Instruct students to write a newspaper article on the difference between providing an enriched environment for babies and teaching babies directly.

## Activities to Stimulate the Senses

28. **RT**  Review with students the changes in babies' perceptual preferences (as presented in chapter 8). Students should write a list of these changes.

29. **RT**  *Sensory Stimulation Activities*, reproducible master 10-2. Use this master to show students sensory stimulation activities that are easy to do with babies. Encourage them to try to think of others.

30. **ER**  As an individual or small-group project, suggest that students make the materials for one or more "games," such as a mobile, wind chime, face hoop, play quilt, or sound can. Students can then donate their projects, with instructions and safety rules, to an infant program, parent, or hospital.

## Problem-Solving Activities

31. **RT**  *Spatial Concepts*, color transparency CT-10. Use this transparency to introduce one example of the relationship of objects within space.

32. **RT**  *Problem-Solving Activities*, reproducible master 10-3. Use this master to show students various types of problem-solving activities. This may help students think of other ways babies can solve problems.

33. **ER**  *Solve Problems*, reproducible master 10-4. Have students try three of the problem-solving activities from this chapter with a baby between the ages of six months and one year.

## Motor Activities

34. **RT**  Have students explain how motor activity aids babies' intellectual and social-emotional development.

35. **RT**  *Gross-Motor and Fine-Motor Games*, reproducible master 10-5. Use this master to show students various ways babies can use their gross- and fine-motor skills. Ask students to brainstorm other ways babies can use their motor skills.

## Language Activities

36. **RT**  Discuss with students the importance of reading to and talking with babies (as well as older children) daily.

37. **RT**  *Action Rhymes*, transparency master 10-6. Use this master to show students a number of action rhymes. Encourage students to think of others to add to the list.

38. **ER**  Instruct students to plan to try one or more of the language games from this chapter with a baby. Students should then carry out their plans, carefully recording their observations. Have students present their findings in class.

## Social-Emotional Needs

39. **RT**  Have students review the key interactions of babies in their social worlds during the first year as discussed in chapter 9.

40. **RT**  Discuss with students how parents can help infants meet their social-emotional needs.

## Baby-Adult Interaction

41. **RT**  Discuss with students the typical adult-child interactions with babies of the following temperaments: easy, slow to warm up, and difficult.

42. **ER**  *How's the Baby-Adult Interaction?* Activity E, SAG. Explain to students this is an informal observation in which they are simply getting a brief impression of types of both positive and negative interactions between parents and children. Students should share their observations in class. (Remind students not to record or reveal the names of the parents or children they observed.)

43. **RT**   Discuss with students how adults come to feel loved and valued by their children. Ask students whether they think a baby's love that grows out of the love and attention of the adult differs from the origin of adult love for someone.

## Helping Babies Develop Their Self-Awareness

44. **RF**   Ask students to define *self-awareness*. Students should list what a person learns about himself or herself to develop self-awareness. Students should also describe what babies learn about themselves to learn self-awareness.

45. **RT**   Have the class discuss why a baby must feel "possession" before he or she can "share." Students should discuss the following questions: Are there possessions you do not want to share with anyone? How do you think babies or young children feel when they are asked to share everything?

46. **RT**   *Meeting Infant's Developmental Needs*, reproducible master 10-7. Ask students to suggest answers to each of the situations presented.

## Handling Special Problems

47. **ER**   Invite students to interview a pediatrician about recognizing serious health problems that call for professional medical help.

48. **EX**   Have students explain the benefits for adults and children of finding alternate care for the baby sometimes so the adult can take a short break from child care responsibilities.

## Recognizing Developmental Delays

49. **RT**   Ask students to list common developmental delays in infants.

50. **ER**   Invite a pediatrician to speak to the class about how he or she recognizes developmental delays in infants. Have students prepare a list of questions for the speaker in advance.

# Answer Key

## Text

### Reviewing Key Concepts, page 286

1. physical
2. (List three): a baby cannot digest complex nutrients found in solids; starting solids too early may cause allergy problems; some solids have too much sodium; solids may be too high in calories; jaw and throat muscles must develop before swallowing solids is easy and safe; during spoon feeding, a baby cannot be held and given the warm feeling of physical closeness received during formula- or breast-feeding; babies do not need solids for nutritional reasons in the first half-year

3. A and C
4. false
5. (List three. Student response. See pages 271 to 272 in the text.)
6. true
7. A. watching for signs of each baby's interest in certain experiences
   B. repeating games many times over several months
   C. letting babies try things for themselves
8. false
9. true
10. (List two): talk to a baby; ask questions as you talk; pronounce words correctly; talk about baby's everyday world as babies begin to understand their world
11. (List three. Student response. See pages 280 to 281 in the text.)

## Student Activity Guide

### Foods Babies Should Not Eat, Activity A

See chart 10-4 in the text for answers.

## Teacher's Resources

### Chapter 10 Test

| | | | |
|---|---|---|---|
| 1. F | 11. T | 21. B | 31. I |
| 2. F | 12. T | 22. A | 32. E |
| 3. T | 13. F | 23. C | 33. J |
| 4. T | 14. T | 24. D | 34. C |
| 5. T | 15. T | 25. D | 35. K |
| 6. F | 16. F | 26. B | 36. D |
| 7. F | 17. F | 27. A | 37. B |
| 8. T | 18. F | 28. D | 38. H |
| 9. T | 19. T | 29. D | 39. A |
| 10. F | 20. D | 30. F | 40. G |

41. Physical needs must be met in order for a baby to survive, grow, and develop. Babies are helpless to meet these needs and rely on parents and other caregivers for help.

42. (Give three:) Babies should sleep away from major activities. The sleeping area should be large enough for a full-sized crib and other

furnishings. Play spaces need to accommodate mess, be safe, be bright and cheerful, have a low-nap carpet or tile floor coverings for wheeled toys and blocks. All spaces need to be planned for frequent and economical changes as the baby grows.

43. (Describe three:) Adults should talk to babies about all aspects of their world. Routines are a great time for language activities. Pronounce words clearly and correctly. Singing, chanting, and using inflections while speaking aid baby's interest. Encourage babies to talk by smiling and responding to their attempts. Read to babies. Play language games.

44. Using the baby's name helps the baby connect the name to himself or herself. Using the baby's name during happy times also gives the baby positive feelings about his or her name.

# Successful Caregiving Survey

**Name** _____ **Date** _____ **Period** _____

Interview caregivers to learn helpful hints to ease difficulty or solve problems in caring for infants. Focus your interview on hints in one of the following areas: feeding, weaning, clothing, diapering, bathing, providing rest and sleep time, establishing routines, providing sleep and play spaces, meeting intellectual needs, and meeting social-emotional needs. The following questions will help you. (Be sure to focus your specific questions on one of the areas listed above.)

1. Are there needs of your infant (such as feeding or bathing) that were difficult for you to meet at first but are easier now?
2. What are some techniques you tried to make those tasks easier?
3. Were some of the techniques more successful than others?
4. How did the successful techniques make tasks easier?
5. Which of these techniques would you recommend to other caregivers?

## Interview Notes

_____

_____

_____

_____

_____

_____

_____

_____

## Helpful Hints

(For each hint, give the area of care to which the hint applies.)

_____

_____

_____

_____

_____

_____

_____

_____

# Sensory Stimulation Activities

The following activities can be used with children to help them learn to notice and discover more about their environment.

## Activity

## Senses

*Music*

Sing and play music from an instrument, the radio, a tape, or a compact disc.

*Hearing*

*Play Quilts*

Make a play quilt for baby using fabrics with many different patterns, colors, and textures.

*Sight and touch*

*Find the Bell*

Ring a bell while the baby is not watching. When the baby looks in the right direction, show him or her the bell while ringing it again.

*Hearing*

*Sound Tour*

Carry the baby on a sound tour of the house. Do not make loud sounds, such as turning on a vacuum cleaner. Instead, use sounds like a note or two on the piano, wind chimes, a music box, a clock that strikes on the hour, a closing cabinet door, and a doorbell.

*Hearing*

*Floating Toys*

Babies enjoy watching toys in the bathtub. Use clean, empty measuring cups as well as toys made for the tub.

*Sight*

*Feeling Tour*

Help the baby feel and touch objects with different textures.

*Touch*

*Food*

As babies eat solid foods, talk about the senses they are using. You may say statements like, "This smells good." or "See the orange carrots."

*Sight, touch, smell, and taste*

# Problem-Solving Activities

The following activities can be used to help children see the relationship of objects within space or the relationship of a person's body to objects in space.

## Spatial Relationship Activities

*Get the Toy*
Place a toy between two objects, such as between two chairs or a chair and a wall. Then have the baby get the toy. Each time you play the game, change the space between the two objects. The baby should learn when there is enough space to crawl between two objects and when there is only enough space to reach for the toy.

*Right Side Up*
Show the baby a known object–such as a doll or picture–that is upside-down. See whether the baby will turn the object or picture right side up. Try this while reading books, too.

*Up, Down, and Around*
Lift the baby and say, "Up (baby's name) goes." As you lower the baby, say, "Down (baby's name) comes." Repeat several times. (Never toss and catch a baby.) Next, hold the baby close to your body and as you turn, say, "Around and around (baby's name) goes."

## Object Permanence Activities

The following activities help children see that objects, people, and places still exist even when they can no longer be seen, heard, or felt.

*Hide the Teddy Bear*
Hide a teddy bear or another object in a place where it is easy to find. Gradually hide it in a more difficult place as the baby watches you hide it. Then say, "Where did the bear go? Here's the bear!" Reveal the bear's hiding place.

*Peek-a-Boo*
Cover your eyes and say, "Where did (baby's name) go?" Uncover eyes and say, "Peek-a-boo, I see you!" Repeat several times. Then cover baby's eyes lightly with your hand or a small cloth draped over the baby's head and eyes. Say, "Where did (given name, such as Daddy) go?" Then uncover the baby's eyes and say, "Peek-a-boo, here I am." After a few times the baby will remove the eye cover. Older infants may reach up to cover your eyes.

## Using Objects as Tools

The following activities help children see and understand how objects can be used in different ways to help them reach their goals.

*Cause and Effect*
Use a drum and drumsticks to help baby learn the cause and effect of the beating. An oatmeal box and stick can also be used for drum beating. The sound can be made louder or softer.

*Using a Stepping Stool*
Baby can use a small step stool or chair to reach other objects. Be sure the baby is safe and only reaches safe objects.

# Babies Solve Problems

**Name** _____ **Date** _____ **Period** _____

As sights, sounds, textures, odors, and tastes reach a baby's senses, the world must seem confusing. Because babies do not like confusion, they try to order their world by making rules about how their world works. Look at the problem-solving activities from this chapter. Choose one from each category to try with a baby between the ages of six months and one year. In the space below, record the baby's actions and the rule he or she may have learned from the activity.

Age and gender of baby _____

1. Spatial Relationship
   Activity chosen _____

   Actions observed _____

   _____

   _____

   Rule baby may have learned _____

   _____

   _____

2. Object Permanence
   Activity chosen _____

   Actions observed _____

   _____

   _____

   Rule baby may have learned _____

   _____

   _____

3. Using Objects as Tools
   Activity chosen _____

   Actions observed _____

   _____

   _____

   Rule baby may have learned _____

   _____

   _____

# Gross-Motor and Fine-Motor Games

The following activities can help improve and strengthen baby's large muscles and help with small-muscle coordination.

## Gross-Motor Games

### Getting Objects

While the baby is watching, roll or move any toy or safe object out of the baby's reach. Encourage the baby to get the object. As the baby's motor skills improve, increase the distance between the baby and the object.

### Splashing in Water

Splashing in a tub or pool helps the baby improve motor skills. Babies should be supervised by an adult at all times when in or near water. The adult can hold the baby and encourage the baby to splash and kick.

### Rolling the Ball

Use a large ball for baby to roll or push, then run after it.

## Fine-Motor Games

### Crib Gym

Adults can buy a commercial crib gym or make one using safe objects like squeeze toys or rattles. Change objects to keep the baby's interest.

### Pick up Cereal

After the baby is eating solids, place soft dry cereal on the high chair tray or in a bowl. Baby needs to use finger dexterity to pick up each piece and place it in the mouth.

### Pull on the String

Tie a plastic ring to a string. Make sure the ring is secure so the baby cannot remove the ring and place it in the mouth. On the other end of the string tie one of the baby's toys. The baby has to pick up the string with the ring in order to pull the toy.

### Play with Blocks

Stack blocks on top of each other. After stacking the blocks, gently push them over and watch them tumble.

# Action Rhymes

### "Jack Be Nimble"

Jack be nimble, Jack be quick,

Jack jump over

(Lift baby to imitate a jump on the word *jump.*)

The candlestick.

### "Humpty Dumpty"

Humpty Dumpty sat on a wall.

Humpty Dumpty had a great fall.

(Lower baby from lap on the word *fall.*)

All the king's horses and all the king's men

Couldn't put Humpty together again.

### "Pop Goes the Weasel"

All around the carpenter's bench

The monkey chased the weasel.

The monkey thought 'twas all in fun,

POP goes the weasel.

(Lift baby high or clap on the word *POP.*)

### "London Bridge"

London bridge is falling down,

Falling down, falling down.

London bridge is falling down,

My fair lady (or gentleman).

(Two people hold hands while others walk under the "bridge".
Then the "bridge" falls down and catches one person.)

# Meeting Infant's Developmental Needs

**Name** _____ **Date** _____ **Period** _____

Describe how to handle each of the following situations:

1. You are going to bathe seven-month-old Carissa. Describe the room and supplies you will need.

   _____
   _____
   _____

2. One-year-old Alec is weaned from his bottle. Every night he wakes up crying, and only his mother can comfort him. What should the parents do?

   _____
   _____
   _____

3. Nine-month-old Caylin has a wet diaper. Explain what you will do to change her.

   _____
   _____
   _____

4. Your friend has a 10-month-old son, Devan. Suggest ways you can play with the baby.

   _____
   _____
   _____

5. How can you help babies begin to develop their self-awareness?

   _____
   _____
   _____
   _____
   _____

_____
_____
_____
_____
_____
_____
_____
_____
_____

_____

# Providing for the Infant's Developmental Needs

Name _____

Date _____ Period _____ Score _____

## Chapter 10 Test

True/False: Circle *T* if the statement is true or *F* if the statement is false.

T   F   1. The body grows three times faster in the second and third years than during the first year of life.

T   F   2. An adult cannot understand a baby's crying or calling signals; thus, caring for a baby is, to a great extent, guesswork.

T   F   3. First solid foods for infants should be of a semi-liquid texture.

T   F   4. Adults need to watch for signs of food allergies and intolerance in babies.

T   F   5. Babies should be fed on demand rather than on a set schedule.

T   F   6. Weaning should be done quickly so babies know they are really growing up.

T   F   7. Parents should teach babies it is impolite to reject food by spitting the food back or turning their head away from the food.

T   F   8. The age at which babies sleep through the night may vary widely from baby to baby.

T   F   9. Experts recommend the back position for a sleeping infant to reduce chance of SIDS.

T   F   10. A baby's bed should be located near the major activity areas of the house so parents can check on the baby often.

T   F   11. Watching for signs of a baby's interest in a game or toy as a clue for adult-child play is a good way to aid a baby's mental development.

T   F   12. Sensory stimulation activities are important for the first year.

T   F   13. Babies learn language by watching TV.

T   F   14. Infant social-emotional development centers on baby-adult interaction.

T   F   15. Fostering good feelings in babies leads to love and joy between adults and babies.

T   F   16. Babies do *not* develop understandings of themselves as unique people.

T   F   17. Babies need to learn to share rather than being possessive about objects.

T   F   18. Because babies are so young, they do *not* have problems that call for professional help.

T   F   19. New parents tend to seek advice more often than do experienced parents, particularly on minor problems.

Multiple Choice: Choose the best response. Write the letter in the space provided.

_____ 20. Feeding times for babies should provide _____.
   A. nourishment for growth and development
   B. nourishment for energy needs
   C. close physical contact with an adult
   D. All of the above.

*(Continued)*

**Name** _____

_____ 21. Feeding guidelines for a baby's needs should come from _____.
A. diets printed in books and pamphlets
B. advice from a physician or dietitian
C. adult caregivers' judgments
D. baby's likes and dislikes

_____ 22. Which of the following points about spoon-feeding is true?
A. Spoon-feeding is a developmental task.
B. Spoon-feeding teaches the child how to handle a spoon.
C. Babies will eat from a spoon if they get "hungry enough."
D. Spitting food out is a baby's way of being naughty.

_____ 23. Clothing selections for babies should mainly be based on _____.
A. cost
B. decorative quality and fine fabrics
C. safety, comfort, and ease of care
D. name brand or designer label

_____ 24. Which of the following does *not* increase the risk of SIDS?
A. Placing pillows, stuffed toys, and fluffy blankets in the crib.
B. Smoking during pregnancy and around the baby.
C. Placing the baby on the stomach to sleep.
D. Using a firm mattress in the baby's bed.

_____ 25. Which of the following statements about routines is true?
A. Routines are more important for adults than for babies.
B. Establishing a routine is not healthy because babies need change.
C. Routines can make adults nervous because they have difficulty sticking to the clock.
D. None of the above.

_____ 26. All of the following statements are true about an enriched environment *except* _____.
A. Adults provide learning experiences for their babies soon after birth.
B. Adults should do planned activities regardless of the baby's interest in them.
C. Adults should make constant judgments about the baby's interest in activities.
D. Activities should occur during daily routines.

_____ 27. Problem-solving activities include _____.
A. exploring spatial relationships
B. viewing a mobile
C. smiling at a caregiver
D. saying first words

_____ 28. Adults who have good relationships with babies _____.
A. respect babies' temperaments
B. give babies adequate physical contact
C. realize babies do not give as much love as they receive
D. All of the above.

_____ 29. Which tip for handling their babies' problems should parents ignore?
A. Get help if the problem is not temporary.
B. Get expert advice when needed.
C. Take some time off from your baby, such as an afternoon or evening out.
D. Let your baby cry it out; giving into a baby spoils him or her.

*(Continued)*

**Name** _____

Matching: Match the following terms and identifying phrases.

_____ 30. Substances in food that help growth and provide energy.

_____ 31. Semi-liquid, mushy foods for feeding an infant by spoon.

_____ 32. A negative physical reaction caused by eating a food.

_____ 33. Substances that speed up the functions of vital organs and the nervous system.

_____ 34. Substances that slow down functions of the vital organs and the nervous system.

_____ 35. Gradual process of taking a baby off the bottle or breast.

_____ 36. Foods used for self-feeding.

_____ 37. Surroundings that promote learning.

_____ 38. Learning to notice and find out more about objects in the world through the five senses.

_____ 39. The working together of muscles in movement.

_____ 40. A baby's understanding of himself or herself as a unique person.

A. coordination
B. enriched environment
C. depressants
D. finger foods
E. intolerance
F. nutrients
G. self-awareness
H. sensory stimulation
I. solids
J. stimulants
K. weaning

Essay Questions: Provide complete responses to the following questions or statements.

41. Explain why it is important for adults to meet a baby's physical needs.

42. Give three guidelines for providing sleep and play spaces for infants.

43. Describe three guidelines for stimulating language learning in infants.

44. Why is using the baby's name important to developing self-awareness?

# Physical Development of the Toddler

# 11

## Objectives

After studying this chapter, students will be able to
- describe the physical changes that occur between the first and third years of life.
- identify the toddler's major gross-motor and fine-motor skills.

## Bulletin Boards

**Let's Cover Toddler Growth**

Physical

Intellectual

Emotional

Social

### Title: *Let's Cover Toddler Growth*

Place a picture of a large umbrella with the title above it on the bulletin board. Mount the words *Physical, Intellectual, Social,* and *Emotional* beside or inside the raindrops.

### Title: *Growing Physically*

Draw a large picture of a toddler with a sprinkler can. On the board place paper flowers that students have labeled with key phrases depicting areas of growth and motor skill development (such as *walks upright without support*).

## Teaching Materials

**Text**, pages 290-303
   *Reviewing Key Concepts*
   *Using Your Knowledge*
   *Making Observations*
   *Thinking Further*

**Student Activity Guide**
   A. *Growth Slows and Slows*
   B. *Motor Skills Continue to Develop*
   C. *Motor Skills of a Toddler on the Go*

**Teacher's Resources**
   *Growth for Toddlers*, transparency master 11-1
   *Toddlers Develop New Motor Skills*,
     color transparency CT-11
   *Growth and Practice Go Hand-in-Hand*,
     reproducible master 11-2
   Chapter 11 Test

## Introductory Activities

1. Before reading the chapter, have students (as a class or individually) observe one or more toddlers. Students should then list ways toddlers differ from infants in terms of skeletal growth and motor development. As students study the chapter, have them check those points that correspond with the book. At the bottom of the list, students can add other points made in the text. If possible, students should observe toddlers again and look for examples of the points they added while reading the text.

2. Make or have some of your students bring videotapes of children who are in the toddler stage. Have the class view the tapes and try to find identifying characteristics of this age group, such as skills in walking, climbing, jumping, and playing.

# Strategies to Reteach, Reinforce, Enrich, and Extend Text Concepts

## Body Growth and Development

3. **RT** Review with students the growth of the various organ systems in the first year as presented in chapter 7.
4. **RF** Instruct students to read and record the definitions in at least three other sources for the term *early childhood*. Students should compare the definitions.

## Height and Weight

5. **RF** *Growth Slows and Slows*, Activity A, SAG. Instruct students to chart height and weight increases from birth to three years. Use charts 7-1 and 11-2 in the text for references.
6. **RT** Discuss with students the meaning of the phrase "Premature babies catch up physically in the toddler years." Address with students the following questions: With whom or what are these toddlers catching up? Why do premature children often lag behind their potential, at least for a period?
7. **RF** *Growth for Toddlers*, transparency master 11-1. Have students figure the height and weight changes common in the first two years. Each student may select birth length and weight individually, or you may want to select a birth length and weight for all students to use.
8. **RT** Discuss with students the developmental picture that is emerging when, on the average, girls grow to 53 percent of their adult height by two years of age and boys grow to 50 percent of their adult height by the same age. Have students calculate a girl's adult height if she is 35 inches tall at age two years and a boy's adult height if he is 36 inches tall at age two years.
9. **ER** Guest speaker: Invite a pediatrician to discuss with the class normal and abnormal levels of physical growth in toddlers.

## Other Body Changes

10. **RF** Ask students to write a paper describing the "toddler look."
11. **RT** Students should identify the growth and development principle that explains why the fontanels are closed or almost closed at age two years but the leg and foot bones will not ossify for many years. (People develop from head to toe.)

12. **EX** Students should speculate on how mental and language development would be affected if a person matured from "toe to head" instead of from "head to toe."
13. **EX** Discuss with students what is probably true of a 30-month-old toddler who is extremely chubby.

## Motor Development

14. **RF** Instruct students to look up the term *refined* in a dictionary. Students should explain how a refined skill is different from a new skill.
15. **RT** *Toddlers Develop New Motor Skills*, color transparency CT-11. Use this transparency to point out new skills that are developing in the gross- and fine-motor areas.
16. **RF** *Motor Skills Continue to Develop*, Activity B, SAG. Have students match each gross- and fine-motor skill with the approximate age in which it occurs. Students also should identify the refined and new gross- and fine-motor skills of the toddler years.
17. **ER** *Motor Skills of a Toddler on the Go*, Activity C, SAG. Students should observe and record a toddler's gross- and fine-motor skills.
18. **EX** Discuss with students how practicing a skill at the time when the needed physical growth and development are complete compares with the meaning of the term *developmental task* as described in chapter 1.
19. **RF** *Growth and Practice Go Hand-in-Hand*, reproducible master 11-2. Instruct students to write a newspaper article on how the development of motor skills depends on both the child's growth and development and the child's practice. Student articles should include quotes from written resources as well as from pediatricians and caregivers.

## Large-Muscle Development

20. **RT** Students should identify the growth and development principle that explains why skills involving large muscles mature before skills involving small muscles. (People develop from the center to the extremities.)
21. **RT** Based on the principle of developing from center to extremities, have students explain when fine-motor skills could be expected to mature if toddlers are in the gross-motor stage.
22. **EX** Discuss with students why a healthy 14-month-old may not yet be walking.

23. **RF**   Have students look up the word *toddle* in a dictionary. Students should explain why the word *toddler* fits a child in this stage of physical development.

## Small-Muscle Development

24. **RT**   Ask students to observe the fine-motor skills of a younger toddler and an older toddler playing at home or at a child care center. After the observation, have students describe how the toddlers' skills differed and how their observation findings compared with the text information.

25. **EX**   Have students suggest ways the fine-motor skills of toddlers increase the need for making the home and yard safer.

26. **EX**   Have students discuss how society pressures more and more children to settle on the right hand as their preferred hand instead of the left hand.

27. **ER**   Interview a left-handed person. What tasks are more difficult for this person because of equipment and teaching methods? How could society do more to help people who are left-handed?

# Answer Key

## Text

*Reviewing Key Concepts,* page 302

1. heredity; environment
2. true
3. true
4. B
5. false
6. (List two:) some toddlers are frustrated or fearful when they try to walk and fall; children who creep quickly may not walk early because creeping gets them where they need to be; girls often begin walking before boys; lighter babies may walk earlier than heavier babies
7. Toddlers must visually monitor their foot placement to keep from falling. If they are distracted from their monitoring task, they are apt to fall.
8. walking—F; running—B; jumping—A; climbing—D; throwing—E; catching—C
9. false
10. false

## Student Activity Guide

*Growth Slows and Slows,* Activity A

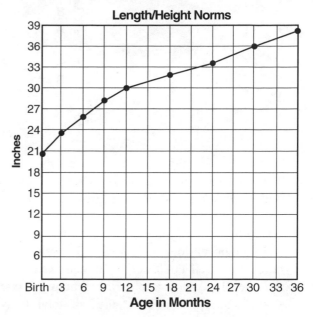

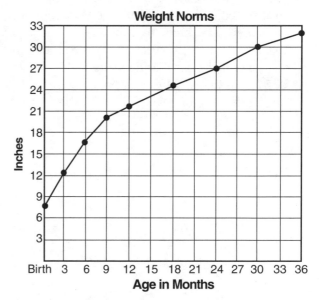

## Motor Skills Continue to Develop, Activity B

Gross-motor skills:

| | | |
|---|---|---|
| 1. RS | 6. NS | 11. A |
| 2. NS | 7. C | 12. B |
| 3. NS | 8. C | 13. D |
| 4. RS | 9. D | |
| 5. RS | 10. B | |

Fine-motor skills:

| | | |
|---|---|---|
| 1. RS | 5. NS | 9. D |
| 2. NS | 6. A | 10. B |
| 3. NS | 7. C | 11. C |
| 4. RS | 8. B | |

## Teacher's Resources

### Chapter 11 Test

| | | |
|---|---|---|
| 1. F | 10. F | 19. B |
| 2. T | 11. F | 20. A |
| 3. F | 12. T | 21. D |
| 4. T | 13. B | 22. C |
| 5. F | 14. C | 23. B |
| 6. T | 15. B | 24. D |
| 7. T | 16. D | 25. A |
| 8. T | 17. C | |
| 9. T | 18. C | |

26. The toddler's growth slows when compared with prenatal and first-year growth. Toddlers tend to grow two to three inches and gain about six pounds per year after the second year throughout childhood. Most girls reach 53 percent of their adult height by age two years. Boys reach 50 percent of their height by age two years. The head is one-fourth of total body length. The chest and abdomen of a two-year-old are about the same size. The bones continue to harden. The brain becomes more and more mature. Other body systems mature at a slower rate than the brain. Fat deposits under the skin decrease rapidly. Muscle development is slow during the toddler years.

27. Toddlers refine their walking (or almost walking), climbing, and throwing skills that emerged in the first year. Many new motor skills are also emerging, such as running, jumping off objects, and catching objects. Fine-motor skills are emerging from the thumb and forefingers grasping skill of the first year, such as holding spoons and drawing tools, turning doorknobs and book pages, stringing beads, stacking two or three blocks, and hitting pegs with a plastic hammer.

28. Children must be able to use the hands and eyes together in order to perform fine-motor skills, such as grasping and manipulating objects.

# Growth for Toddlers

## Length/Height

### First Year

Birth...................... [ ]

Add 9 inches
based on norms..... [ ]

Total length......... [ ]

### Second Year

12 months............ [ ]

Add half the
growth from
first year................ [ ]

Total height......... [ ]

Total height
increase from
birth to end of
second year........... [ ]

## Weight

### First Year

Birth..................... [ ]

Triple birth
weight...................... [ ]

Total .................... [ ]

### Second Year

12 months............ [ ]

Add ¼ of total
weight at
12 months.............. [ ]

Total.................... [ ]

Total weight
increase from
birth to end of
second year........... [ ]

# Growth and Practice Go Hand-in-Hand

**Name** _____ **Date** _____ **Period** _____

In the space below, write a newspaper article on how the development of motor skills depends on the child's physical growth and development and on the child's practice. (Use your own paper if you run out of space.) Before you begin writing, consider the questions below. Research the topic using books, magazines, pamphlets, or Internet resources. Also, interview people with knowledge on the subject, such as pediatricians, professional caregivers, and parents. (Be sure to list all your resources at the end of your article.)

## Questions to Consider

If the child is not mature in his or her development:

1. How can practice be frustrating and unsafe for a child who does not have adequate physical growth and development for learning a motor skill? How could premature practice later affect the desire to learn a skill when growth and development are adequate? What should an adult do if a child is not ready to learn a skill?

If the child is mature in his or her development:

2. What happens when a child has the needed growth and development to learn a skill but does not practice? Should an adult encourage practice? If so, in what way(s) can an adult encourage practice?

_____

_____

_____

_____

_____

_____

_____

_____

_____

_____

_____

_____

_____

_____

_____

_____

_____

_____

_____

_____

# Physical Development of the Toddler

**Name** _____ .

**Date** _____ **Period** _____ **Score** _____

## Chapter 11 Test

True/False: Circle *T* if the statement is true or *F* if the statement is false.

T    F    1. Growth rate increases in the toddler stage.

T    F    2. The fontanels are closed, or almost closed, by the toddler years.

T    F    3. The degree of ossification of the bones is the same throughout the body.

T    F    4. The toddler's brain is closer to maturity than other body organs.

T    F    5. Fat deposits under the skin increase during the toddler years.

T    F    6. Pushing a baby to walk early will not help, and it may even delay walking.

T    F    7. The 18-month-old toddler assumes an adult walking posture.

T    F    8. Usually toddlers show almost no weight shift in throwing.

T    F    9. Toddlers often close their eyes when playing catch.

T    F    10. Fine-motor skills are skills, such as running and jumping, that are mastered to an advanced degree.

T    F    11. After two years, many toddlers can hold crayons or pencils with the thumb on one side and fingers on another.

T    F    12. Most children begin to show hand preference by two years of age.

Multiple Choice: Choose the best response. Write the letter in the space provided.

_____ 13. A person's weight is mainly influenced by _____.
A. genes
B. environment
C. emotions
D. None of the above.

_____ 14. A toddler's height tends to _____ in the second year as compared to height changes in the first year.
A. stay pretty much the same
B. increase at the same rate
C. increase half as much
D. increase twice as much

_____ 15. Which of the following statements is the most accurate concerning the second year weight gain?
A. Toddlers add about one-fifth of their first year's gain.
B. Toddlers add about one-fourth of their first year's gain.
C. Toddlers add about one-half of their first year's gain.
D. Toddlers double their first year's gain.

_____ 16. First steps in walking can be described as _____.
A. uneven
B. weaving
C. taken in any direction, such as forward, backward, and sideways
D. All of the above.

*(Continued)*

**Name** _____

_____ 17. When running, toddlers hold their arms _____.
A. stiffly at their sides
B. swinging alternately with foot movement
C. up or out to the sides
D. above their heads

_____ 18. The most difficult climbing for toddlers is going _____.
A. up stairs with alternating feet
B. up stairs without alternating feet
C. down stairs with alternating feet
D. down stairs without alternating feet

_____ 19. When the toddler is two or three years old, catching an object is done by _____.
A. trapping it between outstretched legs while sitting
B. extending arms with rigid elbows
C. grasping between the hands
D. None of the above.

_____ 20. Pencils or crayons are first held _____.
A. in the fist
B. between the index and middle fingers
C. between the index finger and thumb
D. in no certain way

_____ 21. Which of the following tasks is most difficult for most toddlers to master?
A. Turning a doorknob.
B. Removing shoes.
C. Hitting pegs with a hammer.
D. Holding a crayon the way adults do.

Matching: Match the following terms and identifying phrases.

_____ 22. Lengthening and thickening of muscles.

_____ 23. Development of the muscles of the trunk, arms, and legs.

_____ 24. Development of the muscles of the hands and fingers.

_____ 25. The ability to coordinate what is seen with movements of the hands.

A. eye-hand coordination

B. large-muscle development

C. muscle development

D. small-muscle development

Essay Questions: Provide complete responses to the following questions or statements.

26. What descriptive words or phrases best describe a toddler's physical development?

27. Briefly describe motor developments that occur in the toddler years.

28. Explain why hand-eye coordination is needed for the development of fine-motor skills.

# Intellectual Development of the Toddler
## 12

## Objectives

After studying this chapter, students will be able to
- describe how and what toddlers learn.
- describe the sequence of language development.

## Bulletin Boards

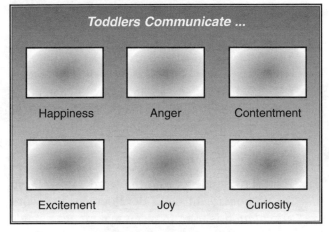

**Toddlers Communicate ...**

| | | |
|---|---|---|
| Happiness | Anger | Contentment |
| Excitement | Joy | Curiosity |

### Title: *Toddlers Communicate*

Have students brainstorm ways toddlers communicate. These might include crying, smiling, pointing, and using words and sentences. Place examples of common first words on the bulletin board. Have students find pictures of young children communicating through their facial expressions. Under each picture write emotions the children could be communicating, such as anger, unhappiness, happiness, curiosity, excitement, contentment, joy.

### Title: *Learning Language: From Concrete to Abstract*

On the board, display one object from the concrete example to examples that become more and more abstract. For instance, the display could begin with a real ball for the concrete object. (This could be displayed in a clear bag attached to the board.) Successive examples could be a photograph of the ball; a clay model of the ball; a sewn, stuffed ball; a drawing of the ball; and the word ball written on a card.

## Teaching Materials

**Text**, pages 304-317
*Reviewing Key Concepts*
*Using Your Knowledge*
*Making Observations*
*Thinking Further*

**Student Activity Guide**
    A. *Toddlers Are Scientists*
    B. *Toddlers Learn by Throwing Objects*
    C. *Toys Are Tools for Thinking*
    D. *Toddlers Begin to Think*

**Teacher's Resources**
*Toys Help Toddlers*, color transparency CT-12A
*Observation: Thinking and Toddlers*, reproducible master 12-1
*Language Sequence*, color transparency CT-12B
*Common Vocabulary Problems*, reproducible master 12-2
Chapter 12 Test

## Introductory Activities

1. Ask students why they think toddlers get into mischief by exploring household objects, such as wastebaskets and dresser drawers. Are children naturally destructive, or do they have other reasons for exploring?
2. Discuss with students the meaning of baby talk. Ask students how to respond to toddlers who use the wrong words or use incorrect words, such as *wa-wa* for water.

## Strategies to Reteach, Reinforce, Enrich, and Extend Text Concepts

### How and What Toddlers Learn

3. **EX** Ask students to describe the characteristics of adults who are eager learners.
4. **RF** *Toddlers Are Scientists*, Activity A, SAG. Students should list traits of scientists and observe and record similar traits in toddlers.

5. **RF** *Toddlers Learn by Throwing Objects*, Activity B, SAG. Have students list all the learnings toddlers may acquire from throwing objects.

6. **RT** Ask students to explain how the maturation of sensory organs and motor skills aids toddlers' learnings.

## Discovering New Ways to Solve Problems

7. **RT** *Toys Help Toddlers*, color transparency CT-12A. Use this transparency to show various ways toys help toddlers learn. Students should give examples of types of toys that might fit each area.

8. **RF** *Toys Are Tools for Thinking*, Activity C, SAG. Instruct students to consider some of the learnings that toddlers may acquire from common toys.

## Beginning of Thought

9. **ER** Have students observe a toddler who is 18 to 24 months old and identify deferred actions in the toddler's play. Students should share examples in class.

10. **EX** Ask students how deferred imitation relates to the concern about influences of negative models on young children, including those seen on TV and other media. Explain that Albert Bandura, a noted child development theorist, explained the impact of modeling in this way: Seeing negative models does not guarantee a given child will imitate. Seeing models does mean the child has the "know-how" for imitation. In Bandura's research, children imitated aggressive models more frequently than non-aggressive ones.

11. **ER** *Observation: Thinking and Toddlers*, reproducible master 12-1. Have students observe a toddler who is 15 to 24 months old and answer the questions about their observations.

12. **RF** Ask students to choose an object and write a description of the object. After the description is written, ask them to underline words that are attributes. Note the importance of using attributes in identifying objects. Ask what parts of speech attributions usually are (adjectives and adverbs).

13. **ER** *Toddlers Begin to Think*, Activity D, SAG. Have students interview a caregiver who works with children between ages 15 and 24 months and ask about the kinds of thinking skills toddlers display.

14. **RT** Discuss with students the reason(s) toddlers are interested in solving practical problems in their world, such as feeding and dressing themselves and opening doors. Ask students to explain why a toddler might be more interested in opening and closing a door than in playing with an expensive toy.

## Language Abilities

15. **RF** Students should list all the reasons that language skills are important to humans.

16. **RT** *Language Sequence*, color transparency CT-12B. Use this transparency to outline the general sequence of language development. Have students give examples of words toddlers often use as nouns, action verbs, and descriptive words. Students may also give examples of toddlers' typical one-, two-, and multiple-word sentences.

17. **ER** Invite students to interview a parent or caregiver about some of the babbled sounds or first words they have heard toddlers use.

## Learning Spoken Language

18. **RF** Have students find the word *articulate* in the dictionary. In child development the word *articulation* is used to mean making the sounds of words. Ask students how the dictionary definition says these sounds are to be made. Point out how the definition is carried further when people speak of an "articulate person."

19. **RF** Have students add to the chart "Our Brains Are Wired" that was begun in chapter 6. (See teaching strategies in chapter 6 of this *Teacher's Resource* product for description.) Students should list *Toddler* as the stage and list descriptions of what is wired in this first year of life. If needed, have students conduct Internet to help them complete the chart. (This chart can be continued in upcoming chapters.)

20. **EX** Ask students why it is logical for spoken language abilities to be wired in the toddler years than at an earlier stage. (Toddlers have learned so much they have lots of reasons to talk.)

21. **RT** *Common Vocabulary Problems*, reproducible master 12-2. Have students read the list of common vocabulary problems of young children and identify the problem in each of the situations given at the bottom.

22. **ER** Instruct students to record the speech of toddlers at play with other toddlers. Listen to the tape and answer these questions: What sound substitutes do you hear? Do you hear single

words, two-word sentences, and longer sentences? Give some examples. What incorrect grammar do you hear? What concepts seem to be correctly understood by the children? What, if any, wrong meanings of words do the toddlers express?

## Different Rates of Learning to Talk

23. **RT** Have students explain why talking at a very late age could be a handicap to a toddler intellectually and socially.

24. **EX** Instruct students to role-play a response to a friend who is concerned that her almost three-year-old toddler still is not talking. The friend wants to know why some toddlers may not talk and how parents can encourage them.

# Answer Key

## Text

### Reviewing Key Concepts, page 316

1. E
2. true
3. C
4. true
5. (Give two. Student response. See pages 310 to 315 in the text.)
6. Articulation means to make the sounds of language.
7. common
8. false
9. A—daddy; B—bye-bye; C—kitty
10. (Describe three:) hearing loss, greater interest in motor skills than in learning to talk, mental disabilities, getting what one wants or needs without speech, living in an environment that is not interesting, having little or no freedom to explore one's environment, being a boy

## Teacher's Resources

### Common Vocabulary Problems, reproducible master 12-2

1. D
2. A
3. C
4. E
5. B
6. C
7. A
8. E
9. D
10. B

## Chapter 12 Test

| | | |
|---|---|---|
| 1. T | 13. F | 25. C |
| 2. F | 14. F | 26. B |
| 3. F | 15. T | 27. C |
| 4. F | 16. T | 28. D |
| 5. T | 17. F | 29. D |
| 6. T | 18. F | 30. B |
| 7. T | 19. T | 31. F |
| 8. F | 20. F | 32. G |
| 9. T | 21. D | 33. A |
| 10. T | 22. C | 34. C |
| 11. T | 23. D | 35. E |
| 12. T | 24. D | |

36. Toddlers show their thinking skill of recall through deferred imitation. They think of ways to reach their own goals. Thinking is also evident in hiding games in which toddlers think where adults have hidden objects, show object permanence, and use spatial concepts as they look for objects. In exploring new objects, toddlers use their knowledge of the attributes of similar objects. Toddlers show thinking skills as they associate words with the people or objects to which they refer. They can recall these words as noted in their passive and active vocabularies.

37. Toddlers communicate to achieve a goal, identify an object, and create a bond with another person. (Examples are student response.)

38. Although toddlers often have some articulation problems, they make major steps in learning to pronounce many words and even their inaccurate articulation can often be understood by others. Toddlers learn to associate words and meanings although they experience errors as they use words. Vocabulary growth is the fastest around 30 months. First words are usually nouns and simple action verbs. Next words learned are descriptive words. About six months after talking begins, grammar begins with one-word sentences. As the vocabulary increases, one-word sentences are gradually replaced with two-word and multiple-word sentences.

39. (Name four:) hearing, interest, mental abilities, gender, need for speech, and interesting environment

40. If a significant delay is present, parents should seek professional help for their child.

# Observation: Thinking and Toddlers

**Name** _____ **Date** _____ **Period** _____

According to Piaget, toddlers begin to think—with their minds rather than with their actions—between their first and second birthdays. Spend 30 minutes to 1 hour observing a 15- to 24-month-old toddler in a home or child care environment. After your observation, answer the following questions, using complete sentences.

Toddler's name and age: _____

1. What, if any, goal did you observe the toddler trying to achieve (for example, get a toy off a high shelf, remove shoes, work a puzzle)? _____

   _____

   _____

   _____

   What actions, if any, did the toddler take to achieve this goal (for example, climbing or stacking objects)?

   _____

   _____

   _____

2. Give an example you observed of the toddler figuring out how to make something work._____

   _____

   _____

   _____

3. Does the toddler search for a hidden object (for example, in games in which the adult hides an object, in cases where the toddler misplaces a toy)? If so, describe. _____

   _____

   _____

   _____

4. Does the toddler imitate (for example, rock a doll like a baby, repeat sounds)? If so, describe some of the imitations. _____

   _____

   _____

   _____

   _____

*(Continued)*

5. What are some of the words the toddler said? _____

_____

_____

_____

   Did the toddler use all these words correctly? If not, give some examples._____

_____

_____

_____

6. Did the toddler respond to any words used by others? If so, describe. _____

_____

_____

_____

# Common Vocabulary Problems

**Name** _____ **Date** _____ **Period** _____

Learning language is a difficult task. Toddlers make many mistakes as they learn to speak. For each situation given below, write the letter of the problem it illustrates. (Each letter may be used more than once.)

## Problems

A. **Overextending:** Referring to different objects with the same or similar features by the same name.

B. **Overrestricting:** Using a general term to mean a specific person or object.

C. **Word substitution:** Using a known word in the wrong way because the child cannot say or recall the correct word.

D. **Sound substitution:** Using one sound for another, such as *t* for *k* or *w* for *r*. May say, *tite* instead of *kite*.

E. **Holophrase:** A single word used to mean different ideas at different times. The word *bye* may mean an animal came but is now gone, or it may mean, "I want to go."

## Situations

_____ 1. Jody says, "See my *wed* box."

_____ 2. Chris calls all tall, four-legged animals *cows*.

_____ 3. Carrie hands her father a spoon and says, "Take my plate."

_____ 4. Shelly points to a sore on her arm and says, "Boo-boo." When her mother bumps her head on the door, Shelly runs to her father and says, "Boo-boo."

_____ 5. As Sarah points to roses in her neighbor's flower bed she asks her mother, "What zat?" Her mother replies, "Those are roses." Sarah shakes her head, and says, "No, No! Roses at *my* house."

_____ 6. Malia is almost three years old. She loves going to children's concerts with her mother. Malia and her mother have stage-level seats to make it easier for Malia to see her father, the concert master. She turns and points to the balconies filled with people and says, "I want to sit in the basket."

_____ 7. Josh's grandmother gave him a quarter. He proudly shows his "penny" to everyone.

_____ 8. When Alicia hears someone unlock the door, she looks up and asks, "Daddy?" Later as her father leaves, she stands by the door and cries, "Daddy."

_____ 9. As his mother tucks him into bed, Carlos says he wants his *pidda* (pillow).

_____ 10. Susan loves her new puppy, Governor. She follows Governor around the house, calling him *doggie*.

# Intellectual Development of the Toddler

Name _____

Date _____ Period _____ Score _____

## Chapter 12 Test

True/False: Circle *T* if the statement is true or *F* if the statement is false.

T    F    1. Toddlers have a sense of curiosity about their world.

T    F    2. Toddlers use an object in the same way each time.

T    F    3. When toddlers repeatedly throw toys from their high chairs, their main goal is to see whether their parents will keep picking up the toys.

T    F    4. Toddlers work toward goals set by their parents or other adult caregivers.

T    F    5. Toddlers like to solve their own problems of self-feeding and dressing themselves.

T    F    6. Between 18 and 24 months, a toddler's thinking is linked mainly to his or her actions.

T    F    7. Hiding games require thinking ability because toddlers must know an object still exists, think about where the adult might have hidden it, and use spatial concepts to find it.

T    F    8. Noting the difference between dogs and cats is a simple visual skill.

T    F    9. If a toddler has played with a ball, he or she will likely know that an orange will roll.

T    F    10. If words did not have meanings, language would *not* exist.

T    F    11. To understand the meaning of a word, the child must see the association between the word and the object.

T    F    12. Memory is important in language learning.

T    F    13. If a child can articulate a sound in one position of a word, he or she can articulate the sound in other positions of a word.

T    F    14. For the most part, toddlers who use sound substitutions have a serious speech problem and need immediate help.

T    F    15. Brain wiring for language is very active in the toddler years.

T    F    16. Many words go with a toddler's actions.

T    F    17. The fastest vocabulary growth occurs between one and two years.

T    F    18. Toddlers' first words are generally descriptive words, such as *big, little*, and *pretty*.

T    F    19. Toddlers figure out some of the rules of grammar.

T    F    20. Instead of using words for affection, toddlers just hug and kiss others.

Multiple Choice: Choose the best response. Write the letter in the space provided.

_____ 21. Between ages one and two years, most toddlers _____.
  A. discover new ways to solve problems
  B. use deferred imitation
  C. note differences in the attributes of objects
  D. All of the above.

*(Continued)*

**Name** _____

_____ 22. Deferred imitation is an important thinking skill because it means the toddler will _____.
A. accept the values of positive models
B. reject the aggression or violent acts of negative models
C. recall the actions of a model and repeat the actions at a later time
D. ignore what is seen on television, movies, and computer games

_____ 23. As toddlers play, they learn _____.
A. about shapes, colors, sizes, textures
B. what happens when objects are manipulated
C. Neither of the above.
D. Both A and B.

_____ 24. Language requires which of the following skills?
A. Must associate the word with the person or object to which it refers.
B. Must recall the word and its meaning when they hear the word or want to say it.
C. Neither of the above.
D. Both A and B.

_____ 25. As toddlers learn to articulate sounds, they do all of the following *except* _____.
A. substitute one sound for another
B. change the sound order of a word
C. use the correct words and sounds all the time
D. drop a sound

_____ 26. All of the following are important for vocabulary growth *except* _____.
A. hearing the correct articulation of words
B. being forced to repeat the word until it is said correctly
C. having a given word repeated many times
D. understanding the meaning of the word

_____ 27. Language serves as a tool for _____.
A. communication
B. thinking
C. communication and thinking
D. None of the above.

_____ 28. The first words of toddlers are often _____.
A. animal sounds
B. possessive words (*me* or *my*)
C. descriptive words
D. nouns

*(Continued)*

**Name** _____

Matching: Match the following terms and identifying phrases.

_____29. The ability to recall someone's behavior and later reproduce (mimic) it.

_____30. Distinctive characteristics of objects, such as color, size, shape, and texture.

_____31. A symbol system in which words are imitation used as labels for people, objects, and ideas.

_____32. High-pitched style in which parents commonly speak to very young children.

_____33. Making the sounds of a language.

_____34. The skill needed to understand others and to be understood by them.

_____35. The preferred word usage and order of a language.

A. articulation

B. attributes

C. communication

D. deferred imitation

E. grammar

F. language

G. parentese

Essay Questions: Provide complete responses to the following questions or statements.

36. Explain some of the ways experts can tell that 18- to 24-month-olds are thinking.

37. List the three purposes of toddler's communication and give an example of each.

38. Briefly describe the milestones in the toddlers' language learnings.

39. Name four factors that might affect the rate of language development.

40. What should parents do if a toddler lags far behind others in the rate of language development?

# Social-Emotional Development of the Toddler

## Objectives

After studying this chapter, students will be able to
- describe how toddlers develop self-will.
- explain the way toddlers extend their social relationships with others.
- describe how toddlers develop a sense of self-worth.
- identify how toddlers reveal their emotions.

## Bulletin Boards

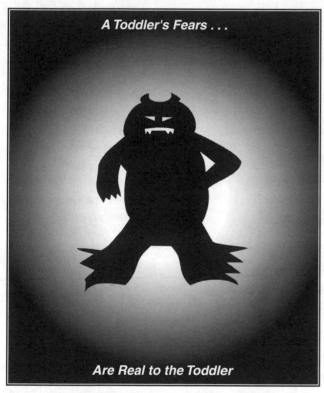

A Toddler's Fears . . .

Are Real to the Toddler

### Title: A Toddler's Fears Are Real to the Toddler

Have students draw a silhouette of a monster (or enlarge one of the silhouettes in Figure 13-12 of the text) to place in the center of the board. Students should write descriptions of toddlers' typical fears around the silhouette.

### Title: Typical Toddler Thinking

Place a large circle in the middle of the bulletin board. In the center of the circle, place a small circle with the words "I am special!" written on it. Place a picture of a two- or three-year-old child near it. With lines radiating out from the circle, place phrases that are typical of the way a toddler thinks and feels, such as the following:

> "I want to do it myself."
> "Sometimes I am dependent."
> "I like to explore new places."
> "It bothers me when others hurt."
> "I like to give hugs and kisses to special people."
> "I don't like monsters. They scare me."
> "When are you coming back?"
> "If I don't get my way, I may throw a temper tantrum."

## Teaching Materials

**Text**, pages 318-331
>*Reviewing Key Concepts*
>*Using Your Knowledge*
>*Making Observations*
>*Thinking Further*

**Student Activity Guide**
> A. *Toddlers View Themselves Through Adults*
> B. *Toddlers Are Being Socialized*
> C. *Helping Toddlers Gain Self-Esteem*
> D. *Observation: Toddlers and Separation Anxiety*
> E. *Temper Tantrums and Toddlers*

**Teacher's Resources**
>*Toddlers Are Dependent and Independent*, reproducible master 13-1
>*Toddlers' Social Worlds Expand*, reproducible master 13-2
> Chapter 13 Test

## Introductory Activities

1. *Toddlers Are Dependent and Independent*, reproducible master 13-1. Students are asked to interview the parent of a toddler and record examples of the toddler's dependence and independence. Have students discuss findings in class.

2. Ask students to describe events that make them feel important. Students should contrast this with events that might make a toddler feel important.

3. Students should identify the types of emotions observed in toddlers. Discuss with students whether toddlers express their emotions differently than any other age group.

# Strategies to Reteach, Reinforce, Enrich, and Extend Text Concepts

## Self-Awareness

4. **EX**  Ask students to give example that explain how adults' motor and language skills influence their social relations. Students should compare the adult situation to the toddler's situation.

5. **RF**  *Toddlers View Themselves Through Adults*, Activity A, SAG. Have students give some examples of how toddlers may react to both positive and negative responses of adults.

## Achieving Autonomy

6. **RT**  Students should find the word *autonomy* in a dictionary. Have students contrast the dictionary definition of autonomy with the definition of autonomy derived from Erikson's theory in chart 13-2 in the text.

7. **RT**  Discuss with students Erikson's statement that the successful achievement of the previous stage helps a child master the present stage. Students should explain how the feeling of trust would help a toddler develop a feeling of autonomy.

8. **RF**  Have students list some specific ways adults may help toddlers gain a feeling of autonomy. How can adults help toddlers feel autonomous and still say no when they must?

9. **RF**  Instruct students to write a paper speculating on the possible personality traits of an older child or adult who developed a feeling of shame and doubt (rather than autonomy) and never overcame the feeling.

10. **EX**  Ask students: What do you think are the long-term consequences of overprotecting a child? What do you think are the long-term consequences for a child whose parents do not set limits? Explain that Erikson felt achieving autonomy and avoiding shame and doubt as a young child would set the stage for the healthy development of independence in the teen years.

## Extending Social Relations

11. **RF**  *Toddlers Are Being Socialized*, Activity B, SAG. Students should match the categories of the socialization process with the examples.

12. **ER**  Invite students to interview an older child about caring for and having fun with his or her sibling who is a toddler. Students should write a newspaper or magazine-style article based on their findings.

13. **ER**  Instruct students to develop a videotape presentation featuring an older child caring for and having fun with a sibling who is a toddler.

14. **RF**  Discuss with students how an adult's loving feelings for a toddler often lead to a toddler's empathetic feelings for others.

15. **ER**  *Toddlers' Social Worlds Expand*, reproducible master 13-2. Invite students to interview the parent of a toddler about the important people in the toddler's expanding social world. Students should present their findings to the class. You may ask students to develop visual aids for their presentation.

16. **ER**  Panel discussion: Invite three adults in your community—one elderly, one middle-aged, and one recent high school or college graduate—to speak to the class. Ask panelists to address how they were raised concerning clothes, chores, obedience, schooling, dating, spending money, and similar issues. Students should note changes in the way the three generations were reared and explain how time affects socialization of children. (Resource persons from other countries may also share child rearing practices in their cultures. Students may then note how cultures may be alike in some ways and different in others.)

17. **RF**  Ask students to list ideas toddlers may develop about themselves, such as the size concept "I am big!"

18. **RT**  Instruct students to contrast the traits of adults who have high amounts of self-esteem to adults who lack self-esteem. Can these variances be observed in toddlers?

19. **EX**  *Helping Toddlers Gain Self-Esteem*, Activity C, SAG. Ask a group of students to plan and perform a skit in which a toddler makes a mistake and an adult causes the toddler to lose self-esteem. Using the same toddler's mistake as the basis, have a second group of students perform a skit where the adult causes the toddler to gain self-esteem. Have students use the activity sheet in their planning process.

## Emotions

20. **RF**   Students should make a poster that depicts emotional changes in the toddler years.
21. **RT**   Discuss with students possible reasons that toddlers do not "talk out" their fears and anxieties.

## Affection

22. **RT**   Discuss with students why children who have had loving adult care are usually less aggressive than children who have not had loving care from adults.
23. **ER**   Have students ask toddlers in a children's program to name those they love. Students should note how toddlers' affectionate feelings extend to many people and objects. Have students discuss their findings in class.

## Fear

24. **EX**   Ask students to explain why it may be unwise to stop or discourage a toddler who is pretending to be a monster.
25. **EX**   Ask students what may happen when toddlers are teased about their fears.

## Anxiety

26. **ER**   *Observation: Toddlers and Separation Anxiety*, Activity D, SAG. Have students observe and record displays of separation anxiety and "reunions" following separations.
27. **EX**   Ask students to suggest how adults may decrease separation anxiety.
28. **RT**   Ask students to share their thoughts about the following situation: Dave is the father of two-year-old Randy. Randy has cried every day for two weeks when Dave leaves the child care center. Dave decides to stay for a half hour and then sneak out. What effects might this have on Randy, and why?

## Anger

29. **RT**   Discuss with students why toddlers use tantrums rather than other means, such as talking, to get adults' attention.
30. **EX**   Discuss with students reasons some refer to the toddler stage of development as the "terrible twos." Students should develop a more accurate term or phrase and justify it.

31. **EX**   *Temper Tantrums and Toddlers*, Activity E, SAG. Have students compare causes and expressions of anger in toddlers and high school students.

# Answer Key

## Text

*Reviewing Key Concepts,* page 330

1. false
2. true
3. true
4. A. Autonomy often happens during routines.
   B. Autonomy often involves trying to work beyond the ability level.
5. (List three. See Figure 13-4 in the text.)
6. false
7. C
8. does
9. physical
10. Toddlers react to a wider range of stimuli. They can better read emotions in others. They have a wider range of responses to feelings. Their abilities to think, and thus imagine, increase the number of emotions that are difficult to handle.
11. (List three:) imagined creatures, animals, darkness, nightmares, bad people, injury, gestures or noises made to frighten toddlers
12. Adults should stay calm and not give too much attention to the tantrum. After the tantrum, adults should be loving and reassuring to the toddler.

## Student Activity Guide

*Toddlers Are Being Socialized,* Activity B

1. E and/or B
2. C
3. C and/or F
4. C
5. D
6. A and/or C
7. B
8. E and/or C
9. C and/or F
10. B

(Students may be able to justify additional categories.)

# Teacher's Resources

## Chapter 13 Test

| | | |
|---|---|---|
| 1. F | 10. T | 19. D |
| 2. T | 11. T | 20. C |
| 3. F | 12. F | 21. B |
| 4. F | 13. T | 22. D |
| 5. T | 14. F | 23. B |
| 6. F | 15. F | 24. B |
| 7. T | 16. F | 25. A |
| 8. F | 17. T | 26. D |
| 9. T | 18. F | 27. C |

28. Infants' needs are mainly physical in nature, such as being fed, being kept warm and clean, and being kept safe. Although toddlers have physical needs that must be met, their needs center on intellectual and social-emotional areas, such as finding out about their worlds of people and objects and discovering their ability to cope in their world.

29. To promote autonomy, caregivers must recognize the toddler's desire to be more independent and do what he or she is capable of doing at his or her own pace. On the other hand, when caregivers are impatient (overly critical) or do for toddlers what they can do for themselves (overprotective), shame and doubt develops.

30. Toddlers want to be independent, yet they depend on adults in many ways. Conflicts between the adult and toddler often occur because of toddlers' desires to be independent in ways beyond their abilities or at times when independence is not convenient. The toddler stage is difficult because self-esteem is beginning to develop and is most fragile. Toddlers' expressions of emotions are difficult to handle. Toddlers also express anger in a very physical way—the temper tantrum.

# Toddlers Are Dependent and Independent

**Name** _____ **Date** _____ **Period** _____

Sometimes toddlers demand help from adults, but at other times they wave a banner of independence. Interview the parent of a two- or three-year-old toddler. Ask the parent to share examples of the toddler's dependence and independence. Record the examples in the space below.

Age and gender of child: _____

| Examples of Dependence | Examples of Independence |
|---|---|
|  |  |

# Toddlers' Social Worlds Expand

**Name** _____ **Date** _____ **Period** _____

Toddlers love people—both adults and children—who adore them. Playing, talking, and just snuggling with others are the ways toddlers socialize. Interview a parent or caregiver of a toddler about people important in the toddler's social world. Then record the responses in the space below. Plan an oral presentation based on your findings and present it to the class.

1. Age and gender of toddler: _____

   Person interviewed (mother, father, caregiver): _____

2. Describe some of the specific activities the toddler does with other adults in the family, such as the other parent or adult relatives who live in the home or visit frequently.

| Relationship | Activities |
|---|---|
| Relationship | Activities |
| Relationship | Activities |

3. Describe some of the specific activities the toddler does with other children in the family.

| Relationship and age | Activities |
|---|---|
| Relationship and age | Activities |
| Relationship and age | Activities |

*(Continued)*

4. Describe some of the specific activities the toddler does with adults outside the family, such as relatives who visit less often than daily, friends, caregivers, or babysitters.

| Relationship | Activities |
|---|---|
| Relationship | Activities |
| Relationship | Activities |
| Relationship | Activities |

5. Describe some of the specific activities the toddler does with other children outside the family.

| Relationship and age | Activities |
|---|---|
| Relationship and age | Activities |
| Relationship and age | Activities |
| Relationship and age | Activities |

# Social-Emotional Development of the Toddler

**Name** _____

**Date** _____ **Period** _____ **Score** _____

## Chapter 13 Test

True/False: Circle *T* if the statement is true or *F* if the statement is false.

T    F    1.  Toddlers find out the world is solely devoted to meeting their needs as they see them.

T    F    2.  Trust is the needed foundation for the toddler's social-emotional development.

T    F    3.  Self-awareness is focused in feelings of dependence.

T    F    4.  Toddlers are unaware of others' feelings toward them.

T    F    5.  Autonomous toddlers want to do tasks by themselves.

T    F    6.  Toddlers often ask for help when they don't know how to do a task.

T    F    7.  Conflicts of adults and toddlers will occur mainly during daily routines.

T    F    8.  According to Erikson, toddlers develop doubt and shame unless they are allowed to have their way at all times.

T    F    9.  Autonomy is a form of self-control in which toddlers seek to develop a will of their own.

T    F   10.  Socialization begins with the main caregivers.

T    F   11.  Experiences with several adults help toddlers to expect differences in people.

T    F   12.  Toddlers will share their toys with others most of the time.

T    F   13.  Becoming aware of his or her body influences a toddler's self-esteem.

T    F   14.  Toddlers respond to fewer stimuli; thus, they fear fewer things than infants.

T    F   15.  Toddlers do not sense emotions in others.

T    F   16.  Toddlers never experience separation anxiety.

T    F   17.  Toddlers respond to emotions both physically and verbally.

T    F   18.  Having temper tantrums is often a sign of developmental problems in a toddler.

Multiple Choice: Choose the best response. Write the letter in the space provided.

_____ 19. Toddlers' self-awareness includes _____.
        A.  how they look
        B.  what belongs to them and doesn't belong to them
        C.  what they can and cannot do, especially physically
        D.  All of the above.

_____ 20. Erikson's second stage of social-emotional development is called _____.
        A.  trust versus mistrust
        B.  initiative versus guilt
        C.  autonomy versus shame and doubt
        D.  dependence versus independence

*(Continued)*

**Name** _____

_____ 21. Erikson would recommend that toddlers _____.
   A. be punished for negative behaviors
   B. be encouraged to do what they are capable of doing at their own pace
   C. not have limits placed on their actions so they can learn from mistakes
   D. be protected from taking any risks

_____ 22. Toddlers' social world should be centered on _____.
   A. parents only
   B. parents and other adults only
   C. other children only
   D. None of the above.

_____ 23. Feeling good about yourself and what you can do is called _____.
   A. self-awareness
   B. self-esteem
   C. self-image
   D. self-doubt

_____ 24. Changes in emotions from infancy to the toddler years include _____.
   A. reacting to a smaller range of stimuli
   B. "reading" emotions in others
   C. having a smaller range of responses to feelings
   D. All of the above.

_____ 25. Toddlers' nightmares stem from _____.
   A. anxieties
   B. poor relations with other children their own age
   C. childhood mental health problems
   D. memories of bad experiences

_____ 26. Temper tantrums _____.
   A. occur when events do not go according to a toddler's plan
   B. are done to get attention
   C. are not directed at anyone
   D. All of the above.

_____ 27. Which of the following should be an adult's main concern during a temper tantrum?
   A. Worrying whether the child will embarrass them in public.
   B. Getting the tantrum to stop.
   C. Keeping everyone safe.
   D. Making the child happy.

Essay Questions: Provide complete responses to the following questions or statements.

28. How do a child's needs change as the child moves from infancy to the toddler stage?

29. How do caregivers promote a toddler's desire for autonomy and prevent shame and doubt?

30. Why is the toddler stage difficult for the adult caregiver?

## Objectives

After studying this chapter, students will be able to
- plan ways to meet toddlers' physical needs.
- stimulate toddlers' growing mental abilities.
- help toddlers adjust to their first social controls.

## Bulletin Boards

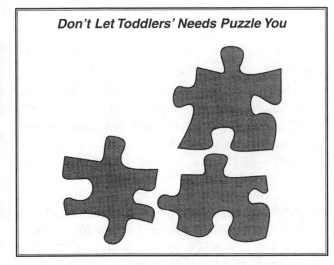

**Don't Let Toddlers' Needs Puzzle You**

Title: *Don't Let Toddlers' Needs Puzzle You*

Cut three large, interlocking puzzle pieces from poster board. Students should cover these with magazine pictures depicting toddlers' needs. Each piece may contain needs in one area—physical, intellectual, and social-emotional—or needs may be mixed on the pieces. Place puzzle pieces on the bulletin board almost ready to slip together but with a little space between them.

Title: *How to Encourage Learning*

Ask students to brainstorm ways to help toddlers learn. Have them write phrases on large pieces of paper suggesting ways parents and care-givers can encourage young children to learn. Place these suggestions under the title. (An example is *Provide a stimulating setting.*) Students may find pictures from magazines to illustrate a number of the suggestions.

## Teaching Materials

**Text**, pages 332-371
   *Reviewing Key Concepts*
   *Using Your Knowledge*
   *Making Observations*
   *Thinking Further*

**Student Activity Guide**
   A. *Bedtime Rituals*
   B. *Toilet Learning*
   C. *Learning Happens in Everyday Experiences*
   D. *Planned Activities for Sensory Stimulation*
   E. *Planned Activities for Problem Solving*
   F. *Planned Motor Activities*
   G. *Modeling Language for Toddlers*
   H. *Planned Language Activities*
   I. *Transition Stages Are Difficult*
   J. *Planned Activities for Self-Awareness*

**Teacher's Resources**
   *Learnings of Toddlers*, reproducible master 14-1
   *Meal/Snack Pattern for Toddlers*,
        reproducible master 14-2
   *Sensory Stimulation Activities*,
        reproducible master 14-3
   *Problem-Solving Activities*, reproducible
        master 14-4
   *Motor Activities*, reproducible master 14-5
   *Language Activities*, reproducible master 14-6
   *Self-Awareness Activities*, reproducible master 14-7
   Chapter 14 Test
   *Happy Mealtimes*, color transparency CT-14

## Introductory Activities

1. *Learnings of Toddlers*, reproducible master 14-1. Instruct students to unscramble the words describing the learnings of toddlers. Then have them list the circled letters to find the word describing persons who have these characteristics.
2. Panel discussion: Invite three to five fathers who care for and play with their toddlers to speak to the class. Panelists should address the following questions: What care do you provide? How do you play with your toddlers? Do you feel that playing with and caring for toddlers will help your parent-child relationship in the future? (You may have students write other questions for the panelists.)

# Strategies to Reteach, Reinforce, Enrich, and Extend Text Concepts

## Physical Needs

3. **RF** Ask students to give examples of this concept as stated in the text, "Caregivers must meet toddlers' physical needs to keep them healthy and safe. Meeting physical needs also keeps toddlers mentally and socially fit."

4. **RT** Ask students for examples of other ways toddlers may help take care of themselves besides self-feeding, self-cleaning, and toileting.

5. **ER** Instruct students to set up a display illustrating ways to foster independence through self-help devices. Examples of such devices include child-sized eating equipment, potty chairs, and elastic waistbands in pants.

6. **EX** Ask students to locate books written for toddlers about how they can help take care of themselves, such as eating, dressing, sleeping, bathing, and toilet learning. Share the books in class. Ask students these questions: What is the author/illustrator trying to "teach" toddlers? Would they use the books if they were parents? Why or why not?

## Feeding

7. **RF** Discuss with students why it is unwise to insist that a toddler eat everything served. Students should discuss the possible long-term consequences of this practice.

8. **ER** Have students observe a toddler eating. Students should share their observations in class. Discuss with students how the toddler grasped finger food (palm grasp or thumb and index finger grasp). Did the toddler attempt to use a fork or spoon? If so, how well did the toddler manage these tools? What foods did the toddler enjoy? Was the feeding process messy?

9. **RF** Ask students to look at the Food Guide Pyramid for Young Children, Figure 14-3 in the text. Explain how it is read. Ask students why the pyramid shape is a good choice to depict the concept. (Point out how the number of servings in a food group decreases as they read from the base to the point.) Point out the tip is not a food group so servings are not indicated. Ask these questions: How do toddlers get fats and sweets from foods in the food groups? How could a parent or caregiver "follow" the Pyramid and still possibly offer an unhealthy diet to a toddler? (Food preparation techniques, such as deep fat frying, adding salt or sugar, and using sauces high in fat, can have a major impact on an otherwise healthy diet.)

10. **RT** Using the text, have students plan and evaluate a sample day's menu for a toddler. Students might find the following method a simple way to check the menu plus reinforce the number of servings in the food groups: Prepare the following list and darken a "pyramid" each time a food in a given category is listed:

milk △△
meat △△
fruits △△
vegetables △△△
grains △△△△△△

(Use this activity to prepare for the first *Using Your Knowledge* activity on page 370 in the text.)

11. **EX** Give the class a sample day's menu (three meals and two snacks) for a toddler using the Pyramid. Divide the class into four groups assigning each group to breakfast, lunch, dinner, or snacks. Have each group prepare the planned foods, cut or mash as needed, measure, and attractively arrange on toddler or toddler-size dishes (plates should be about 9" diameter).

12. **EX** *Meal/Snack Pattern for Toddlers,* reproducible master 14-2. Point out that, like the Pyramid, this meal/snack pattern was developed by the USDA. Schools and child care programs can apply for government funding to support their food programs. To get this money, they must follow regulations, such as following this pattern in the meals and snacks they provide to children daily. Ask students to compare groupings, serving sizes and number of servings for each group on this meal/snack pattern with the Pyramid's recommendations.

13. **EX** Ask students to measure one serving size of several foods listed on the Pyramid. Each food should be on a separate plate (or bowl) of the same size. Tell students that busy parents and caregivers need to learn to estimate to save time and mess. Looking at each serving, ask students to supply the name of a familiar object as their estimate references. For example, ⅓ cup of cooked cereal is about the size of a (an) _____.

14. **EX** Ask students to compare the recommended serving size for fruits, vegetables, rice, or pasta based on the USDA's Pyramid with that of the ADA (one measuring tablespoon per year of age.)

15. **RT** *Happy Mealtimes*, color transparency CT-14. Use this transparency to lead a discussion on ways parents and caregivers can make mealtimes for toddlers happier and less stressful. Discuss with students other suggestions that may help toddlers with their self-feeding and perhaps avoid some mealtime problems.

16. **ER** Guest speaker: Invite a pediatrician or an allergist to speak to the class on foods, food additives, and preservatives often associated with allergies in toddlers. The speaker should also address foods high in sodium and sugar.

## Clothing

17. **EX** Using Figure 14-6 in the text as a guide, students should evaluate a toddler's garment and share the evaluation in class.

18. **ER** Have students ask a toddler to tell them about his or her clothing. (If the student can interview in a toddler's home, perhaps toddlers can show and describe their favorite garment.) Students should share their findings in class. Listing the features and keeping a tally might prove interesting.

19. **RT** Instruct students to observe a toddler dressing in dramatic play clothes. Students should answer the following questions: What dressing tasks did the toddler find easy? Which tasks were more difficult? Did the toddler ask for help? Did the toddler resist help when offered?

## Rest and Sleep

20. **RF** Have students find the term *nightmare* in a dictionary. Ask students to explain the origin of the word *mare*.

21. **EX** Discuss with students why it is important to return toddlers to their bed when they awaken during the night. Ask students the following questions: What are the long-term consequences for children who become "night owls?" How do their actions affect parents?

22. **RF** *Bedtime Rituals*, Activity A, SAG. Students are asked to plan a bedtime ritual for a toddler. They should ask a parent to implement the ritual and provide feedback. Students should report the results to the class.

## Hygiene

23. **EX** Ask the students to make (from a household object) or collect a suitable bath item or toy for a toddler. For example, students could make a bath mitt as described in the text or use a woman's anklet and brush paint the decoration with acrylic paint mixed with a textile medium (available in any craft store or department). Thin sponges may be cut with scissors in the shape of familiar animals. Other toys can be made, too.

24. **ER** Guest speaker: Ask a dentist to explain professional care for toddlers' teeth. The dentist should also recommend and show how to best clean toddlers' teeth at home.

## Toilet Learning

25. **RF** *Toilet Learning*, Activity B, SAG. Have students write 10 tips for making toilet learning easier and less stressful for adults and toddlers.

26. **RT** Discuss with students what happens to a toddler's self-concept when he or she has a toileting accident and an adult refers to the toddler as "bad" or "a baby."

27. **EX** Instruct students to evaluate toilet-learning equipment in terms of the following categories: (a) ease of self-use by toddler, (b) ease of cleaning, (c) floor space required, (d) attractiveness of design, and (e) price.

## Indoor and Outdoor Spaces

28. **RF** Have students list some items appropriate for toddlers' outdoor play spaces.

29. **ER** Field trip: As a class, visit one or more homes that have well-planned bedrooms or play spaces for toddlers. Ask students to sketch or list ideas while in the home. Discuss the features after returning to class.

## Intellectual Needs

30. **RF** *Learning Happens in Everyday Experiences*, Activity C, SAG. Students should list concepts that toddlers can develop while bathing or dressing and explain what adults can say or do to help the toddler develop these concepts.

31. **EX** Review with students the toddler's desire to have some independence and make decisions of his or her own. Create a master list of choices parents might offer their toddlers.

32. **EX** Discuss with students the types of shopping trips that might be appropriate or inappropriate for toddlers. Ask students to describe an appropriate shopping trip in terms of the store, its merchandise, and how to make the trip interesting for the toddler. Ask students to name possible toddler learnings.

## Learning Through Activities

33. **EX** Tell students that *in* and *out, push* and *pull,* and *open* and *close* are important concepts for toddlers to learn. Ask students to give examples of how these words can be taught in all homes. Ask why these concepts are intellectually appropriate for a toddler. (These concepts are connected to actions and they are also opposites.) Ask what other learning beside vocabulary is being developed (coordination in movement).

34. **EX** Explain that toddlers are interested in sounds and need to identify sources. As a class, list "sound-making" household items that would gain a toddler's interest. Make a similar list of noisemakers outside of homes.

## Learning Through Play

35. **EX** Explain that "on the go" toddlers enjoy action games and play is the best way to learn. Ask students to list actions parents can have their toddlers do, such as sitting and standing. (The game could be a simplified "Simon Says" renamed "Mommy Says.") Remind students that combining thoughts (words) with actions is appropriate for toddlers.

36. **EX** Explain that as toddlers approach 18 months, they can begin to drop their toys in a basket or put them on a shelf. To make this skill fun and to aid toddlers in ending play before lunch time or bedtime "picking up" should be a game. Ask students to write a couple of games of "pick-up" and share with class. Have students note other skills that are being taught with their games (following directions, names and attributes of objects, motor skills).

## Sensory Stimulation Activities

37. **RT** As a class, have students take turns describing objects in the classroom or school. Other class members should guess the objects being described. Discuss with students the types of words they used to describe objects. Also discuss why words that describe the attributes of objects are important for toddlers to learn and use.

38. **RT** *Sensory Stimulation Activities,* reproducible master 14-3. Use this master to present other sensory stimulation ideas for students to use when working with children. Students should create activities of their own.

39. **ER** *Planned Activities for Sensory Stimulation,* Activity D, SAG. Students should select a sensory stimulation activity to try with a toddler and record the results. This can be done as a small group activity, if desired.

## Problem-Solving Activities

40. **RT** Have students explain why problem-solving activities should begin early in a child's life, such as in the toddler years.

41. **RT** *Problem-Solving Activities,* reproducible master 14-4. Use this master to show students other types of problem-solving activities that can be used when working with children. Students should create activities of their own.

42. **ER** *Planned Activities for Problem Solving,* Activity E, SAG. Students should select a problem-solving activity to try with a toddler and record their results.

## Motor Activities

43. **RT** *Motor Activities,* reproducible master 14-5. Use this master to present motor activities appropriate to use with children. Students should create activities of their own.

44. **ER** *Planned Motor Activities,* Activity F, SAG. Have students select a motor activity to try with a toddler. Students should record their results.

## Language Activities

45. **EX** Discuss with students why the toddler's world of action needs an overlay of language.

46. **RF** *Modeling Language for Toddlers,* Activity G, SAG. Using descriptions of a toddler's language, students should expand what the toddler has said to model pronunciation and grammar, add a new word, and correct meaning.

47. **RT** *Language Activities,* reproducible master 14-6. Use this master to present other language activities students could try with toddlers. Have students brainstorm other activities to encourage language development.

48. **ER** *Planned Language Activities,* Activity H, SAG. Students should select a language activity to try with a toddler and then record their results.

49. **RF** With a librarian's help, students should list quality picture books that are appropriate for children younger than three years.

50. **ER** Instruct students to try "reading" a picture book to a toddler. Students should share their experience with class members.

## Social-Emotional Needs

51. **RT**  Have students find the word *transition* in a dictionary. Students should compare the dictionary and text definitions.
52. **RF**  *Transition Stages Are Difficult*, Activity I, SAG. Have students compare the transition that occurs in the toddler stage with the transition that occurs in the teen years prior to the young adult stage.

## Discipline

53. **EX**  Discuss with students how adults need to balance self-assertion and obedience in their own lives. How does this compare to a toddler's need for discipline?
54. **RF**  Instruct students to write a paper comparing the four needs of toddlers (as discussed in the text) with the needs of adults. Students should give examples of the ways adults and toddlers must have their needs met.

## Guidance: Helping Toddlers Control Their Emotions

55. **RT**  Instruct students to find the term *devil's advocate* in the dictionary. (The dictionary will give the origin of the term as well as its more common usage.) Do toddlers and adults say no at times for argument's sake?
56. **RT**  Ask students to give some specific examples of situations that may trigger a temper tantrum.
57. **RT**  Ask students for examples of how adults can lessen toddlers' fears. (An example is suggesting toddlers sleep with favorite stuffed animals.)

## Planning Self-Awareness Activities

58. **ER**  *Self-Awareness Activities*, reproducible master 14-7. Use this master to show students other types of self-awareness activities that can be used when working with children. Students should create activities of their own.
59. **RT**  Discuss with students reasons a toddler's self-awareness centers on physical rather than intellectual or social-emotional aspects of the self.
60. **ER**  *Planned Activities for Self-Awareness*, Activity J, SAG. Students should select one or more self-awareness activities to try with a toddler. Have them record the results and share with the class.

## Recognizing Developmental Delays

61. **RT**  Ask students to prepare a list of the more common developmental delays in toddlers.
62. **ER**  Ask a pediatrician to speak to the class about how he or she recognizes developmental delays in toddlers. Have students prepare a list of questions in advance.

# Answer Key

## Text
*Reviewing Key Concepts,* page 370
1. true
2. B, E
3. taking off
4. false
5. (Give four:) have a definite hour for bedtime and use a neutral stimulus to signal the hour; set up a ritual that is relaxing; choose a comfortable place for sleep; tell toddlers who resist they do not have to sleep right away, but just stay in bed; if toddlers show fear, tell them where you'll be while they sleep; provide a night-light; offer a stuffed toy or doll to take to bed; tell toddlers you will check on them often to see they are all right; and follow through with checks every 10 to 15 minutes until they are asleep
6. 15 months
7. false
8. B
9. (Give two:) tell the toddler what is going to happen five minutes in advance; play a pretend game of obedience; allow the toddler to make a few decisions when the results are not harmful
10. (Describe three:) reduce or avoid demands when the toddler is tired; make requests in a pleasant tone of voice; remove difficult toys or play equipment that seems to frustrate; have enough toys to prevent boredom; offer help when the toddler seems to need it; give in on small demands; praise the toddler for signs of control
11. false

## Student Activity Guide
*Modeling Language for Toddlers*
Activity G
(Exact sentences should be student response.)
1. purpose: B. correct grammar, corrected word: ran
2. purpose: A. correct pronunciation, corrected word: pillow

3. purpose: C. correct grammar, corrected word: are
4. purpose: D. correct meaning, corrected word: duck
5. purpose: B. correct grammar, corrected word: feet
6. purpose: C. add a new word to vocabulary, corrected word: flies
7. purpose: A. correct pronunciation, corrected word: roses
8. purpose: D. correct meaning, corrected word: cello
9. purpose: D. correct meaning, corrected word: whiskers
10. purpose: C. correct grammar, corrected word: I

## Teacher's Resources

### Learnings of Toddlers,
reproducible master 14-1

1. safety limits
2. toilet learning
3. self-feeding
4. self-dressing
5. language
6. health habits
7. self-awareness
8. simple problem solving

Term formed from circled letters: toddlers

### Chapter 14 Test

| | | |
|---|---|---|
| 1. T | 16. F | 31. D |
| 2. T | 17. T | 32. A |
| 3. F | 18. T | 33. C |
| 4. T | 19. T | 34. E |
| 5. F | 20. T | 35. B |
| 6. T | 21. F | 36. G |
| 7. F | 22. T | 37. K |
| 8. T | 23. C | 38. F |
| 9. F | 24. D | 39. L |
| 10. F | 25. B | 40. J |
| 11. T | 26. C | 41. M |
| 12. F | 27. A | 42. I |
| 13. F | 28. D | 43. H |
| 14. T | 29. A | 44. D |
| 15. T | 30. B | 45. A |

46. The toddler makes the transition from almost total dependence on the adult to some independence from the adult. Independence is mainly seen in self-care skills. The second transition occurs in mental development as the toddler moves from an infant who communicates and thinks mainly in terms of actions to a toddler who communicates with words and who thinks with words that are mentally paired with concrete objects and actions.

47. Mental abilities of toddlers can be stimulated by: involving the toddler in routine daily activities; giving the toddler time for play in order to check and recheck learnings; providing a few enriching materials and activities based on a toddler's own interest and learnings; and providing an overlay of quality language for all activities. Harmful effects involve criticizing the toddler's mistakes and pushing the toddler beyond his or her own abilities which gives rise to shame and doubt.

48. Toddlers often feel very contrary. They oppose adults and other children. Self-assertion and anger give rise to temper tantrums that are a toddler's way of releasing stress and getting adult attention. Fears and anxieties come from both real and unreal insecurities.

49. The toddler has more skills and can express himself or herself better using language. There are more developmental milestones which the child should have reached. The child's development can be compared with these milestones, making a pattern of delays more evident. Also, toddlers often interact with more people than infants do, which increases the likelihood of someone noting the delay.

# Learnings of Toddlers

**Name** _____ **Date** _____ **Period** _____

Toddlers must learn many tasks and concepts. Unscramble the words below that describe some of the learnings of toddlers. (Necessary hyphens and spaces between words are already inserted.) Then arrange the circled letters to form the term describing persons having the characteristics listed.

1. FTESAY MSITLI    __ __ __ __ Ⓞ __    __ __ __ __ __ __ __

2. LTETOI GINARNLE    __ Ⓞ __ __ __ __    __ __ __ __ __ __ __

3. LFES-DEFNIEG    __ __ __ __ – __ __ Ⓞ __ __ __ __

4. LFES-RNISEGSD    __ __ __ __ – Ⓞ __ __ __ __ __ __

5. NAGEUALG    Ⓞ __ __ __ __ __ __ __

6. LTAHEH BTISAH    __ Ⓞ __ __ __ __    __ __ __ __ __

7. LSEF-WESRSANAE    __ __ __ __ – __ __ Ⓞ __ __ __ __ __

8. LMISPE LMBOERP IGVNSOL    __ __ __ __ __ __ __ __ __ __ __
        Ⓞ __ __ __ __ __ __

**Term from circled letters:**    __ __ __ __ __ __ __ __

# Meal/Snack Pattern for Toddlers

### Breakfast—Toddlers

1 milk component

1 fruit/vegetable component

1 grains/bread component

### Lunch and Dinner—Toddlers

1 milk component

2 fruit/vegetable components

1 grains/bread component

1 meat/meat alternate component

### Snack—Toddlers

Each day, two snacks must be served halfway between meals. For each snack, choose two from the following:

1 milk component

2 fruit/vegetable components

1 grain component

1 meat/meat alternate component

USDA Child Care Food Program

## Milk Component

½ cup fluid milk

## Fruit/Vegetable Component

¼ cup full-strength fruit or vegetable juice[1]

¼ cup fruit or vegetable

Note:
[1] Juice cannot be served at snack if milk is the only other snack component.

## Grain/Bread Component[2]

½ slice bread

½ roll, biscuit, muffin, or cornbread serving

¼ cup cold dry cereal

¼ cup hot cooked cereal

¼ cup pasta, noodles, or grains

Note:
[2] Breads and grains must be made from whole-grain or enriched meal or flour. Cereals must be whole-grain, enriched, or fortified.

## Meat/Meat Alternate Component

### Lunch/Dinner

1 oz. meat, poultry, or fish[3],
or alternate protein product

1 oz. cheese

½ egg

¼ cup cooked, dry beans or peas

2 tbsp. peanut butter
(or other seed or nut butters)

½ oz. nuts or seeds[4]

4 oz. yogurt[5]

Notes:
[3] Only the edible portion of cooked lean meat, poultry, or fish counts toward the requirement.

[4] For lunch and dinner, nuts and seeds may only meet half of the total meat/meat alternate serving and must be combined with another meat/meat alternate to fulfill the requirement.

[5] Yogurt may be plain or flavored, sweetened or unsweetened.

### Snack

½ oz. meat, poultry, or fish[3],
or alternate protein product

½ oz. cheese

½ egg

⅛ cup cooked, dry beans or peas

1 tbsp. peanut butter
(or other seed or nut butters)

½ oz. nuts or seeds

2 oz. yogurt[4]

Notes:
[3] Only the edible portion of cooked lean meat, poultry, or fish counts toward the requirement.

[4] Yogurt may be plain or flavored, sweetened or unsweetened.

USDA Child Care Food Program

# Sensory Stimulation Activities

**Name** _____ **Date** _____ **Period** _____

Read the following examples of sensory stimulation activities and then write two activities of your own. Focus one of your activities on taste and the other on smell.

## Sensory Stimulation Activities

### Dark and Light
You will need a shoebox or other small box with a lid. Cut a nickel-sized hole in the center of the lid. Put a small toy in the box and cover with the lid. Tell the child to look through the hole and tell you what he or she can see. Explain that it is dark inside the box when the lid is on. Tell the child to take the lid off and look through the hole again. Ask the child whether he or she can see the object. Explain that it is light inside the box when the lid is off. Try looking at other objects in the same way.

### Which Sound Maker?
Play with a toddler using a bell, whistle, and drum. Cover the toddler's eyes while you make one of the sounds. Ask the toddler which sound maker he or she heard.

*Variation: You may record sounds, then play them for the toddler. After the toddler listens to each sound, ask him or her to point to the sound maker.*

### A Feeling Tour of the Yard
Help the toddler find rough and smooth objects in the yard. The toddler may feel smooth and rough rocks, rough tree bark, a smooth blade of grass, and a smooth rose petal.

**Taste activity title:** _____

_____

_____

_____

_____

_____

_____

**Smell activity title:** _____

_____

_____

_____

_____

_____

_____

# Problem-Solving Activities

Name _____ Date _____ Period _____

Read the following examples of problem-solving activities and write two activities of your own.

## Drop-In Toys
In the lid of a box, cut a circle that is large enough for a ball to fit. Place the lid on the box and show the toddler how to drop balls or other small objects through the hole. Retrieve the objects from inside the box.

## Puzzles
Very simple puzzles are fun for toddlers. Begin with one-piece puzzles and work up to puzzles with five or six pieces during the toddler years. For toddlers, each puzzle piece should depict an entire object or picture of an object. A knob on the puzzle piece will help the toddler's motor control.

## Where Is the Toy?
Wrap a toy in newspaper and hide it in a box. You may also hide a toy in a box and place this box inside another box or boxes. Ask the child to find the toy.

Activity title: _____

_____

_____

_____

_____

_____

_____

_____

_____

_____

Activity title: _____

_____

_____

_____

_____

_____

_____

_____

_____

_____

# Motor Activities

**Name** _____ **Date** _____ **Period** _____

Read the following examples of motor activities, and write a gross-motor activity and a fine-motor activity of your own.

## Gross-Motor Activities

### Pick up the Ball

(The child must be able to bend at the waist before playing this game.) As the toddler stands, roll the ball and say, "Pick up the ball." Model bending at the waist.

### Climb and Sit

Place the toddler facing the front of a chair or sofa. The toddler's hands should rest on the seat. Raise the toddler's knee to the chair or sofa and give him or her a slight boost. Turn the toddler if he or she needs more help. Help the child less and less each time you try this activity. (If the chair or sofa seems too high, remove the seat cushion.)

**Activity title:** _____

_____

_____

_____

_____

_____

_____

_____

## Fine-Motor Activities

### Scribbling

Tape paper (even newspaper will do) to a table or high chair feeding tray. Give the toddler a crayon. Show him or her how to make marks on the paper. (Remember, the toddler cannot yet hold the crayon with a mature grasp.)

### Getting Dressed

Toddlers can learn to put on mittens and zip zippers. (They cannot start jacket zippers.) Special items, such as dressing dolls and books, can make this learning even more fun.

**Activity title:** _____

_____

_____

_____

_____

_____

_____

_____

# Language Activities

**Name** _____ **Date** _____ **Period** _____

Read the following examples of language activities. Then write two activities of your own.

## "Here We Go 'Round the Mulberry Bush"

Acting out the meaning of words helps the toddler learn. This song allows you to sing and act out such lines as, "This is the way we eat our soup," and "This is the way we wash our hands." You may use many other verses.

## Follow Directions

Give the toddler simple directions using familiar objects. For example, say to the toddler, "Bring me the ball." Praise the toddler for following directions properly.

**Activity title:** _____

_____

_____

_____

_____

_____

_____

_____

_____

_____

_____

**Activity title:** _____

_____

_____

_____

_____

_____

_____

_____

_____

_____

_____

_____

# Self-Awareness Activities

**Name** _____ **Date** _____ **Period** _____

Read the following examples of self-awareness activities. Then write two activities of your own.

## Name the Parts of the Face

Place the toddler's hands on your face. Name aloud each part of your face as the child feels it. Then have the toddler name the parts.

## A Book About Me

Photograph the toddler's daily activities. Place the pictures in a photo album or in plastic bags that are fastened together with string.

**Activity title:** _____

_____

_____

_____

_____

_____

_____

_____

_____

_____

**Activity title:** _____

_____

_____

_____

_____

_____

_____

_____

_____

# Providing for the Toddler's Developmental Needs

**Name** _____

**Date** _____ **Period** _____ **Score** _____

## Chapter 14 Test

True/False: Circle *T* if the statement is true or *F* if the statement is false.

T    F    1. Toddlers are still rather dependent on adults to meet their physical needs.

T    F    2. Self-care skills influence toddlers' mental and social-emotional development.

T    F    3. Toddlers' appetites continue to increase as they grow.

T    F    4. Healthy toddlers are inclined to skip a meal every now and then.

T    F    5. During the toddler years, complementary table foods make up three-fourths of the toddler's daily caloric intake.

T    F    6. The Food Guide Pyramid for Young Children is designed for children from two to six years of age.

T    F    7. New clothes should be bought a size or two larger to allow room for growth.

T    F    8. Height and weight are more reliable indicators of size for a toddler's garments than age.

T    F    9. Adults should discuss nightmares with toddlers in order to discover the anxiety that triggers them.

T    F    10. Once toddlers are able to sit, they can safely stay alone while bathing.

T    F    11. Bathing is a good time for water play.

T    F    12. Brushing teeth is *not* important for toddlers because they will lose their deciduous teeth anyway.

T    F    13. All children should begin toilet learning at the same age.

T    F    14. Both the adult and the toddler influence the success of toilet learning.

T    F    15. Toddlers, more than infants, enjoy specially planned bedrooms and play spaces.

T    F    16. Toddlers *cannot* solve any problems on their own.

T    F    17. Toddlers' gross-motor skills are developed mainly through their high activity level rather than through planned activities.

T    F    18. For toddlers, language learning comes from hearing the language as adults talk, share books, and sing songs with them.

T    F    19. Adults need to help toddlers learn to balance self-assertion with obedience.

T    F    20. Toddlers have a difficult time socially and emotionally because they are in a transitional stage.

T    F    21. Adults *cannot* reduce the contrariness of toddlers because contrariness is just toddlers' nature.

T    F    22. Recognizing developmental delays among toddlers involves assessing gross- and fine-motor skills as well as language learnings.

*(Continued)*

**Name** _____

Multiple Choice: Choose the best response. Write the letter in the space provided.

_____ 23. Which of the following statements about the Food Guide Pyramid for Young Children is true?
A. The food groups with the most servings are located on the higher sections of the Pyramid.
B. The Pyramid allows for no flexibility in food preferences.
C. The Pyramid recommends the number and size of servings in each of the five food groups.
D. The Pyramid forbids fats and sweets.

_____ 24. When purchasing toddlers' garments, the adult should consider _____.
A. quality of construction
B. ease for self-dressing
C. special features that toddlers enjoy
D. All of the above.

_____ 25. A suggestion for avoiding bedtime problems is to _____.
A. have active play just before bed to make the toddler tired
B. tell the toddler where you'll be while he or she is sleeping
C. keep the room dark to keep toddlers from getting out of bed
D. All of the above.

_____ 26. Successful toilet learning involves the toddler's _____.
A. physical maturity
B. emotional readiness
C. Both A and B.
D. Neither A nor B.

_____ 27. Adult-planned games should fit _____.
A. toddlers' own interest and learnings
B. toys that adults have purchased or made
C. what adults know toddlers should learn at a certain stage
D. the adult's preferences

_____ 28. Adult guidance of language mainly involves _____.
A. talking during play and routines
B. modeling the language for toddlers
C. sharing books, rhymes, and songs
D. All of the above.

_____ 29. The most important way to show toddlers they are loved is by _____.
A. frequently hugging and telling them
B. buying them toys
C. letting them do whatever they want
D. having surprises for them on birthdays and other special occasions

_____ 30. Consistency in discipline does *not* refer to sameness in _____.
A. limits
B. activities offered each day
C. punishment for a given behavior
D. rewards for a given behavior

_____ 31. Toddlers are helped in controlling their emotions by _____.
A. letting them have some choices
B. letting the toddler know about upcoming changes in activities in advance
C. playing pretend games of obedience
D. All of the above.

*(Continued)*

**Name** _____

_____   32. The roots of self-awareness form in the _____ years.
  A. toddler
  B. early elementary
  C. teen
  D. young adult

Matching: Match the following terms and identifying phrases.

_____ 33.   Level of vitamins, minerals, proteins, and other needed substances in a food compared to the level of calories in the food.

_____ 34.   People with special training in nutrition and diet who meet the qualifications of the American Dietetic Association.

_____ 35.   A child-friendly version of the plan for healthy eating and physical activity developed by the USDA.

_____ 36.   A pattern of activities repeated at a set time each day, such as bedtime.

_____ 37.   Process by which adults help children learn to use the toilet to manage their elimination needs.

_____ 38.   Going back to an earlier stage of development.

_____ 39.   Garment made of disposable diaper material or cotton with a multi-layered cotton crotch.

_____ 40.   Pertaining to space.

_____ 41.   A stage of development in which a person is passing from one stage to another.

_____ 42.   The ability to control oneself.

_____ 43.   To do as one chooses.

_____ 44.   To act within the limits set by others.

_____ 45.   Tendency to oppose others.

A. contrariness

B. Food Guide Pyramid for Young Children

C. nutrient density

D. obedience

E. registered dietitians

F. regression

G. ritual

H. self-assertion

I. self-restraint

J. spatial

K. toilet learning

L. training pants

M. transitional stage

Essay Questions: Provide complete responses to the following questions or statements.

46.  Describe two major transitions made in the toddler years.

47.  What are the most effective and least harmful ways to stimulate a toddler's growing mental abilities?

48.  Describe three emotions often seen in toddlers.

49.  Why is it easier to note a developmental delay in the toddler years than it is during infancy?

# Physical Development of the Preschooler

# 15

## Objectives

After studying this chapter, students will be able to
- describe the physical development that occurs in preschool children.
- describe preschool children's gross-motor and fine-motor skills.

## Bulletin Boards

Stepping Stones to Maturity

### Title: *Stepping Stones to Maturity*

Place a large drawing or picture of a preschooler on the bulletin board as shown. Place paper stepping stones in a path on the board. As students progress through the chapter, they should write descriptive words or phrases to indicate growth and motor skill developmental changes on each stone.

### Title: *Good Diet Equals Strong Bones and Teeth*

On the bulletin board, place pictures of children who look healthy. Surround the children with pictures of foods that are appropriate for growing bodies.

## Teaching Materials

**Text**, pages 374-385
   *Reviewing Key Concepts*
   *Using Your Knowledge*
   *Making Observations*
   *Thinking Further*

**Student Activity Guide**
   A. *Average Heights and Weights of Preschoolers*
   B. *Preschoolers' Bodies Mature*
   C. *Observation: Strength and Coordination Increase*

**Teacher's Resources**
   *Observation: Small-Muscle Control*, reproducible master 15-1
   *Refining Preschoolers' Fine-Motor Skills*, reproducible master 15-2
   Chapter 15 Test

## Introductory Activities

1. Ask students to suppose residents of a far-away planet asked them to describe the growth and motor skill development of preschool "earthlings." Ask each student to list descriptive words and phrases, such as *on the go*, that describe preschoolers. Have class members read their lists aloud and tally the most common words and phrases. Have students compare the descriptions with those in the text as they study the chapter.

2. Explain to students the meaning of the term *preschool* in describing this age group. Many three- to five-year-old children attend nursery schools, child care centers and other group programs for children. Ask students what level of schooling is implied in the term *preschool*.

# Strategies to Reteach, Reinforce, Enrich, and Extend Text Concepts

## Body Growth and Development

3. **RT**  Ask students to explain the difference in the rate of growth between toddlers and preschoolers.

4. **RF**  Have students explain the meaning of the following statement from the text and give examples that support or refute it: "Children who are larger than their peers at age three years will probably be larger than their peers at age five years, too."

## Height and Weight

5. **RF**  *Average Heights and Weights of Preschoolers*, Activity A, SAG. Using Figures 15-1 and 15-2 in the text, have students average the heights and weights of boys and girls from ages three to five years. Students should then plot the averaged heights and weights on the graphs. The graphs should depict the height and weight increases of children between ages three and five years.

6. **RT**  Students should explain why boys tend to be slightly heavier than girls. (Boys have a higher muscle mass than girls do.)

7. **RT**  Discuss with students how preschool children's weight gains may not show or cause changes in clothing sizes. (Typical weight gain in preschool children is mainly due to growth of muscle tissues.)

## Other Body Changes

8. **RF**  *Preschoolers' Bodies Mature*, Activity B, SAG. Instruct students to write descriptive phrases that summarize major body changes that occur in the preschool years.

9. **RT**  Have students find the term *deciduous* in a dictionary. Students should explain why children's first teeth are referred to as deciduous teeth.

10. **RF**  Using a nutrition book, students should list foods that preschoolers particularly need to develop healthy bones and teeth.

11. **RF**  Using a nutrition book, students should list foods high in fiber and seasonings that may irritate the digestive tract of preschool children.

## Motor Development

12. **EX**  Instruct students to choose a skill (such as throwing or catching) in a sport with which they are familiar. Students should explain how success in the sport requires refined eye-hand coordination and quick reaction time.

13. **EX**  Discuss with students why, in order for children's motor skills to develop, play is just as essential as physical maturation. (Specialized skills require both maturation and experience.)

14. **ER**  Have students observe the physical play of preschool children. Ask students what activities the children enjoyed most.

## Gross-Motor Development

15. **EX**  Help students note the effects of eyes on balance by doing the following: (a) stand behind their chairs with their eyes closed; (b) stand on one foot, eyes open, and arms outstretched; and (c) repeat b with hands folded across chest. (These activities are all examples of static balance.) Ask, "Why do you think tight rope performers use a long, flexible pole in their acts?"

16. **EX**  Ask students who participate in sports, dance, gymnastics, and cheerleading to explain some of the strategies they use to maintain balance.

17. **EX**  Share with students another word for a person's balance (*equilibrium*) and other words for problems with balance (*disequilibrium, dizziness,* and *vertigo*).

18. **RT**  Ask students to explain whether they would expect preschool children to show more interest and have more success in gross-motor or fine-motor activities. Students should justify their answers. (Gross-motor activities should be more developed according to the center-to-extremities principle.)

19. **RT**  Students should explain the sequence of throwing and catching a ball from early preschool age to later preschool age. What three body maturation developments have occurred that have increased skill? (Preschoolers develop body rotation, weight shift, and increases in strength, balance, and coordination.)

20. **RF**  *Observation: Strength and Coordination Increase*, Activity C, SAG. Have students observe and record the gross-motor skills of a preschool child.

21. **RT**  Ask students to explain why a preschooler can catch a ball he or she has bounced more easily than a ball someone else has thrown to him or her.

22. **EX** Students should observe preschool children trying to skip. Have students compare the preschoolers' attempts with the text discussion.

## Fine-Motor Development

23. **RT** Discuss with students why some preschoolers may lag in fine-motor development.
24. **RF** *Observation: Small-Muscle Control,* reproducible master 15-1. Have students closely observe preschool children performing everyday tasks that involve small muscles, such as eating and dressing. Students describe in as much detail as they can the way the child performed the task.
25. **RF** *Refining Preschoolers' Fine-Motor Skills,* reproducible master 15-2. Have students test the fine-motor skills of a preschooler and record their results. Students should present their findings to the class as an oral report.

26. **ER** Invite a preschool teacher to discuss the kinds of gross- and fine-motor activities used in the teacher's preschool program.

## Answer Key

### Text

*Reviewing Key Concepts,* page 384

1. false
2. C
3. true
4. digestive tract
5. true
6. false
7. false
8. walking—D; running—C; jumping—A; throwing—B; balancing—E
9. (List four. Student response. See pages 381 to 382 in the text.)
10. false

### Student Activity Guide

*Preschoolers' Bodies Mature,* Activity B

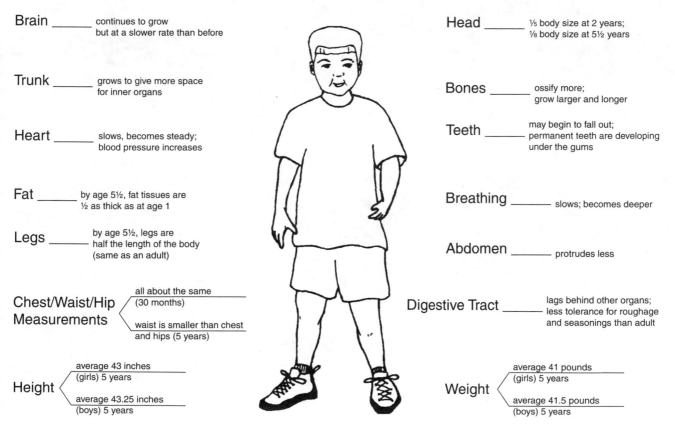

Brain _____ continues to grow but at a slower rate than before

Trunk _____ grows to give more space for inner organs

Heart _____ slows, becomes steady; blood pressure increases

Fat _____ by age 5½, fat tissues are ½ as thick as at age 1

Legs _____ by age 5½, legs are half the length of the body (same as an adult)

Chest/Waist/Hip Measurements — all about the same (30 months) / waist is smaller than chest and hips (5 years)

Height — average 43 inches (girls) 5 years / average 43.25 inches (boys) 5 years

Head _____ ⅕ body size at 2 years; ⅛ body size at 5½ years

Bones _____ ossify more; grow larger and longer

Teeth _____ may begin to fall out; permanent teeth are developing under the gums

Breathing _____ slows; becomes deeper

Abdomen _____ protrudes less

Digestive Tract _____ lags behind other organs; less tolerance for roughage and seasonings than adult

Weight — average 41 pounds (girls) 5 years / average 41.5 pounds (boys) 5 years

# Teacher's Resources
## Chapter 15 Test

| | | |
|---|---|---|
| 1. T | 13. T | 25. C |
| 2. F | 14. C | 26. A |
| 3. T | 15. C | 27. E |
| 4. T | 16. B | 28. C |
| 5. T | 17. D | 29. F |
| 6. F | 18. B | 30. B |
| 7. T | 19. C | 31. G |
| 8. T | 20. D | 32. A |
| 9. T | 21. A | 33. H |
| 10. F | 22. B | 34. D |
| 11. T | 23. D | |
| 12. F | 24. B | |

35. Growth rate slows; body proportions appear less "babyish"; organ systems continue to mature; fat decreases while muscle fibers increase.

36. Rapid development of gross- and fine-motor skills occurs in the preschool years due to: (a) an increase in muscular strength and balance skills; (b) more refinement of eye-hand coordination; and (c) an shorter reaction time. These physical abilities are often coupled with a desire to engage in gross- and fine-motor activities.

# Observation: Small-Muscle Control

**Name** _____ **Date** _____ **Period** _____

Similar to gross-motor skills, the fine-motor skills of preschoolers are much more mature than those of toddlers. However, preschoolers still have problems with fine-motor coordination as they work at various tasks. Observe preschool-age children as they eat, dress (button or unbutton clothing), or play. Try to observe a younger child and an older child performing the same activities. Note how they perform the task and differences in their coordination. Record your results.

Child's first name and age_____

Tasks observed _____

How did the child perform the tasks? _____

Child's first name and age_____

Tasks observed _____

How did the child perform the tasks? _____

_____

_____

_____

_____

_____

_____

_____

_____

What differences did you see in the way they performed each task? Any similarities? Other than age, why do you think one child performed the task a little easier than the other? _____

_____

_____

_____

_____

_____

_____

_____

_____

_____

# Refining Preschoolers' Fine-Motor Skills

**Name** _____ **Date** _____ **Period** _____

Just as the preschoolers' gross-motor abilities increase with each year, so do their fine-motor abilities. Ask two preschoolers, one who is between 3 and 3½ years old and the other who is between 5 and 5½ years old, to do each of the following activities.

→ Work on puzzles.
→ Cut out copies of the predrawn two-inch square and circle with a two-inch diameter shown below.

→ Trace with a crayon over the given letters.
→ Draw a picture of themselves using a pencil (no crayons) and a three-by-five-inch piece of plain paper.

Record observations in the space below. Then prepare an oral presentation to share your findings with the class.

## Results

### Working on Puzzles

Three-year-old: Describe any problems with task. _____

_____

_____

_____

_____

Five-year-old: Describe any problems with task. _____

_____

_____

_____

_____

*(Continued)*

**Name** _____

## Cutting Squares and Circles

Mount the completed cuttings below.

### Three-Year-Old

### Five-Year-Old

Describe any problems either or both of the children had in handling the scissors. _____

_____

_____

_____

*(Continued)*

**Name** _____

## Tracing Letters

Have children trace the letters below.

M S

**Three-Year-Old**

M S

**Five-Year-Old**

Describe any problems either or both of the children had in handling crayons. _____

_____

_____

_____

*(Continued)*

**Name** _____

Drawing of Self

Mount pictures in the space below.

Three-Year-Old

Five-Year-Old

Describe any problems either or both of the children had drawing themselves. _____

_____

_____

_____

# Physical Development of the Preschooler

**Name** _____

**Date** _____ **Period** _____ **Score** _____

## Chapter 15 Test

True/False: Circle *T* if the statement is true or *F* if the statement is false.

T   F   1. Preschoolers' rate of growth slows.

T   F   2. The preschool child's head grows more than the face.

T   F   3. Both the trunk and the legs grow rapidly in the preschool years.

T   F   4. Between four and five years of age, many preschool children begin to lose their deciduous teeth.

T   F   5. Health problems can damage both teeth and bones.

T   F   6. The internal organs reach maturity during the preschool years.

T   F   7. A preschooler's ratio of fat to muscle decreases.

T   F   8. The motor development of preschoolers greatly improves.

T   F   9. Balancing skills developed in the preschool years aid gross-motor development.

T   F   10. For most children, weight shift while throwing an object begins at age five years.

T   F   11. Preschoolers achieve the skill of hopping before skipping.

T   F   12. Fine-motor development in preschoolers has "caught up" with gross-motor development.

T   F   13. Eye-hand coordination is greatly improved in most children by five years of age.

Multiple Choice: Choose the best response. Write the letter in the space provided.

_____ 14. Of the total weight gain in the preschool years, muscle development accounts for _____ percent.
A. 25
B. 50
C. 75
D. 100

_____ 15. Boys tend to weigh more than girls because boys tend to have _____.
A. more fat deposits
B. greater bone ossification
C. more muscle tissue
D. more water in the body

_____ 16. The abdomen of preschool children protrudes less due to the _____.
A. tightening of abdominal muscles
B. growth of the trunk
C. receding of fat tissue
D. straighter walking posture

_____ 17. Problems with bones may be due to _____.
A. malnutrition
B. diseases
C. injury
D. All of the above.

© Goodheart-Willcox

*(Continued)*

**Name** _____

_____ 18. Of the following, the _____ is the least mature in the preschool years.
   A. liver
   B. digestive tract
   C. heart
   D. lungs

_____ 19. Skeletal muscles increase in size and strength due to _____.
   A. more protein in muscle fiber
   B. increase in size of muscle fiber due to exercise
   C. Both A and B.
   D. Neither A nor B.

_____ 20. As compared with toddlers, preschool children are more skillful in play activities because they have _____.
   A. increased muscle development
   B. more refined eye-hand coordination
   C. a shorter reaction time
   D. All of the above.

_____ 21. Balance is due to all of the following *except* _____.
   A. ability to think about body position
   B. signals from the movement of fluid in the inner ears
   C. brain signals to the muscles
   D. signals from the eyes

_____ 22. Preschool children's ability to climb is *not* aided by _____.
   A. better balance
   B. improved running ability
   C. greater courage
   D. All of the above.

_____ 23. Improvement in running speed is most noticeable by age _____ years.
   A. two
   B. three
   C. four
   D. five

_____ 24. Skills in hopping usually begin at _____ years.
   A. two
   B. three
   C. four
   D. five

_____ 25. The preschooler's throwing ability is helped by _____.
   A. body rotation
   B. weight shift
   C. Both A and B.
   D. Neither A nor B.

_____ 26. The first geometric shape that can be drawn is the _____.
   A. circle
   B. square
   C. rectangle
   D. triangle

*(Continued)*

**Name** _____

Matching: Match the following terms and identifying phrases.

_____27. Children between the ages of three and five years.

_____28. Parts inside of the body, such as the heart, lungs, and liver.

_____29. Time required to take action in response to a change in the environment, such as a sight or sound.

_____30. Balance maintained while moving.

_____31. Balance maintained while being still.

_____32. Turning the trunk of the body to the one side when the hand of the other side is used to throw.

_____33. Shifting the body from the back foot to the front foot.

_____34. To work an object by using the hands.

A. body rotation

B. dynamic balance

C. internal organs

D. manipulate

E. preschool children

F. reaction time

G. static balance

H. weight shift

Essay Questions: Provide complete responses to the following questions or statements.

35. What are three major changes that occur in body growth and development during the preschool years?

36. Describe the basic motor development of preschool children.

# Intellectual Development of the Preschooler

16

## Objectives

After studying this chapter, students will be able to
- relate how new thinking skills emerge in preschool children.
- identify the major concepts learned at this stage of mental development.
- chart the increasing language skills of preschoolers.

## Bulletin Boards

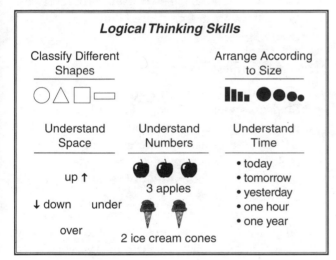

**Logical Thinking Skills**

Classify Different Shapes

Arrange According to Size

Understand Space

up ↑

↓ down    under

over

Understand Numbers

3 apples

2 ice cream cones

Understand Time
- today
- tomorrow
- yesterday
- one hour
- one year

Title: *Logical Thinking Skills*

Under the title place the phrases Classify Different Shapes, Arrange According to Size, Understand Space, Understand Time, Understand Numbers. As indicated, place symbols and terms under the appropriate columns.

Title: *Beginning to Think*

Select or have students bring in cartoons or anecdotes in which a young child uses illogical thinking. Display these on the board. Have students share their experiences with young children who have used illogical thinking.

## Teaching Materials

**Text**, pages 386-403
*Reviewing Key Concepts*
*Using Your Knowledge*
*Making Observations*
*Thinking Further*

**Student Activity Guide**
A. *Preschoolers Lack Complete Logical Thought*
B. *Using Symbols in Play*
C. *Fairy Tales and Children*

**Teacher's Resources**
*Piaget's Tasks for Logical Thinking,* reproducible master 16-1
*Observing a Preschooler's Thinking Skills,* reproducible master 16-2
*Concepts of Preschool Children,* reproducible master 16-3
*Following Directions,* color transparency CT-16
*Observation: Preschoolers and Grammar Problems,* reproducible master 16-4
Chapter 16 Test

## Introductory Activities

1. Have students observe children in dramatic play. About how old were the children observed? What kinds of symbols did the children use in their pretend play? How could students tell that the children were pretending and not imitating?
2. Guide students through a logical thinking example. You may ask students, "If you have a term paper due next week, what sequence of work must take place in order to finish it on time? If you don't finish it what happens?" Have students give other examples of people using logical thinking skills. How might young children react to a series of events that must be placed in sequence?

## Strategies to Reteach, Reinforce, Enrich, and Extend Text Concepts

### How Preschool Children Learn

3. **RF** Ask students to give an example of a mental action versus a physical action. (Note: Computing 2 + 2 = 4 in the head is a mental action; putting two blocks on the table, putting two more blocks together, and counting the four blocks is a physical action.)

4. **RT** Discuss with students why the child's short memory for images of objects and persons causes many concepts to be incomplete or illogical. Ask students why the quickly fading image of a particular object or person (such as several apples, several horses, or several Santas) would cause the child to see different members of the same class as identical.

5. **RT** Ask students to give examples of some of the ways preschool children learn intuitively. Students should give examples of what a child might learn intuitively about space or time relationships.

## Obstacles to Logical Thinking

6. **RT** After students look up the term egocentric in a dictionary, ask them the following questions: When Piaget uses the term *egocentric*, does he mean viewing everything in relation to oneself or self-centered? (viewing everything in relation to oneself) In which way is the term *egocentric* more commonly used? (to mean self-centered) Have students share examples of children's egocentric thoughts.

7. **RT** Have students explain how children center their attention on one part instead of looking at all parts. This is an obstacle to logical thought for the preschooler.

8. **RT** Discuss with students the typical reactions of older children and adults to a movie that is run backwards. Ask students why people usually laugh at such a movie. Have students use this example to explain why the concept of reversibility is difficult for preschool children to understand. (Examples of physical concepts like texture are seen and felt before the person develops a mental concept of texture. Conversely, the concept of reversing or reversals is only mental because examples of reversing or reversals are seldom seen in real life.)

9. **RT** Ask students to give examples of obstacles to logical thought they have observed in children. Students should try to identify with which of the obstacles each situation might be associated: egocentrism, centering their attention on only one part, focusing on individual steps or events, not being able to mentally reverse actions, or associating actions without using logic.

10. **RF** *Preschoolers Lack Complete Logical Thought*, Activity A, SAG. Ask students to match the stories with the types of obstacles to complete logical thought.

11. **ER** *Piaget's Tasks for Logical Thinking*, reproducible master 16-1. Explain that Piaget developed many (more than shown here) tasks

to determine the thinking of children of different ages. After planning these tasks, Piaget administered them to children individually and carefully recorded their verbal responses. From the children's responses, he developed his theory of cognitive development. As students look at three transparencies, demonstrate how each task is conducted. Point out that Piaget did not consider answers as right or wrong but as typical for a given age child. He realized that immature answers would become mature just as children mature in other ways. (Use this to prepare students to do reproducible master 16-2.)

12. **EX** *Observing a Preschooler's Thinking Skills*, reproducible master 16-2. Instruct students to select one of the tasks developed by Piaget (as shown in reproducible master 16-1), gather the materials, write and practice the procedure, try the task with a four-year-old, and record the results.

## New Abilities Emerge

13. **ER** *Using Symbols in Play*, Activity B, SAG. Students should observe and record examples of the symbolic play of preschool children.

14. **ER** Guest speaker: Invite a nursery school or child care teacher to speak to students about some of the imitations they observe in preschool children.

15. **RF** Choose two familiar words, such as *dog* and *flower*. Ask students to write what they mentally "see" as you say the words. Have students describe their images and share whether they recall examples of their childhood mental images that contrasted with reality.

16. **RF** Collect or have students collect drawings of preschool children. Label each drawing with the child's verbal description of his or her drawing. Display the drawings. Discuss with students how the drawings are more realistic in intent than visually accurate.

17. **RF** Have students recall any word (foreign or native) for which they did not know the meaning. After they discovered the meaning, how did this help their thinking?

## What Preschool Children Learn

18. **EX** Have students find the terms *physical* and *logical* in a dictionary. Students should contrast the meanings of these terms.

19. **RF** Ask students to explain with examples why logical knowledge concepts lag behind physical knowledge concepts in children's mental development.

20. **RT**  Discuss with students why young children believe humans and human-like beings cause all happenings.
21. **RF**  *Fairy Tales and Children*, Activity C, SAG. Ask students to give some examples of children's stories that give life to inanimate objects. How do these stories affect children's thinking? (These stories can make it difficult for children to separate reality from make-believe.)

## Concepts Children Learn

22. **RT**  Have students list the attributes of various classroom objects. Students should contrast their thinking with the concepts children need to learn in order to differentiate attributes.
23. **RT**  Ask students to give examples of possible attributes children need to learn to classify, such as color or shape.
24. **RT**  Discuss with students the problems children may have with number concepts even if they can count to 10 or 20.
25. **EX**  *Concepts of Preschool Children*, reproducible master 16-3. Have students try to complete the chart on common concepts developed by preschool children. Discuss their responses. As students study the chapter, have them adjust their charts as needed.

## Language Abilities Increase

26. **RT**  Discuss with students how advanced speech affects social relationships and emotional expressions.
27. **RF**  Students should listen to several preschool children talk. They should note whether the problems the children have in articulation closely match those given in Figure 16-13 of the text. Students should discuss their observations with classmates.
28. **RF**  Record the words, phrases, and sentences of preschool children as they play. Play the recording in class. Ask students the following questions: Do the children use more words to describe the attributes of objects (color, texture, shape, size) or more words to describe logical concepts (space relations, time relations, numbers, classes of objects)? Students should give examples to support answers.
29. **RT**  *Following Directions*, color transparency CT-16. Use this transparency to illustrate the advanced language comprehension skills of four- and five-year-olds.

30. **ER**  Invite students to interview a parent or an adult who works with preschool children. Ask the person to share examples of how preschool children give their own meanings (as opposed to standard meanings) to words. Have students write a short paper based on their findings.
31. **ER**  *Observation: Preschoolers and Grammar Problems*, reproducible master 16-4. Have students observe and record some preschool children's problems with grammar.
32. **RT**  Ask students to explain why making some grammatical errors, such as adding an *-ed* sound to irregular verbs and adding *-s* or *-es* to all nouns, is actually a sign of the child's growing intellect.
33. **ER**  Instruct students to research stuttering in the preschool years. Have each student write a short summary and present the paper in class.

# Answer Key

## Text

*Reviewing Key Concepts,* page 402

1. A
2. false
3. true
4. B
5. B, D, C, A
6. (Student response for A through D. See pages 394 to 396 in the text.)
7. true
8. true
9. false
10. A. "Mommy fixed my toy."
    A. "I'm never going no more to your house."
    A. "I like food. I like apples best."

## Student Activity Guide

*Preschoolers Lack Complete Logical Thought,* Activity A

1. C
2. A
3. E
4. B
5. B
6. A
7. D

# Teacher's Resources

## Chapter 16 Test

| | | |
|---|---|---|
| 1. T | 15. F | 29. D |
| 2. F | 16. T | 30. B |
| 3. T | 17. F | 31. K |
| 4. F | 18. F | 32. J |
| 5. T | 19. T | 33. F |
| 6. T | 20. T | 34. D |
| 7. F | 21. D | 35. H |
| 8. T | 22. B | 36. E |
| 9. T | 23. B | 37. A |
| 10. F | 24. C | 38. G |
| 11. T | 25. D | 39. B |
| 12. F | 26. C | 40. I |
| 13. T | 27. D | 41. C |
| 14. T | 28. D | |

42. (Give three of the following:). Children: (a) are egocentric and cannot see ideas from another's perspectives; (b) center on only one part of an object or event; (c) focus on single steps, stages, or events and thus do not pay attention to the order of changes that occur; (d) cannot follow a line of reasoning back to where it starts; and (e) link actions without using logic

43. (Student response.)

44. Children exchange ideas with words and thus learn from others. Thinking with words is much faster than thinking through physical actions; thus, language makes thinking more efficient.

45. (List two:) using pronouns incorrectly, using negatives incorrectly, incorrect word order for questions; incorrect verb forms; incorrect plural formation

# Piaget's Tasks for Logical Thinking

## Rotation of Beads

Show a child three beads strung on a wire and insert the beads into a hollow cardboard tube to hide them. Hold the tube vertically and remind the child which color is on top. Turn the tube upside down and ask which color bead is now on top. Next, turn the tube end over end and have the child again tell which color bead is on top. Show the child the top bead after each guess.

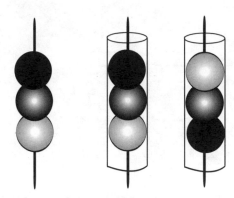

## Conservation of Number

Start with the circles placed in two equal rows and ask the child whether the two rows have the same number of circles. Then, move the bottom row of circles together so they touch. Ask the same question. Finally, space the bottom row of circles wider apart than the top row, and ask the question again.

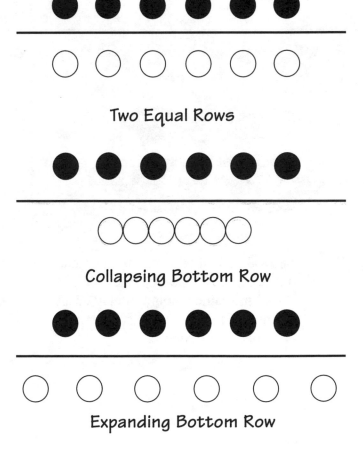

**Two Equal Rows**

**Collapsing Bottom Row**

**Expanding Bottom Row**

*(Continued)*

# Piaget's Tasks for Logical Thinking

## Conservation of Liquid

Step 1. Show the child two glasses that are exactly the same and contain exactly the same amount of colored water. Ask the child, "Is there the same amount of water in both glasses or are they different?" If the child agrees they are equal in amount, begin Step 2.

Step 2. With the child watching, pour water from one glass into a taller but thinner glass or into a shorter but wider glass. Ask the child, "Do the glasses have the same amount of water or are they different? How do you know?"

## Conservation of Mass

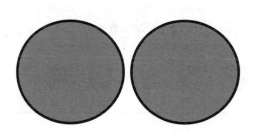

Step 1. Show the child two balls of clay that are of equal size and shape. Ask the child, "Do the balls have the same amount of clay or are they different?" If the child agrees they are equal in amount, begin Step 2.

Step 2. With the child watching, flatten one ball of clay. Ask the child, "Do these two pieces have the same amount of clay or are they different? How do you know?"

*(Continued)*

# Piaget's Tasks for Logical Thinking

## Conservation of Length

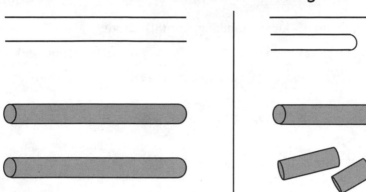

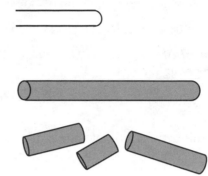

Step 1. Show the child two pieces of string (or two rods) that are exactly the same length. Ask the child, "Are the two strings (or rods) the same length or are they different?" If the child agrees they are equal in length, begin Step 2.

Step 2. With the child watching, curve one string (or break one rod into three pieces). Ask the child, "Are the two strings (or the three pieces of the rod as compared to the whole rod) the same length or are they different? How do you know?"

## Conservation of Area

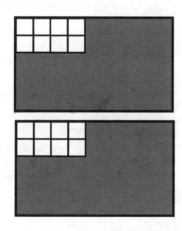

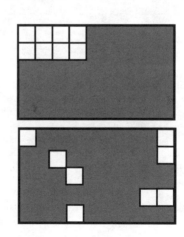

Step 1. Show the child two sheets of cardboard with the same number of white blocks on each sheet placed in exactly the same way. Ask the child, "Do the two sheets have the same amount of uncovered space or are they different?" If the child agrees the uncovered space is equal, begin Step 2.

Step 2. With the child watching, move the blocks on one sheet of cardboard apart. Ask the child, "Do these two pieces have the same amount of uncovered space or are they different? How do you know?"

# Observing a Preschooler's Thinking Skills

**Name** _____ **Date** _____ **Period** _____

Piaget designed many tasks to test children's logical thinking. For this activity, do each of the following:

1. Select one task developed by Piaget (as shown on *Piaget's Tasks for Logical Thinking*).

2. Using *Piaget's Tasks for Logical Thinking,* collect or make the materials, write the procedure on note cards, and practice giving the task.

3. Select a four-year-old child, try the task, and record his or her responses.

As you work on this activity, complete the following information:

1. Name of task _____

2. Materials collected or made _____

   _____

   _____

3. Describe the basic procedure _____

   _____

   _____

4. Age and gender of child _____

5. Describe child's responses _____

   _____

   _____

   _____

   _____

   _____

   _____

   _____

6. Did the child have problems with logical thought as expected for this age? Explain._____

   _____

   _____

   _____

   _____

   _____

# Concepts of Preschool Children

**Name** _____ **Date** _____ **Period** _____

Concepts are learned in stages that begin with general ideas and become more and more refined over time. For each item listed below, try to determine what concepts a toddler, a young preschool child, and an older preschool child might have. An example is provided for you. As you study the chapter, you can adjust your original answers as needed.

| Topic Concept | Toddler | Younger Preschool Child | Older Preschool Child |
|---|---|---|---|
| Dog | *Dog* refers to all fuzzy, furry creatures, such as all small, furry animals and stuffed animals. | *Dog* refers to animals that are small and bark. (May include seals but exclude large dogs.) | Child can explain how a dog differs from other animals. For example, "Dogs bark, but cats meow." |
| Daddy or Mommy | | | |
| Baby | | | |
| Car | | | |
| Ball | | | |
| Water | | | |

# Observation: Preschoolers and Grammar Problems

**Name** _____ **Date** _____ **Period** _____

Preschool children experience problems with grammar. Common mistakes include the following:
(1) adding -ed to make all verbs—including irregular verbs—past tense, (2) making plurals by adding -s
or -es to certain nouns (for example, *childs*), (3) asking questions with incorrect word order, (4) using
negatives incorrectly, and (5) using pronouns incorrectly. Listen to a group of preschool children talk
with each other and with adults. In the space below, record phrases or sentences that illustrate these
grammatical problems. Share your findings with classmates.

Incorrect Past Tense Verb Form

Incorrect Plurals

Incorrect Word Order for Questions

Incorrect Use of Negatives

Incorrect Use of Pronouns

# Intellectual Development of the Preschooler

**Name**_____

**Date** _____**Period** _____**Score** _____

## Chapter 16 Test

True/False: Circle *T* if the statement is true or *F* if the statement is false.

T    F    1.  The advancing motor skills of preschoolers aid their intellectual development.

T    F    2.  During the preoperational stage, preschoolers can think as logically as adults do.

T    F    3.  Preschool children may *not* be able to solve all concepts mentally.

T    F    4.  Preschoolers can retrace the steps to undo a task.

T    F    5.  Pretend play has intellectual value for preschoolers.

T    F    6.  Children must be able to imitate before they can create symbols to use in pretend play.

T    F    7.  Preschool children often choose the subject of their drawing before they begin to draw it.

T    F    8.  The symbols used in language are the most abstract of all symbols.

T    F    9.  Physical knowledge concepts pertain to attributes of objects and what happens when objects are acted upon.

T    F    10. Preschool children only see a figure as a whole rather than noting its parts.

T    F    11. Sorting is an easier task than classifying.

T    F    12. Being able to count signifies that a child has learned the concept of numbers.

T    F    13. Inaccurate spatial concepts can be seen in preschoolers' drawings.

T    F    14. Time is a logical thinking concept.

T    F    15. If adults give preschool children correct scientific answers to their questions about natural happenings, children will develop correct cause and effect concepts.

T    F    16. Because preschool children often talk without really communicating with others, their speech in referred to as egocentric.

T    F    17. Articulation is slow to progress in the preschool years.

T    F    18. When learning vocabulary, children learn words for abstract ideas before they learn words for concrete ideas.

T    F    19. Preschool children learn some rules of grammar.

T    F    20. Brain wiring for grammar occurs during the preschool period.

Multiple Choice: Choose the best response. Write the letter in the space provided.

_____    21. Intellectual development consists of _____.
  A. how people learn
  B. what people learn
  C. how people express what they know through language
  D. All of the above.

_____    22. The major theorist who described children's mental development is _____.
  A. Havighurst
  B. Piaget
  C. Maslow
  D. Erikson

*(Continued)*

**Name**_____

_____ 23. Preschool children figure out problems mainly by _____.
   A. trial and error
   B. intuitive thinking
   C. abstract reasoning
   D. All of the above.

_____ 24. Piaget claims children are egocentric because they _____.
   A. are self-centered
   B. do not care how others feel
   C. believe everyone thinks like they do
   D. All of the above.

_____ 25. Children *cannot* always think logically because they _____.
   A. view everything in relation to themselves
   B. do not see the sequence of events that bring about changes
   C. cannot follow a line of reasoning back to where it started
   D. All of the above.

_____ 26. Symbolic play for the child _____.
   A. involves changing the "real" world into the desired world
   B. is a mental activity
   C. Both A and B.
   D. Neither A nor B.

_____ 27. Mental images are _____.
   A. symbols
   B. private and internalized
   C. triggered by words or other events
   D. All of the above.

_____ 28. Logical thinking concepts include _____.
   A. classifying objects
   B. arranging objects by size
   C. number, spatial, and time concepts
   D. All of the above.

_____ 29. The speech of four- and five-year-olds includes _____.
   A. problems with the use of pronouns
   B. sentences that use conjunctions and prepositions
   C. asking questions in the correct word order
   D. All of the above.

_____ 30. Major grammatical errors of preschool children include all of the following *except*
   _____.
   A. choosing the wrong vocabulary word
   B. using negatives incorrectly
   C. asking questions without inverted word order
   D. making irregular verb forms regular

*(Continued)*

**Name**_____

Matching: Match the following terms and identifying phrases.

_____31.   The second stage in the mental development of children as described by Piaget.

_____32.   The first substage of the preoperational stage in which children ages two to four years are developing some concepts.

_____33.   The second substage of the preoperational stage in which children can solve many problems correctly by imagining how they would act out the solution.

_____34.   Preschooler's belief that everyone thinks in the same way concepts and has the same ideas as he or she does.

_____35.   Symbols of objects and past experiences that are stored in the mind.

_____36.   Something that is only thought about and not shared with others.

_____37.   Words that do not relate to what they represent.

_____38.   Concepts that are not directly experienced through the senses but are developed through thought.

_____39.   Ability to choose an attribute and group all the objects from a set that possess that attributes.

_____40.   Talking to oneself as though thinking aloud.

_____41.   Talking to another person without listening to what the other person has said.

A.  abstract

B.  classifying

C.  collective monologue

D.  egocentrism

E.  internalized

F.  intuitive substage

G.  logical thinking

H.  mental images

I.  monologue

J.  preconceptual substage

K.  preoperational stage

Essay Questions: Provide complete responses to the following questions or statements.

42.  Give three examples of preschool children's problems in logical thinking.

43.  Use your own words to explain what Piaget meant by the term *egocentric* and why this is an obstacle to logical thinking.

44.  How do the preschool child's developing language skills aid his or her mental abilities?

45.  List two grammar problems common among preschoolers.

# Social-Emotional Development of the Preschooler

## Objectives

After studying this chapter, students will be able to
- analyze the problems preschoolers face as they develop initiative.
- explain how adults can help children become more responsible.
- describe how preschool children learn gender roles.
- discuss the growing importance of friends.
- describe how feelings and emotions change during the preschool years.

## Bulletin Boards

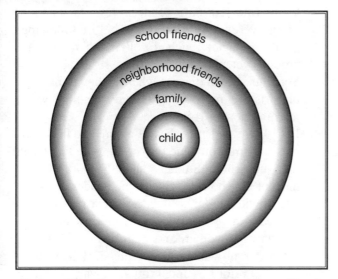

**Title:** *The Preschooler's Expanding Circle of Friends*

Cover the bulletin board with paper. In the center of the paper, draw a small circle on which the word *child* appears. The words *family, neighborhood friends,* and *school friends* appear on the subsequent circles, as indicated, showing the ever-widening circle of friendships.

**Title:** *Initiative Means*

Ask students for examples of preschoolers' acts that show initiative within limits and without guilt. Have students clip and mount magazine or other pictures that show some of the acts. Place the pictures on the board. Students should label their pictures.

## Teaching Materials

**Text**, pages 404-417
*Reviewing Key Concepts*
*Using Your Knowledge*
*Making Observations*
*Thinking Further*

**Student Activity Guide**
A. *A Dependable Adult*
B. *Friends Are Important*
C. *Learning from Play*
D. *Observation: Children at Play*

**Teacher's Resources**
*Preschoolers Show Responsibility*, color transparency CT-17
*Sex Typing and Gender Roles*, transparency master 17-1
*Observation: Aggression in Preschoolers*, reproducible master 17-2
Chapter 17 Test

## Introductory Activities

1. Have students write a poem or paragraph from a preschool child's point of view. Direct students to use social and emotional development as the focus of this creative-writing piece.
2. Ask students to cite examples of times when parents or caregivers have had to set limits on a child's exploration, curiosity, and independence in order to keep him or her safe from harm.

## Strategies to Reteach, Reinforce, Enrich, and Extend Text Concepts

### Developing Social Awareness

3. **RT** Instruct students to list words and phrases that relate to social awareness.
4. **RT** Ask students to recall their first friends. Were they relatives, neighborhood children, preschool playgroups, or others? What do they remember about their play activities with others? How important to them were their friends?

## Taking the Initiative

5. **RT**  Have students use the following diagram to explain Erikson's theory of personality development. Students should use examples in their explanations. Diagram: trust (leads to) autonomy (leads to) initiative

6. **EX**  Ask students to think of examples of times they tried something and failed. How did this make them feel? Contrast this with how their successes made them feel. How can adults help to keep children from feeling like they are failures?

7. **EX**  Have students role-play a group of adults planning a fund-raising project (or another activity of your choice). Some of the adults should "take initiative beyond their ability or beyond reasonable limits," some should "take initiative within reasonable limits," and some should "act afraid to show initiative due to past failures."

8. **ER**  Panel discussion: Invite three or four parents to discuss activities their children tried in the preschool years. Have the parents be prepared to share some of the funny and dangerous consequences of the children's explorations.

## Showing Responsibility

9. **RF**  *A Dependable Adult*, Activity A, SAG. Have students list some examples of dependable adults and describe some advantages of being dependable as an adult.

10. **RT**  *Preschoolers Show Responsibility*, color transparency CT-17. Use this transparency to indicate ways preschoolers show responsibility. Ask students to brainstorm other ways children can demonstrate they are learning responsibility.

11. **RF**  Students should plan some tasks a preschool child might be able to do in the home setting. Students should draw or illustrate five of these tasks on three-by-five-inch cards so a preschooler could "read" these cards with little help. Have students ask a parent to try these tasks with his or her preschooler, helping as needed. After a week, the parent should report results.

12. **ER**  Field trip: Arrange for students to visit and observe a group program for preschool children. After the visit students should explain the ways in which the adult encouraged the children to show responsibility.

## Learning Gender Roles

13. *Sex Typing and Gender Roles*, transparency master 17-1. Explain to students that learning gender roles is an important part of preschoolers' social-emotional development. Sex typing aids gender-role learning. Gender roles may be defined strictly or broadly depending on the culture and priorities of the people who surround children. Using the transparency, have students discuss areas of difference in the treatment of boys and girls. Write their responses on the transparency. Discuss with students how these differences affect the social-emotional development of boys and girls.

14. **EX**  For each of the following gender-role expectations, students should give an example of a specific learning society may expect of a male and a female: (a) physical behaviors, such as style of dress, speech, walking, and sitting; (b) priorities and attitudes, such as how a person treats members of the same or opposite gender; (c) various roles, such as in the family, community, and workplace.

15. **RT**  Ask students for examples of overexaggerations when learning gender roles. (An example of an overexaggeration might be the following: A boy will not touch a doll if other boys are around, yet plays dolls with a sister at home.) Students should discuss whether they think boys or girls are more apt to overexaggerate when learning gender roles.

16. **ER**  Have students ask several three- to five-year-olds to name someone they want to be like when they are grown. Students should report whether most of the choices reflect same-gender models.

17. **ER**  Invite students to interview a person over 60 years of age. Students should ask the older person how women and men were expected to act differently in terms of physical behaviors, personal priorities and attitudes toward the same and opposite genders, and roles in the family, community, and workplace when they were younger. Instruct each student to write an article on the differences.

18. **RF**  Ask students to discuss in pairs whether they agree that boys tend to be more physical and girls tend to be more verbal? Ask each partner to provide two examples that prove or disprove this statement.

19. **ER**  *Observation: Children at Play*, Activity D, SAG. Students should observe a group of children at play and record their observations. Students are asked to pay particular attention to gender-role modeling in play activities and conversation.

## Extending Social Relations

20. **RT**   Ask students for examples of how adults serve as social models.
21. **RF**   *Friends Are Important*, Activity B, SAG. Students should observe and record characteristics of preschool children's friendships.
22. **RT**   Ask students for examples of how preschool children's peer groups aid learning in the following ways: (a) by enriching play experiences; (b) by teaching children to be fair; (c) by helping children to see from other children's perspectives; and (d) by providing fun times.
23. **RF**   *Learning from Play*, Activity C, SAG. Students should describe possible learning from a number of play activities.

## Feeling and Controlling Emotions

24. **RT**   Discuss with students why preschool children react to stressors (illness, moving, death, adult quarrels, divorce) in more serious ways than toddlers.
25. **RT**   Discuss with students ways that adults can positively foster children's feelings and help them control emotions.

## Dependency

26. **ER**   Invite students to interview a parent concerning his or her preschool child's level of dependence. Students should then share the following in class: (1) Explain how the child shows dependence. (2) Does the child's dependence ever upset the parent? If so, explain the circumstances. (3) How does the parent handle the dependence?
27. **EX**   Ask students to describe the different forms of dependence (physical, financial, and emotional). Discuss with students how emotional dependence on others at various points in the individual life cycle can be both good and bad.

## Fear and Anxiety

28. **RF**   Instruct students to make a poster that depicts changes in fears from the toddler to the preschool years. (Students may leave space to depict school-aged fears and complete the poster while studying the chapter on school-age children.)

29. **RT**   Discuss with students why fears change over the years. Students should give examples of adult fears of which preschool children would likely be unaware.
30. **RT**   Ask students for examples of how fear can lead to more danger in some situations and to less danger in other situations.
31. **ER**   Students should ask a group of preschoolers how they feel about the characters in the movie, *The Wizard of Oz*. Do they fear any of the characters at all? Do they like scary stories? Find out whether any TV shows frighten them. How do their parents help them overcome their fears? Have students share findings in class.

## Anger and Aggression

32. **RT**   Ask students to list possible causes of anger and aggression in preschoolers.
33. **RT**   Discuss with students reasons some experts are concerned about aggression depicted in books, comics and cartoons, television, and movies.
34. **RT**   Ask students to describe how anger can be used to get one's way, intentionally hurt another, and gain attention.
35. **RT**   Ask students to explain why children direct their anger more toward other children than toward adults.
36. **ER**   *Observation: Aggression in Preschoolers*, reproducible master 17-2. Have students observe a group of preschool children at play and record information about their aggressive behavior. Students should present their findings orally to the class.

## Jealousy

37. **EX**   Have students describe situations where teens feel jealous. At whom do they generally aim their jealousy? How do they feel toward that person or object? When they realize they must share something or someone, are children's feelings similar or different from those of teens?
38. **ER**   Invite students to interview a parent concerning his or her preschool child's expressions of sibling jealousy. Students may ask the following questions: How long did the jealousy last? How did the child express jealousy? How did the parent(s) handle the situation? Students should use the information to write a paper about sibling jealousy.

# Answer Key

## Text

### Reviewing Key Concepts, page 416

1. false
2. true
3. true
4. true
5. true
6. false
7. C
8. Peers make play experiences richer. Children are taught how to behave by peers. Children become less egocentric in peer groups. Children see friends as fun.
9. B, C, F
10. false
11. known
12. true

## Teacher's Resources

### Chapter 17 Test

| | | |
|---|---|---|
| 1. T | 14. T | 27. D |
| 2. T | 15. T | 28. C |
| 3. T | 16. T | 29. D |
| 4. F | 17. D | 30. C |
| 5. T | 18. A | 31. B |
| 6. T | 19. B | 32. G |
| 7. T | 20. A | 33. H |
| 8. F | 21. B | 34. E |
| 9. T | 22. D | 35. I |
| 10. T | 23. B | 36. A |
| 11. T | 24. A | 37. F |
| 12. F | 25. D | |
| 13. F | 26. A | |

38. Children who take the initiative achieve many goals by exploring, experimenting, and questioning. Self-control is learned, too, because initiative should be taken within the limits defined by adults. Also, initiative in childhood leads to ambitions and purpose in life as an adult.

39. The adult must select tasks, often household tasks, with the child's ability and time in mind. The adult must carefully explain and demonstrate how the tasks are to be done. If a child does a task correctly, praise is needed. If the child does not complete the task or do it to a satisfactory level, the adult must provide additional encouragement or help, such as to reteach the task. Adults should not redo the child's work or criticize.

40. Children may have nightmares or physical problems, such as upset stomachs, headaches, fevers, and changes in appetite.

# Sex Typing and Gender Roles

| Areas of Difference | Boys | Girls |
|---|---|---|
| Birth announcement cards; greeting cards | | |
| Clothes | | |
| Popular games | | |
| Toys | | |
| Party decorations | | |
| Bedroom/playroom decor | | |

# Observation: Aggression in Preschoolers

**Name** _____ **Date** _____ **Period** _____

Aggression, both physical and verbal, occurs often in preschool groups. Although aggressive acts are often short-lived and soon forgotten by the "combatants;" adults who care for children feel as though they spend much of their time helping children avoid and resolve aggression. Observe a group of preschool children at play and give information requested below. Then plan and present to the class an oral presentation on your findings.

1. Describe the ages of children, number of children, and the play setting (indoor/outdoor; activity or activities). _____
_____
_____
_____
_____

2. Observe the play group for five minutes. Keep a tally of the number of aggressive acts you observe. How many did you note? _____

3. Observe again for an indefinite period. Record information on five aggressive acts using the chart on the following page. _____

4. Note the traits of children who seem to be frequently involved in aggressive acts. How would you describe these aggressive children's personalities? _____
_____
_____
_____
_____
_____

5. Note the traits of children who seem to have reasons to be aggressive at times but who often avoid aggressive acts. How would you describe these nonaggressive children's personalities? _____
_____
_____
_____
_____

6. Compare your findings with the text discussion on the "take charge" children and the more carefree children. _____
_____
_____
_____
_____

*(Continued)*

| Child Involved (first name) | Subject of Aggressive Act (first name) | Form of Aggression | Probable Cause | How Resolved |
|---|---|---|---|---|
|  |  |  |  |  |
|  |  |  |  |  |
|  |  |  |  |  |
|  |  |  |  |  |
|  |  |  |  |  |

# Social-Emotional Development of the Preschooler

**Name** _____

**Date** _____ **Period** _____ **Score** _____

## Chapter 17 Test

True/False: Circle *T* if the statement is true or *F* if the statement is false.

T  F  1. For preschoolers too much failure can result in feelings of guilt.

T  F  2. Through their own examples adults help children become dependable and accept responsibility.

T  F  3. Preschool children often learn responsibility by performing household tasks.

T  F  4. By two years of age children know whether they are male or female.

T  F  5. Preschoolers learn their gender roles.

T  F  6. Preschoolers learn to think about the feelings of others through social interactions.

T  F  7. Adults are still important to preschool children.

T  F  8. Preschool children rarely extend their social relationships beyond their family.

T  F  9. Learning to be dependable involves successes and failures before mastery is achieved.

T  F  10. Stressors in a preschooler include the real and the unreal.

T  F  11. Preschoolers are expected to control many of their intense emotional feelings.

T  F  12. Once children go to preschool and are involved with other children, they stop depending on parents for emotional support.

T  F  13. Fears remain the same from the toddler years through the preschool years.

T  F  14. A shove may be a preschool child's sign of affection.

T  F  15. Anger and aggression is more often directed at other children than at adults.

T  F  16. Jealousy often develops over stress regarding the preschool child's attachment.

Multiple Choice: Choose the best response. Write the letter in the space provided.

_____ 17. As children develop initiative, they _____.
A. like to ask questions
B. like to explore
C. may feel they are bad when they fail
D. All of the above.

_____ 18. Initiative in the preschool years later leads to _____.
A. ambition and purpose for one's life
B. happiness in marriage
C. curiosity about the world
D. better self-control

_____ 19. Too many failures can cause a child to _____.
A. turn to earlier behaviors
B. be afraid to try new experiences
C. cling to their parents
D. yell at their friends

*(Continued)*

**Name** _____

_____ 20. Children need some limits placed on their initiative for all of the following reasons *except* _____.
A. keeping them from disturbing adults
B. preventing some failures and the resulting feelings of guilt
C. keeping them safe
D. reducing the fear of trying new things

_____ 21. Good parenting involves all of the following *except* _____.
A. encouraging children to take the initiative for their own learning
B. punishing children and making them feel guilty when they make mistakes
C. giving children opportunities to show they can be dependable and responsible
D. minimizing feelings of guilt when children do tasks that are too difficult for them to do

_____ 22. Preschoolers' gender role-learning depends on _____.
A. how they are treated
B. how they see men and women treated in their home, community, and on television
C. their cultural patterns
D. All of the above.

_____ 23. The ease of making friends depends on _____.
A. preschooler's friendliness
B. ability to follow group rules
C. lack of dependence on adults
D. All of the above.

_____ 24. Friendship is seen by preschool children from _____.
A. a selfish point of view
B. an unselfish point of view
C. a mutual interest point of view
D. None of the above.

_____ 25. Stressors occurring in preschool children compared to those in toddlers are characterized as _____.
A. lasting for a shorter amount of time
B. less serious
C. Both A and B.
D. Neither A nor B.

_____ 26. Which of the following statements is *not* true about preschoolers' emotions?
A. Preschoolers' emotions as compared with those of toddlers are less intense.
B. Preschoolers are expected to control expressions of their emotions.
C. Preschoolers often admit their underlying feelings to themselves and others.
D. Preschoolers feel many emotions.

_____ 27. Preschoolers show fears and anxieties about _____.
A. monsters and other unreal beings
B. criminals
C. injuries or pain to their own bodies
D. All of the above.

_____ 28. Sibling jealousy begins when preschool children realize the _____.
A. new baby usually gets his or her way
B. parent loves the older child less
C. new baby will claim some of the parent's attention which he or she once had
D. All of the above.

*(Continued)*

**Name** _____

Matching: Match the following terms and identifying phrases.

_____ 29.  The ability to think or act without being urged.

_____ 30.  Blaming oneself for something done wrong.

_____ 31.  Knowing what behavior is expected of a male or female.

_____ 32.  Treating boys and girls differently.

_____ 33.  A statement or hint that men and women always do or should do certain tasks.

_____ 34.  Unrelated people who are near the same age.

_____ 35.  Situations that cause feelings of tension.

_____ 36.  Seeking attention, approval, comfort, and contact from another person.

_____ 37.  Feelings of envy that are not directly expressed and may even be denied.

A. emotional dependency
B. gender-role learning
C. guilt
D. initiative
E. peers
F. repressed jealousy
G. sex typing
H. sexual stereotyping
I. stressors

Essay Questions: Provide complete responses to the following questions or statements.

38. Why do preschool children need to take initiative?

39. How does a preschool child learn responsibility?

40. How may repressed jealousy be harmful for a child?

# Providing for the Preschooler's Developmental Needs

## Objectives

After studying this chapter, students will be able to
- plan ways to meet the developmental needs of preschool children.
- help preschool children care for their own physical needs.
- stimulate preschool children's mental thinking.
- assist preschoolers in meeting their social and emotional needs.

## Bulletin Boards

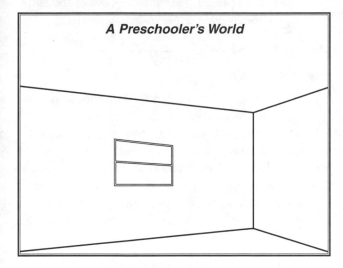

**A Preschooler's World**

Title: *A Preschooler's World*

Draw the outline of an empty room on the board. Have students select pictures of furniture and accessory items that are designed for a preschool child's bedroom or play space. Students should display these items on the board.

Title: *Preschoolers Can Group Objects That Are Alike*

Students should group various shapes together, such as squares, triangles, and colors, under the title.

## Teaching Materials

**Text**, pages 418-455
  *Reviewing Key Concepts*
  *Using Your Knowledge*
  *Making Observations*
  *Thinking Further*

**Student Activity Guide**
  A. *Special Foods Are Fun*
  B. *Evaluating Garments for Preschoolers*
  C. *Planned Observation Activities for Preschoolers*
  D. *Problem-Solving Games—A Step Toward Logic*
  E. *Observation: Let's Pretend*
  F. *Vocabulary Grows from Everyday Activities*
  G. *Helping with Tasks*

**Teacher's Resources**
  *Helping Preschoolers Gain Independence,* reproducible master 18-1
  *Meal/Snack Pattern for Preschoolers,* reproducible master 18-2
  *Helpful Features Encourage Self-Dressing,* color transparency CT-18
  *Intellectual Development Activities for Preschoolers,* reproducible master 18-3
  *Motor Development Activities for Preschoolers,* reproducible master 18-4
  *Harnessing Preschoolers' Energy,* reproducible master 18-5
  *Helping Preschoolers Develop Computer Skills,* transparency master 18-6
  *Evaluating Gender Roles,* reproducible master 18-7
  Chapter 18 Test

## Introductory Activities

1. Ask students to contrast the physical, intellectual, and social-emotional development of preschoolers with that of toddlers.
2. *Helping Preschoolers Gain Independence,* reproducible master 18-1. For each dependence problem given, have students brainstorm ways that adults could foster independence.
3. Students should list ways that adults can help preschoolers meet their developmental needs. They may add to the list as they progress through the chapter.

# Strategies to Reteach, Reinforce, Enrich, and Extend Text Concepts

## Physical Needs

4. **RT** Ask students for examples of how each of the following developmental changes equip children to better meet their physical needs: (a) maturation of the body; (b) refinement of many motor skills; and (c) the growing mind.
5. **RT** Discuss with students how the adult-child relationship deepens when adults help children meet their physical needs.

## Meeting Nutritional Needs

6. **RF** Ask students to make a poster depicting the importance of good nutrition for the preschool child.
7. **EX** *Meal/Snack Pattern for Preschoolers*, reproducible master 18-2. Ask students to compare both serving sizes and the number of servings for each food group on this menu pattern with the recommendations based on the Food Guide Pyramid for Young Children.
8. **EX** Invite students to ask a preschool child what foods he or she likes and dislikes. Keeping the child's preferences in mind, students should plan a week's menu that meets a preschooler's general needs. (Note: You may use Figure 18-3 in the text as a guide.) Students should critique one another's menus in class.
9. **EX** *Special Foods Are Fun*, Activity A, SAG. Have students plan and prepare one nutritious and attractive-looking meal or snack. Students should try serving their meal to a preschooler and evaluate it according to the preschooler's response.

## Selecting the Right Clothes

10. **RT** *Helpful Features Encourage Self-Dressing*, color transparency CT-18. Use this transparency to lead a discussion about self-dressing features that help children learn to dress themselves.
11. **RF** *Evaluating Garments for Preschoolers*, Activity B, SAG. Students should choose and evaluate a garment for a preschooler.
12. **EX** Instruct students to choose a pair of shoes for a preschool child and compare the shoes with the criteria in Figure 18-11 in the text.

13. **ER** Students should collect photos of clothing for preschool children. They should show these photos to a child and ask what the child likes and does not like about the clothes. Students should record the child's responses and share them in class discussion.

## Handling Sleep and Toileting Problems

14. **RT** Instruct students to review the bedtime ritual planned in SAG Activity 14A. Have students list ways they would change the toddler's bedtime ritual to meet a preschooler's needs.
15. **RT** Discuss with students how they would handle a preschooler's bedtime toileting accidents. Have them explain how they would handle daytime accidents of a preschooler, too.
16. **ER** Guest speaker: Invite an adult who works in a preschool program to share ways he or she helps preschool children avoid toileting accidents.

## Providing Needed Space and Furnishings

17. **RF** Students should list the benefits of having storage spaces for preschool children's possessions. Discuss with students the qualities of good storage spaces.
18. **ER** Field trip: Arrange to visit several preschool facilities to look at the storage spaces for preschool group programs. Have students discuss how parents could adapt some of the storage spaces for home use.

## Learning Responsibility

19. **RT** Ask students to find a picture of a playroom or bedroom designed for a preschooler. Have students list evidence of self-help features and perhaps some impractical features for the more independent preschooler.
20. **EX** Visit a child care and education program. Ask each student to make a descriptive list of furnishings designed to help preschoolers become more independent.
21. **EX** Explain to students that in homes, unlike child care centers, spaces must grow with the child. Ask students to draw how a bedroom closet might be remodeled as the child grows from the preschool through teen years. (The class will need to investigate on the easy reaching heights of children at different ages.)

## Intellectual Needs

22. **EX**  Discuss the following question with students: How do divergent thinkers benefit society?
23. **RT**  Have students discuss how adults can stimulate children's mental abilities while going for ice cream, shopping, and going to the park.
24. **RT**  Students should explain why the home and neighborhood are just as beneficial if not more so when it comes to providing opportunities for learning.
25. **RT**  *Intellectual Development Activities for Preschoolers*, reproducible master 18-2. Use this master to present activities for students to use while working with preschool children on the following intellectual development areas: observation skills, sorting and classifying skills, ordering skills, transformation skills, and reversal skills. For each category, students are asked to create an activity of their own.

## Learning Through Observing

26. **RF**  *Planned Observation Activities for Preschoolers*, Activity C, SAG. Have students select one or more of the observation activities to try with a preschool child and record the results.
27. **RF**  Instruct each student to observe a preschooler watching a children's TV program alone. Note the child's actions and comments. Observe another preschooler watching a similar program with an involved adult. Again record the child's actions and comments. Discuss the differences between the two situations in class. Also discuss ways in which passive viewing may contribute to a child's short attention span, focus attention on minor details, and promote incorrect understandings.

## Learning Through Problem Solving

28. **ER**  Have students interview a preschool teacher and ask the teacher to explain or demonstrate activities and materials he or she uses to help the children learn problem-solving skills.
29. **RF**  *Problem-Solving Games—A Step Toward Logic*, Activity D, SAG. Have students select one activity from each of the following areas: classification, putting objects in order, transformation, and reversals. Use the activities with a preschool child. Students should record their observations of the preschool child's interest in the activities and learnings.

## Learning Through Symbolizing

30. **ER**  Instruct students to prepare an article for a local newspaper explaining the types of symbols preschool children need to experience before they begin to read and write words.
31. **RF**  *Observation: Let's Pretend*, Activity E, SAG. Students should observe children in pretend play. Have students record their observations and report in class.

## Learning Through Motor Skills

32. **RT**  *Motor Development Activities for Preschoolers*, reproducible master 18-4. Use this master to identify motor skill activities appropriate for preschoolers. Students are also asked to create one gross-motor activity and one fine-motor activity of their own.
33. **RF**  Instruct students to observe a toddler and a preschool child playing with equipment that requires fine-motor skills, such as scissors, crayons, beads, or building sets. (The equipment should be a toddler-safe style and size.) Students should contrast the children's skills and share observations with class members.
34. **RF**  Ask students to show and explain how children's building toys can accommodate the different stages in children's development. (Building toys for younger children come in larger piece sizes and have fewer total pieces. For older children the piece size is smaller and the total number of pieces increases.)
35. **RF**  *Harnessing Preschoolers' Energy*, reproducible master 18-5. Students should observe and record adult-child interactions during times when preschoolers are expected to be quiet or still. Students should then offer suggestions on how to use the preschoolers' energies during quiet activities.

## Learning Through Language

36. **RT**  Discuss with students why children of multiple births often have more problems with language than single-birth siblings.
37. **RF**  *Vocabulary Grows from Everyday Activities*, Activity F, SAG. Students should list words children might learn when adult-child talk becomes part of daily activities.
38. **RT**  Have students discuss why some parents and caregivers allow preschool children to watch television for many hours each day and what the consequences of this might be.

39. **RF** With the help of a librarian, students should choose a quality book for a preschool child. Students should list new words and concepts the child may learn by hearing the story and talking about the illustrations.

40. **RF** A first-grade teacher said he could quickly tell which children beginning first grade had been read to and which children had mainly watched TV in their preschool years. (The teacher did not receive this information from parents or other adult caregivers.) Ask students to explain how this could be true.

## Computers and Learning

41. **RF** Make arrangements for students to visit a store that sells or a classroom or computer lab that has computer programs for preschoolers. Working in groups, have each group examine software designed for preschoolers. Programs that have been especially recommended for this age group include: Reader Rabbit Toddler and Reader Rabbit I from The Learning Company, Disney's Mickey Mouse from Disney Interactive, and Jumpstart Pre-School from Knowledge Adventure.

42. **EX** *Helping Preschoolers Develop Computer Skills*, transparency master 18-6. Use this transparency as a discussion starter on helping preschoolers use a computer. Students may interview staff members of child care and education programs and ask for additional tips.

43. **ER** Have students visit the following Web sites to review children's products: *Children's Software Revue* magazine online at **www.childrenssoftware.com** and the *Children and computers* Web site, **www.childrenandcomputers.com.**

## Social-Emotional Needs

44. **RT** Discuss with students possible reasons that preschool children have more fragile self-concepts than adults do.

45. **ER** Guest speaker: Invite an adult who is employed in a preschool program to share with the class some examples of social progress children have made since beginning the program. (Note: Ask the speaker to avoid using children's names.)

## Discipline: Helping with Initiative and Mistakes

46. **ER** Share with students the following case study: Tomi is a curious five-year-old who likes to do tasks on his own. While his mother is on the phone, he climbs onto the kitchen cabinet to reach a box of cereal. On his way down he breaks his mother's favorite vase. Have students suggest a positive statement his mother could use to discourage him from doing something like this again.

47. **ER** Do research on spanking. Have students read different books and articles and summarize their opinions and reasons. Report to the class.

48. **EX** Instruct students to role-play the parts of parents making a mistake, admitting it, and telling or showing children that making mistakes doesn't make a person bad.

49. **EX** Instruct students to role-play the parts of adults setting limits for children concerning how much TV they may watch, where and how long they can play, and when they should go to bed.

## Sharing Responsibility

50. **RF** Have students make an item to help a child learn a task. (For example, students may make some placemats that picture the basic positions for a plate, cup and saucer, glass, three pieces of flatware, and napkin.)

51. **ER** *Helping with Tasks,* Activity G, SAG. Students are asked to identify parts of household tasks preschoolers can help adults do and describe how they would explain each task so that a preschooler could understand.

52. **ER** Panel discussion: Invite several parents of preschool children to discuss tasks their children have done successfully. Panelists should focus on how they explained the tasks to the child, to what standards they expected the tasks to be completed, and how much and what kind of adult help was needed.

## Aiding Gender Role Learning

53. **ER** Have students look at children's books and toys about various occupations. Students should find examples of how some of the books and toys promote traditional gender roles and how others promote nontraditional gender roles.

54. **ER** *Evaluating Gender Roles,* reproducible master 8-7. Students are asked to choose three children's books and use the questions provided to evaluate the gender roles presented in each book.

55. **RT** Panel discussion: Invite an equal number of mothers and fathers to discuss teaching gender roles. Mothers should discuss some of

the activities they do with their daughters; fathers should discuss some of the activities they do with their sons. Panelists and class members should discuss what the children are learning about gender roles as they participate in the activities.

## Providing Time for Friendships

56. **RT** Discuss with students why showing concern for a hurt child is a more effective guidance technique than punishing the aggressor.
57. **ER** Instruct students to plan and present a skit depicting two children who want the same toy. Students should show several positive ways in which adults can handle the situation.

## Helping Children with Emotional Control

58. **RF** Ask students to list some specific ways that parents and teachers can encourage independence among preschoolers.
59. **RT** Discuss with students why adults never should laugh at or belittle children's fears. How can adults be models of courage even when they themselves are fearful?
60. **RF** Ask students to list as many ways as they can to reduce competitive situations among children. Students should observe examples of how adults working in preschool programs attempt to reduce competition.
61. **RF** Have students list tasks a preschool child could perform to help with a new baby.
62. **EX** Students should role-play how to best prepare a child for a new brother or sister.

## Recognizing Developmental Delays

63. **RT** Ask students to prepare a list of common developmental delays in preschoolers.
64. **ER** Ask a pediatrician to speak to the class about how he or she recognizes developmental delays in preschoolers. Have students prepare a list of questions in advance.

# Answer Key

## Text

*Reviewing Key Concepts,* page 454
1. B, C
2. true

3. C, D, E
4. (List three:) long shoelaces; no reflective tape on clothes worn after dark; nondetachable hoods; floppy headwear and/or pant legs; long, wide sleeves; drawstring ties; long scarves and sashes; too large clothes
5. (List two:) restrict bedtime liquids; remind children to use the toilet when they wake up, before they go to bed, and before they leave the house; make certain children's clothes are easy to put on and take off
6. true
7. false
8. B, C, D, F
9. are
10. adults
11. should not
12. (List two:) give positive statements when children are successful; give children the freedom to try things on their own; give children reasonable limits; admit their own mistakes to children
13. true
14. (List two:) teach children they do not always have to share any more than adults do; model concern for the hurt rather than shame the aggressor; explain feelings of both children wanting the same toy or wanting to do the same thing
15. false

## Teacher's Resource Guide
### Chapter 18 Test

| | | |
|---|---|---|
| 1. T | 17. F | 33. H |
| 2. T | 18. F | 34. M |
| 3. F | 19. A | 35. N |
| 4. T | 20. B | 36. P |
| 5. F | 21. C | 37. E |
| 6. T | 22. A | 38. F |
| 7. T | 23. D | 39. O |
| 8. T | 24. B | 40. K |
| 9. F | 25. D | 41. I |
| 10. T | 26. C | 42. J |
| 11. T | 27. D | 43. B |
| 12. T | 28. B | 44. C |
| 13. F | 29. D | 45. A |
| 14. F | 30. D | 46. D |
| 15. T | 31. L | |
| 16. F | 32. G | |

47. Adults expect preschool children to become more independent by meeting more of their own physical needs. Adults expect preschoolers to grow more slowly than before and to continue to refine their motor skills.

48. (Describe three. Student response. See pages 431 to 443 in the text.)

49. (List four. Student response. See pages 442 and 443 in the text.)

50. Parents can support social-emotional development by encouraging independence, helping children show responsibility, and setting an example of how to control hurtful expressions of feelings.

# Helping Preschoolers Gain Independence

**Name** _____ **Date** _____ **Period** _____

**Problem:**   Susan is three years old and waits for her mother to
dress her completely.

**Possible Solutions:**




**Problem:**   When anyone speaks to Chris, he hides behind his parent
or babysitter.

**Possible Solutions:**




**Problem:**   Debbie, a 4½-year-old, sobs each time her mother takes
her to the child care center (even though she is well cared for
and has been attending the program for several months).

**Possible Solutions:**




**Problem:**   During any creative activity at kindergarten, Richard hesitates and
will not begin until he sees how his classmates are doing the activity.

**Possible Solutions:**

# Meal/Snack Pattern for Preschoolers

## Breakfast—Preschoolers

1 milk component

1 fruit/vegetable component

1 grain component

## Lunch and Dinner—Preschoolers

1 milk component

2 fruit/vegetable components

1 grain component

1 meat/meat alternate component

## Snack—Preschoolers

Each day, two snacks must be served halfway between meals. For each snack, choose two from the following:

1 milk component

2 fruit/vegetable components

1 grain component

1 meat/meat alternate component

*(Continued)*

## Milk Component

### Meals
¾ cup fluid milk

### Snack
½ cup fluid milk

## Fruit/Vegetable Component

½ cup full-strength fruit or vegetable juice[1]

½ cup fruit or vegetable

Note:
[1] Juice cannot be served at snack if milk is the only other snack component.

## Grain/Bread Component[2]

½ slice bread

½ roll, biscuit, muffin, or cornbread serving

⅓ cup cold dry cereal

¼ cup hot cooked cereal

¼ cup pasta, noodles, or grains

Note:
[2] Breads and grains must be made from whole-grain or enriched meal or flour. Cereals must be whole-grain, enriched, or fortified.

## Meat/Meat Alternate Component

### Lunch/Dinner

1½ oz. meat, poultry, or fish[3], or alternate protein product

1½ oz. cheese

¾ egg

⅜ cup cooked, dry beans or peas

3 tbsp. peanut butter (or other seed or nut butters)

¾ oz. nuts or seeds[4]

6 oz. yogurt[5]

Notes:
[3] Only the edible portion of cooked lean meat, poultry, or fish counts toward the requirement.

[4] For lunch and dinner, nuts and seeds may only meet half of the total meat/meat alternate serving and must be combined with another meat/meat alternate to fulfill the requirement.

[5] Yogurt may be plain or flavored, sweetened or unsweetened.

### Snack

½ oz. meat, poultry, or fish[3], or alternate protein product

½ oz. cheese

½ egg

⅛ cup cooked, dry beans or peas

1 tbsp. peanut butter (or other seed or nut butters)

½ oz. nuts and seeds

2 oz. yogurt[4]

Notes:
[3] Only the edible portion of cooked lean meat, poultry, or fish counts toward the requirement.

[4] Yogurt may be plain or flavored, sweetened or unsweetened.

USDA Child Care Food Program

# Intellectual Development Activities
# for Preschoolers

**Name** _____ **Date** _____ **Period** _____

For each category given, read the sample activity and then write an activity of your own that would be suitable for preschoolers.

## Observation Activities

**Little Bits of Big Objects:** Give the child a paper towel tube or small mailing tube to use as a telescope. Show the child how to look through the tube with one eye while the other eye is closed. (You might explain that a real telescope helps people see objects that are far away.) Point to a rather large object, such as a chair. Ask the child to look at it through the tube. Help the child move the tube until he or she sees the object. Then say, "Which part of the chair do you see?" Name parts for the child to find and ask questions about each part, such as questions about its color and shape.

Activity title: _____

_____

_____

_____

_____

## Sorting Activities

**Red Here, Blue There:** Gather red and blue objects (balls, blocks, and other items) and two pieces of paper (one red and one blue). Begin by placing a red object on the red paper. Say, "I am putting the red block on the red paper." Repeat with a blue item. Then pick up a red or a blue object and ask, "Where does this blue block (or red block) go?" If the child understands, give the object to the child to put on the paper. The child may continue until all objects are sorted. If the child does not understand, repeat the first step.

Activity title: _____

_____

_____

_____

_____

## Classifying Activities

**Two Houses:** Show the child a group of small blocks that may be classified by color or shape. Ask, "Are any of these alike in some way?" The child may say that some of the objects are blue, some are red, or some are round. If the child does not single out an attribute, say, "Would you like to find all the red or all the blue or all the round ones?" (Let the child choose.) Then, get out two small boxes and say, "Let's put all the blue blocks in this box. We will put all the blocks that are not blue in this other box." After the child has grouped the blocks correctly, point to the other box and say, "This is the house for items that are not blue."

Activity title: _____

_____

_____

_____

_____

*(Continued)*

**Name** _____

## Ordering Activities

**Little, Bigger, Biggest:** Gather three boxes—one small, one medium, and one large. Set the boxes in front of the child so the smallest box is to the child's left, the medium one is in front of the child, and the largest is to the child's right. Ask the child to find the little box, then the bigger box, and finally the biggest box. If the child makes a mistake and does not correct it, try nesting the boxes to help him or her.

Activity title: _____

_____

_____

_____

_____

_____

## Transformation Activities

**Growing Plants:** Help the child plant a fast-growing seed, such as a bean. You may also put a sweet potato in water. Observe it daily and talk about the changes taking place. Taking pictures can help the child recall past states.

Activity title: _____

_____

_____

_____

_____

_____

## Reversal Activities

**Water and Sand Play:** Gather two containers of different sizes. Put some water into one container. Let a child pour the water from one container into the other and back again. The child can do a similar reversal with sand.

Activity title: _____

_____

_____

_____

_____

_____

## Symbolizing Activities

**Pantomime:** Have the child act out an action as chosen by the child or suggested by the adult. Have others try to guess what the action is.

Activity title: _____

_____

_____

_____

_____

_____

# Motor Development Activities for Preschooolers

**Name** _____ **Date** _____ **Period** _____

Read the following motor development activities and then write one gross-motor and one fine-motor activity of your own.

## Gross-Motor Skills

**Sliding:** Teach the child to slide by moving one foot to the side and bringing the other foot to it. Do not let the body bounce. Once the child masters the step, have him or her slide through narrow spaces. The child may also slide to music.

**Bending, Twisting, and Swaying:** Have the child try movements with feet in place, such as bending, twisting, and swaying. Use such movements to pretend to be the wind, a rocking boat, a swaying tree, or any other object.

Activity title: _____

_____

_____

_____

_____

_____

_____

_____

## Fine-Motor Skills

**Tracing:** Have the child practice tracing around various objects, such as plastic cookie cutters with knobs. The child can do this tracing on paper with a pencil, on dampened sand with a finger, or on a flattened piece of clay with a plastic tool.

**Cutting:** Have the child practice cutting using child-sized, blunt-tipped safety scissors. Start with cutting blank paper, and progress to cutting out shapes drawn on the paper.

Activity title: _____

_____

_____

_____

_____

_____

_____

_____

# Harnessing Preschoolers' Energy

**Name**_____**Date**_____**Period** _____

Preschoolers are increasingly asked to "sit still" or "walk quietly" in group programs for young children. Parents want children to keep still at home, too. Parents and other adults must learn to use the preschoolers' energy even in "quiet" activities. In the space below, respond to each of the following questions.

1. Observe four- or five-year-old children in a group setting, such as kindergarten, while the adult reads a story or involves the children in another "quiet" activity. After observing, respond to the items below.

    Did the adult ask or tell the children to be quiet or sit still? _____

    If so, describe what the adult asked or said. _____

    _____

    _____

    Did all the children really sit quietly by the adult's standards? If not, describe what the children did.

    _____

    How did the adult try to maintain quietness? _____

    _____

    _____

2. Using the same or another group of preschoolers, observe a group of children walking from one part of the building to another part or to an outside door. After observing, respond to these items.

    How did the children walk? _____

    _____

    _____

    Where did they put their hands? _____

    _____

3. Pretend you are a parent, babysitter, or teacher of preschoolers. You want the preschoolers to do some quiet activities. Suggest ways to use the preschoolers' energies while engaging in these "quiet" activities.

    Listening to a story _____

    _____

    _____

    _____

    Painting _____

    _____

    _____

    _____

*(Continued)*

**Name**_____

Singing a song _____

_____

_____

Sharing ideas in a group time _____

_____

_____

_____

Walking in a line or cluster _____

_____

_____

_____

4. "Sit perfectly still, feet flat on the floor, hands in your lap, and keep your eyes on the speaker." Try this posture, then respond to these items.

Did you concentrate on what the speaker was saying or on your posture? Explain. _____

_____

_____

_____

Did you become more tired than usual although you were sitting "perfectly still?" _____

_____

_____

_____

Do you think it is reasonable for adults to expect or demand that preschoolers be "perfectly still" for relatively long periods? Justify your answer. _____

_____

_____

_____

# Helping Preschoolers Develop Computer Skills

## General Learnings:
- → Wash hands before using a computer
- → Learn computer terms (through adult use, not drill)
- → Never unplug or turn off a computer; ask for help

## Skills for Three-Year-Olds
- → Talk or sing with program characters
- → Use directional arrows with software until child is about 42 months old (Arrows develop spatial concepts of up, down, left, and right.)
- → Introduce mouse. (Mouse develops fine-motor skills and spatial concepts.)
- → Help child position hands over mouse with one or more fingers extended over left button only (for PCs)
- → Move mouse randomly while watching cursor
- → Move mouse purposefully to large icon areas
- → Steady mouse and click
- → Explore icons on screen

## Skills for Four-Year-Olds
- → Start a program from the desktop
- → Use a CD in the CD-Rom drive
- → Click and drag on objects; move objects around
- → Work through simple programs

## Skills for Five-Year-Olds
- → Start the computer
- → Exit a program
- → Use the print function
- → Match letters on cards with keyboard letters; press with pointer finger
- → Use sign-in options once child can enter name
- → Work through more advanced programs
- → Explore a children's Web site, using back and forward commands and the Escape key

# Providing for the Preschooler's Developmental Needs

Name _____

Date _____ Period _____ Score _____

## Chapter 18 Test

True/False: Circle *T* if the statement is true or *F* if the statement is false.

T   F     1. Preschoolers' rate of growth may vary from month to month.

T   F     2. Poor nutrition may cause irritability and restlessness among preschoolers.

T   F     3. The Food Guide Pyramid for Young Children does *not* include recommendations for preschoolers' diets.

T   F     4. If foods are attractive looking, preschoolers are more apt to eat them.

T   F     5. Foods should be served at extreme temperatures because preschoolers like food that is very hot or very cold.

T   F     6. Some clothing can be dangerous for preschool children.

T   F     7. Preschoolers still need bedtime rituals.

T   F     8. Preschoolers need some space or furnishings of their own.

T   F     9. Television viewing provides many opportunities for active interaction.

T   F   10. Problem-solving tasks require seeing mental relationships, which is difficult for preschoolers.

T   F   11. Pretend play and creative artwork are good for the mental development of preschoolers.

T   F   12. Preschool children enjoy materials requiring fine-motor skills.

T   F   13. Purchasing computer software should be based solely on the child's interest and skills.

T   F   14. A preschool child should *not* be allowed to make mistakes because mistakes damage the child's fragile self-concept.

T   F   15. Friendships help preschoolers see from another's perspective and be less self-centered.

T   F   16. Preschoolers should learn to control their underlying feelings associated with emotions.

T   F   17. Laughing at children's fears is helpful because it makes children see how silly their fears really are.

T   F   18. Spanking for aggression helps the child see that aggression is not good.

Multiple Choice: Choose the best response. Write the letter in the space provided.

_____ 19. Mealtime should *not* be spent _____.
A. disciplining children
B. modeling table manners
C. playing language games
D. sharing news about the day's activities

*(Continued)*

**Name** _____

_____ 20. Self-dressing is aided by all of the following *except* _____.
   A. large openings at the neck and sleeves
   B. complicated fasteners
   C. front buttons or snaps
   D. easy-to-recognize fronts and backs

_____ 21. Being able to place objects in order is made easier by _____.
   A. adding more items
   B. having smaller differences among items
   C. having greater differences among items
   D. None of the above.

_____ 22. Building and then helping a child take down a tower of blocks one by one helps the child to understand _____.
   A. reversals
   B. classification
   C. placing objects in order
   D. transformations

_____ 23. Examples of transformations include _____.
   A. growth of people over the years
   B. freezing water to make ice
   C. mixing paints to make new colors
   D. All of the above.

_____ 24. A play activity that helps develop a child's imagination, creativity, and thinking processes is _____.
   A. cutting pictures from magazines
   B. using construction sets
   C. drawing an outline of an animal by connecting dots
   D. coloring by number

_____ 25. The most abstract symbols are _____.
   A. using dolls to represent family members
   B. preschooler's use of his or her body to imitate actions, such as jump like a frog
   C. pictures the child draws
   D. words the child uses

_____ 26. Motor skills aid _____.
   A. health
   B. mental development
   C. Both A and B.
   D. Neither A nor B.

_____ 27. Children learn through their _____.
   A. attempts
   B. mistakes
   C. successes
   D. All of the above.

_____ 28. Which of the following statements is *not* true?
   A. Preschool children enjoy doing tasks.
   B. Preschool children often do tasks on the parent's schedule.
   C. Preschool children need praise for tasks they have done well.
   D. Tasks for preschoolers need to be scaled to their size and abilities.

*(Continued)*

**Name** _____

_____ 29. Emotional control in children is aided when an adult _____.
  A. sets a good example of control
  B. helps children understand the difference between feelings and expressions of feelings
  C. explains that controlling emotions is difficult for everyone, even adults
  D. All of the above.

_____ 30. Adults can reduce conflicts among children by _____.
  A. not insisting on sharing
  B. modeling concern for the harmed or wronged child
  C. explaining feelings of both children
  D. All of the above.

Matching: Match the following terms and identifying phrases.

_____ 31. Involuntary urination of a child older than three years.

_____ 32. To see how objects are alike.

_____ 33. To see how objects are different.

_____ 34. Watching another's actions without interacting.

_____ 35. Having the ability to note a problem and the skills to solve it.

_____ 36. Changes that occur between one state and another.

_____ 37. A group of items that has an attribute in common.

_____ 38. Any item that does not belong within the class being considered.

_____ 39. Mentally doing and undoing an action.

_____ 40. Coming up with different possible ways to solve a problem.

_____ 41. Coming up with only one right solution.

_____ 42. Working in a joint effort.

_____ 43. Concern for others.

_____ 44. An emotion caused by frustration.

_____ 45. An attempt to hurt or an act of hurting another person.

_____ 46. The act of speaking out, standing up for one's rights, and defending oneself.

A. aggression
B. altruistic behavior
C. anger
D. assertion
E. class
F. class complement
G. compare
H. contrast
I. convergent thinking
J. cooperation
K. divergent thinking
L. enuresis
M. passive observing
N. problem solving
O. reversals
P. transformation

Essay Questions: Provide complete responses to the following questions or statements.

47. What should adults expect of preschoolers based on their physical development?

48. Describe three ways adults can aid a preschooler's intellectual development.

49. List four tips for parents regarding arranging a physically safe computer work station for their preschoolers.

50. What is an adult's role in aiding a preschooler's social-emotional development?

# School-Age Children

## Objectives

After studying this chapter, students will be able to
- describe the physical development of school-age children.
- describe the intellectual development of school-age children.
- describe the social-emotional development of school-age children.
- explain how adults and parents can help school-age children meet their developmental needs.

## Bulletin Boards

School Jitters

new friends

new routine

separation from parents

Title: *School Jitters*

Draw a large schoolhouse—either traditional or modern—on a bulletin board. Around the school students should list problems children must cope with when they enter school.

Title: *Picture Me Growing*

Have two or three volunteers from the class bring in pictures of themselves that span from first through sixth grades. Place each set of pictures on the board arranged from youngest to oldest. Label each picture by age. Have students discuss ways each child changed.

## Teaching Materials

**Text**, pages 457-497
*Reviewing Key Concepts*
*Using Your Knowledge*
*Making Observations*
*Thinking Further*

## Student Activity Guide

A. *Sports, Games, and Physical Qualities*
B. *Proper Diets Are Important in Middle Childhood*
C. *A School-Age Child's Bedroom*
D. *I Do and I Understand*
E. *Children's Humor: A Reflection of Mental and Language Development*
F. *Industry Is Important in the School Years*
G. *Peers Are Important*
H. *School-Age Children Want to Be Accepted*
I. *Helping Children Deal with Rejection*

## Teacher's Resources

*The Brain Becomes Specialized*, color transparency CT-19A
*Meal/Snack Pattern for School-Age Children*, transparency master 19-1
*Intellectual Development Activities for School-Age Children*, reproducible master 19-2
*Showing Relationships*, color transparency CT-19B
*Preparation for School*, transparency master 19-3
*Handling Friendship Problems*, reproducible master 19-4
Chapter 19 Test

## Introductory Activities

1. Adults who see a child daily may not notice his or her physical changes because they occur so gradually. Perhaps while looking at photos or seeing children dressed in certain ways, adults see these familiar children as suddenly seeming more grown up. For example, Philip's mother was looking at her eight-year-old son in a suit. She exclaimed, "I no longer have a baby; you look just like a little man!" Have students defend or refute Philip's mother's statements that her son looks like a "little man."

2. Have students view an educational television program for preschool children and one for school-age children. Students should give examples of methods the programs use to stimulate learning. What do the differences in these methods say about the differences in the thinking abilities of preschool and school-age children?

# Strategies to Reteach, Reinforce, Enrich, and Extend Text Concepts

## Physical Development of School-Age Children

3. **RT** Ask students why the school-age years are called middle childhood. What stages do they fall between? (early childhood and adolescence)
4. **EX** Discuss with students whether they ever felt physically awkward during the school-age years. Ask how the ever-changing body size affects motor skills, clothing fit, and comfort with space and furnishings.

## Body Growth and Development

5. **RT** Ask students to explain the difference between the rate of growth and development and total growth and development. Would students expect more total growth in middle childhood than in the preschool years? Why? (Although the rate of growth and development is almost the same per year, there are twice as many years in middle childhood than in the preschool years, so more total growth is expected.)
6. **RT** Discuss with students why the changes in proportions during the school-age years makes athletic activities easier for school-age children than for preschool children.
7. **RF** Instruct students to observe children in the fourth, fifth, or sixth grade. Students should note whether they see almost constant movement, such as wiggling and moving of arms and legs. Ask students to explain why these children move so continuously.
8. **EX** *The Brain Becomes Specialized,* color transparency CT-19A. Use this transparency to examine the various areas of brain specialization. Review the order and approximate ages of brain wiring for various areas. Specialization of the brain has benefits because due to frequently activated areas, the brain has stronger connections and responds more quickly and accurately. Specialization of the brain also has disadvantages because this makes it much more difficult for parts of the brain to compensate for one another in the case of an injury or illness. Rewiring takes years of therapy and is not totally successful.

## Motor Development

9. **RF** *Sports, Games, and Physical Qualities,* Activity A, SAG. Students should name sports or games in which certain players need certain physical attributes.
10. **RT** Have students explain why boys tend to perform better than girls in tasks requiring speed, power, and force.
11. **RT** Students should name some of the physical needs of school-age children that adults must help meet.

## Encouraging Health Practices and Safety

12. **RF** Have students design a poster to display in an elementary classroom that shows the need for an adequate diet in the school-age years.
13. **RF** *Proper Diets Are Important in Middle Childhood,* Activity B, SAG. Using Figure 19-6 in the text, have students plan a week's menu for a school-age child.
14. **EX** *Meal/Snack Pattern for School-Age Children,* reproducible master 19-1. Ask students to compare both the serving sizes and the number of servings for each food group on this USDA Child Care Program menu pattern with the recommendations based on the Food Guide Pyramid.
15. **EX** Ask students to list factors that contribute to the lack of fitness among today's school-age children. Ask students to list ideas for aiding fitness.

## Selecting the Right Clothing

16. **RT** Discuss with students why school-age children become concerned about how peers view their clothing selections.
17. **ER** Have students interview school-age boys and girls to identify their clothing preferences and influences on their choices. Ask students to report their findings to the class.

## Providing Needed Space and Furnishings

18. **RF** Using advertisement photos and other pictures, have students make a poster or bulletin board showing different types of bedroom accessories (such as bedspreads, curtains, lamps) that would appeal to both school-age boys and girls.

19. **RF**   *A School-Age Child's Bedroom*, Activity C, SAG. Students are asked to plan a room for a school-age child using the furniture patterns and floor plan provided.

20. **ER**   Interview a school-age child about his or her space. Have the child describe the space, furnishings, decorations, storage, and functions of the space.

## Intellectual Development of School-Age Children

21. **RF**   Have students find the term *logic* in a dictionary. Students should explain how using perception and using logic involve different ways of thinking.

22. **RF**   *I Do and I Understand*, Activity D, SAG. Have students explain why doing (action) is important to understanding (learning) in middle childhood.

23. **ER**   *Intellectual Development Activities for School-Age Children,* reproducible master 19-2. Use this master to show students various activities to do with school-age children to enhance skills in the following areas: physical knowledge, perception, logic, and language. For each area, students are asked to create one activity of their own. You may wish to have students try the activities with school-age children and report results in class.

## How School-Age Children Think

24. **EX**   Discuss with students why Andersen's *The Ugly Duckling* is better understood by school-age than preschool children. (The story involves the transformation of a swan.)

25. **RT**   Ask students to give an example of deductive reasoning and an example of inductive reasoning. Students should explain why inductive reasoning is used in scientific investigations rather than deductive reasoning.

## What School-Age Children Learn

26. **ER**   Have students ask several fifth- or sixth-grade children how they memorize a list, the number of days in each month, and other similar items. Students should note whether they use memory aids, such as rhymes.

27. **EX**   Ask students to repeat the activity based on Piaget's intellectual tasks (reproducible master 16-2 of this *Teacher's Resource* product) with seven- and eight-year-old children. Ask them to contrast the differences in logic used by four-year-olds with these older children.

28. **RT**   *Showing Relationships*, color transparency CT-19B. Use this transparency to show students how children can match two series of objects that correspond.

## Language Is Mastered

29. **RT**   Discuss with students why children with articulation problems are often referred for special speech services as early as possible.

30. **RF**   *Children's Humor: A Reflection of Mental and Language Development*, Activity E, SAG. Have students find and record examples of humor enjoyed by primary-grade and elementary-grade children. Students should note differences in the type of humor enjoyed by these two age groups.

## Helping School-Age Children Meet Their Intellectual Needs

31. **ER**   Have students share what their hobbies were as school-age children. What have they learned from these hobbies, and are there any of these hobbies they have continued?

32. **ER**   Have students list on the chalkboard some everyday home activities. Below each activity, list some learning experiences that could result from that activity.

## Guiding Intellectual Growth

33. **RT**   Discuss with students how adults may encourage children without overusing praise and rewards. Do students think that less dependence on praise and rewards for productivity is good training for the adult years? Explain why or why not.

34. **RF**.  *Preparation for School*, transparency master 19-3. Use this transparency as a basis for discussing the social-emotional transition from home to school. For each building block that depicts the needed preparation for entrance to school, have students give examples of how adults may provide the needed experiences.

35. **RF**   Have students list school-like tasks that parents could encourage children to do when they are not assigned homework.

36. **RF**   Each student should select a different television program and analyze its content for violence, unfavorable behavior, and other negative effects.

37. **EX**   Interview two elementary school teachers about what information they provide for parents concerning computer use for doing homework or enriching children's learnings.

## Social-Emotional Development of School-Age Children

38. **EX** Invite students to recall their middle childhood years and share some fun times they had with peers and some difficulties they experienced.
39. **EX** Ask students whether they agree or disagree with this statement from the text: "In many ways, social development becomes the most important aspect of development in middle childhood." Ask them to explain why they agree or disagree.

## Developing the Self-Concept

40. **RT** Discuss with students the likely differences in adults' personalities and successes if they are self-confident versus if they have much self-doubt.
41. **RT** Ask students to explain why school-age children are concerned with how others feel about them. Students should explain how such concern is good or bad.

## Showing Social Awareness

42. **RT** Have students explain what the term *social awareness* means. How does this compare to the term *self-awareness*?
43. **ER** *Industry Is Important in the School Years*, Activity F, SAG. Invite students to interview an upper-grade elementary child concerning the importance of industry. Students should explain how the child's responses compare with the text.
44. **RT** Ask students for examples of some important skills in today's culture.
45. **RF** *Peers Are Important*, Activity G, SAG. Students should write examples that illustrate each of the purposes of friendships.
46. **EX** *Handling Friendship Problems*, reproducible master 19-4. Students should work individually or in groups to consider the listed friendship problems and suggest ways to resolve them. Students should share results in class.

## Controlling Emotions

47. **RF** Using one emotion as an example, have students show how it affects physical well-being and intellectual development.
48. **RT** Discuss with students why being loved helps people experience other emotions, such as joy, grief, and guilt.

49. **RF** *School-Age Children Want to Be Accepted*, Activity H, SAG. Instruct students to write an essay on (a) what it means to be accepted as you are and (b) why acceptance without too many strings attached is necessary for the development of good relationships with others.
50. **ER** Have students interview several school-age children concerning their fears and anxieties. Students should write a news feature or magazine-style article comparing the children's answers with the discussion of fears and anxieties in the text.
51. **RT** Discuss with students how each of these behaviors can be a form of anger: impertinence, sulkiness, and scapegoating.
52. **ER** Assign students to research the life of a person who saw wrongs in a society and worked to correct them. Students should then write an essay on this person. Much of the essay should focus on how the person turned anger into positive social action.

## Helping School-Age Children with Their Social-Emotional Needs

53. **ER** Instruct students to write a short essay on the aspect of development (physical, intellectual, social-emotional) they think is the most difficult for parents to meet. Students should give reasons for their answer.
54. **RT** Discuss with students how adults can let go and also be available for school-age children. Students should explain what may happen when adults do not find a balance between letting go of and being there for children.

## Guiding and Modeling Behavior

55. **EX** Explain that school-age children often admire parents and other adults. Ask students to consider people they admired and list characteristics they think are needed by adult models for school-age children.
56. **ER** Divide the class into two groups. Members of one group should create skits that illustrate a personal priority or attitude modeled by an adult. The other group should discuss what the child might be learning. (Students should keep in mind the way something is said or the actions of adults may speak louder than words.)
57. **RF** Divide the class into small groups. Have each group create a list of "Rules for Good Communication." Share with the class.

## Enjoying Family Ties

58. **ER** Invite students to interview a parent about ways he or she helps his or her school-age child. Students should write a short report on their findings.
59. **ER** Ask students to give examples of ways they helped during family times, including family rituals, when they were school-age children.

## Providing Time for Friendships

60. **EX** Discuss with students why feelings of rejection are serious in the middle childhood years, especially if the feelings are long lasting.
61. **RF** *Helping Children Deal with Rejection*, Activity I, SAG. Ask students to explain how they would respond to the given situations in which children experience various forms of rejection.

## Helping Children Control Their Emotions

62. **RT** Discuss with students why talking about feelings is important.
63. **RT** Students should explain why psychological discipline works better than discipline through physical control with school-age children.

## Helping Children Improve Their Self-Concept

64. **EX** Ask students to contrast how children with a good self-concept versus those with a poor self-concept. How can self-concept affect learning and social development?
65. **ER** Instruct students to write a paper on how adults and parents may help children improve their self-concept.

## Recognizing Developmental Delays

66. **RT** Ask students to prepare a list of common developmental delays in school-age children.
67. **ER** Ask a pediatrician to speak to the class about how he or she recognizes developmental delays in school-age children. Have students prepare a list of questions in advance.

# Answer Key

## Text

*Reviewing Key Concepts, page 496*

1. false
2. false
3. An adequate diet is needed to meet growth needs. Foods are needed to meet the great energy demands caused by school-age children's physical activities. Proper diets help children resist infections. School-age children must store nutrients for the rapid growth of the teen years.
4. possibly wrong
5. true
6. (Give two. Student response.)
7. Goals for kindergarten and first grade are unlike the goals of preschool programs, and children must learn independently, follow directions, stay on one task, and put a teacher's desires ahead of their own wishes. There is a switch from the home and preschool program of learning about real objects through direct experiences and some symbolic play to the school program of learning abstract symbol systems. Children must cope with peers for many hours.
8. Social
9. to do their best
10. Close friendships are formed from peer groups. Friendships with peers provide school-age children the chance to join rather formal groups, such as 4-H. Peers help children become less dependent on adults. Peers provide emotional support. Peers share information with each other. Peers affect each child's self-concept.
11. B, C

## Teacher's Resources

### Chapter 19 Test

| | | | |
|---|---|---|---|
| 1. T | 14. T | 27. B | 40. O |
| 2. T | 15. T | 28. D | 41. D |
| 3. F | 16. T | 29. C | 42. A |
| 4. T | 17. T | 30. B | 43. E |
| 5. T | 18. C | 31. C | 44. C |
| 6. T | 19. D | 32. A | 45. I |
| 7. F | 20. B | 33. C | 46. B |
| 8. T | 21. D | 34. R | 47. H |
| 9. F | 22. B | 35. L | 48. S |
| 10. F | 23. B | 36. F | 49. J |
| 11. T | 24. C | 37. N | 50. K |
| 12. F | 25. A | 38. M | 51. Q |
| 13. F | 26. D | 39. G | 52. P |

53. Growth tends to be at the same steady growth seen in the preschool years. Height increases more steadily than weight. Toward the end of middle childhood, some children begin a growth spurt. Body proportions are becoming more and more like those of adults. Organ systems mature.

54. School-age children's perceptual refinement and their growing ability to use logic allow for improved physical knowledge concepts and logical thinking concepts. Children are now able to classify, order, understand number and spatial concepts, and resolve many cause and effect relationships. However, they still have difficulty in handling problems involving distance, time, and speed. Language is mastered and even enjoyed during this stage.

55. Friendships help children learn to give and take; provide opportunities for them to join formal groups; help them depend less on adults as friends provide emotional support and become a way to gain information and skills; and have a profound effect on their self-concepts.

# Meal/Snack Pattern for School-Age Children

## Breakfast—School-Age Children

1 milk component

1 fruit/vegetable component

1 grains/bread component

## Lunch and Dinner—School-Age Children

1 milk component

2 fruit/vegetable components

1 grains/bread component

1 meat/meat alternate component

## Snack—School-Age Children

Each day, two snacks must be served halfway between meals. For each snack, choose two from the following:

1 milk component

2 fruit/vegetable components

1 grain component

1 meat/meat alternate component

## Milk Component

1 cup fluid milk

## Fruit/Vegetable Component

½ cup full-strength fruit or vegetable juice[1]

½ cup fruit or vegetable

Note:
[1]Juice cannot be served at snack if milk is the only other snack component.

## Grain/Bread Component[2]

1 slice bread

1 roll, biscuit, muffin, or cornbread serving

¾ cup cold dry cereal

½ cup hot cooked cereal

½ cup pasta, noodles, or grains

Note:
[2]Breads and grains must be made from whole-grain or enriched meal or flour. Cereals must be whole-grain, enriched, or fortified.

## Meat/Meat Alternate Component

### Lunch/Dinner

2 oz. meat, poultry, or fish[3], or alternate protein product

2 oz. cheese

1 egg

½ cup cooked, dry beans or peas

4 tbsp. peanut butter
(or other seed or nut butters)

1 oz. nuts or seeds[4]

8 oz. yogurt[5]

Notes:
[3] Only the edible portion of cooked lean meat, poultry, or fish counts toward the requirement.
[4] For lunch and dinner, nuts and seeds may only meet half of the total meat/meat alternate serving and must be combined with another meat/meat alternate to fulfill the requirement.
[5] Yogurt may be plain or flavored, sweetened or unsweetened.

### Snack

1 oz. meat, poultry, or fish[3], or alternate protein product

1 oz. cheese

½ egg

¼ cup cooked, dry beans or peas

2 tbsp. peanut butter
(or other seed or nut butters)

1 oz. nuts and seeds

4 oz. yogurt[4]

Notes:
[3] Only the edible portion of cooked lean meat, poultry, or fish counts toward the requirement.
[4] Yogurt may be plain or flavored, sweetened or unsweetened.

USDA Child Care Food Program

# Intellectual Development Activities for School-Age Children

**Name** _____ **Date** _____ **Period** _____

For each category given, read the sample activity and then write an activity of your own that would be suitable for school-age children.

## Perceptual Activities

**Memory Chain:** Memory chain games are good for travel times or when playing jump rope. Children should choose a category. One person says a word in the category. The next person names this word and adds another word to the chain. Words are added until a person cannot repeat the entire chain.

Activity title: _____

_____

_____

_____

_____

## Logic Activities

**Problems of Relationships:** Figuring relationship is hard for many people. Logic problems can help children understand relationships better. An example of this type of problem would be, "My father is the brother of your sister. What relative am I of yours?"

**Math Logic:** Many logic problems are math problems. An example is, "A rabbit farmer dies, leaving his 17 rabbits to his three sons. The will states the first son should receive half of the rabbits. The second son is to receive one-third of the rabbits. The third son is to receive one-ninth of the rabbits." How are the rabbits divided among the heirs?

Activity title: _____

_____

_____

_____

_____

## Language Activities

**Anagrams:** In anagrams the letters in words are rearranged to form other words. For example, *won* can be rearranged to form *now*. An adult can write a coded message using anagrams and ask the child to decode it. For example, the anagrams in this nonsense phrase *Pots the looped form braking* can be decoded as *Stop the poodle from barking*.

Activity title: _____

_____

_____

_____

_____

# Preparation for School

Help the child overcome separation anxiety

Teach the child to accept the authority of adults other than parents

Teach the child to accept the authority of adults other than parents

"Let go" some to help the child become more independent

# Handling Friendship Problems

**Name** _____ **Date** _____ **Period** _____

Pretend you are the parent of a school-age child who is having some friendship problems. For each problem given below, use the space provided to write what you would do to help your child solve it.

Your child very much wants to have friends but doesn't know how to make friends with others.

_____
_____
_____
_____
_____
_____
_____
_____

Your child has few friends because he has other interests and cares little about friendships.

_____
_____
_____
_____
_____
_____
_____
_____

Your child has friends whose priorities are very different from your own.

_____
_____
_____
_____
_____
_____
_____
_____

*(Continued)*

**Name** _____

Your child has a popular friend who has committed an offense that should be reported to school authorities. Your child does not want to report the friend for fear she will lose the friendship. Your child realizes, however, people are being hurt by her friend's actions.

_____

_____

_____

_____

_____

_____

_____

Your child feels she would be more acceptable to the group if she had money to buy new clothes like the other girls in school seem to own. Your limited family budget will not allow this.

_____

_____

_____

_____

_____

_____

_____

Your child lives several miles from his school friends and cannot be with them often after school hours.

_____

_____

_____

_____

_____

_____

# School-Age Children

**Name** _____

**Date** _____ **Period** _____ **Score** _____

## Chapter 19 Test

True/False: Circle *T* if the statement is true or *F* if the statement is false.

T  F  1. After the girls' growth spurt in the middle childhood years, size differences between boys and girls show mainly between slow-maturing boys and fast-maturing girls.

T  F  2. The body's center of gravity is lower in middle childhood, which gives these children better balance.

T  F  3. The muscles and heart are less prone to stress in middle childhood than are other organs.

T  F  4. Nutritious food choices are highly important in the school-age years.

T  F  5. School-age children often have definite clothing preferences.

T  F  6. Communicating with others helps children overcome egocentric thinking.

T  F  7. Perceptual accuracy reaches its peak in the preschool years and declines in the school-age years.

T  F  8. Logic aids the ability to form more accurate physical knowledge and logical thinking concepts.

T  F  9. Scientific reasoning is another name for deductive reasoning.

T  F  10. School-age children can communicate at an adult level.

T  F  11. Articulation of all English sounds should be mastered in the school-age years.

T  F  12. School-age children take language seriously; thus, they do *not* play with words.

T  F  13. Adults can best encourage children to meet their own needs by rewarding them for their efforts.

T  F  14. Computer use can aid mental development.

T  F  15. Peer groups assign children to certain roles, such as leadership ones.

T  F  16. Adults often have problems finding the balance between being there for their children and letting go.

T  F  17. Adults should discipline children privately rather than in front of others.

Multiple Choice: Choose the best response. Write the letter in the space provided.

_____ 18. Which of the following does *not* grow in relation to the overall size of a school-age child?
A. The brain.
B. The eyes.
C. The heart.
D. The lungs.

_____ 19. Motor skills become easier for school-age children due to _____.
A. faster reaction time
B. more precision
C. strength and flexibility
D. All of the above.

*(Continued)*

**Name** _____

_____ 20. As compared to boys, girls are better at tasks that require _____.
   A. faster reaction time
   B. flexibility
   C. precision
   D. speed

_____ 21. School-age children need adequate nutrition to _____.
   A. meet present and future growth needs
   B. meet great energy demands
   C. help resist infection
   D. All of the above.

_____ 22. Adults can help children develop good health habits by doing all of the following *except* _____.
   A. giving reasons for good health habits
   B. forcing children to clean their plates
   C. providing opportunities for practice
   D. setting examples

_____ 23. The name *concrete operations* means that children _____.
   A. handle materials to solve problems
   B. use what they have experienced to solve problems
   C. reason abstractly to solve problems
   D. All of the above.

_____ 24. Being able to think ahead and plan strategies is an ability developed in the _____ stage.
   A. preoperational
   B. concrete operational
   C. formal operational
   D. abstract

_____ 25. In the concrete operational stage, children become free of _____.
   A. egocentric thought
   B. use of concrete materials
   C. perception
   D. None of the above.

_____ 26. Following a line of reasoning back to where it started is called _____.
   A. decentering perceptions
   B. noting transformations
   C. using deductive reasoning
   D. using reversibility logic

_____ 27. The most advanced form of reasoning is _____.
   A. deductive
   B. inductive
   C. transductive
   D. None of the above.

*(Continued)*

**Name** _____

_____ 28. School-age children still have difficulty understanding _____.
A. distance
B. speed
C. time
D. All of the above.

_____ 29. Which of the following statements is *not* true of language development in middle childhood?
A. Children give more exact definitions of words.
B. Articulation is often mastered by eight years of age.
C. Changing children's grammar is rather easy.
D. Children have fun with words.

_____ 30. Adults should meet children's intellectual needs in all of the following ways *except* _____.
A. treating the child's entry to school as a developmental task
B. treating school entry as a very special occasion
C. staying in close contact with the schools
D. guiding television viewing and computer use to promote success in school and in other mental learnings

_____ 31. School-age children are interested in doing activities with _____.
A. adults
B. peers
C. Both A and B.
D. Neither A nor B.

_____ 32. School-age children need adults to _____.
A. encourage them to test their abilities
B. tell them what to do
C. evaluate them by adult standards
D. make them redo actions until they are correctly performed

_____ 33. As compared to adults, peer rules are more _____.
A. flexible
B. geared toward what group members should do
C. geared toward what group members should not do
D. geared toward what adults should do

*(Continued)*

**Name** _____

Matching: Match the following terms and identifying phrases.

_____ 34.  Children between ages 6 and 12 years.

_____ 35.  Another name for the school-age years.

_____ 36.  A period of rapid physical growth.

_____ 37.  Teeth that are meant to last a lifetime.

_____ 38.  Problems pertaining to bones and muscles.

_____ 39.  Aches that occur when the muscles try to catch up to skeletal size.

_____ 40.  The ability to perform motor skills accurately.

_____ 41.  Ability to move, bend, and stretch easily.

_____ 42.  Piaget's third stage of mental development when children begin to think logically, but base logic on past experiences.

_____ 43.  Piaget's last stage of mental development in which people can reason in more abstract ways.

_____ 44.  Reasoning process by which one goes from the general to the specific.

_____ 45.  Reasoning process by which one goes from specific facts to general conclusions.

_____ 46.  The concept that changing an object's shape, direction, or position does not alter the quantity.

_____ 47.  Having classes within other classes; that is, having subclasses.

_____ 48.  Areas in which a person wants or needs to improve.

_____ 49.  Term used by Erikson to describe a child who joins others in striving to become a competent member of society.

_____ 50.  Term used by Erikson to describe a child who feels left out and incompetent as a member of society.

_____ 51.  Blaming someone else for personal mistakes.

_____ 52.  Feeling that someone cares and will help when needed.

A. concrete operational stage

B. conservation

C. deductive reasoning

D. flexibility

E. formal operations

F. growth spurt

G. growth pains

H. hierarchical classification

I. inductive reasoning

J. industry

K. inferiority

L. middle childhood

M. orthopedic problems

N. permanent teeth

O. precision

P. psychological security

Q. scapegoating

R. school-age children

S. shortcomings

Essay Questions: Provide complete responses to the following questions or statements.

53.  What major changes are seen in physical growth and development during the school-age years?

54.  What are the major intellectual accomplishments during middle childhood?

55.  Why are friendships considered a necessity in the school-age years?

## Part 6 · Guiding and Caring for Children

# Teaching Through Play

# 20

## Objectives

After studying this chapter, students will be able to
- describe the importance of play and play activities in children's lives.
- explain how adults can help children learn through play, art, music, science, and reading.

## Bulletin Boards

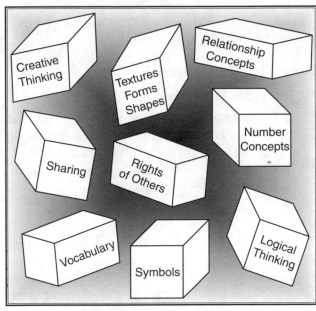

Creative Thinking

Textures Forms Shapes

Relationship Concepts

Number Concepts

Sharing

Rights of Others

Vocabulary

Symbols

Logical Thinking

### Title: *Learning Through Play*

Cut block-like squares from various colors of construction paper. On each block write a concept children learn through play, such as sharing, use of symbols, vocabulary, and logical thinking concepts. Students may add others as they study about the value of children's play.

### Title: *My Collage*

As an introduction to art for children, have students design their own collage by using alphabet cereal, dried beans or peas, seeds, boxes, cloth, yarn, ribbon, leaves, and other objects glued to a flat surface.

## Teaching Materials

**Text**, page 500-531
*Reviewing Key Concepts*
*Using Your Knowledge*
*Making Observations*
*Thinking Further*

**Student Activity Guide**
    A. *Learning Through Play*
    B. *Development Through the Visual Arts*
    C. *Learning Science Through Cooking*

**Teacher's Resources**
*Stages of Development in Symbolic Play,*
    transparency master 20-1
*Choosing Toys Wisely,* transparency
    master 20-2
*Art Activities,* reproducible master 20-3
*Music Activities,* reproducible master 20-4
*Science Activities,* reproducible master 20-5
*Making Children's Book Selections,*
    transparency master 20-6
Chapter 20 Test

## Introductory Activities

1. On the chalkboard write the phrase *Play is the child's....* Each student should finish the sentence and then share his or her ideas with the class. Record some responses on the chalkboard below the phrase.
2. Ask students to recall play activities from their earlier years. What kinds of activities do they remember enjoying most? Have them contrast their memories with activities parents and grandparents considered play in their day.

293

# Strategies to Reteach, Reinforce, Enrich, and Extend Text Concepts

## Children and Their World of Play

3. **RT** Ask students why the term *play* is difficult to define. Students should discuss how work for one person may be play for another.
4. **RT** Have students list some words used to describe play, such as *dawdle*, that make play seem unimportant.

## Importance of Play

5. **RF** *Learning Through Play*, Activity A, SAG. Students should give examples of how play may promote mental development.
6. **RT** Discuss with students the value of play for children. How does it differ from adults' concepts of play?
7. **RT** Ask students to explain how play affects physical, intellectual, and social-emotional development.
8. **ER** *Stages of Development in Symbolic Play*, reproducible master 20-1. Use the master to describe the stages in young children's symbolic play. (The stages begin about 18 months to 2 years, and the last stage begins in the late preschool or early school-age years.) Remind students these stages prepare the child mentally to understand more abstract symbols, such as words. Have them watch a group of young children play and identify these stages. Explain to students that children engage in more than one stage of symbolizing because children continue to use earlier learnings in later stages.

## Stages of Play

9. **RT** Discuss with students why play must mirror development.
10. **RF** Instruct students to observe children playing as an outside assignment. In class, students should give examples of play they observed. Students should try to match examples of stages of play with objects and people.

## Types of Play

11. **RF** As a class or small-group project, students should ask children to describe their favorite games. Instruct students to record the types of age trends they note in the preferred types of play.

12. **ER** Instruct students to design a pamphlet or newsletter for parents suggesting appropriate toys for each type of play.

## The Adult's Role in Children's Play

13. **ER** Students should observe a preschool teacher during playtime, then share examples of how the teacher enriched the children's play.
14. **ER** Instruct students to display or list good travel toys for a baby, toddler, preschooler, and school-age child.
15. **ER** Have students ask a librarian to show them some books on toys that children can make.
16. **RF** As a class or small-group project, students should make a "good consumer checklist" adults can use when shopping for children's toys.
17. **RT** *Choosing Toys Wisely*, transparency master 20-2. Use the transparency master as a stimulus for a discussion. Ask students to bring several toys to class and evaluate them using the criteria listed on the transparency.

## Providing Enrichment Activities for Children

18. **RT** Ask students to explain the meaning of the word *enrichment* as it refers to activities aiding children's growth and development.
19. **RT** Have students list other enrichment activities besides playing with toys.

## Art

20. **RT** Discuss with students why painting, construction, and photography are called visual arts.
21. **RF** *Development Through the Visual Arts*, Activity B, SAG. Students should observe a child involved in an art project and note the developmental skills, learnings, and feelings that result from the project.
22. **RT** Using the chalkboard, have students list headings for each stage of art development. Then have them list art activities that fit each stage.
23. **ER** Have students collect the artwork of children of various ages. Students should try to categorize each work by the stages of creative development in the visual arts. Display the works with the stages labeled. Students should then examine the artwork and find examples of ways children show spatial relationships, exaggerated sizes, transparencies, and other designs discussed in the text.

24. **RT**   Discuss with students how adults can stimulate children's art experiences and how they should react to children's artwork.
25. **ER**   *Art Activities*, reproducible master 20-3. Students should read the listed art activities and then create one of their own. They may try an activity of their choice with children and report results in class.
26. **ER**   Field trip: Students should prepare some clay recipes for a children's program. Arrange for the class to observe children using the clay. Students should evaluate how well the clay worked and how the children enjoyed the materials.

## Music

27. **RT**   Ask students for examples of how music creates feelings.
28. **RF**   Students should observe a toddler playing with toys that make musical sounds and then share their observations in class.
29. **RF**   Instruct students to listen to songs composed for young children. What features did they note in these songs that make them suitable for children?
30. **ER**   Have students demonstrate some rhythm instruments for children.
31. **ER**   *Music Activities*, reproducible master 20-4. Students should read the music activities, and then create one of their own. They may test the activity on children and discuss results in class.
32. **RT**   Have students explain why adults do not need to be musicians in order to enjoy music activities with children.

## Science

33. **RT**   Discuss with students how helping a child wonder differs from telling a child facts.
34. **RF**   Ask students to list some of nature's beautiful creations they could share with a child.
35. **RT**   Discuss with students that science is sometimes presented as a "magic show." Students should give reasons it is important for children to see science as a part of everyday life.
36. **RF**   Students should list 10 books suitable for preschool children and 10 books suitable for school-age children that might help them understand the scientific world.
37. **ER** *Learning Science Through Cooking*, Activity C, SAG. Have students plan and conduct a cooking lesson with a 9- to 12-year-old child. Students should incorporate in an informal way as many science concepts as they can.

38. **RF**   Ask students to list everyday situations during which they could introduce science concepts.
39. **ER**   *Science Activities*, reproducible master 20-5. Students should read the listed science activities and create one of their own. Then have them try one or more of the activities with children. Students should share their observations with other class members.

## Literature

40. **EX**   Instruct students to develop a criteria list to use when selecting books for children.
41. **ER**   Invite students to observe storytime at a local library. Students should explain what techniques the adult used to make the story interesting.
42. **ER**   Guest speaker: Ask an elementary teacher to share with the class some stories and poems children have written. Students should discuss the writing in terms of concepts, humor, emotions expressed, and complexity of sentences.
43. **RT**   *Making Children's Book Selections*, transparency master 20-6. Ask students to bring several picture books to class. Have students evaluate the books using the criteria listed on this transparency master. In addition, mention to students it is good to choose books that have won or been nominated for the following awards: The Caldecott Medal (for picture books), The Newberry Medal (for older-children's books), and the International Reading Association's Book Award.
44. **ER**   Guest speaker: Invite a librarian to visit your classroom and show some award-winning children's books. Ask the librarian to explain how to choose quality children's books.

# Answer Key

## Text

*Reviewing Key Concepts,* page 530
1. D
2. active-physical play—C; manipulative-constructive play—B; imitative-imaginative play—A; language-logic play—D
3. true
4. false
5. false
6. true
7. false
8. can
9. true

10. false
11. true
12. (Student response.)

# Teacher's Resources

## Chapter 20 Test

| | | |
|---|---|---|
| 1. T | 17. T | 33. D |
| 2. T | 18. T | 34. A |
| 3. F | 19. F | 35. D |
| 4. T | 20. T | 36. B |
| 5. T | 21. D | 37. H |
| 6. F | 22. D | 38. C |
| 7. F | 23. A | 39. I |
| 8. T | 24. C | 40. N |
| 9. T | 25. C | 41. E |
| 10. F | 26. A | 42. L |
| 11. T | 27. D | 43. J |
| 12. F | 28. B | 44. M |
| 13. F | 29. C | 45. G |
| 14. T | 30. C | 46. K |
| 15. F | 31. B | 47. F |
| 16. T | 32. B | |

48. By learning about the various stages of children's development, adults can provide appropriate activities and materials for children. Children should be encouraged to explore and learn. Reacting to children's growing competence by praising and displaying products is helpful. Adults should also talk with children about their learnings and help them find answers to their questions.

49. Active physical play uses children's gross-motor skills; manipulative-constructive play uses children's fine-motor skills; imitative-imaginative play uses children's ability to pretend to be objects or persons other than themselves; language-logic play uses children's mental abilities as they play language, word, and logic games.

50. (List two. Student response. See pages 511 to 514 in the text for toy selection criteria. See pages 527 and 528 in the text for book selection criteria.)

# Stages of Development in Symbolic Play

| Stage | Example |
|---|---|
| Directs pretense toward self | Child pretends to drink from a cup. |
| Recognizes concrete representation | Child thinks of toy duck as a duck; identifies pictures of ducks. |
| Directs pretense toward another | Child feeds doll a bottle. |
| Uses substitution | Child uses a block as a truck. |
| Uses imaginary objects | Child pretends to pour coffee using an imaginary coffeepot and imaginary cups. |
| Engages in imitation | Child makes animal sounds and moves like an animal. |
| Animates toy (toy engages in pretense) | Child has toy dogs chase each other and talk in words. |
| Uses same actions with different receivers | Child drinks from a toy cup offers same cup to stuffed animals and dolls. |
| Uses more than one related role in unplanned pretense | Child pretends to be mother who feeds her baby, cooks, and shops. |
| Develops planned roles and props including signs and engages in dramatic play | Child can explain plans to make a grocery store, collect props, make signs, and play various roles with peers. |

# Choosing Toys Wisely

**Parents and caregivers should choose toys and play materials that are**

Well-constructed, durable, and safe

Easy to clean (and sanitized for infants and toddlers)

Age/stage appropriate
- should match child's knowledge, skills, and interests

- open-ended materials (many possibilities to work material) over closed ended materials (one way to work material)

Anti-bias and anti-violence
- dolls and other people images should reflect all kinds of diversity (gender; age; ethnic, socioeconomic, and cultural groups; family type) positively

- should not be associated with or encourage aggression or violence

# Art Activities

**Name** _____ **Date** _____ **Period** _____

Read the art activities listed below and then create two of your own activities.

## Sponge Painting

Cut sponges into various shapes. Attach a spring-type clothespin to each sponge. Have children dip sponges into tempera and stamp on paper.

## Collages

A collage is a picture or design made by gluing flat objects on a background. Supply children with paper, small objects, and fabrics. Have children arrange and attach them to a piece of paper or cardboard. Using objects with some thickness will produce a three-dimensional effect.

## Clay Work

Have children work with a soft, pliable modeling compound. Plasticine® is best for young children. Clay work should first be done with hands only. Do not allow children to use plastic knives, rolling pins, cookie cutters, or other gadgets in the beginning.

Activity title: _____

Age of child activity suits: _____

Activity description: _____

_____

_____

_____

_____

_____

_____

Activity title: _____

Age of child activity suits: _____

Activity description: _____

_____

_____

_____

_____

_____

_____

_____

# Music Activities

**Name** _____ **Date** _____ **Period** _____

Read the music activities listed below and then create two activities of your own.

## Echoing Rhythms

Tap a simple rhythmic pattern using the body or a rhythm instrument. Have the child repeat the pattern. After doing several patterns, have the child start and you can repeat the pattern.

## Learning About Tones

Use a xylophone or a bell set. Show children the longest bar or largest tube makes the lowest sound and the shortest bar or smallest tube makes the highest sound. (Because many instruments have the lowest notes to the left of the musician, the lowest tones should be to the child's left as you demonstrate.

Activity title: _____

Age of child activity suits: _____

Activity description: _____

_____

_____

_____

_____

_____

Activity title: _____

Age of child activity suits: _____

Activity description: _____

_____

_____

_____

_____

_____

_____

# Science Activities

**Name** _____ **Date** _____ **Period** _____

Read the science activities listed below and then create two activities of your own.

## Magnify Nature

Through a magnifying glass, have children look at leaves, bugs, bark of trees, and other objects in nature. Study the shapes, sizes, color, and textures. Observe and talk about the differences.

## Dissolve Solids into Liquids

Through observation and participation, note what materials dissolve in water. Provide materials like sugar cubes, salt, and baking soda. Also, supply materials that do not dissolve in water, such as cooking oil, rice, and margarine. Let each child stir the mixture. Ask what happens and why.

## Attach Magnets

As children work and play with magnets, have them observe the materials that magnets pull and those that get pushed away. Note which magnets are stronger than others. Talk about what materials the magnets will attract and why.

Activity title: _____

Age of child activity suits: _____

Activity description: _____

_____

_____

_____

_____

_____

_____

Activity title: _____

Age of child activity suits: _____

Activity description: _____

_____

_____

_____

_____

_____

_____

# Making Children's Book Selections

📖 Safe and durable for age

📖 Appealing for age/stage

📖 Shows and respects all types of diversity

📖 Promotes nonviolence

📖 Text has one main theme (no subplots)

📖 Child can anticipate the ending

📖 Is either fantasy or reality, but not both in the same story

📖 Uses one main character or a group treated as one

📖 Placement and content of pictures matches the text

📖 Art medium fits the spirit of the story

# Teaching Through Play

**Name** _____

**Date** _____ **Period** _____ **Score** _____

## Chapter 20 Test

True/False: Circle *T* if the statement is true or *F* if the statement is false.

T    F    1. Children's play and artistic expressions mirror their learnings.

T    F    2. Humor is mental play.

T    F    3. Stages of development and stages of play do *not* interact.

T    F    4. Spatial concepts can be learned through active-physical play.

T    F    5. Play helps children become more coordinated.

T    F    6. Babies do *not* develop any fine-motor skills.

T    F    7. *Socio-dramatic play* and *dramatic play* are two names for the same skill level of imitative-imaginative play.

T    F    8. Board games can be classified as language-logic play.

T    F    9. Adults should give children some ideas for play.

T    F    10. Selecting toys for children is mainly a matter of asking children what they want.

T    F    11. A magnetic game board is a good toy to take on car trips.

T    F    12. Art activities help children express their ideas and feelings but *not* grow mentally.

T    F    13. Children's artistic expressions begin with representations.

T    F    14. Spatial representations are difficult for children to understand.

T    F    15. Children's ability to sing on pitch is mastered before they start to move rhythmically to music.

T    F    16. Children's first instruments are usually percussion instruments.

T    F    17. Children have many attitudes that are similar to those of professional scientists.

T    F    18. Children need to learn to care for their environment.

T    F    19. Children *cannot* create stories and poems until about middle childhood.

T    F    20. Children enjoy various follow-up activities (discussions, art projects, cooking experiences, picture reading) after enjoying stories and poems.

Multiple Choice: Choose the best response. Write the letter in the space provided.

_____ 21. Play is most important in promoting which area of development?
A. Physical development.
B. Intellectual development.
C. Social-emotional development.
D. All areas of development equally.

_____ 22. Mentally, play aids _____.
A. logical relationship concepts
B. symbols systems including language
C. humor and creative thinking
D. All of the above.

*(Continued)*

**Name** _____

_____ 23. Through playing games with others, children learn all of the following *except* _____.
  A. how to get their own way
  B. acceptable and unacceptable behavior
  C. rules
  D. how to settle disagreements

_____ 24. Stages of play can be seen with _____.
  A. pets
  B. toys
  C. objects and people
  D. None of the above.

_____ 25. Active-physical play aids all of the following *except* _____.
  A. gross-motor skills
  B. ability to protect oneself from injury
  C. fine-motor skills
  D. balance and reaction time

_____ 26. Playing with small blocks is most often classified as _____ play.
  A. manipulative-constructive
  B. imitative-imaginative
  C. language-logic
  D. active-physical

_____ 27. Through play therapy, children get to act out their _____.
  A. fears
  B. resentments
  C. hostilities
  D. All of the above.

_____ 28. Scribbling is part of the _____ stage in visual art development.
  A. random marks
  B. manipulative
  C. transition
  D. representation

_____ 29. Children in the representation stage of visual arts do *not* produce _____.
  A. baselines
  B. folding over
  C. scribbling
  D. transparencies

_____ 30. Musical experiences for young children begin with _____.
  A. listening to music
  B. playing instruments
  C. moving to music
  D. singing

_____ 31. Singing aids all of the following skills *except* _____ skills.
  A. language
  B. motor
  C. listening
  D. pitch

*(Continued)*

**Name** _____

_____ 32. In science, children need guidance in _____.
A. learning how many objects are in a certain quantity
B. appreciating beauty and caring for the world
C. seeing science as magic
D. All of the above.

_____ 33. The values of reading quality books to children include _____.
A. appreciation of beauty and learning
B. development of vocabulary and language skills
C. increase in the child's self expression
D. All of the above.

Matching: Match the following terms and identifying phrases.

_____ 34. Play that uses gross-motor skills.

_____ 35. Play that uses fine-motor skills.

_____ 36. Play in which children pretend to be objects or people.

_____ 37. Use of play between a child and trained counselor to help the child resolve certain problems.

_____ 38. A form of mental play that is seen most often in school-age children.

_____ 39. Container that holds a collection of real objects related to a certain role for children's use in play.

_____ 40. Forms of art that create products that appeal to the sense of sight.

_____ 41. Playing with art materials as opposed to creating with art materials.

_____ 42. The drawing of dots, straight and curved lines, loops, spirals, and imperfect circles.

_____ 43. Stage in drawing in which children create symbols to show objects, experiences, and feelings.

_____ 44. Artwork that shows the inside and outside of an object at the same time (also called X-ray pictures).

_____ 45. Instruments whose tones are produced by striking them.

_____ 46. Instruments that when struck produce indefinite pitches.

_____ 47. Instruments that when struck produce definite pitches.

A. active-physical play
B. imitative-imaginative play
C. language-logic play
D. manipulative-constructive play
E. manipulative stage
F. melody percussion instruments
G. percussion instruments
H. play therapy
I. prop box
J. representation stage
K. rhythm instruments
L. scribbling
M. transparencies
N. visual arts

Essay Questions: Provide complete responses to the following questions or statements.

48. How can adults help children enrich their lives through art, music, science, and books?

49. Name and describe the four types of play.

50. List three tips for adults when choosing play materials or books for children.

# Protecting Children's Health and Safety

## Objectives

After studying this chapter, students will be able to
- explain ways to protect children from diseases and illnesses.
- create a safe environment for young children.
- teach young children simple safety practices.
- discuss the steps in preparing a child for medical care in the doctor's office, in the hospital, and at home.

## Bulletin Boards

**Shield Children from Illness with...**

Cleanliness

Nutrition

Physical Activity

Rest

### Title: *Shield Children from Illness with...*

Draw a large shield with a child peeking from behind it as shown. Divide the shield into four sections and label the sections *Nutrition, Rest, Cleanliness,* and *Physical Activity*. Under each heading have students write reasons that care in these areas helps to prevent illness and disease.

### Title: *Be Wise to Safety Problems*

Use transparency master 21-1 as a pattern for the bulletin board. Have students write causes of accidents on the branches as suggested in the first introductory activity.

## Teaching Materials

**Text**, pages 532-581
  *Reviewing Key Concepts*
  *Using Your Knowledge*
  *Making Observations*
  *Thinking Further*

**Student Activity Guide**
  A. *Adults Model Health Practices*
  B. *Supervision Decreases Accidents*
  C. *Childproofing Is Essential*
  D. *Toys Should Not Hurt*
  E. *Making Computers Child-Friendly*
  F. *Ill Children Need Quiet Activities*

**Teacher's Resources**
  *Be Wise to Safety Problems,*
      transparency master 21-1
  *Specific Immunities Matrix,*
      transparency master 21-2
  *Adults' Roles in Children's Computer Use,*
      transparency master 21-3
  *Accidents Can Be Prevented,* color
      transparency CT-21
  *Hospital Kit,* reproducible master 21-4
  Chapter 21 Test

## Introductory Activities

1. *Be Wise to Safety Problems,* transparency master 21-1. Have students brainstorm causes of accidents for children of all ages. Write causes on the tree branches. (As noted in the bulletin board instructions, you might choose to enlarge the master and use it as a bulletin board pattern.)
2. Have students give examples of general practices that help prevent health problems.

# Strategies to Reteach, Reinforce, Enrich, and Extend Text Concepts

## Protecting Children from Disease and Illness

3. **EX** Ask students to explain how a disease, injury, or problem may harm a child's self-esteem.
4. **RT** Discuss with students what a doctor can tell about a child's health and development from the child's eating, sleeping, and playing habits.

## Nutrition, Rest, Cleanliness, and Physical Activity

5. **RT** Ask students to explain why self-care should be considered a necessity rather than a luxury.
6. **RF** *Adults Model Health Practices*, Activity A, SAG. Students should list ways adults can serve as models of good health practices for children.

## Medical and Dental Care

7. **RT** Ask students to explain why a physician needs to check a child's growth and development from time to time even when the child appears to be healthy.
8. **ER** Guest speaker: Invite a dentist to speak to the class about reasons dental care should begin with the primary teeth.

## Immunization

9. **RT** *Specific Immunities Matrix,* transparency master 21-2. Begin by reviewing with students how to read a matrix. Review single classifications first by reading columns and noting two types of naturally acquired immunities and two types of artificially acquired immunities. Then, read the rows noting two types of both active and passive immunities. Finally, look for the two-way classifications by finding the intersections of the column and row. Note particularly the intersection of artificially acquired and active immunities. This matrix cell contains immunizations, in which the child receives an antigen and develops the needed antibodies to protect from a specific disease.
10. **ER** Students should research how certain immunizations were discovered, such as smallpox, diphtheria, tetanus, and infantile paralysis (polio). Report results in class.

11. **RF** Instruct students to find the terms *vaccination, inoculation,* and *immunization* in a dictionary. Students should determine the origin of each of these terms.
12. **RT** Ask students why a child should be healthy at the time of immunization and should be carefully watched for a few days after an immunization.
13. **RT** Instruct students to use the Internet to research immunizations requirements for entry into child care and school in your state.
14. **RT** Ask students to explain why some immunizations have been discontinued for the general public in the United States.
15. **EX** Discuss the need for "booster shots" in the early teen and adult years. Explain how the lack of booster shots has led to measles outbreaks on college campuses recently. Ask why many adults who were children before a given immunization was created would not need booster shots. (These adults contracted the disease, which resulted in lifelong immunity.)

## Medical Attention During Illness

16. **RT** Discuss with students why it is beneficial to write down symptoms before calling a physician or making an office visit. Ask students how written instructions can help parents care for children who are ill.
17. **RF** As a class or small group project, have students make forms suitable for recording symptoms and noting physicians' instructions. Students should use the text as a guide. Students might also ask a physician or nurse to make other suggestions.
18. **ER** Instruct students to ask a pharmacist to clarify common prescription terminology, such as *before meals* (How long before?), *with food* (how much food? what kind of food?), or *three times daily* (three times in 24 hours or three times in a waking day?). Students should share their findings with the class.

## Childhood Diseases

19. **RT** Discuss childhood diseases with students. Ask students to describe some of the childhood diseases they have experienced or observed others experiencing.
20. **ER** Have students ask a doctor or nurse how to prevent the spread of various childhood diseases. Ask students to report their findings to the class.

## Allergies

21. **RT** Have students create one or three posters showing common food, pollen, and animal/pet allergens.

22. **ER** Ask students to search the Internet and write a report on one of these topics: *Why the Incidence of Allergies Is Increasing; Childhood Illnesses Associated with Allergies; Family History of Allergies—The Genetic Connection; Treatment Options;* or *Avoidance and Control Measures for Children with Allergies.*

## Accident Prevention

23. **RT** Ask students to differentiate between *accidents* and *illnesses.*

24. **RT** Discuss with students why teaching safety (modeling, showing, and explaining) does not provide enough protection for children.

## How Do Accidents Happen?

25. **RT** *Accidents Can Be Prevented,* color transparency CT-21. Use this transparency to lead a discussion on ways to prevent accidents in the home. Have students add other preventative methods to use when small children are in the home.

26. **RF** *Supervision Decreases Accidents,* Activity B, SAG. Students should think of ways adults may increase supervision during difficult times.

## Anticipating Possible Hazards

27. **RT** Ask students how understanding child development can help adults anticipate possible hazards.

28. **EX** Have students find the terms *risk* and *hazard* in a dictionary. Ask the students to explain the difference between a hazard and risk-taking that is needed for learning.

29. **RT** Ask students to explain why adults must be one step ahead of children's development if they are to reduce potentially dangerous situations.

## Helping Children Meet Goals in a Safe Way

30. **RT** Divide students into four groups representing the following four age groups: infants, toddlers, preschoolers, and school-age children. Ask each group to list for its chosen age group what goals children might commonly have. Discuss the risks associated with these goals. Have students think of a way or ways to meet the goals while avoiding the risks.

31. **ER** Ask students what are the consequences of overprotecting children during infancy, toddler, preschool, and school-age years. (Students might want to review the negative aspects of Erikson's first four stages.)

## Childproofing the Environment

32. **RF** *Childproofing Is Essential,* Activity C, SAG. Have students list childproofing measures they would need to take in various areas of a home.

33. **RT** Discuss with students the reasons behind each of the following statements: (a) Never refer to medicine as *candy*. (b) Do not give children medicine in baby bottles or juice glasses. (c) Do not take medicine, even vitamins, in front of children. (d) Carry a limited amount of medicine in a purse or pocket, and place medicine in a childproof container.

34. **RT** Ask students to explain why doors should be removed from old kitchen appliances and cars before they are discarded, even in salvage yards.

35. **RF** Students should identify common poisonous plants in their area.

36. **RF** Instruct students to examine various approved car restraint systems for children. Then have students work as teams to shop for a certified child safety seat. (This can be done in a store, online, or by catalog.) Compare seats for weight limits, cost, ease of use, harness style, and safety features. Based on their comparison, which seats would each group recommend?

37. **EX** *Toys Should Not Hurt,* Activity D, SAG. Have students evaluate a toy from a safety standpoint.

38. **RF** Students should create a display of devices parents may use to childproof a home and yard.

39. **ER** Ask a local veterinarian to speak to your class about choosing pets for children, the usual expenses involved in pet care, and suggestions for teaching children how to care for pets properly.

40. **RT** *Adults' Roles in Children's Computer Use,* transparency master 21-3. Have students discuss how parents and other adults have protective and guidance responsibilities concerning children's computer use.

41. **RF** *Making Computers Child-Friendly,* Activity E, SAG. Have students interview a parent about how he or she is making the computer "child-friendly." Students should bring their recorded responses to class and discuss their findings. For example, discuss whether the physical or content aspects of computer use are more of a parental concern.

## Safety Devices, Safety Measures, and Safety Lessons

42. **EX** Have students give hypothetical examples of adults modeling unsafe practices.
43. **ER** Instruct students to plan and give a series of short skits in which an adult attempts to teach a child a safety practice.

## Preparing a Child for Routine or Hospital Care

44. **RT** Discuss with students why it is important to relieve the stress of doctor and dental visits. Do students think this stress in the childhood years could have lasting effects?
45. **EX** Have students speculate why pain and feeling sick frightens children.

## Preparing a Child for Routine Care

46. **RT** Have students explain what the term *routine care* means.
47. **RF** Discuss with students why it is not wise to tell a child, "As soon as you see the doctor, you'll feel better." (Many medications require time before they reduce symptoms.)

## Preparing a Child for Hospital Care

48. **EX** *Hospital Kit*, reproducible master 21-4. Have students develop and evaluate a kit a child could take along to the hospital to make the trip more comfortable. (Students should arrange to have the kit given to a child entering the hospital, if possible.)
49. **ER** Arrange for the class to visit a local or nearby hospital with a pediatric wing or a children's hospital. Students should note how the hospital tries to relieve stress by its decor and services to children and parents.
50. **RF** Have students read several children's books on hospital care. Then ask them to write a story about visiting the hospital that would help reduce a child's anxieties.

## Caring for an Ill or Injured Child

51. **EX** Have students list some advantages of caring for a sick or injured child at home.
52. **ER** Display and demonstrate the use of various accurate measuring devices for medicine. Have students practice measuring colored water using these devices.

53. **ER** *Ill Children Need Quiet Activities*, Activity F, SAG. Have students plan some quiet activities for an ill toddler, preschool child, and school-age child.

## Caring for a Terminally Ill Child

54. **RT** Discuss with students how the terminal illness of a child may affect other children in the family.
55. **ER** Students should read a personal account of a family who faced the terminal illness of a child. (Personal accounts may be found in books and magazines.) Ask students to discuss in small groups their reactions to the accounts they read.
56. **ER** As a class project, students should get involved in a local effort to help a family with a terminally ill child.

# Answer Key

## Text

*Reviewing Key Concepts, page 580*

1. true
2. B, E
3. true
4. The adult's ability to supervise changes with the time of day. For instance, more accidents happen when adults are busy with supper or other tasks in the late afternoon and early evening hours.
5. 50 percent
6. true
7. D
8. A baby sharing a seat belt with an adult is likely to be crushed by the adult's force in an auto crash, even at a rather low speed.
9. (List five:) design computer areas for comfortable and safe posture and vision; have children take frequent breaks; select and monitor all computer use and software; filter unacceptable Web sites; set rules and guidelines for computer use; provide a balance among all daily activities; encourage and help children use the computer in more beneficial ways than browsing; communicate with children about their computer activities; model appropriate computer behaviors
10. (List four:) select a physician or dentist with care; take along books, toys, and clothing changes (if necessary) in case you must wait; be prepared with information or questions to save

time; reassure the child it is all right to feel sick; explain just a little about procedures and relate them as much as possible to everyday life; during the examination, stay in view of the child, use a soft, soothing voice, hold the child as the doctor requests, do not say things will not hurt, and do not distract the child by making sounds; never threaten a child with a doctor's visit or a shot

11. (Give three:) hospitals, in general, may be seen as a place where people experience separation from loved ones, pain, and even death; hospitals may seem large and impersonal. Parents are no longer in charge of the care of their children; parents are often asked to assist with painful tests and treatments; parents or other adults may feel guilty about the cause for the needed hospital care

12. false

13. (List two:) families need the help of support groups; friends can help by listening and carefully choosing words to express concern and sorrow; suggest concrete ways to help

# Teacher's Resources
## Chapter 21 Test

| | | |
|---|---|---|
| 1. T | 19. T | 37. E |
| 2. T | 20. A | 38. O |
| 3. T | 21. C | 39. A |
| 4. T | 22. B | 40. S |
| 5. T | 23. D | 41. V |
| 6. F | 24. B | 42. J |
| 7. F | 25. D | 43. C |
| 8. F | 26. C | 44. B |
| 9. T | 27. A | 45. I |
| 10. T | 28. A | 46. T |
| 11. T | 29. D | 47. G |
| 12. F | 30. C | 48. U |
| 13. F | 31. K | 49. P |
| 14. F | 32. R | 50. H |
| 15. T | 33. N | 51. M |
| 16. F | 34. D | 52. L |
| 17. F | 35. Q | 53. W |
| 18. T | 36. F | |

54. (Give five. Accept valid student responses and/or the following:) note possible dangers; help the child meet goals in a safe way; childproof indoor and outdoor areas; use a restraint system when traveling; check toys and baby items for safety; monitor computer use for physical and content safety; teach and model safety

55. (List three:) remember that adults are models for the child; carefully explain the boundaries of play; practice safety measures, such as fire drills; read books or stories on safety or watch special segments on safety in children's television programs; insist on obedience to safety rules; explain the importance and use of safety devices

# Be Wise to Safety Problems

# Specific Immunities Matrix

|  | Naturally Acquired | Artificially Acquired |
|---|---|---|
| **Active** | Infection (causes a person's body to develop antibodies as a reaction to the illness) | Immunization (causes a person's body to develop antibodies as a reaction to the antigen) |
| **Passive** | Antibodies are passed to unborn through placenta or to newborn through colostrum | Antibodies are transferred to the person as an anti-serum |

# Adults' Roles in Children's Computer Use

## Guiding Children Toward Benefits

- Introduce computer use during preschool years
- Select (and later monitor child's selection) of quality software and Web sites
- Provide a balance among daily activities
- Plan special Internet projects for child
- Communicate with child about computer activities
- Model appropriate computer use

## Protecting Children from Dangers

- Design computer areas for child's comfortable and safe use
- Adjust monitor and reduce glare to protect child's eyes
- Have child take frequent breaks
- Monitor all computer use
- Use filtering programs to block unacceptable content
- Set and enforce rules for child's computer use

# Hospital Kit

**Name** _____ **Date** _____ **Period** _____

Children are often anxious about staying in the hospital. While in the hospital, they may wish for some special comforts to make them feel better about their stay. Create a hospital kit for a child to use during a hospital stay. Include in the kit items that are fun and easy for a child to play with in bed. The following suggestions will help you get started on your kit.

A. Plan items for specific age groups, such as a simple picture book for a three-year-old or a word-find book for a school-age child.

B. You may purchase items, such as pencils, fancy erasers, books, or a small flashlight. You may make items, such as a picture book (of pictures cut from magazines) or puzzle (picture mounted on a piece of cardboard and then cut into a few pieces). You may collect items, too, such as a few plastic, miniature animals or cars from a set long outgrown or some leftover activity sheet from a teacher.

C. The kit should contain only a few items because most hospital stays are only a few days. You might want to plan several surprises for a child who must be hospitalized for a longer stay.

D. The child may unwrap the package as a present. A handmade or purchased card is a nice touch, too.

E. On a separate card secured to the kit, list the contents of the kit and the age of child for which the kit is suited. (This will help the hospital match the gift with a child.)

After assembling your kit answer the following questions.

What did your kit include? _____

_____

_____

_____

_____

What age child did your kit suit? _____

What special features made your kit able to help the child feel more comfortable in the hospital?

_____

_____

_____

_____

_____

_____

_____

_____

_____

_____

# Protecting Children's Health and Safety

**Name** _____

**Date** _____ **Period** _____ **Score** _____

## Chapter 21 Test

True/False: Circle *T* if the statement is true or *F* if the statement is false.

T    F      1. Good nutritional status may aid children's recovery from disease or injury.

T    F      2. Babies should receive regular physical checkups more frequently than young adults.

T    F      3. Having straight teeth decreases the chance of tooth and gum disease.

T    F      4. Antigens are injected into a person's body to help him or her develop immunity.

T    F      5. Immunizations are often part of well-baby checkups.

T    F      6. Because physicians check children, they do *not* need to know symptoms adults note or hear how adults have treated these symptoms.

T    F      7. Allergies are caused by a failure of the immune system to react.

T    F      8. Children of all ages are likely to have the same types of accidents.

T    F      9. Adults must consider childproofing every part of the child's world.

T    F    10. Children can eat medicines and poisonous plants without an adult's knowledge.

T    F    11. Children who weigh 40 to 80 pounds should ride in a booster seat.

T    F    12. A toy that is labeled as safe by a manufacturer or distributor would be safe for all children within the recommended age range.

T    F    13. The amount and type of space in which a child has to play with a toy does *not* affect safety.

T    F    14. Kittens and puppies make better children's pets than adult cats and dogs.

T    F    15. Adults need to plan ways to make children's computer use physically safe.

T    F    16. Filtering programs can replace the need for adults to monitor Internet use.

T    F    17. Safety devices make an area or object completely safe.

T    F    18. Adults must teach and model safety lessons for children.

T    F    19. Hospital care is rather frightening to both the child and the parent.

Multiple Choice: Choose the best response. Write the letter in the space provided.

_____ 20. Adults are almost totally responsible for the child's _____.
    A. health and safety
    B. motor skills
    C. intellectual skills
    D. All of the above.

_____ 21. Physical health may be damaged by all of the following *except* _____.
    A. abnormal conditions
    B. injury
    C. physical activity
    D. disease

*(Continued)*

**Name** _____

_____ 22. Professional dental care should begin at _____.
A. birth
B. one year of age
C. three years of age
D. the early school-age years

_____ 23. Immunity may develop from _____.
A. developing antibodies by having a disease
B. receiving antibodies from the mother in the prenatal and neonatal stages
C. developing antibodies from an immunization
D. All of the above.

_____ 24. Which of the following statements about childhood diseases is *not* true?
A. Immunizations have been developed to protect against several childhood diseases.
B. These diseases cannot be contracted after childhood.
C. Many childhood diseases are contagious and require adults to keep an infected child away from other children.
D. Childhood diseases vary in severity, symptoms, and treatments.

_____ 25. Allergies are treated by _____.
A. removing or limiting contact with the allergen
B. using medications
C. using desensitization therapy
D. All of the above.

_____ 26. Adults can help protect children from accidents by doing all of the following *except* _____.
A. creating a safe environment
B. modeling and teaching safety practices
C. relying on safety devices
D. supervising children carefully

_____ 27. More than _____ percent of all poisonings involve children under five years of age.
A. 50
B. 75
C. 90
D. 99

_____ 28. Certified child safety seats should *not* be used _____.
A. in the front seat of a car
B. for infants weighing less than 20 pounds
C. for airline trips
D. when adults can hold children securely

_____ 29. Many toy injuries can be prevented by _____.
A. careful choice
B. supervision
C. proper maintenance
D. All of the above.

_____ 30. A computer filtering program does *not* block _____.
A. inappropriate Web sites
B. inappropriate software programs
C. glare on the monitor
D. inappropriate e-mail

*(Continued)*

**Name** _____

Matching: Match the following terms and identifying phrases.

_____31. Decayed places in teeth.

_____32. A dentist who specializes in correcting irregular teeth.

_____33. Having agents that prevent a person from developing a disease.

_____34. Proteins in the blood that fight diseases.

_____35. Type of immunity developed through direct contact with an infection or by receiving antibodies from the mother during pregnancy or breast-feeding.

_____36. Immunity formed as a reaction to antibodies or an antigen received through medical care.

_____37. Substances made in a laboratory and transferred to people in the form of an injection to help their bodies form antibodies against a disease.

_____38. Giving protection from disease through the injection of an antigen.

_____39. Immunity due to developing one's own antibodies.

_____40. Immunity due to receiving antibodies from another person.

_____41. Signs of an illness or injury.

_____42. Disease that can be caught from another person.

_____43. An overreaction of the immune system to contact with a given substance.

_____44. Substances that cause allergies.

_____45. The process of removing objects from a child's reach or preventing dangerous situations.

_____46. Car seats, seat belts, and other devices designed to protect people during a vehicle accident.

_____47. Restraint systems for infants and young children that have been tested and approved by federal agencies.

_____48. Issuing of a notice by a product manufacturer stating the product is unsafe.

_____49. Special anchors and tethers installed in new cars to aid the use of certified child safety seats.

_____50. Professional who provides information on child safety seats and inspects them after installation.

_____51. Emergency treatment that is given for an accident or illness before professional help arrives.

_____52. Identifying the cause of a person's illness.

_____53. Having a disease that will result in death.

A. active immunity

B. allergen

C. allergy

D. antibodies

E. antigens

F. artificially acquired immunity

G. certified child safety seats

H. child passenger seat technician

I. childproofing

J. contagious disease

K. dental caries

L. diagnosis

M. first aid

N. immunity

O. immunization

P. LATCH system

Q. naturally acquired immunity

R. orthodontist

S. passive immunity

T. restraint system

U. safety recall

V. symptoms

W. terminally ill

*(Continued)*

**Name** _____

Essay Questions: Provide complete responses to the following questions or statements.

54. Give five tips for parents on creating a safe environment for children.

55. List three ways parents and other adults can teach children safety.

# Child Care and Education in Group Settings

## Objectives

After studying this chapter, students will be able to
- trace the history of the major types of group programs for young children.
- describe what to look for when choosing a quality program.
- explain the effects of group care and education on children's development.
- describe ways to help children adjust to group settings.

## Bulletin Boards

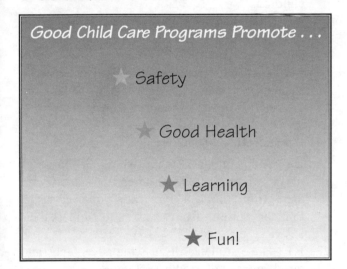

*Good Child Care Programs Promote . . .*

⭐ Safety

⭐ Good Health

⭐ Learning

⭐ Fun!

Title: *Good Child Care Programs Promote...*

Under the title, place large gold stars in front of the words: *safety, good health, learning,* and *fun.*

Title: *Home Life and Group Life Differ*

On large sheets of paper, write *Home life is....* On another large sheet, write *Group life is....* Have students list differences in the two, such as environment, number of playmates, contact with adults, types of experiences, and number and kinds of toys.

## Teaching Materials

**Text**, pages 582-617
*Reviewing Key Concepts*
*Using Your Knowledge*
*Making Observations*
*Thinking Further*

**Student Activity Guide**
A. *The Shapes and Sizes of Children's Programs*
B. *Local Child Care and Education Facilities*
C. *Family Communication and Participation Opportunities*
D. *Good Programs Help Children Grow*
E. *Finding a Quality Group Program*

**Teacher's Resources**
*Benefits of Group Programs,* transparency master 22-1
*A Rich Tradition,* reproducible master 22-2
*Share Your Talent,* reproducible master 22-3
Chapter 22 Test

## Introductory Activities

1. *Benefits of Group Programs,* transparency master 22-1. For each category have students list typical group program activities that could benefit the area of development.
2. Have students visit the Web sites of the following professional organizations dealing with the care and education for children: American Montessori Society (www.amshq.org); Association for Childhood International (www.acei.org); and National Association for the Education of Young Children (www.naeyc.org).

## Strategies to Reteach, Reinforce, Enrich, and Extend Text Concepts

### Types of Group Programs

3. **RF** Have students explain how the term *group program* differs from the term *babysitting.*
4. **RF** *The Shapes and Sizes of Children's Programs,* Activity A, SAG. As students read the chapter, have them complete each section on the chart concerning the basic features of each group program.
5. **ER** *A Rich Tradition,* reproducible master 22-2. As students read this section of the chapter, have them complete the corresponding section of the chart. (Note: For the section "Nursery Schools," you may need to explain that "nurses" were female caregivers of children.) Then discuss

commonalities among programs, such as activity programs as opposed to drill, sensory-perceptual learnings as appropriate for young children, and quality materials.

## Child Care Programs

6. **RT**  Ask students why child care programs are in great demand today.
7. **RF**  Students should plan and present a skit in which several couples (or individual parents) are discussing the pros and cons of various types of child care.
8. **EX**  Explain that *au pair* is French for "on the par." This name suggests that host families should treat au pairs as members of the family.
9. **RT**  Ask students to compare and contrast the advantages and disadvantages of child care provided by housekeepers, au pairs, and nannies.
10. **RT**  Share with students that not-for-profit programs have a main purpose other than making a profit. These programs should and do make some profit, however. These profits generally go back into the program for its operation and expansion. (In this way, not-for-profit programs differ from nonprofit programs, which are not allowed under the law to make a profit.)
11. **EX**  Ask students about their care during their elementary school years. Compare their care with the types of SACC programs now available locally. Ask students whether they think SACC programs should be mainly for diversion/recreation or for education. Have students explain the reasons for their answers.
12. **RT**  Have students brainstorm reasons for the high cost of infant-toddler programs.
13. **ER**  Invite a person from the local CCR&R agency to the classroom. Ask them to share information on their services and the general need for and the availability of local child care programs.

## Kindergartens

14. **RT**  Discuss with students Froebel's idea that young children are different from adults and should be treated in special ways. Discuss whether they think children are different from adults based on their study of child development.
15. **ER**  Instruct students to review some historical materials about early kindergartens in the United States and write a report on their findings.
16. **EX**  Explain that kindergartens in Froebel's day served children three to seven years of age. Tell

students that Froebel introduced blockbuilding as the most important activity for young children. From these blocks, which he called *gifts*, children learned many skills. Look at some of these blocks online at www.froebelgifts.com. Tell students that Frank Lloyd Wright, a noted American architect, used those blocks as a child and felt they were the foundation for his skills.

17. **ER**  Have students interview a kindergarten teacher about the types of activities he or she provides for students.

## Nursery Schools

18. **ER**  Point out the word *nursery* means attentive care. Ask students to name the ways we use the term today, such as nursery for plants, nursery at hospitals, nursery for baby animals at zoos, a young child's bedroom, a school or program for young children, and a rhyme or story for young children.
19. **RT**  Ask students to explain how the historical roots of nursery schools differ from those of child care.
20. **ER**  Ask students to read about the work of Rachel and Margaret McMillan in developing the English nursery school in the early 1900s.

## Montessori Schools

21. **EX**  Ask students what Maria Montessori meant when she said children can absorb and learn from the world as they work at tasks. Students should give examples to support their answers.
22. **RT**  Have students discuss the advantages and disadvantages of grouping children in three-year age spans.
23. **ER**  Take a field trip to a local Montessori school. Ask students to write a description of Montessori materials.
24. **EX**  Have students read about the life of Montessori who had to overcome many obstacles to become Italy's first female medical doctor and later founded the Montessori schools.
25. **RF**  Discuss some differences between a traditional Montessori program and some of the American Montessori programs. (The newer American Montessori programs include creative art, dramatic play, science activities, and gross-motor play using playground equipment. Traditional Montessori programs do not have these components.)

# Head Start

26. **RT**   Discuss with students what the name *Head Start* implies.
27. **RT**   Discuss with students why children from low-income families often need special help for maximum development.
28. **ER**   Invite a Head Start director to speak to the class about some of the services that Head Start provides.

# Choosing a Group Program

29. **RT**   Ask students to explain why parents should carefully consider group programs for children.
30. **EX**   Ask students for some hypothetical examples of how family needs differ and therefore require different types of programs for children.
31. **RF**   *Local Child Care Facilities*, Activity B, SAG. Students are asked to pretend they have moved into a community and are searching for group child care for an infant. They are asked to research local not-for-profit centers and for-profit centers.

# Regulations

32. **RT**   Borrow from a local provider or order from your state's licensing agency a manual for center-based child care programs. Assign small groups of students to read one or two areas of regulations (such as housing or staff) and share their findings with the class.
33. **ER**   Invite a public school administrator of a kindergarten program, a director of a private program for young children, and a director of a Head Start program to speak to the class. Panelists should discuss how and by whom they are regulated. Panelists should share a few examples of regulations they must meet.
34. **RT**   Discuss with students how parents can know whether private programs are meeting state regulations.

# Housing and Equipment

35. **RT**   Ask students for examples of how housing and equipment can enhance or hamper group programs.
36. **RT**   Instruct students to explain why quality play equipment is important in a program for children.
37. **ER**   Field trip: Arrange for the class to visit a program for children in your area. Students should note the housing arrangements and equipment.

# Staff

38. **RT**   Ask students to describe some dangers of having too large of groups or inadequate adult-child ratios in child care programs.
39. **RT**   Ask students to list characteristics needed by staff members working in programs for young children.
40. **ER**   Invite a teacher of young children to talk about the physical and other personal characteristics needed to work in programs for young children. Compare the teacher's remarks with the class list of needed characteristics.
41. **RT**   Discuss with students ways that adults make children feel safe and secure.
42. **RT**   Instruct students to define the term *guidance*. Students should discuss ways adults guide children.

# Parent Communication and Participation

43. **RF**   *Family Communication and Participation Opportunities*, Activity C, SAG. Instruct students to visit one or two programs for young children and ask caregivers to describe specifically how they communicate with and involve families. In addition to recording the information, tell students to attach any samples they may be able to share with the class, such as a newsletter, handbook, list of parent program meetings for the year, or a printed page from a program Web site.
44. **ER**   Invite a director of a program for young children to share with the class ways staff from the program communicate with family members and involve them in the program.
45. **ER**   Invite a teacher of young children who uses children's portfolios as a way to sharing a child's accomplishments with a parent. Ask the teacher to explain how meaningful this approach is to parents. (It would be helpful if the teacher could bring samples of various portfolios with each child's identity removed.)

# Program Activities

46. **ER**   Students should browse through a curriculum guide for kindergarten or another group program for young children. Instruct them to list some examples of activities that help children with language learnings, math learnings, social learnings, science learnings, creativity, and motor skills.

47. **RT**   Adults who are not on the staff of a group program but who share their skills and interests with children are often called *resource people*. Have students explain why this term is appropriate.

48. **ER**   *Share Your Talent*, reproducible master 22-2. Have students complete the form by listing some of the skills or interests they have and could share with others.

49. **EX**   Have students obtain schedules from two or more group programs for children. For each schedule students should construct a large clock and place it on a poster board. Using the schedule, students should draw symbols to represent the various activities at the corresponding times. Students should present their posters to the class and compare and contrast activities various programs use.

50. **RF**   *Good Programs Help Children Grow*, Activity D, SAG. Instruct students to visit a program for young children and describe how the program uses both routine and specially planned activities to help children grow.

## Cultural Diversity in Group Programs

51. **RT**   Ask students how they have felt in settings or situations in which they thought of themselves as somewhat "out of place." Ask them how they think young children and also their families feel when they enter programs in which the language or other aspects of culture differ from their own cultures. What can caregivers and teachers do to help children of other cultures feel more welcome?

52. **ER**   Have students visit a toy store that sells school supplies and a bookstore or library and find two or three items that would promote cultural diversity. Share the descriptions of the items in class. (Catalogs or Web sites of suppliers of equipment or books may also be used to locate items.)

53. **ER**   Ask students to role-play adults helping children handle culture shock and expressions of bias from others.

## Providing Child Care and Education for Children with Special Needs

54. **ER**   Visit a classroom in which housing and furnishings have been adapted for children with special needs. Note similarities and differences in this classroom with classrooms that have not made accommodations for children with special needs.

55. **ER**   Point out to students the law states that children with special needs must have the "least restrictive placement." Ask what this means. Discuss how inclusion is often the best way to meet this requirement.

56. **EX**   Ask students to describe possible advantages of inclusion for children with and without special needs.

## Other Considerations

57. **ER**   Have students interview a director of a work-related child care program. Students should ask the director to explain how the business meets the needs of parents through its child care program. Instruct students to write a report based on their findings.

58. **ER**   Encourage students to investigate the costs of group programs in your area. Students should examine: (a) costs for different ages of children; (b) costs if more than one child per family is enrolled; (c) costs for drop-in care; (d) costs for various special services. Students should also list hidden added costs.

## Quality of Group Programs

59. **ER**   Assign students to write a newspaper-style article on why children have the right to quality programs and possible ways parents may locate quality programs.

60. **RF**   *Finding a Quality Group Program*, Activity E, SAG. Have students find the problems in the program described and suggest possible ways to correct them.

## Effects of Group Care and Education on Children

61. **RT**   Have students discuss the following questions: Do you feel a quality program would be good for any child? Do you feel a below-standard program would be good for any child? Do you think the cost of a program is an indication of its quality?

62. **RF**   Ask students to list some aspects of development that parents should note after their children enter any group program.

## Effects on Health

63. **ER**   Invite a pediatrician to speak to the class about how group programs for young children can affect their health. Ask the pediatrician how parents and teachers can help protect children's health while the children are in group settings.

64. **ER** Invite a teacher of young children or a director of a child care and education program to share ways his or her program helps prevent illnesses. (Topics could include vaccination requirements, sanitary food handling, cleaning, policies on hand washing and use of gloves, and policies concerning ill children.)

## Effects on Mental Development

65. **EX** Have students speculate why gains in intellectual development in the preschool years must be followed with enrichment if the gains are to remain stable. Ask students to give examples of how skills can decline due to lack of practice.

66. **ER** Discuss with students how parents can determine whether preschool programs challenge children mentally or are "pushy" programs. Ask how "pushy" programs are harmful to children. (Review Figure 22-16 on DIP.)

## Effects on Social Development

67. **RT** Discuss with students the dangers of allowing even a quality program to totally (or almost totally) replace family life rather than enrich family life for the child.

68. **ER** Ask students to list ways parents and other family members can maintain closeness with their children despite having to use group programs.

69. **ER** Ask students to interview a teacher or director of a group program on how he or she helps children learn to control aggression. Ask students what other sources of aggression parents should note. Review with students how to note unhealthy aggression in young children. Ask what measures parents should take regarding aggression.

## Helping Children Adjust to Group Care

70. **RT** Ask students why adults should be casual when they introduce the idea that a child will soon enter a group program.

71. **RT** Discuss with students why it is natural and even good for parents to be anxious about children's enrollment in group programs. Have students list signs that indicate parents should take action because problems likely exist with the care.

# Answer Key

## Text
### Reviewing Key Concepts, page 616
1. number; type
2. housekeepers; au pairs; nannies
3. A, D, A, E, B, D, C, A, D, B
4. false
5. (List four:) based on knowledge of development; based on the strengths, needs, and interests of each child within the group; based on knowledge of the social and cultural contexts in which children in a given program live; promotes all areas of development; uses both planned activities and day-to-day routines to help children learn; planned in ways that help children develop
6. materials; activities; people
7. true
8. (Name one hidden added cost:) costs of transportation, supplies, and disposable diapers and formulas for babies; donations made for services given to the program. (Name one hidden cost credit) money that may be added from a second income; money saved in the cost of utilities and food for at-home care; child care tax credits
9. (List five. See Figure 22-23 in text.)
10. false
11. (Suggest three:) make the adjustment seem casual; realize adults can be anxious as well as children; show you are sure of the child's ability to adjust; about one month before enrolling a child in a group program, explain what the new program is like and visit the program, if possible

## Student Activity Guide
### The Shapes and Sizes of Children's Programs, Activity A

**In-home child care**

*Children served:* babies through school-age children

*Sponsorship:* N/A

*Major purposes of program:* to provide care for children for extended hours

**Family child care**

*Children served:* babies to school-age children, possibly even school-age children before and after school and school holidays

*Sponsorship:* family served

*Major purposes of program:* to provide care for children for extended hours, usually between 9 and 12 hours per day

**Center-based child care**

*Children served*: babies to school-age children, possibly even school-age children for after school and school holidays

*Sponsorship*: varies from for-profit businesses to not-for-profit organizations to businesses who offer programs for employees

*Major purposes of program:* to provide care for children for extended hours, usually between 9 and 12 hours per day

**Kindergartens**

*Children served*: four- and five-year-old children

*Sponsorship*: the public education system of the United States

*Major purposes of program*: to prepare children for school education, to give children the chance to play and develop through various games, and to meet the needs of children without causing undue stress

**Nursery schools**

*Children served*: children under age five years

*Sponsorship*: private ownership or part of a public school or research institution

*Major purposes of program*: to provide education as well as physical care for children, to study children and provide career training, and to provide first-hand learning experiences that build on life within the family

**Montessori schools**

*Children served*: children between the ages of two-and-one-half and seven years

*Sponsorship*: private ownership

*Major purposes of program*: to allow children to absorb and learn from their world as they work at tasks; to guide children but allow them to be more in charge of their own learnings; and to teach through sensory learnings, daily living activities, and language activities

**Head Start**

*Children served*: children from families with low income

*Sponsorship*: federal grants with support from individual communities

*Major purposes of program*: to provide any food, medical care, and learning help that cannot be obtained at home; to involve parents and families of the enrolled children; to help build children's self-esteem; and to help children and their families work together to solve problems

## Finding a Quality Group Program, Activity E

**Problems:** Parents are not allowed to visit at any time; adults who supervise may not be experienced (the sixteen-year-old); the ratio of adults to children is not high enough when one adult is involved in tasks other than child care (Mr. Green should not be preparing snacks); there may be too much pressure on children if every toddler is required to read.

(Student response for ways to correct the problems.)

# Teacher's Resources

## A Rich Tradition, reproducible master 22-2

1. Play is important for all areas of development.
2. According to Piaget, sensorimotor and preoperational children need to manipulate objects. Even in the concrete operational stage, children think in terms of their experiences in manipulating objects.
3. Parents play the most important role in their children's lives and thus need to be educated about child development.
4. Piaget's first stage of development is the sensorimotor stage.
5. Language is the means by which humans both communicate and think. Brain wiring for most aspects of language occurs early in life.
6. Erikson's second stage of development deals with autonomy.
7. Emotional stress causes pruning of brain connections and physical symptoms. Too much or prolonged stress hampers all areas of development.
8. Brain wiring for certain abilities occurs at a specific time. During this time parents and teachers need to take advantage of the window of opportunity.
9. (Same as # 4 above.)
10. Self-help skills are most important to develop beginning in the Erikson stage of "autonomy versus self-doubt."
11. (Same as # 2 above.)
12. A child-sized and orderly environment promotes self-help skills and hence autonomy.

## Chapter 22 Test

| | | |
|---|---|---|
| 1. F | 19. B | 37. F |
| 2. F | 20. C | 38. Q |
| 3. T | 21. D | 39. U |
| 4. F | 22. B | 40. L |
| 5. T | 23. D | 41. T |
| 6. T | 24. C | 42. R |
| 7. T | 25. A | 43. M |
| 8. T | 26. C | 44. V |
| 9. F | 27. A | 45. A |
| 10. F | 28. C | 46. H |
| 11. T | 29. E | 47. I |
| 12. F | 30. P | 48. K |
| 13. T | 31. B | 49. G |
| 14. F | 32. S | 50. C |
| 15. F | 33. J | 51. N |
| 16. F | 34. D | 52. O |
| 17. D | 35. X | |
| 18. C | 36. W | |

53. (Describe three:) parent room or reception area; group meetings and workshops; open house; individual conferences; home visits; parent visitation of program; newsletters; informal notes; serve on an advisory board; volunteer in program

(Student response for description.)

54. Affirm each child's identity by pronouncing name correctly, providing self-awareness activities, and by responding positively to questions and comments; make the program culturally rich by selecting culturally diverse materials, activities, and role models; help children learn that bias hurts

55. Make needed physical accommodations for children with special needs; adapt activities to meet needs of all children; team teach

Children: The Early Years Teacher's Resources

# Benefits of Group Programs

| Physical Development | Intellectual Development | Social-Emotional Development |
|---|---|---|
|  |  |  |

# A Rich Tradition

**Name** _____ **Date** _____ **Period** _____

Many ideas for today's child care and education programs are based on programs of the past. Explain how each of these early ideas has relevance today based on what you have learned about children's development and their needs.

| Idea | Relevance Today |
|------|-----------------|
| **Froebel's Kindergarten** | |
| 1.  Play is the highest level of child development. | |
| 2.  Children learn best through hands-on activities. | |
| 3.  Mothers and other caregivers need to be educated about children's needs. | |
| **Nursery Schools** | |
| 4.  Children need perceptual-motor activities. | |
| 5.  Language activities are very important. | |
| 6.  Children should begin the process of detaching from parents. | |
| 7.  Teachers must guard against emotional stress. | |
| **Montessori Schools** | |
| 8.  Children have "sensitive periods" in which they are ready to learn certain concepts. | |
| 9.  Sensory perceptions are the basis of all learnings. | |
| 10. Self-help skills are important for children. | |
| 11. Children learn mainly through working with materials. | |
| 12. Children need a child-sized and orderly environment. | |

# Share Your Talent

**Name** _____ **Date** _____ **Period** _____

Almost all adults have a hobby or a skill they can share with young children in a group program. Resource persons can add so much sparkle to a classroom. Pretend you have received the following form from a group program. Complete the form.

## The Early Years Child Care Center
### Volunteer Inventory

Name: _____

Address: _____

Phone: _____

List hobbies or skills you could share with children. _____
_____
_____
_____

How could these skills enhance our program? _____
_____
_____
_____

Define a presentation you could make to children involving your hobbies or skills. _____
_____
_____
_____

For what age children would your presentation be most suited? _____
_____

How many children could participate with you at one time (1 child, 4 or 5 children in small groups, 15 to 20 children in a large group)? _____
_____

What special arrangements for your presentation would you need (such as furniture arrangement or equipment)? _____
_____
_____

What time(s) could you serve as a resource person? _____
_____

How may we contact you? _____

# Child Care and Education in Group Settings

**Name** _____

**Date** _____ **Period** _____ **Score** _____

## Chapter 22 Test

True/False: Circle *T* if the statement is true or *F* if the statement is false.

T    F    1. The need for child care is decreasing rapidly because most families today have at least one parent staying home with the children.

T    F    2. The main purpose of child care centers is to provide educational services for children.

T    F    3. Family child care is often a good option for infants and toddlers.

T    F    4. Very few families need school-age child care.

T    F    5. The founder of the kindergarten emphasized play as important for learning.

T    F    6. One purpose of nursery schools is to serve as sites for experts to research child development.

T    F    7. Montessori felt that children absorb much from the world as they work at tasks.

T    F    8. A major strength of Head Start is its focus on children's families and cultures.

T    F    9. Meeting the regulations for child care and education programs means the program has met the highest standards possible.

T    F    10. Adult-child ratio is another name for group size.

T    F    11. Good parent communication requires knowledge of each family's culture.

T    F    12. Children do *not* need to understand or appreciate cultural diversity.

T    F    13. Inclusionary programs care for and teach children with special needs in the same classroom as children without disabilities or gifts.

T    F    14. Not-for-profit programs charge the highest fees to parents.

T    F    15. Parents can judge the quality of a program just by meeting the staff and taking a quick walk through the facility.

T    F    16. All studies agree that children in group programs have more serious illnesses than children cared for in their own homes.

Multiple Choice: Choose the best response. Write the letter in the space provided.

_____ 17. Parents might choose to enroll their children in group programs for which of the following reasons?
A. They want their children challenged in all areas of development.
B. They work outside the home.
C. They need relief from providing full-time child care themselves.
D. All of the above.

_____ 18. Which of the following statements is true?
A. For-profit programs operate for the purpose of making money for the owners.
B. Not-for-profit programs are designed to serve purposes other than making money.
C. Both A and B are true.
D. Neither A nor B is true.

*(Continued)*

**Name** _____

_____ 19. Benefits of SACC programs include all of the following *except* _____.
   A. more enrichment than self-care
   B. lower cost than self-care
   C. lower safety risks than self-care
   D. more reliable care than self-care

_____ 20. Trends in child care do *not* include _____.
   A. an increased demand for infant and toddler programs
   B. the creation and use of child care resource and referral agencies
   C. a rapid decrease in center-based child care programs available
   D. an increase in school-age child care programs available

_____ 21. Program activities of the nursery school are planned to build on life within the _____.
   A. family
   B. peer group
   C. school
   D. All of the above.

_____ 22. Head Start is primarily funded through _____.
   A. community organization donations
   B. federal monies
   C. individual donations
   D. state monies

_____ 23. Regulations _____.
   A. are often minimum standards
   B. may or may not be easy to check
   C. may simply be on record with little or no enforcement
   D. All of the above.

_____ 24. Staff members who work with children need to _____.
   A. teach young children usable skills, such as reading and math
   B. meet only the physical needs of children
   C. work well with adults, too
   D. All of the above.

_____ 25. Developmentally appropriate practices are primarily based on all of the following *except* _____.
   A. offering the same activities to all children
   B. being culturally relevant
   C. being age/stage appropriate
   D. serving each child's needs and interests

_____ 26. In quality group programs, children learn through _____.
   A. day-to-day routines
   B. specially planned activities
   C. Both A and B.
   D. Neither A nor B.

_____ 27. Quality group programs tend to enhance intellectual development most in children from families with _____.
   A. below-average income
   B. average income
   C. above-average income
   D. all income groups equally

_____ 28. Children who attend group programs seem to be _____.
   A. just as attached to their parents as children who do not attend group programs
   B. more aggressive than children who do not attend group programs
   C. Both A and B.
   D. Neither A nor B.

*(Continued)*

**Name** _____

Matching: Match the following terms and identifying phrases.

_____ 29.  Programs that operate to care for children for extended hours.

_____ 30.  Care that takes place in the child's own home.

_____ 31.  Persons who provide in-home child care for a host family as part of a cultural exchange program.

_____ 32.  Professionals who contract with a family to provide in-home child care.

_____ 33.  Care provided by a person for a small number of children in his or her own home.

_____ 34.  Large group care that is not provided in a home.

_____ 35.  Group programs funded by businesses for employees.

_____ 36.  Care programs provided for older children.

_____ 37.  Programs that promote local care programs and help parents find child care.

_____ 38.  Publicly and privately operated programs for four- and five-year-old children that serve as an entrance to school education.

_____ 39.  Programs owned that are not owned by the government.

_____ 40.  Rhymes or poems with actions.

_____ 41.  Programs that offer education and care for children under age five years.

_____ 42.  Programs that educate children to work independently through the use of materials.

_____ 43.  Programs that provide care, education, and other services to children from families with low income.

_____ 44.  Programs funded through government monies.

_____ 45.  Number of adults (excluding support staff) per number of children.

_____ 46.  Group program that bases its services on knowledge of child development and children's individual needs.

_____ 47.  Group program that has less-than-desirable practices and activities.

_____ 48.  Outings that take children off a program's property.

_____ 49.  An uncomfortable response to an unfamiliar culture.

_____ 50.  Belief or feeling that results in an unfair treatment of another person or makes such a treatment by others seem right.

_____ 51.  Unseen costs that are part of total cost.

_____ 52.  Unseen assets that lower the direct costs.

A. adult-child ratio

B. au pairs

C. bias

D. center-based child care

E. child care programs

F. Child Care Resource and Referral agencies

G. culture shock

H. developmentally appropriate practices

I. developmentally inappropriate practices

J. family child care

K. field trips

L. fingerplays

M. Head Start

N. hidden added costs

O. hidden cost credits

P. in-home child care

Q. kindergarten

R. Montessori schools

S. nannies

T. nursery schools

U. private programs

V. public programs

W. school-age child care

X. work-related child care

Essay Questions: Provide complete responses to the following questions or statements.

53. Describe three ways child care and education programs can communicate with and involve families.

54. What can group programs do to create an environment where cultural diversity is appreciated?

55. Explain how children's special needs are met through inclusionary programs.

# Children with Special Needs

## Objectives

After studying this chapter, students will be able to
- define the term *children with special needs.*
- explain why children with and without special needs are more alike than different.
- describe some of the common forms of special needs in children.
- outline steps people can take to help children with special needs.

## Bulletin Boards

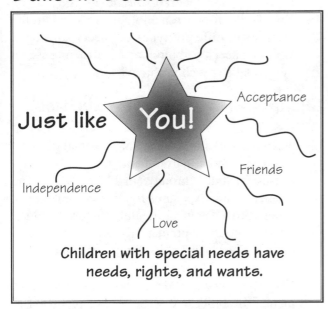

Just like **You!**

Acceptance

Independence

Friends

Love

**Children with special needs have needs, rights, and wants.**

Title: *Just Like You!*

From gold or other brightly colored paper make a large star. Mount the word *You!* on the star. Around the edges of the star write the words *Acceptance, Love, Friends,* and *Independence.* Under the star, write the sentence *Children with special needs have needs, rights, and wants.* Have students identify other similarities between children with special needs and themselves. Post other characteristics around the star.

Title: *Spotlight on People with Special Needs*

Have students bring in pictures of famous gifted or disabled people. Place each picture on the board labeled with the person's name and achievements. Have students discuss each person's background.

## Teaching Materials

**Text**, pages 618-637
*Reviewing Key Concepts*
*Using Your Knowledge*
*Making Observations*
*Thinking Further*

**Student Activity Guide**
A. *A More In-Depth View*
B. *A Special Classroom*
C. *Community Resources*

**Teacher's Resources**
*Parents Can Assess Development,*
transparency master 23-1
*Delays and Problems: Common Myths,*
transparency master 23-2
*Bibliotherapy Helps*, reproducible master 23-3
Chapter 23 Test

## Introductory Activities

1. Students should brainstorm a list of highly intelligent, artistic, or musical people. Ask students whether they think their gifts and talents are products of heredity or environment.
2. Discuss with students how the development of children with special needs differs from the development of children at an average pace. (The rate of development, sometimes the pattern of development, and the degree of development differ for children with special needs.)

## Strategies to Reteach, Reinforce, Enrich, and Extend Text Concepts

### Children Are More Alike Than Different

3. **RT** After reading this section, have students make a poster with pictures or drawings showing how children are alike.
4. **EX** Point out that teachers of even severely disabled children often say they see these children as more "abled than disabled." Ask students to describe their feelings about the statement. Is such an attitude healthy? Students should explain why or why not.

5. **RF**   Ask students for examples of people with gifts in one area and disabilities in another area. (One example is Itzhak Perlman, a famous Israeli violinist who performs sitting down because he has been permanently disabled since he was four years old. He walks with crutches and leg braces.)

6. **RT**   Review from chapter 1 the vocabulary words *developmental acceleration* and *developmental delay*. Remind students these terms describe the rate of development.

7. **ER**   Have students search the Internet for information on atypical patterns of development called pervasive developmental disorders (PDDs).

8. **RT**   Ask students to explain what the terms *borderline* and *profound* mean. Explain to students these terms refer to the degree of talents or disabilities. Then look up the terms *limited, extensive,* and *pervasive.* These terms are used to describe the amount of help or supervision needed.

## Children with Special Needs

9. **ER**   *Parents Can Assess Development,* transparency master 23-1. Use this transparency to outline aspects of development parents should watch. Ask students what parents need to know in order to assess their children's development. (Parents must understand expected or typical behaviors of certain ages and stages.) Ask students to indicate what each behavior could indicate.

10. **RF**   *A More In-Depth View*, Activity A, SAG. Have students obtain more information on one type of giftedness and one type of disability.

## Gifted and Talented Children

11. **RF**   The degree of giftedness is often referred to as *talented, gifted,* or *very gifted*. However, many words can describe development that is faster and beyond average. Instruct students to list and define as many of these words as they can.

12. **RF**   Ask students to give examples of people who have excelled in areas such as general mental ability, specific academic areas, creative or productive thinking, leadership, visual or performing arts, and psychomotor areas.

13. **EX**   Discuss with students how culture affects giftedness.

## Children with Physical Disabilities

14. **RT**   Have students list examples of physical disabilities.

15. **RT**   Discuss with students that children with physical disabilities do not need overprotection.

16. **ER**   Students should read a story of someone who struggled to overcome a physical disability. Students should share parts of the story with other class members.

17. **EX**   Ask students to name some of the environmental conditions that have been addressed to promote independence for people with physical disabilities. Point out some of these adaptations on a visit to a playground or park designed to accommodate the needs of children with physical disabilities.

## Speech Disorders

18. **ER**   Instruct students to research a speech disorder, such as stuttering or stammering, and to write a short report about the disorder.

19. **ER**   Invite a speech pathologist to speak to the class about different types of speech disorders. How do speech pathologists work to improve an individual's speech problem?

## Children with Mental Disabilities

20. **RT**   Discuss with students causes of mental disabilities. Point out that some mental disabilities result from environmental factors. (Prenatal causes include chromosomal disorders, gene problems, and exposures to toxins or infections. After birth, environmental factors include complications of prematurity, low birthweight, or infections; lead poisoning; metabolic disorders; and head trauma.)

21. **ER**   Have each student choose one type of mental disability and write a brief report on it. Examples include Down syndrome, Fragile X syndrome, Rett syndrome, and lead poisoning. Ask students to present their reports orally.

22. **EX**   Invite a teacher of children with mental disabilities to the classroom. Have her demonstrate how tasks are broken down into smaller parts.

## Children with Learning Disabilities

23. **ER**   Instruct students to research one type of learning disability and present findings in class.

24. **RT**   Discuss with students why children's learning disabilities are rarely discovered before they start school.

25. **ER**   Students should report on help that benefits children who are learning disabled.

## Children with Behavior Disorders

26. **RT**  Ask students to differentiate between aggressive behavior and hyperactivity.
27. **ER**  Invite a classroom teacher who has served children with ADD or ADHD. Ask some of the techniques used to help these children.

## Help for Children with Special Needs

28. **ER**  *Delays and Problems: Common Myths,* transparency master 23-2. Use this transparency to address common myths that persist about developmental delays and other problems. Discuss the typical results if children do not get the assistance they need.
29. **EX**  Read the story of a family faced with learning their child has a special need. Report on the challenges and joys faced by the family.

## How Many Children Have Special Needs?

30. **ER**  Have students use the Internet to research the number of IEPs and IFSP written for children locally, statewide, and nationally. These figures can be further broken down by age groups served and types of special needs.
31. **EX**  Interview a special education teacher about the community's efforts to identify and assist children with special needs.

## What Kinds of Help Are Needed?

32. **ER**  Invite a professional who provides assistance for children with special needs to discuss provisions of IDEA (Individuals with Disabilities Education Act) and IFSP. Students can learn some of the terminology associated with the services provided by IDEA and IFSP. They could also see the IEP and IFSP forms.
33. **ER**  *Bibliotherapy Helps,* reproducible master 23-3. Instruct students to read a book designed to help a child with special needs. Students should then answer the questions about the book.
34. **ER**  *A Special Classroom,* Activity B, SAG. Have the students visit a special education classroom and compare it to their own classroom.

35. **ER**  Invite students to interview a special education supervisor or someone from a local organization serving people with special needs about special events or programs, such as the Special Olympics. Encourage students to volunteer with one such organization.
36. **RF**  *Community Resources,* Activity C, SAG. Students should list some community resources for children with special needs.

# Answer Key

## Text

### Reviewing Key Concepts, *page 636*

1. are
2. true
3. rate
4. (Name three:) general mental ability (high IQ), specific academic aptitude, creative or productive thinking, leadership ability, visual or performing arts ability, psychomotor ability
5. A, C, D, B, F, E, F, A, G, A, G, A, E
6. (Name three:) reverses words in reading; writes numerals out of order given; reverses sounds; has poor spatial orientation; seems awkward or clumsy; has short attention span; is hyperactive; acts disorderly; is inflexible
7. 1—referral for testing; 2—testing; 3—finding a suitable program to help the child; 4—writing an IEP; 5—retesting and writing a new IEP from time to time

## Teacher's Resources

### Chapter 23 Test

| | | |
|---|---|---|
| 1. T | 17. D | 33. R |
| 2. T | 18. D | 34. P |
| 3. T | 19. B | 35. U |
| 4. F | 20. B | 36. Q |
| 5. T | 21. A | 37. O |
| 6. T | 22. C | 38. T |
| 7. F | 23. B | 39. I |
| 8. T | 24. B | 40. H |
| 9. F | 25. D | 41. D |
| 10. F | 26. B | 42. A |
| 11. T | 27. E | 43. V |
| 12. F | 28. S | 44. C |
| 13. T | 29. F | 45. L |
| 14. T | 30. G | 46. B |
| 15. F | 31. K | 47. M |
| 16. D | 32. J | 48. N |

49. Children with and without special needs are alike except in the areas affected by the needs of those children with special needs. All children have the same basic needs and most, but not all, follow the same developmental patterns. Children with special needs differ from those without in terms of the rate and degree of development for the most part although some vary in the pattern of development.

50. The children must be referred, often by a doctor or teacher, for needed tests. The parents must give their consent. Once testing is completed, parents and others involved develop a written IEP or IFSP. The plans are carried out, and the progress toward meeting the goals are periodically checked at which time a new IEP or IFSP is developed.

# Parents Can Assess Development

→ Unusual sleeping, eating, and toileting habits

→ Frequent physical complaints

→ Lack of self-help skills

→ Lack of curiosity and little interest in activities

→ Short attention span for age

→ Restless or hyperactive behavior

→ Is careless or rarely completes tasks

→ Does not listen or seem to understand

→ Speech problems

→ Engages often in repetitive behaviors

→ Shows little variation in play

→ Cannot initiate or maintain friendships; hurts playmates

→ Prefers to be alone

→ Is too dependent

→ Does not show emotion or a range of emotions;
   rarely shows spontaneous affection

→ Seems overly sensitive or sad

→ Never gets into mischief or constantly does the "forbidden"

→ Resists positive guidance and discipline attempts of adults

# Delays and Problems: Common Myths

**If they suspect a problem or delay, adults should seek help rather than believing the following myths:**

The child will outgrow the problem.

The child is imitating a sibling or peer.

We should wait until the child starts school and see if it improves.

The child is just stubborn, lazy, or immature.

The child is just neglected or deprived.

He's a boy!

Even if there's a problem, we can't change things.

The child is too young to be evaluated.

# Bibliotherapy Helps

**Name** _____ **Date** _____ **Period** _____

One of the problems many children with special needs face is the feeling of being alone. These children may think no other children experience their same joys or struggles. Special classrooms, special events, and caring adults help. In addition, bibliotherapy is often helpful (*biblio-* means book and *-therapy* means aid). Many books are now written to show children with special needs (and their families) how real and fictitious children meet their challenges. Ask your librarian to help you choose a book written for a child with special needs. Read the book and answer the questions below.

Name of book _____

Author(s) _____

Publishing company _____

Intended audience age _____

Type of special need depicted _____

Summary of story _____

_____

_____

_____

_____

_____

_____

_____

_____

List point(s) the book was trying to convey. _____

_____

_____

_____

_____

_____

_____

_____

_____

Define other good features of the book. _____

_____

_____

# Children with Special Needs

Name _____

Date _____ Period _____ Score _____

## Chapter 23 Test

True/False: Circle *T* if the statement is true or *F* if the statement is false.

T    F    1. When a child's development differs from the development of most other children of the same age, the child is said to have special needs.

T    F    2. Tests can often determine the type and the degree of a talent or problem.

T    F    3. Children with and without special needs are more alike than different.

T    F    4. All children follow the same pattern of development.

T    F    5. Children with special needs can be both above average in one area of development and below average in another area.

T    F    6. Developmental problems are sometimes called impairments, disabilities, and disorders.

T    F    7. Giftedness results solely from genetic factors.

T    F    8. A child may be gifted in one or more of six key areas.

T    F    9. A physical disability *never* involves the nervous system.

T    F   10. A speech disorder only affects the child's speaking ability.

T    F   11. Children who are learning disabled are often undiagnosed until the school-age years.

T    F   12. Children who *cannot* sit still for long periods are always hyperactive.

T    F   13. Retesting from time to time is needed to monitor the progress of children with special needs.

T    F   14. When it comes to education, state and federal laws determine which children are defined as having special needs and what kinds of services these children are eligible to receive.

T    F   15. An IFSP would be appropriate for a child age 10 years and an IEP would be appropriate for an infant.

Multiple Choice: Choose the best response. Write the letter in the space provided.

_____ 16. Developmental differences may occur in which of the following areas of development?
    A. Physical development.
    B. Mental development.
    C. Social-emotional development.
    D. All areas of development.

_____ 17. Children with special needs may differ from other children in the _____ of their development.
    A. rate
    B. pattern
    C. degree
    D. All of the above.

*(Continued)*

**Name** _____

18. Special needs may be identified by _____.
    A. observing the child at birth
    B. noting some of the child's behaviors
    C. testing the child's abilities in various areas
    D. All of the above.

19. IQ tests measure all of the following *except* how _____.
    A. quickly a person can learn
    B. well a person will do in school
    C. easily a person can find solutions to problems
    D. well a person can reason

20. Giftedness _____.
    A. occurs in about half of all children
    B. can be enhanced by a child's environment
    C. refers only to higher mental ability
    D. is measured only by IQ testing

21. A person who is visually impaired _____.
    A. has problems seeing
    B. is totally blind
    C. cannot wear contact lenses
    D. sees perfectly without corrective lenses

22. Speech disorders include all the following *except* _____ problems.
    A. articulation
    B. voice
    C. grammar
    D. rhythm

23. Mental disabilities can result from all the following *except* _____.
    A. inherited disorders
    B. not studying hard enough
    C. prenatal and birth problems
    D. injuries and infections

24. Children with learning disabilities often _____.
    A. have low IQs
    B. have problems when using symbol systems such as reading or mathematics
    C. are lazy
    D. come from schools that have used the wrong method of teaching

25. Behavioral disorders include _____.
    A. aggressive behaviors
    B. withdrawn behaviors
    C. ADHD and ADD
    D. All of the above.

26. Which of the following is *not* a criticism of medications given to treat behavioral disorders?
    A. These medications are sometimes given to children who do not have behavioral disorders.
    B. These medications can help calm hyperactivity.
    C. These medications are often the first treatment tried for a behavioral disorder.
    D. These medications have unpleasant side effects.

*(Continued)*

**Name** _____

Matching: Match the following terms and identifying phrases.

_____ 27. • Identifies a problem as mild or an ability as just above average.

_____ 28. Identifies a problem as severe or an ability as extreme.

_____ 29. Indicates that a problem may exist for a long time, perhaps a lifetime.

_____ 30. Indicates that a problem may be overcome with the appropriate support.

_____ 31. Having a hearing loss.

_____ 32. Children who show high performance in one or more of six key areas.

_____ 33. A limitation of a person's body or its function.

_____ 34. Indicates that a person meets the legal definition that qualifies persons to receive services for vision loss.

_____ 35. Indicates a person has speech problems.

_____ 36. A condition in which a person's intellectual abilities are more than a year delayed when compared with the abilities of other people of the same age.

_____ 37. Problems in one or more areas of spoken or written language, mathematics, and spatial orientation.

_____ 38. The ability to see relationships between objects in space.

_____ 39. Learning disability that affects child's ability to read.

_____ 40. Learning disability that affects child's mathematical abilities.

_____ 41. Pattern of problems that surfaces in a child's behavior.

_____ 42. Outward behavior disorder that initiates problem behaviors toward others.

_____ 43. Inward behavior disorder that causes children *not* to relate well to others.

_____ 44. Disorder that involves a lack of attention with extremely active physical behaviors.

_____ 45. A pattern of behavior in which a person is overactive, restless, and has a short attention span.

_____ 46. Disorder that involves a lack of attention but *not* extremely active physical behaviors.

_____ 47. An educational plan designed to meet a child's special educational needs.

_____ 48. A plan designed to coordinate all the services needed by a family in the effort to assist a child younger than three years of age with special needs.

A. aggressive behavior

B. attention-deficit disorder (ADD)

C. attention-deficit hyperactivity disorder (ADHD)

D. behavioral disorders

E. borderline

F. chronic

G. correctable

H. developmental dyscalculia

I. dyslexia

J. gifted and talented children

K. hearing impaired

L. hyperactivity

M. Individualized Education Plan (IEP)

N. Individualized Family Service Plan (IFSP)

O. learning disabilities

P. legally blind

Q. mental disability

R. physical disability

S. profound

T. spatial orientation

U. speech impaired

V. withdrawn behavior

Essay Questions: Provide complete responses to the following questions or statements.

49. How are children with and without special needs alike? How are they different?

50. What are the steps involved in the process of providing help to a child with special needs?

## Objectives

After studying this chapter, students will be able to
- describe four sibling relationships and explain how a child's birth order affects development.
- describe how parental employment affects children.
- explain how stress from family moves can hurt children and how to lessen these effects.
- describe ways adults can help children handle divorce, remarriage, and death.
- point out problems single parents and teen parents face.
- describe ways to protect children from neglect and abuse.
- list resources available for helping children in crisis.

## Bulletin Boards

## Title: *Abusive Behavior Is OUT*

On the bulletin board place a picture of a baseball pitcher in a throwing position. Mount pictures of three large baseballs in front of the pitcher. On each baseball write a way to protect children from child abuse, such as *Report child abuse; Learn parenting skills;* and *Remember that children are special.*

## Title: *Make Moving Less Stressful*

Draw or enlarge a picture of a moving van with a ramp leading from the back loading area of the truck to the ground. On and around the ramp and van, place phrases that help make a move less stressful, such as *Have a positive attitude; Emphasize chances for making new friends; Take children to see the new home; Have children help with packing; Pack a few favorite toys to travel with children; Plan special treats;* and *Plan more time with children.*

## Teaching Materials

**Text**, pages 638-685
> *Reviewing Key Concepts*
> *Using Your Knowledge*
> *Making Observations*
> *Thinking Further*

**Student Activity Guide**
> A. *The Roles of Siblings*
> B. *Working Parents Must Be Good Managers*
> C. *Planning Ahead for Self-Care*
> D. *Grief and Other Reactions to Death*
> E. *Teen Parenting: A Major Risk*
> F. *Traits of Child Abusers*

**Teacher's Resources**
> *A Special Brother or Sister*, reproducible
>> master 24-1
> *At Risk: Children in Self-Care*, color
>> transparency CT-24
> *Teen Parents' Financial Cycle*, transparency
>> master 24-2
> *Act Now to Prevent Child Abuse*, reproducible
>> master 24-3
> *Resources for Helping Children*, reproducible
>> master 24-4
> Chapter 24 Test

# Introductory Activities

1. Ask students to brainstorm ways that family life has changed in the last 25 years. What stressors have entered family life and affect the life of children? What situations or stressors were rare years ago that are now common sources of concern for families?

2. Each student should visit a library and check out one children's book on family problems or situations like divorce, death, or adoption. Students should bring these books to class for other class members to review.

# Strategies to Reteach, Reinforce, Enrich, and Extend Text Concepts

## Sibling Relationships

3. **RF** On the top of a large sheet of paper, write *Siblings are special because….* Mount the paper to a wall or bulletin board. Ask class members to write thoughts on the paper that complete the sentence.

4. **RF** Have students list some activities that siblings do together for fun.

5. **EX** Discuss with students problems that may occur when parents or other adults ask older siblings to babysit younger siblings.

6. **RT** Ask students to explain how some sibling rivalry may be positive and suggest ways that parents can help keep sibling rivalry under control.

7. **RF** *The Roles of Siblings*, Activity A, SAG. Students should give examples of how siblings fill each of the roles listed.

8. **RF** Ask students to share their views of their birth order. How do their views compare with the text information?

9. **EX** Students should speculate on advantages only children gain from spending some time alone.

10. **RT** Ask students to explain how parents can encourage children of multiple births to develop separate identities.

11. **ER** *A Special Brother or Sister*, reproducible master 24-1. Students should read about the personalities of multiple-birth children, interview a person from a multiple birth, and record his or her responses in the space provided.

## Parental Employment

12. **ER** *Working Parents Must Be Good Managers*, Activity B, SAG. Invite students to interview a working parent and record his or her comments in the space provided. Students then should compare interview responses with the text discussion.

13. **RF** Have students list examples of conflicts that might arise between family and work roles when parents work outside the home.

14. **EX** Ask students to share their views on the following: If a mother wants to return to work after staying home for a while with a child, when do you think it is best for her to do so?

15. **RT** Ask students for examples that illustrate how the children of working parents may have broader gender role concepts than other children.

16. **RT** Have students identify problems adults may have in balancing multiple roles of parent and worker. What actions can they take to lessen stress and achieve a better balance?

17. **ER** Students should survey parents about their feelings concerning role strain or role guilt. Have students share their findings in class.

18. **RT** Ask students to give examples of ways in which working parents can spend quality time with their children.

19. **EX** Have the class role-play a television talk show in which the audience and guests debate the pros and cons of children in self-care. The students may want to bring in an expert to clarify the issues and make suggestions.

20. **RT** *At Risk: Children in Self-Care*, color transparency CT-24. Use this transparency to emphasize the concerns that parents and society have about children who stay home alone while their parents work.

21. **RF** *Planning Ahead for Self-Care*, Activity C, SAG. Have students review concerns for the well-being of a child in self-care and then list possible solutions for each concern.

## Coping with Family Moves

22. **RT** Discuss with students the social and economic factors that tend to increase the likelihood of family moves.

23. **ER** Discuss with students that many children move more frequently than indicated by data on family moves. These children include children with parents in the military, children whose divorced parents have split custody, foster children, and adopted children.

## Coping with Death

24. **RT**  Ask students to explain why children's mental development makes it hard for them to understand that life can stop, death is forever, and people and pets cannot come back to life.
25. **RF**  *Grief and Other Reactions to Death,* Activity D, SAG. After reading the anecdotes, students should explain why the adult reactions given are not appropriate. Students should write more appropriate reactions.
26. **RF**  Ask students to give some appropriate responses to a child's grief over the death of a pet.
27. **RT**  Ask students to suggest ways a child can express grief over the death of a loved one.
28. **EX**  Discuss with students whether they think children should attend funerals. What role does the child's age play?

## Coping with Divorce

29. **RT**  Ask students why they feel today more people are unwilling to stay in unhappy relationships than they were in the past.
30. **EX**  Discuss with students why teen marriages have a greater risk of failure.
31. **RF**  Have students list factors that contribute to divorce.
32. **RF**  Students should write a paragraph describing how divorce affects family members, including children.
33. **EX**  Have students compare and contrast how divorce affects children of different ages.
34. **RT**  Discuss with students how much parents should tell children about the problems that lead them to divorce. What boundaries must parents set in the information they share with children?

## Single Parenting

35. **RT**  Emphasize that single-parent families headed by females tend to face financial struggles because women still earn less money than men even for the same work.
36. **EX**  Have students contrast the different types of single-parent families—those headed by divorced parents; those headed by widowed parents; and those headed by never-married single parents.
37. **ER**  Invite a panel of single parents to discuss the challenges and rewards of single parenting.
38. **ER**  Invite a local judge or attorney to explain child support orders. More specifically, ask the speaker to explain laws regarding child support,

how the amount of support is determined, the statistical incidence of failure to pay, difficulties in getting needed support, and what is being done to change the situation.

## Remarriage and Stepparenting

39. **RT**  Ask students for examples of ways children can prepare for a new marriage and family changes.
40. **RT**  Discuss with students why adjusting to a stepparent and stepfamily is difficult.
41. **RF**  Instruct students to research books and/or magazine articles about remarriage and stepparenting. Students should write a report and share information in class.

## Teens as Parents

42. **EX**  Discuss with students why the U.S. has the highest teen birthrate of all industrialized nations in the world.
43. **ER**  Invite a panel of teen parents to talk to the class about their experiences raising children. What daily demands do these parents face? How much time do they have for themselves? How do (or did) they deal with school responsibilities?
44. **RF**  *Teen Parenting: A Major Risk,* Activity E, SAG. Review the text section "Reasons for Not Choosing Parenthood" in chapter 3. Have students relate the reasons for all parents to more specific reasons that teen parenting is a major risk.
45. **RT**  Ask students to explain why serious health risks exist for teen mothers and their babies.
46. **RT**  Discuss with students why it is especially dangerous for teens to become pregnant by older men. (Many older men may have had multiple partners, which makes many of them carriers of sexually transmitted diseases. Also, older males are more likely to have had recent exposure to alcohol, drugs, toxic chemicals, or other environmental pollutants prior to conception that may seriously affect the fetus.)

## Financial Concerns

47. **RF**  *Teen Parents' Financial Cycle,* transparency master 24-2. Use this transparency to discuss how the financial/educational cycle becomes almost impossible to break. Ask students how the cycle might be broken and how this is important to the teen parent, his or her child, the family, and society as a whole.

48. **EX** Discuss with students how much financial support they feel a teen parent's own parents should provide for the teen parent and his or her baby.
49. **RT** Have students discuss in small groups the special challenges teen parents face as they attempt to complete their education.
50. **RF** Instruct students to list problems that may result when children grow up in poverty.
51. **RT** Discuss with students why pregnant teenagers often feel socially isolated.
52. **RT** Discuss with students why teen parents are more likely to abuse their children.

## Child Neglect and Abuse

53. **RF** Using Erikson's theory as a rationale, ask students why child neglect and abuse leaves such emotional scars. (Most neglect and abuse occurs in the home and is done by a person the child knows and trusts. Destroying a child's trust early in life leads to a generalized feeling of mistrust.).
54. **ER** Guest speaker: Invite a local person involved in a prevention or crisis agency to explain the services of the agency and share a few success stories.
55. **RF** *Traits of Child Abusers*, Activity F, SAG. Students are asked to analyze various traits and explain why the trait might lead to child abuse.
56. **RF** Review with students the procedure in your state for reporting known or suspected cases of child abuse.
57. **RF** *Act Now to Prevent Child Abuse*, reproducible master 24-3. Distribute this handout listing actions students can take to prevent child abuse. Use the handout as a discussion starter.
58. **EX** Plan a class project to help educate fellow students or the community about the incidence, causes, effects, and treatments for abuse. Posters, brochures, series of newspaper articles, or presentations to organizations would be worth while.
59. **ER** Guest speaker: Invite a local person who works with child abuse cases, such as a juvenile officer or physician, to speak to the class. The following questions will help the person prepare the presentation: What are the local statistics on reported child abuse? What is the state law regarding the reporting of incidents? What local services aid abusers and abused children? Does the local community have prevention services?

## Resources for Children in Crises

60. **RF** Have students work as a class to make a directory of local resources for children in crisis including the name of the resource, its address and phone number, and basic services offered.
61. **RF** *Resources for Helping Children*, reproducible master 24-4. Distribute this list of Internet resources for families and children in crisis. Assign small groups of students to visit selected Web sites from the list and give an oral report on their findings.

# Answer Key

## Text
*Reviewing Key Concepts,* page 684

1. playmates, teachers and learners, protectors, rivals
2. false
3. false
4. (Name four:) tend to miss fewer days of school; usually enjoy meaningful and well-planned free time with parents; help with household chores and learn home-care skills; may live in homes with more structured times and more clearly stated rules; often show more confidence; interact more with others and spend more time with other adults and with children
5. (Name two positive effects and two negative effects. See Figure 24-10 in the text.)
6. false
7. Life can stop. Death is forever. People and pets cannot come back to life, even if children really want them to come back.
8. false
9. false
10. Neglect is harming or endangering a child by an adult who fails to do something legally expected of him or her. Abuse is an action that harms or threatens to harm a child's well-being.
11. true
12. false

## Student Activity Guide
*Teen Parenting: A Major Risk!* Activity E

**"We're not ready for a child."** Teen parents most often have unplanned pregnancies and are often unmarried. If marriage occurs, it may be shortly before or after the baby's birth. Teen mothers often have another child before age 20 years.

**"A baby costs a lot."** Pregnancy and childbirth are often not covered for teen parents under their parents' insurance plans. Financially, teen parents are not prepared to support themselves and a baby. They have a lower earning potential due to inadequate education.

**"A child will tie us down."** The teen years are often a time of socializing and recreation. Because teen parents must focus on their baby and direct their money to meet baby expenses, they are not able to socialize as much as other teens. They often feel isolated and lonely.

**"A child will interfere with our careers."** The baby's costs mean teen parents must work longer hours. Work and baby care limit study time. High-school dropout rates for teen parents are high. Few teen parents complete college. This greatly restricts the career fields they can enter.

**"Our child could be sick or disabled."** Teen mothers are still growing, may smoke, may have untreated STDs, and may not get medical care. All of these factors increase the health risks for both mother and baby. Babies of teen parents have lower birthweights, higher rates of SIDS, and higher incidence of congenital problems.

**"Our marriage could fail, and I don't want to be a single parent."** Many teen parents do not marry. Because those who do marry often do so for the baby, these couples risk an unhappy marriage and divorce.

**Other reasons.** Teen parenting is stressful for teens and their parents. Living at home is difficult for teen parents. Teen parenting is associated with an increase in family violence.

# Teacher's Resources

## Chapter 24 Test

| | | |
|---|---|---|
| 1. T | 20. T | 39. P |
| 2. T | 21. D | 40. O |
| 3. T | 22. C | 41. E |
| 4. F | 23. B | 42. D |
| 5. F | 24. B | 43. V |
| 6. F | 25. B | 44. L |
| 7. T | 26. D | 45. A |
| 8. F | 27. B | 46. C |
| 9. F | 28. D | 47. N |
| 10. T | 29. C | 48. F |
| 11. T | 30. A | 49. J |
| 12. F | 31. A | 50. K |
| 13. T | 32. D | 51. G |
| 14. T | 33. C | 52. B |
| 15. T | 34. B | 53. M |
| 16. T | 35. D | 54. S |
| 17. F | 36. U | 55. H |
| 18. T | 37. R | 56. T |
| 19. F | 38. Q | 57. I |

58. (Name four:) Parents must carefully budget their time to allow for quality time with the child. Parents must make alternative plans for child care in case it is impossible for the child to use the primary child care. Parents should visit the child's school, and the child should visit the parents' work sites. Parents should set limits for their children. Parents need to understand children's feelings and reactions to their return to work.

59. a relationship built on sex is unstable; people may desire sex for reasons unrelated to intimacy; breakups of relationships are more difficult when sex has been involved; sex has life-altering and permanent consequences, such as pregnancy and STDs; conflicts with parents and other adults occur over these relationships; conflicts within a person occurs over conscience, goals, and personal priorities

60. (List two:) increased awareness of the problem; social changes need to occur, such as rejection of violence; increased professional support for parents; increased education in child development and parenting; recognizing and reporting known or suspected cases of neglect and abuse

# A Special Brother or Sister

**Name** _____ **Date** _____ **Period** _____

Multiple-birth children are special. Some share identical genes. Most share similar environments. To find out how a multiple-birth child feels about having and being a special brother or sister, interview an older child of a multiple birth and record information in the space below. Then write an essay based on your findings.

1. Age of child (or write teen or adult) _____

   Gender _____ Type of multiple birth (identical or fraternal twin, mixed types triplet, etc.)

2. Do others often confuse you with your same-birth sibling? _____

If no, skip to question 3. If yes, answer the following questions:

   Does this bother you? Explain why or why not. _____

   _____

   _____

   _____

   Do you think people mistake you for your same-birth sibling because you look so much alike or because they cannot remember which name goes with which person? _____

3. How similar are your interests with those of your same-birth sibling(s)? Give examples.

   _____

   _____

   _____

   _____

   How similar are your skills to those of your same-birth sibling(s)? Give examples.

   _____

   _____

   _____

   _____

   Can you recall doing something so much like your same-birth sibling(s) that others noticed? Give example(s)._____

   _____

   _____

   _____

   _____

*(Continued)*

4. Do you share a close relationship? _____

  Do you enjoy being close or would you prefer to be more like brothers or sisters born at different times?

  _____

  _____

  How do you try to stay close or somewhat separate? _____

  _____

  _____

  Do your parents and other adults foster your closeness in some ways? Explain. _____

  _____

  _____

  _____

  Do your parents and other adults foster your separate identity in some ways? Explain._____

  _____

  _____

  _____

  Do you think you will be close as adults? Why or why not? _____

  _____

  _____

  _____

5. What do you like best about being from a multiple birth?_____

  _____

  _____

  What is most difficult about being from a multiple birth? _____

  _____

  _____

  _____

  _____

  _____

  _____

  _____

# Teen Parents' Financial Cycle

Baby and other family
expenses increase over time.

Teen parents earn less
money and are less
able to meet expenses.

Teen parents may
work more hours
to meet expenses.

Without a diploma
or degree, teen
parents qualify only
for lower-paying jobs.

Longer work hours
limit time for study
and socialization.

Teen parents may
drop out of high
school or college.

School performance suffers,
and teen parents feel
frustrated and isolated.

# Act Now to Prevent Child Abuse

Learn all you can about child development and parenting.

Do not minimize the effects of abuse.

Get counseling for yourself
- if your stress leads to explosive feelings or behaviors toward anyone or anything.

- if you are (or were) a victim of abuse.

- if you saw abuse in your home.

- if you are (or were) an abuser.

Know the background of a potential spouse and encourage counseling before marriage if abuse is (was) present.

Report suspected or known cases of abuse.

Volunteer to work in a child abuse prevention agency.

Help educate others about causes, effects, and treatments for abuse.

Advocate for legislation
- to educate the public

- to support programs for victims

- to mandate counseling or other services for abusers

- to prevent abusers from working in human service careers

- to support mental health research

# Resources for Helping Children

## General Parenting and Family
Child Welfare League of America
www.cwla.org
Connect for Kids
www.connectforkids.org
Family.com
www.family.go.com
Generations United
www.gu.org
KidsHealth
www.kidshealth.org
MyWholeFamily.com
www.mywholefamily.com
National Parent Information Network
www.npin.org
National Resource Center for Health and
Safety in Child Care
www.nrc.uchsc.edu
Parents Place
www.parentsplace.com
Quality Care for Children
www.qualitycareforchildren.org

## Abuse and Neglect
ARCH National Resource Center for Respite &
Crisis Care Services
www.chtop.com/archbroc.htm
Child Abuse.org
www.childabuse.org
Child Assault Prevention Center
www.ncap.org
The KlassKids Foundation
www.KlassKids.org
National Domestic Violence Hotline
www.ndvh.org
National Foundation for Abused and Neglected
Children
www.gangfreekids.org
Rape, Abuse, Incest National Network
www.rainn.org

## Alcohol and Drugs
Alateen
www.al-anon.alateen.org/alateen.html
Truth: The Anti-Drug
www.theantidrug.com
The Children of Alcoholics Foundation
www.coaf.org
National Child Safety Council
www.healthy.net/pan/cso/cioi/ncsc.htm

## Disabilities
The Kids on the Block
www.kotb.com
The National Center for Children and Youth
with Disabilities
www.nichcy.org

National Fathers' Network
www.fathersnetwork.org

## Adoption
Adoption Network
www.adoptionpro.com
Birthmother.com
www.birthmother.com

## Divorce/Single Parenting
National Fatherhood Initiative
www.fatherhood.org
Parents Without Partners
www.parentswithoutpartners.org

## Stepfamilies
Rainbows
www.rainbows.org
The Stepfamily Association of America, Inc.
www.stepfam.org
The Stepfamily Network
www.stepfamily.net

## Grief
Barr-Harris Children's Grief Center
www.barrharris.org
The Dougy Center (The National Center for
Grieving Children and Parents)
www.dougy.org

## Mental Health
Early Intervention Solutions
www.earlyintervention.com
KidsHealth
www.KidsHealth.org
Kids Peace
www.kidspeace.org
Light for Life Foundation's Yellow Ribbon
Suicide Prevention Program
www.yellowribbon.org
National Network for Family Resiliency
www.nnfr.org
National Runaway Switchboard
www.nrcrisisline.org
Teens Health
www.kidshealth.org/teen

## Multicultural Children and Families
The Jigsaw Classroom
www.jigsaw.org
Multicultural Kids
www.multiculturalkids.com

## Teen Pregnancy
Girls, Inc.
www.girlsinc.org
National Campaign to Prevent Teen Pregnancy
www.teenpregnancy.org

# Concerns of Children and Families

**Name** _____

**Date** _____ **Period** _____ **Score** _____

## Chapter 24 Test

True/False: Circle *T* if the statement is true or *F* if the statement is false.

T    F    1. Siblings are often rivals as well as protectors of each other.

T    F    2. Sibling relationships offer children the chance to learn much social give-and-take.

T    F    3. Personality is somewhat influenced by a person's birth order in the family.

T    F    4. Multiple-birth children view all aspects of their world in the same way that singletons do.

T    F    5. Children whose parents have family and work roles are at a disadvantage mentally and socially.

T    F    6. Self-care is *not* risky for children who are age 12 years and older.

T    F    7. Parents need to spend extra time with children during family moves to lessen their concerns.

T    F    8. When the death of a close friend or relative occurs, it is best *not* to talk about it or show sorrow in front of the child.

T    F    9. Because children *cannot* really understand the concept of death, it is best to quickly dismiss the subject when they mention it.

T    F   10. A child's standard of living usually drops following a divorce.

T    F   11. Parents need to alert teachers and caregivers of changes in the family structure.

T    F   12. For most single parents, their greatest problem is coping with loneliness.

T    F   13. Single-parent families vary in how they were formed.

T    F   14. The younger people are when they become single parents, the more likely they are to remarry.

T    F   15. Discipline of children is a major problem in stepparenting.

T    F   16. The overall birth rate for teens has fallen.

T    F   17. Pregnant teens are more likely to seek medical help early in pregnancy, lowering the health risk to mother and baby.

T    F   18. Abstinence is the only guaranteed way to avoid unwanted pregnancies and STDs.

T    F   19. Shaken Baby Syndrome causes only minor bruising, so it is *not* a serious problem.

T    F   20. Child neglect and abuse can cause physical, mental, and emotional scars for children.

Multiple Choice: Choose the best response. Write the letter in the space provided.

_____ 21. The effects of birth order on personality may be altered by ____.
      A. gender of the siblings
      B. size of the family
      C. attitudes and culture of the family
      D. All of the above.

*(Continued)*

**Name** _____

_____   22. Parents of multiple-birth children need to realize their children _____.
A. will always show a developmental lag
B. are not really different from singletons
C. have perhaps the closest of all human relationships
D. resent not being able to grow up like singletons

_____   23. Children with working parents tend to do all the following *except* _____.
A. miss fewer school days
B. have weaker relationships with their parents
C. live in homes with more structure and clearly stated rules
D. learn home-care skills faster

_____   24. Common among working mothers is _____.
A. having more traditional gender roles than stay-at-home mothers
B. feeling role strain
C. having more interest in career than in family
D. not caring about home-care tasks

_____   25. Which of the following factors *decreases* the stress of a family move for children?
A. Moving as one of many changes in the family, such as a divorce or death.
B. Having parents who are pleased about the move.
C. Moving during the middle of the school term.
D. Having to move often.

_____   26. Which of the following concepts about death is difficult for young children to understand?
A. Life can stop.
B. Death is forever.
C. People and pets cannot come back to life, even if children really want them to.
D. All of the above.

_____   27. Which of the following statements about divorce is false?
A. Even after divorce, parents have a continual relationship to each other and their in-laws.
B. Divorce affects children for only a short time, especially if they were infants at the time of the divorce.
C. Young children are often confused by divorce.
D. A child's age and gender at the time of divorce influences his or her reaction.

_____   28. When parents divorce, children need to _____.
A. have neutral people who can offer emotional support
B. be shielded from unpleasant divorce and custody battles
C. know they are not to blame and that both parents still love them
D. All of the above.

_____   29. All of the following statements about single-parent families are true *except* _____.
A. each family is different depending on its circumstances
B. more of these families are headed by men than in the past
C. most single parents find it quite easy to collect child support reliably
D. almost one-third of all families are headed by single parents

_____   30. When forming a stepfamily, parents should *not* _____.
A. tell children the new marriage will last
B. discipline their stepchildren
C. ever allow stepchildren to call them Mom or Dad
D. All of the above.

*(Continued)*

**Name** _____

_____ 31. Health risks for babies born to teen mothers include _____.
A. low birthweight, higher rate of SIDS, and more learning problems in school
B. increased rate of growth during childhood
C. being born with Rh disease
D. increased susceptibility to rubella

_____ 32. Which of the following are common obstacles for teen parents?
A. Finishing their education.
B. Managing financial matters.
C. An increased risk of family violence.
D. All of the above.

_____ 33. Abstinence is a way of saying *no* to all of the following *except* _____.
A. unwanted pregnancies and STDs
B. conflicts with parents and other adults and with one's conscience
C. all dating relationships
D. emotional scars from a broken relationship

_____ 34. Which the following is *not* a characteristic common among adults who abuse children?
A. They often have been abused or witnessed abuse as children.
B. They are skilled at handling their emotions in an adult way.
C. They can be of any age, gender, occupation, ethnic group, and income level.
D. They may lack self-esteem.

_____ 35. Ways to prevent abuse include _____.
A. rejecting violence in society
B. educating people in child development and parenting
C. reporting cases of suspected child abuse
D. All of the above.

*(Continued)*

**Name** _____

Matching: Match the following terms and identifying phrases.

_____ 36.   Children born one at a time.

_____ 37.   Feelings of being a distinct person.

_____ 38.   A feeling of having too many tasks to do at one time.

_____ 39.   A feeling of not doing the best job at work or home.

_____ 40.   Time when parents are totally attentive to their children.

_____ 41.   Children who stay home alone until a parent returns from work.

_____ 42.   Judgment by the court that states how much a parent who does not live with the children should pay toward their expenses.

_____ 43.   Feelings of being alone.

_____ 44.   The number of deaths in proportion to a given population.

_____ 45.   Postponing a sexual relationship until marriage.

_____ 46.   Harm or endangerment of a child caused by an adult's failure to do something legally expected.

_____ 47.   Failing to provide for a child's basic survival needs and supervision.

_____ 48.   Failing to adhere to school attendance laws.

_____ 49.   Failing to provide for a child's treatment for health problems or accidents.

_____ 50.   Failing to teach a child right from wrong.

_____ 51.   Inadequate care and attention, violence, or drug use in the home.

_____ 52.   An act adults commit that harms or threatens to harm children's well-being.

_____ 53.   Violence toward a child that results in pain and/or injuries.

_____ 54.   Sexual acts of any kind between a child and an adult (or older child).

_____ 55.   Act in which an adult makes excessive demands, harasses, belittles, or verbally threatens a child.

_____ 56.   Condition in which a "whiplash" motion causes brain damage and other injuries to infants or young children.

_____ 57.   Professionals legally bound to report suspected or known child neglect and abuse.

A. abstinence

B. child abuse

C. child neglect

D. child support order

E. children in self-care

F. educational neglect

G. emotional neglect

H. emotional/verbal abuse

I. mandated reporters

J. medical neglect

K. moral neglect

L. mortality rate

M. physical abuse

N. physical neglect

O. quality time

P. role guilt

Q. role strain

R. separate identities

S. sexual abuse

T. Shaken Baby Syndrome

U. singletons

V. social isolation

*(Continued)*

**Name** _____

Essay Questions: Provide complete responses to the following questions or statements.

58. List four factors parents must consider in balancing family and work.

59. Why is it beneficial for teens to practice abstinence?

60. Describe two ways neglect and abuse can be prevented.

# Making Career Decisions

## Objectives

After studying this chapter, students will be able to
- identify steps in self-assessment.
- explain how to research careers and develop a career plan.
- describe how to find a job.
- describe careers in child-related fields.
- explain how personal and professional qualifications affect your career choice.
- identify skills needed for job success.

## Bulletin Boards

Open the Door...

to Opportunity

### Title: *Open the Door to Opportunity*

Draw or collect pictures of interests or hobbies that may lead to child-related careers (such as working at a camp, child care program, nursery school, or religious program; babysitting; designing dolls and doll clothes; repairing toys; and entertaining children at a school program, in a hospital setting, or at a party). Draw a large, open door on the board and place the pictures inside the door.

### Title: *Where the Action Is*

Place pictures and brochures on the board with appropriate captions to depict local child-related career opportunities.

### Title: *Learning Skills for Job Success Through FCCLA*

Divide the bulletin board into each of the following sections: human relations, communication, teamwork, leadership, and management of multiple roles. Label each section and place pictures or drawings with captions to depict how these skills are developed through FCCLA. Use the bulletin board to recruit new members.

## Teaching Materials

**Text**, pages 686-723
*Reviewing Key Concepts*
*Using Your Knowledge*
*Making Observations*
*Thinking Further*

**Student Activity Guide**
A. *My Interests, Aptitudes, and Abilities*
B. *Getting Involved*
C. *Presenting Yourself*
D. *Contact with Children in Child-Related Careers*
E. *Satisfactions and Problems in Child-Related Careers*
F. *Meeting Professional Qualifications*

**Teacher's Resources**
*Developing My Career Plan,* reproducible master 25-1
*Child-Related Careers,* color transparency CT-25
*Focus for a Career,* transparency master 25-2
*Developing Overall Job Skills,* reproducible master 25-3
*Is This a Spillover?* transparency master 25-4
Chapter 25 Test

## Introductory Activities

1. Have students discuss the meanings of the terms *job* and *career*. How do the terms differ? Students should find these in a dictionary along with other related terms, such as *profession, specialty, field, occupation, calling, vocation, office,* and *post.*

2. At the top of a large sheet of paper, write the sentence stem *Having a deep concern for children means...* Have each student write a thought on the paper that completes the sentence. Then ask to compare the sentences to other personal qualifications as discussed in the text. Ask students whether a deep concern for children would include all the other qualifications on the list. Students should explain why or why not.

# Strategies to Reteach, Reinforce, Enrich, and Extend Text Concepts

## Heading Toward a Career

3. **RT**  Ask students to describe where they want to be by their mid-thirties in terms of where they want to live, people with whom they want to associate, what free time they desire, and the money they would want to earn. Explain that these factors are called one's *lifestyle*. Ask students to explain how career choices influence lifestyle.

4. **EX**  Discuss with students whether qualifications for careers in child-related fields will likely be increased or decreased in the future.

5. **RT**  Discuss with students how adults who are not qualified to work with children may unintentionally harm them.

## Identifying Your Interests, Aptitudes, and Abilities

6. **ER**  Ask students what people want from their careers besides income. Note that most people want careers that are interesting, that use skills they can readily learn or develop, and that make the most of these skills.

7. **RF**  Emphasize that interests, aptitudes, and general abilities may change throughout life but start to become rather stable by the late teen and early adult years. Thus, self-assessment during these years is the best starting place for making career choices.

8. **RT**  Ask students what it means to have a sense of fulfillment through your career. Ask students to identify other ways in which people find fulfillment.

9. **ER**  Invite a professional in a child-related field to discuss how his or her interests, aptitudes, and abilities led to career success and a sense of fulfillment.

10. **RF**  *My Interests, Aptitudes, and Abilities,* Activity A, SAG. Students are asked to use this activity to help them explore interests, aptitudes, and abilities they might have that would enable them to work in child-related careers.

## Learn About Careers

11. **RF**  Have students choose two careers in a child-related field that might interest them. Have them check the Internet or library for information related to each career. Using Figure 25-3 from the text as a model, have students record as many facts as they can find on the careers.

12. **EX**  Survey training schools and colleges in your community or state for training and education in child-related careers.

13. **RF**  *Getting Involved,* Activity B, SAG. Students should list local contact people who are involved in careers in child-related fields.

14. **ER**  Have two groups of students debate the advantages and disadvantages of entering a career field before completing one's educational or training goals.

15. **EX**  As a class, sponsor a babysitting clinic. (Find resources at the library or through government agencies.) Invite other students to attend.

## Developing a Career Plan

16. **RT**  Explain that developing a career plan helps in preparing for a career and also provides practice in setting life goals.

17. **RT**  Ask students how some people get into careers without going through the decision-making process. What are the probable disadvantages of not making your own decisions?

18. **RT**  As a class, list some human and nonhuman resources that might help a person entering a child-related career.

## Short-Term Goals

19. **RT**  Have the students discuss why short-term goals can be invaluable even when long-term goals have been planned.

20. **ER**  Guest speaker: Invite a local pediatrician or professional in a child-related field. Ask the speaker to explain the many short-term goals that led to fulfillment of long-term goals. Ask whether the person's short-term goals ever caused him or her to modify career plans. Perhaps this person could develop a transparency to illustrate his or her long-term and short-term goals.

## Long-Term Goals

21. **RF** *Developing My Career Plan,* reproducible master 25-1. Have students research a career in a child-related field and write long-term and short-term goals for obtaining this career. Discuss how students can determine how realistic their plans are.
22. **ER** Explain that many people enter a career at an entry-level position and climb a career ladder through more specialized training and education and through experience. Make a career ladder for a nonteaching career similar to the one shown in Figure 25-20. Explain that preparing for advanced-level jobs might be seen as a broad long-term goal.

## Job Search Skills

23. **RF** *Presenting Yourself,* Activity C, SAG. Instruct students to compile the information they need to produce a resume. Students could keystroke the information and print several copies for interviews. Explain why spelling, grammar, and neatness are critical for resumes.
24. **RF** Hold some mock interviews for jobs in child-related fields. Invite one or two employers (such as a child care director or a toy store owner) to conduct the interviews. A few days beforehand, choose four or five students to be interviewed. (Discuss some general interview procedures and possible questions with these students before the interviews.) After the interviews, have the employers share constructive comments on the strengths and weaknesses of the interviews.
25. **RT** Discuss with students how dress, grooming, posture, and other similar attributes affect a job interview. Have students discuss how dress might differ depending on career field or whether the job opening is for an entry-level or higher professional-level career. Talk about clothing, accessories, and other attributes (exceptionally long nails, facial piercings, wildly-colored hair, gum chewing) that could be offensive.
26. **EX** Have students check the child care job ads in the weekend edition of a large newspaper and identify ads of interest. What qualifications and salary are listed? If possible, have students call a contact person for more information, explaining their class assignment. Ask students to report their experiences to the class.
27. **ER** Obtain a blank copy of a job application. Photocopy the application and ask students to fill it out using the points in the text as a guide.

28. **ER** Have students use the computer to compose an application letter for a child care job. Share letters in class and allow students to provide feedback.
29. **EX** Ask students what the expression "marketing yourself" means.

## Careers in Child-Related Fields

30. **EX** Ask the students to develop a bulletin board or poster showing the many advantages of a career in a child-related field.
31. **ER** Use the seven categories of child-related fields described in the text. Help students note these are broad fields in which there are careers that provide for children's needs; thus, they are child-related fields.

## Types of Careers

32. **RT** Ask students to explain why parenting is often considered as a child-related career.
33. **RF** *Contact with Children in Child-Related Careers,* Activity D, SAG. Students should classify each career discussed in the text as direct intervention, consulting, and product development and sales.
34. **RF** *Satisfactions and Problems in Child-Related Careers,* Activity E, SAG. Students should list some possible satisfactions and problems experienced by people in child-related careers.
35. **RF** Instruct students to write an essay on the differences and similarities of the skills needed for parenting and child-related careers.
36. **ER** Panel discussion: Arrange for several professionals in child-related fields to speak to the class about their career. Instruct students to summarize what they learned in the form of a thank-you letter to the panel.
37. **RT** *Child-Related Careers,* color transparency CT-25. Use this transparency to stimulate interest in the many child-related careers. Have students list careers that would fit into each category and add to the list as they study the chapter.

## Health and Protective Services

38. **RT** Ask students to explain what the term *protective services* means. Clarify any misconceptions.
39. **RT** Students should give examples of adults in your community who have careers in health and protective services.
40. **ER** Have students interview one or more adults who practice health and protective services careers. Students should share results with the class.

## Care and Education

41. **RT** Help students differentiate between the terms *education* and *care*. Note that while some careers involve one of these two areas, while many careers involve both care and education.

42. **ER** Students should interview one or more adults who practice careers in the care and education of children. Students should share results with the class.

## Entertainment

43. **RT** Have students give some examples of children's entertainment.

44. **RF** Ask students to identify any adults in your area who have careers in children's entertainment. Discuss with students how society's increasing awareness of child development has affected career opportunities in this field.

## Design

45. **RF** Invite students to list some people or companies that design children's clothing, toys, furniture, and other items.

46. **EX** Instruct students to examine a product designed for children. Students should explain how the design is geared toward children.

47. **RT** Discuss with students why adults who design children's products must know child development. Students should give specific examples.

## Advertising, Marketing, and Management

48. **RT** Have students explain what the terms *advertising, marketing,* and *management* mean.

49. **RT** Discuss with students why advertising and marketing professionals must work as a team.

50. **RT** Students should watch commercials that appear during Saturday morning cartoons. Ask them to note examples of how advertising for children's products is often designed to appeal to adults as well as to children. Discuss notes in class.

## Research and Consulting

51. **RT** Ask students for examples of how research has been or can be useful in each of the following child-related fields: health and protective services, care and education, entertainment, design and advertising, marketing, and managing children's products.

52. **RT** Discuss with students why consultants specialize in certain fields.

53. **RF** Have students identify some adults (locally or nationally) who have research or consulting careers related to children.

## Entrepreneurship

54. **RF** Instruct students to look up the term *entrepreneur* in a dictionary, then list words that describe an entrepreneur.

55. **ER** Invite students to interview an entrepreneur in a child-related career. Students should write a magazine-style article on the rewards and difficulties of entrepreneurship based on their interview.

56. **RF** Have students list skills other than those related to child development that an entrepreneur would need to operate a child-related business.

57. **RF** Students should list child-related careers that would work well as entrepreneurships. Students should also name careers that might not work well as entrepreneurships and explain why.

58. **RF** Instruct students to list some people in your area who are entrepreneurs in child-related fields.

## Personal Qualifications for a Child-Related Career

59. **RT** Discuss with students each personal qualification listed for people who directly work with children. Ask students to explain why each qualification is important.

60. **EX** Students should compare causes of career burnout in various careers to causes of career burnout in child-related careers.

61. **EX** As a group, students should brainstorm ways that students can practice and improve their leadership skills in the school and community. Each student should then write two or three ideas he or she will try.

## Professional Qualifications for a Child-Related Career

62. **ER** *Meeting Professional Qualifications*, Activity F, SAG. Have students find out the specific professional qualifications for any child-related career described in the text.

63. **RF** *Focus for a Career*, transparency master 25-2. Students should take careers discussed in the text and, by placing each career name in its appropriate column, show the area of child development career training would emphasize.

## Skills for Job Success

64. **ER**   Invite a community business leader to talk about how skills needed for job success have changed over the years. Have him or her explain ways students can keep developing skills once they have received their diploma or degree. Also have him or her explain skills that are needed for all careers.

65. **ER**   Have students research the Internet for the meaning of the term *information-age economy.* Share this information in class.

66. **RF**   *Developing Overall Job Skills,* reproducible master 25-3. As students study the text section "Skills for Job Success," instruct them to list competencies they lack and make specific plans for developing each. Have students also list on a separate sheet of paper all the competencies they can identify as their own strengths.

## Human Relations Skills

67. **RF**   Have students brainstorm ways to show initiative on the job. Ask them to explain why loafing or doing personal tasks during work hours is dishonest.

68. **RF**   Discuss with students how the need for good manners is reflected in statements such as, "The customer is always right" or the doctor has a "good bedside manner."

## Communications Skills

69. **RF**   Role-play the correct way to do the following: answer the telephone at work and take messages; write office memos; and, write professional e-mail messages.

70. **RF**   Have each student write a business letter requesting information about a career opportunity in a child-related field. (Because business letters have standard parts, obtain some models for your students.)

71. **EX**   Discuss with students why business policies usually state that "all communication is the property of the employer." Discuss how this policy applies to e-mail and Internet use during business hours and/or on business computers.

## Being a Team Player

72. **RF**   Ask students to define *team.* Ask them to discuss their memberships on teams and what was good and bad in their experiences. Lead the discussion toward describing advantages and disadvantages of teamwork. Write these on the chalkboard or a transparency.

73. **RF**   Ask students to describe the roles different team members play during a problem-solving or decision-making process. (For example, one person may keep the group on task, another person may lead, and others may offer feedback. These roles are often informally determined.)

74. **EX**   Brainstorm with the students careers in child-related fields that are conducted in team situations. (Most teaching of young children is team-teaching; teachers and parents form a partnership; and people in protective services work in a team approach with staff members from various support agencies. Many programs and services for children have boards of directors or advisors that work with the program or service staff in a team effort.)

## Leadership Skills

75. **RF**   Ask how FCCLA membership promotes the development of leadership skills.

76. **RT**   Ask students to name some of the characteristics of high school student leaders. Write these on the chalkboard and compare this list with those given in the text.

## Managing Multiple Roles

77. **RT**   Ask students to explain how stress and poor task-management skills lead to lower productivity in all areas of life.

78. **RF**   *Is This a Spillover?* transparency master, 25-4. Use the transparency to stimulate a discussion of spillover and stress in their lives and how these behaviors often become a habit leading to spillover in the workplace.

## Leaving a Job in the Right Way

79. **RF**   Have each student write a sample letter of resignation. The letter should begin with positive experiences with the business followed by an explanation for leaving, planned termination date, and closing.

80. **EX**   Discuss with the students some acceptable reasons for changing employment, but also explain the disadvantages of job changes for the employer and employee. Explain why "job hopping" is negative.

81. **RF**   Ask students to make a class list of reasons employees are fired or not promoted. By each reason, list the job skill that was lacking. (Students should note that most of the reasons have their roots in lack of general skills for job success as opposed to career-specific skills.)

# Answer Key

## Text

*Reviewing Key Concepts,* page 722

1. interests; aptitudes; abilities
2. long-term; short-term
3. increasing
4. (List 12. Student response.)
5. Consultants
6. (Name three:) clothing; personal care items; dishes and flatware; furniture; books; toys; indoor spaces; outdoor spaces
7. (List two for each career. Student response.)
8. concern for children; flexibility; leadership
9. taught
10. child development
11. true
12. (Describe three:) follow personnel policies regarding terminating employment; provide ample notice; complete a letter of resignation; try to complete all current tasks

# Teacher's Resources

## Chapter 25 Test

| | | |
|---|---|---|
| 1. T | 18. T | 35. D |
| 2. T | 19. T | 36. R |
| 3. F | 20. T | 37. U |
| 4. T | 21. D | 38. O |
| 5. T | 22. C | 39. S |
| 6. F | 23. A | 40. Q |
| 7. F | 24. C | 41. G |
| 8. F | 25. D | 42. F |
| 9. T | 26. A | 43. M |
| 10. F | 27. B | 44. H |
| 11. F | 28. D | 45. C |
| 12. T | 29. B | 46. L |
| 13. T | 30. N | 47. V |
| 14. F | 31. T | 48. E |
| 15. T | 32. P | 49. J |
| 16. T | 33. B | 50. K |
| 17. F | 34. A | 51. I |

52. Self-assessment means carefully examining interests, aptitudes, and abilities.
53. Three ways to get involved are talking to people in the career field, gaining experience by working for or volunteering in the profession or a related area, and joining professional organizations.
54. Factors that have promoted careers in child-related fields include society's desire to improve the quality of life for children; increase in dual-career families and single working parents who need child care and education services; consumers who want more goods and services tailored to children's needs.
55. (List three:) follow correct procedure in notifying the employer; provide ample notice; complete necessary paperwork; try to complete all current tasks

# Developing My Career Plan

**Name** _____ **Date** _____ **Period** _____

After studying Figure 25-5 in the text, research career requirements for a career in a child-related field. Write these as your long-term goals. Then, write some short-term goals based on the long-term goals.

## Long-Term Goals

| Area | Goals |
|---|---|
| Basic Education and Tests | |
| Experiences Required or Desired | |
| Other Skills | |

*(Continued)*

# Short-Term Goals

| Area | Goals |
|------|-------|
| Current Education | |
| Extracurricular Activities | |
| Work or Volunteer Experiences | |

How realistic do you think your career plan is? Explain. _____

_____

_____

_____

_____

_____

_____

_____

# Focus for a Career

| Physical Development | Intellectual Development | Social-Emotional Development |
| --- | --- | --- |
|  |  |  |

# Developing Overall Job Skills

**Name** _____ **Date** _____ **Period** _____

Overall job skill development is an ongoing process. After studying this section, write two competencies you need to develop in each area. Make a specific plan to develop the competency. For example, to grasp oral information (a listening competency), you might practice this skill in planning meetings for your FCCLA chapter by summarizing what someone has said before responding to them (a plan to develop the listening competency).

## Human Relations Skills

| Competency | Plan |
|---|---|
| 1. | |
| 2. | |

## Communication Skills (except computer-based skills)

| Competency | Plan |
|---|---|
| 1. | |
| 2. | |

## Computer-Based Skills

| Competency | Plan |
|---|---|
| 1. | |
| 2. | |

*(Continued)*

## Team Member Skills

| Competency | Plan |
|---|---|
| 1. | |
| 2. | |

## Leadership Skills

| Competency | Plan |
|---|---|
| 1. | |
| 2. | |

# Is This a Spillover?

## Signs of Spillover at School

→ being sleepy or distracted in class

→ being unprepared for class

→ making careless mistakes on tests and assignments

→ being late or absent from school

→ asking teachers to postpone tests, accept late work, extend project deadlines, or even lower course requirements

→ making grades far below your ability

## Signs of Spillover in Non-School Settings

→ losing needed sleep and not taking care of yourself

→ not finding time for or enjoying family life and leisure time

→ trying to study while working or doing other tasks

→ missing work or not fulfilling other tasks

→ canceling plans at the last minute

→ becoming irritable with others

→ engaging in substance abuse and other risky behaviors

# Making Career Decisions

**Name** _____

**Date** _____ **Period** _____ **Score** _____

## Chapter 25 Test

True/False: Circle *T* if the statement is true or *F* if the statement is false.

T     F     1. Lifestyle involves choices such as where you live, skills you will develop, people with whom you associate, and your financial outlook.

T     F     2. Career decisions are crucial to your lifestyle and thus require much careful thought.

T     F     3. Personal priorities are your surface, short-lived interests.

T     F     4. Career-specific abilities are developed in schools, colleges, and on-the-job programs.

T     F     5. A person needs to examine the labor market for career opportunities.

T     F     6. A career plan is a list of professional qualifications required for a career.

T     F     7. A resume is a letter to a potential employer requesting an interview.

T     F     8. Appearance during an interview does *not* matter if you have the right qualifications.

T     F     9. Child-related careers are growing.

T     F     10. All persons who work in child-related careers have direct contact with children.

T     F     11. Teaching is the only career in care and education services for children.

T     F     12. Public support for the education of young children is growing.

T     F     13. Entertainment for children is becoming a big business.

T     F     14. Child-related careers in design will probably decrease.

T     F     15. The growth in children's products and services has created careers in advertising, marketing, and management.

T     F     16. Research is conducted in most, if not all, child-related fields.

T     F     17. Personal qualifications are usually taught.

T     F     18. The professional qualifications necessary for child-related careers are often learned in training.

T     F     19. *Work ethic* refers to having appropriate behaviors for the workplace.

T     F     20. In a sense, manners are involved in leaving a job the right way.

Multiple Choice: Choose the best response. Write the letter in the space provided.

_____ 21. Today's employees need to be able to _____.
A. change and cope with the stress of change
B. learn quickly
C. possess skills that can be used in multiple careers
D. All of the above.

_____ 22. Learning about careers involves all of the following *except* _____.
A. analyzing the labor market
B. securing the required education or training
C. developing a resume
D. getting involved with others in the career

*(Continued)*

**Name** _____

_____ 23. Job search skills do *not* include _____.
   A. getting the required education or training
   B. defining your search
   C. writing a resume
   D. securing interviews

_____ 24. Primarily consultants _____.
   A. do research
   B. work directly with children
   C. serve as a link between researchers and those involved in direct
      intervention or other child-related fields
   D. do not need to understand child development

_____ 25. Health and protective services careers involve _____.
   A. caring for physical health
   B. caring for mental health
   C. identifying and correcting wrongs to children
   D. All of the above.

_____ 26. Advantages of entrepreneurship include _____.
   A. being able to fill a variety of roles
   B. working short hours
   C. being able to depend on others to make decisions
   D. not having to risk personal financial loss

_____ 27. The most important qualification for working in a child-related field is _____.
   A. knowledge of child development theories
   B. deep concern for children
   C. good physical health
   D. None of the above.

_____ 28. Career burnout in working directly with children can come from _____.
   A. the hectic physical pace
   B. the emotional stress of constant changes
   C. lack of knowledge about children
   D. All of the above.

_____ 29. Leadership does *not* involve _____.
   A. motivating others
   B. doing all tasks yourself to be sure they are accomplished
   C. setting goals that will help the group fill its purposes
   D. delegating responsibilities

*(Continued)*

**Name** _____

Matching: Match the following terms and identifying phrases.

_____ 30. The typical way of life for a person, group, or culture.

_____ 31. A step in career planning that includes identifying personal interests, aptitudes, and abilities.

_____ 32. Ideas, beliefs, and objects that are important to a person.

_____ 33. A person's natural talents.

_____ 34. Skills a person has learned or developed.

_____ 35. Detailed list of steps a person must complete in order to enter a chosen career field.

_____ 36. Tools a person can use in achieving his or her goals.

_____ 37. Achievements a person desires in the near future.

_____ 38. Major achievements toward which a person strives.

_____ 39. A short, written history of a person's education, work experience, and other qualifications for employment.

_____ 40. People who know a job applicant well enough to discuss his or her qualifications for a job.

_____ 41. Working directly with children, such as in a teaching career.

_____ 42. Professionals who share their knowledge about children with other adults.

_____ 43. Professionals who check the quality of services provided for children.

_____ 44. A person who creates and owns a business.

_____ 45. Becoming emotionally tired of a career.

_____ 46. A person who influences or motivates the thoughts, feelings, or actions of others.

_____ 47. A personal standard of conduct and priorities for job performance.

_____ 48. Written standards of conduct for workers in a certain career field.

_____ 49. Leading or guiding others after being officially chosen to lead.

_____ 50. Leading or guiding others without being officially chosen to lead.

_____ 51. National organization for students in family and consumer sciences courses.

A. abilities
B. aptitudes
C. career burnout
D. career plan
E. codes of professional ethics
F. consultants
G. direct intervention
H. entrepreneur
I. Family, Career and Community Leaders of America (FCCLA)
J. formal leadership
K. informal leadership
L. leader
M. licensing personnel
N. lifestyle
O. long-term goals
P. personal priorities
Q. personal references
R. resources
S. resume
T. self-assessment
U. short-term goals
V. work ethic

*(Continued)*

**Name** _____

Essay Questions: Provide complete responses to the following questions or statements.

52. List three factors considered when doing a self-assessment regarding career choices.

53. Describe three ways a person can get involved in a career while in high school or college.

54. What factors in society have promoted careers in child-related fields?

55. List three obligations workers have when leaving a job.